Teaching Primary Science

This fully updated third edition brings science subject knowledge and pedagogy together to support, inform and inspire those training to teach primary science.

   Written in a clear and accessible way, *Teaching Primary Science* provides comprehensive coverage of a wide range of science themes. With a brand new chapter on STEM education, additional guidance on where to find the best resources, and increased emphasis on assessment, storytelling and problem-solving, this book shows how science can offer children pleasure and intellectual satisfaction and help them to develop sound scientific minds.

Key features include:

- **Ideas for practice** exemplify how you can help children to acquire and use scientific knowledge to satisfy their curiosity about how the natural world works.
- **Something to think about** scenarios help to extend and develop your own understanding of key ideas.
- **Examples** of classroom situations, dialogues and stories help you see how theory is applied to practice and support you in reflecting on the best methods for teaching.
- **Global dimension** sections offer starting points for discussion and research into how scientific ideas can be positively applied and used to evaluate the impact of human activity on the natural world.
- **Talk skills and science discussion** sections enable you to develop children's scientific knowledge and verbal reasoning skills.

About the authors

The authors, who specialise in primary science and science education, worked together at the University of Northampton. Their main research interests and publications are concerned with promoting the value of social learning, more specifically the effective use of talk for learning and storytelling strategies.

Teaching Primary Science

Promoting Enjoyment and Developing Understanding

THIRD EDITION

Peter Loxley, Lyn Dawes,
Linda Nicholls
and Babs Dore

Routledge
Taylor & Francis Group

LONDON AND NEW YORK

Third edition published 2018

by Routledge
2 Park Square, Milton Park, Abingdon, Oxon OX14 4RN

and by Routledge
711 Third Avenue, New York, NY 10017

Routledge is an imprint of the Taylor & Francis Group, an informa business

Second edition published 2014 by Routledge
First edition published 2010 by Pearson

British Library Cataloguing in Publication Data

A catalogue record for this book is available from the British Library

Library of Congress Cataloging in Publication Data
Names: Loxley, Peter, editor. | Nicholls, Linda, editor. | Dore, Babs, 1952-, editor.
Title: Teaching primary science : promoting enjoyment and developing understanding /
edited by Peter Loxley, Lyn Dawes, Linda Nicholls and Babs Dore.Description: Third
edition. | New York : Routledge, 2017.Identifiers: LCCN 2016051026| ISBN 9781138651838 (hardback)
| ISBN 9781138651821 (pbk.) | ISBN 9781315624594 (ebook)Subjects: LCSH: Science--Study and teaching
(Elementary)Classification: LCC LB1585 .L68 2017 | DDC 372.35/044--dc23LC record available at
https://lccn.loc.gov/2016051026

ISBN: 978-1-138-65182-1 (hbk)
ISBN: 978-1-138-65183-8 (pbk)
ISBN: 978-1-315-62459-4 (ebk)

Typeset in Frutiger
by Fish Books Ltd.

Visit the companion website: **www.routledge.com/cw/loxley**

MIX
Paper from
responsible sources
FSC® C013056

Printed and bound in Great Britain by
TJ Books Limited, Padstow, Cornwall

CONTENTS

v

Contents

LIST OF FIGURES AND TABLES

Figures

Tables

Chapter 11

Chapter 12

GUIDED TOUR

This book is divided into two sections: **Theory and practice** (Chapters 1–10) and **Subject knowledge and ideas for practice** (Chapters 11–22) to develop your understanding of key scientific and teaching concepts.

Theory and practice

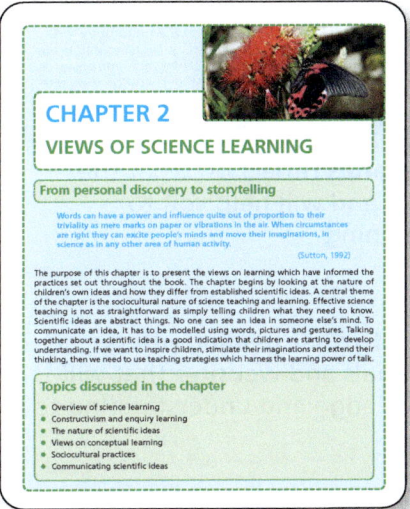

Chapter introductions begin by outlining the key themes of the chapter and highlighting the key topics that the chapter will explore.

Theory is applied to practice in short **Examples**, which present classroom situations, dialogues and stories that allow you to reflect upon best methods for teaching science.

> **Something to think about**
>
> In the transcript 'I think, expand' the teacher intervened to help the children choose useful words to describe how the pupil works. Why are these words effective? What difference did the discussion make to the children's developing ideas? Is it helpful to describe spoken language as a tool for mental modelling?
>
> The differences between the children's initial ideas and the scientific view represent the changes

Something to think about scenarios are designed to help you think creatively about key ideas to help you extend and develop your understanding. Found throughout the text, this feature asks you to pause and reflect, often posing key questions to consider or offering the opportunity to engage in a task.

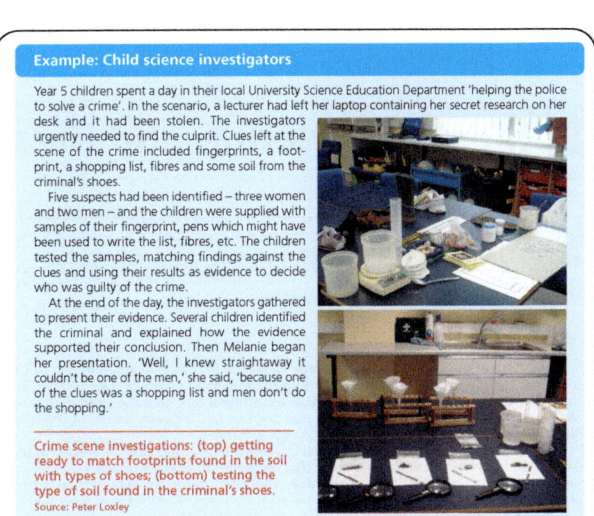

Example: Child science investigators

Year 5 children spent a day in their local University Science Education Department 'helping the police to solve a crime'. In the scenario, a lecturer had left her laptop containing her secret research on her desk and it had been stolen. The investigators urgently needed to find the culprit. Clues left at the scene of the crime included fingerprints, a footprint, a shopping list, fibres and some soil from the criminal's shoes.

Five suspects had been identified – three women and two men – and the children were supplied with samples of their fingerprint, pens which might have been used to write the list, fibres, etc. The children tested the samples, matching findings against the clues and using their results as evidence to decide who was guilty of the crime.

At the end of the day, the investigators gathered to present their evidence. Several children identified the criminal and explained how the evidence supported their conclusion. Then Melanie began her presentation. 'Well, I knew straightaway it couldn't be one of the men,' she said, 'because one of the clues was a shopping list and men don't do the shopping.'

Crime scene investigations: (top) getting ready to match footprints found in the soil with types of shoes; (bottom) testing the type of soil found in the criminal's shoes.
Source: Peter Loxley

Photos and drawings illustrate the scientific concepts explored and show how they are implemented in the classroom.

Further reading

ASE Journals:

* Primary Science 140 (Nov/Dec 2015). *Introducing the TAPS Pyramid Model* by Sarah Earle.
* Primary Science 132 (March/April 2014). *Just Imagine: Using Drama to Support Science Learning with Older Primary Children* by Deb McGregor and Wendy Precious.
* Primary Science 123 (May/June 2012). *Dramatic Science: At Key Stage 1* by Deb McGregor and Wendy Precious.
* Primary Science 123 (May/June 2012). *Using Models to Promote Children's Scientific Understanding* by Jane Maloney and Sheila Curtis.
* Primary Science 123 (May/June 2012). *Making Movies* by Zoe Crompton and Emma Davies.

Books:

* Asoko, H. and de Boo, M. (2001). *Analogies and Illustrations: Presenting Ideas in Primary Science*, Hatfield: Association for Science Education.
* Association for Science Education (2011). *Be Safe! Health and Safety in School Science and Technology for Teachers of 3- to 12-Year Olds (4th edn)*, Hatfield: Association for Science Education.
* Clarke, S. (2008). *Unlocking Formative Assessment*, London: Hodder & Stoughton.
* Harlen, W. and Qualter, A. (2014). *The Teaching of Science in Primary Schools*, London: Routledge.
* Naylor, S., Keogh, B. and Goldworthy, A. (2004). *Active Assessment*, London: David Fulton.

Reports:

* Davies, D., Collier, C., Earle, S., Howe, A. and McMahon, K. (2014). *Approaches to Science Assessment in English Primary Schools*, Bristol: Primary Science Teaching Trust.
* Harlen, W. (2014). *Assessment, Standards and Quality of Learning in Primary Education*, York: Cambridge Primary Review Trust.
* Nuffield Foundation (2012). *Developing Policy, Principles and Practice in Primary School Science*. www.nuffieldfoundation.org/primary-science-assessment
* Primary Science Teachers Trust (2015). *The Teacher Assessment in Primary Science (TAPS)*. https://pstt.org.uk/resources/curriculum-materials/assessment

Peer-reviewed journals:

* Earle, S. (2014). Formative and Summative Assessment of Science, in English Primary Schools: Evidence from the Primary Science Quality Mark, *Research in Science & Technology Education*, 32(2): 216–228.
* Loughland, T. and Kilpatrick, L. (2015). Formative Assessment in Primary Science, *Education 3–13*, 43(2): 128–141.

Summary

The origins of science can be traced back to the time of the ancient Greeks when a small number of radical thinking people began to seek natural, rather than supernatural, explanations for how the physical world works. These first scientists developed new knowledge from experience and reasoned argumentation. The theories developed by the ancient Greeks endured for 2,000 years until many of them proved to be unreliable when rigorously tested in the sixteenth century. Out of this period emerged a new scientific age with more rigorous methodology and greater freedom for people to express their ideas. From that time onwards, our understanding of how the natural world works has developed at an ever-increasing rate.

Short chapter **Summaries** reflect on what the chapter has covered, and will help you to consolidate your learning.

At the end of each chapter, **Further reading** offers suggestions for books, journals and websites that will help you to take your knowledge and understanding to the next level.

Subject knowledge and ideas for practice

Part 1: Subject knowledge

Darwin's theory of natural selection

Who was Charles Darwin?

Charles Darwin was born in 1809, at a time when the Industrial Revolution had just begun in England. The big northern cities were starting to develop, but most of the country was still very rural. The Church was responsible for spiritual and pastoral care, education and spiritual guidance. A Christian view of the natural world was that God had created every species of animal and plant and these species were immutable. They could not change.

Darwin was born into a middle-class and privileged family who were interested in the natural world. His father Robert was a country doctor. His grandfather Erasmus was a surgeon, naturalist and poet who had published his own ideas about the nature of evolution in a book called *Zoonomia*. As a child, Darwin was fascinated by nature and he collected animals and plants. He

Varied, theme-based science **Subject knowledge** covering such topics as the Earth and beyond, the diversity of life, health and well-being, force and motion, light and sound are presented in the first half of each chapter in this section and offer brief historical context and introduce some of the key scientists in the area being explored.

In the second half of each chapter, **Ideas for practice** for different age ranges explore specific topics within the subject knowledge, for example in Chapter 11: Moon craters or phases of the Moon or in Chapter 16: Healthy eating or the benefits of exercise, providing further information on the topic that offers innovative and engaging ways of bringing science to life in the classroom.

Using the **Three-stage framework for teaching science**, specific concepts with practical ideas for making them come alive are presented.

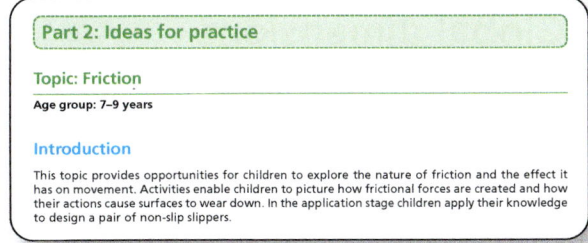

Part 2: Ideas for practice

Topic: Friction

Age group: 7–9 years

Introduction

This topic provides opportunities for children to explore the nature of friction and the effect it has on movement. Activities enable children to picture how frictional forces are created and how their actions cause surfaces to wear down. In the application stage children apply their knowledge to design a pair of non-slip slippers.

- Introducing the framework, **scientific view** summarises the fundamental science behind the topic while **working scientifically** outlines the scientific skills which children can develop.
- **Exploration stage** presents a range of ideas and activities designed to set the scene for children's science learning.
- **Re-describing stage** reinforces children's learning and understanding.
- **Application stage** offers ways for children to use their scientific learning purposefully and creatively in other contexts.

Global dimensions

Learning about the **global dimension** within the primary classroom encourages children to recognise that science is a global activity which impacts upon all our lives. It asks them to engage with complex issues and explore the role of science in the context of both the developed and the developing world. It helps children to begin to consider the ethical, social and political dimensions of science and how scientific exploration and development could contribute to a fairer and more sustainable world. Topics discussed in the Subject knowledge chapters seek to offer suggestions for starting points for discussion and research into how science can shape the future for everyone on the planet.

Talk skills and science discussion

The Primary Science Curriculum has a clear focus on discussion. Children are expected to apply their knowledge by discussing relevant topics with a group and with the whole class. The **Talk skills and science discussion** section in each Subject knowledge chapter provides a structure for building up discussion skills essential to science, in relevant contexts. These discussion sessions enable children to take responsibility for their own learning, as they hypothesise, make tentative suggestions, hear a range of points of view, and try to come to a negotiated agreement. In such exploratory discussion, children in groups have a chance to establish what they do, and do not, know and understand. They can think about what they need to learn or find out about. Discussions based on the Talk skills and science discussion structure involve evaluation of group work, talk skills and ways of learning in collaborative settings, with a focus on scientific ways of working. The contexts are not differentiated into key stages; they can be adapted to suit ages, topics, themes and the needs and interests of specific children and classes. These sections support and reinforce the focus on talk for learning throughout the book.

Additional information and teaching resources for each topic highlight the best books, websites and journals to support and inspire you in enlivening and extending topics.

PREFACE

The purpose of this book is to encourage and guide education students into ways of teaching science which promote the value of scientific learning. It can be used by students and qualified teachers alike to develop their own subject knowledge. The book offers a framework set, where possible, within technological and real-life contexts to foster an appreciation of the relevance of scientific knowledge.

The design of the book is based on the belief that children are more likely to appreciate their science learning if concepts are presented as ideas or useful points of view rather than facts or definitions to be remembered. Learning scientific concepts can be challenging and intellectually hard work for children. If we want them to make the necessary effort, we must ensure that they are rewarded with feelings of satisfaction and achievement.

A key feature of the book is the use of scientific ideas to solve theme-based 'puzzles' as part of a storytelling approach. As in all good mystery stories, the fascinating content of the story and its satisfying resolution provide pleasure and ensure interest. The advantage of narrative is that its familiar and engaging form can carry children along, helping them to generate a real understanding of science and to be able to remember what they have learned.

The book is arranged in two parts. Part 1 presents views of learning which support good classroom practice. Ideas and issues discussed in this part underpin a *three-stage teaching and learning framework*. Sharing ideas, storytelling and working scientifically to solve a 'puzzle', and other questions, are key elements of the *exploratory stage*. The scientific view is introduced in the *re-describing stage* to develop their understanding, and help resolve the puzzle. Following on from the first two stages, children are provided with opportunities in the *application stage* to further develop and make use of their newly-acquired scientific knowledge in other contexts.

Part 2 presents theme-based science subject knowledge to help teachers develop their understanding of key concepts. It also presents what we have called *Ideas for practice*. These exemplify how the three-stage framework can be used to teach particular topics to different age groups. These sections are not lesson plans but suggestions to illustrate how the teaching of particular topics can be organised.

A more comprehensive set of ideas can be found in the companion book entitled *Practical Ideas for Teaching Primary Science: Inspiring Learning and Enjoyment,* also published by Routledge and written by Peter Loxley. The companion book provides theme-based *Ideas for practice* at three age-related levels: key stage 1 (5–7 years), lower key stage 2 (7–9 years) and upper key stage 2 (9–11 years).

The topics and ideas presented in both this book and the companion are consistent with the requirements of the Primary Science National Curriculum for England, and also relevant to the curricula in Scotland, Wales and Northern Ireland.

Peter Loxley, Lyn Dawes, Linda Nicholls and Babs Dore

ACKNOWLEDGEMENTS

The authors would like to thank Mike Dore, Anna Loxley, Neil Mercer and Robert Nicholls for their patience and invaluable help with the book. Special thanks go to the editorial team at Routledge who skilfully and enthusiastically guided us through the writing of this third edition.

Publisher's acknowledgements

We are grateful to the following for permission to reproduce copyright material:

Peter Loxley and Linda Nicholls for photographs; *The Pleasure of Finding Things Out* by Richard Feynman (Penguin Books, 2001). Copyright © Richard Feynman, 2001. Reproduced by permission of Penguin Books Ltd. and reprinted from *The Feynman Lectures on Physics* by Richard P. Feynman, Robert B. Leighton and Matthew Sands; *The Snowman, a haiku* from Sky in the Pie by Roger McGough © Roger McGough reprinted by permission of Peters Fraser & Dunlop (www.petersfraser-dunlop.com) on behalf of Roger McGough; The Untouchable Ones by Charlie Numbulmoore © Charlie Numbulmoore. Viscopy/DACS 2017; Dante's Vision of Heaven, Purgatory and Hell, British Library, London, UK © British Library Board. All Rights Reserved/Bridgeman Images; Mark A. Garlick (www.space-art.co.uk); Kjartan Poskitt for permission for poetry from *The Moon* in *Twinkle Twinkle Chocolate Bar: Rhymes for the Very Young* (Foster, J., 1993), Oxford University Press; © Succession Henri Matisse /DACS 2017/ Tate Picture Library; Photographs of a primrose as seen by the human eye and a bee © Bjorn Rorslett / Science Photo Library Ltd.

Every effort has been made to contact owners of copyright material. In some instances we have been unable to trace owners and we would appreciate any information that would enable us to do so.

PART 1

THEORY AND PRACTICE

CHAPTER 1

THE PLEASURE OF FINDING THINGS OUT

You see? That's why scientists persist in their investigations, why we struggle so desperately for every bit of knowledge, climb the steepest obstacles to the next fragment of understanding; [...it is] part of the pleasure of finding things out.

(Feynman, 1999)

During everyday experience, children observe and interpret for themselves the way the world works. As teachers, we need to find out what children have already experienced, imagined and concluded about scientific ideas. We have the challenge of helping them to come to a more scientific point of view. Children need access to established scientific inform-ation which is based on centuries of careful observation and research. At the same time, we must foster the curiosity which leads children to question theories and the creativity which enables them to generate new thinking. The intrinsic interest of science is in thinking through and resolving the puzzles which are the ways the world works.

Topics discussed in the chapter

- Children's attitudes to science
- Insights into effective science teaching
- The pleasure of finding things out
- Storytelling and science teaching

Children's attitudes to science

What children like about science

Children enjoy practical science; it is interesting to have a puzzle to solve, to set up your own investigation and find out something new. The resources we use in science are intrinsically fascinating – magnets, batteries and bulbs, snails and magnifiers. Excitingly, science happens outdoors or offers a chance to measure or observe things around the school. Such practical activity is motivating and engaging, especially if there is a strong collaborative element. Working with a classmate ensures that there is someone to share ideas, and means that disheartening personal failure is less likely. Children who learn a scientific way of thinking based on reasoning about evidence are learning a life skill. Through the experience of school science, many children acquire an enduring interest in how the world works. Their curiosity is fuelled when they find out enough to know that there are still questions to ask and things to investigate.

Problems with learning concepts

Science is not just about exploration but also about sharing the knowledge and understanding that people have accumulated over time. For children, the problem with science is having to 'learn facts'. There is a lot to learn and it is easy to get things wrong. This includes new words or new uses of words because science, like many other activities, has its own technical vocabulary. A further difficulty is that some scientific explanations are counter-intuitive. Children's everyday observations may lead them to hold firmly established ideas which turn out to be 'wrong' in terms of science. For example, a ball rolling along on grass will slowly come to a stop. If we think that the ball needs force to make it move, then it is reasonable to think that it stops because it has run out of force. A more scientific explanation would be that the ball eventually stops because the forces acting on it cause it to slow down. Children sometimes find science too abstract and separate from their everyday understanding. Force is an abstract idea; the concept of force is a strange notion for children as is the idea that humans are animals made up of little cells or that mass when affected by gravity becomes weight. Confusion arises because these scientific accounts do not map easily onto what children can see, feel and hear.

> ### Something to think about
>
> The Earth-centred model of the universe is an intuitive idea. When we watch the Sun rise in the east and set in the west, common sense tells us that it must be travelling around the Earth. The idea that this is an illusion caused by the spin of the Earth is counter-intuitive. Many scientific ideas are counter-intuitive. What does this mean for the way we need to teach science? Is it feasible to expect children to discover scientific ideas for themselves?

In summary, children may see conceptual learning as hard work, dull and unoriginal. Although they like 'doing experiments', the children in Murphy and Beggs' (2003) study reported disliking writing, learning facts and technical vocabulary. Learning facts for examinations can have a negative effect on attitudes; children tend to enjoy and value science more when they have opportunities to discuss and debate ideas and issues. Research has shown that there is the need to teach concepts in ways which relate to everyday life and appeal to children's interests (Osborne et al., 2003; Simon, 2000; Cerini et al., 2003).

How can we make conceptual learning more rewarding?

In this book we offer a theory-based, practical approach to the teaching of science which we believe will help to overcome some of the difficulties children have with learning concepts. This approach involves teaching science as a collection of interrelated stories. Children are familiar with stories. They know that stories have a beginning, maybe with a puzzle or problem; a middle where events happen and may even become complicated or problematic; and a resolution, after which all becomes clear – although there may be other stories to be told subsequently. The process of science maps easily onto this narrative structure. The advantage of narrative is that it is a familiar and engaging form that can carry children along, helping them to generate a memorable understanding of science concepts, as ideas are framed in interesting and accessible contexts and explained in realistic terms.

A narrative approach to the teaching and learning of science can generate real enthusiasm for learning. Children can develop positive attitudes to the concepts they explore. A powerful mix of story and science can help children to develop a rewarding understanding of why and how things happen as they do.

Something to think about

What do you think the authors mean when they talk about presenting the scientific view as a narrative rather than a series of facts or definitions? What are the differences between the two approaches?

Insights into effective science teaching

Richard Feynman was one of the twentieth century's most brilliant scientists, achieving the Nobel Prize for Physics in 1965. He had an infectious enthusiasm for science and loved sharing his ideas with anyone who wanted to listen. His ability to talk about science in accessible ways made him a popular and entertaining public speaker. In a lecture for teachers Feynman spoke about the teaching of scientific definitions (Feynman, 1999). He thought that, although children need to be taught certain scientific words and definitions, the learning of these words and definitions does not mean they are learning science. To illustrate the point, he described a picture of a wind-up toy dog he had seen in a science textbook with the question '*What makes it move?*' written underneath. The answer the author of the book was looking for was that '*Energy makes it move*'. Feynman pointed out that this answer was meaningless for young people who are just learning about the concept of energy. He suggested that it would be equally meaningful to them to say that 'God makes the toy move' or 'spirits make it move'. He then asked what the teacher would do if the children said that they did not think energy made the toy move. He wanted to know how the teacher would persuade them that the energy explanation is valid. Why not God? Why not spirits? Why is 'energy' the best explanation?

The point Feynman wanted to make was that '*Energy makes things move*' is a definition which only makes sense to children *after* they understand the concept of energy. He suggested that children would learn more about how the toy worked by taking it apart to see how the spring is wound and how it releases to make the wheels go round. They could think about the effect of winding a spring and what has to happen to create a wound spring. They could learn how the Sun enables plants to grow and how eating plants provides people with the capacity to wind up the toy and make it move. For Feynman, the answer to the question *'What makes it move?'* was that sunshine makes the dog move. And if children do not believe this, then teachers and children have a lot of interesting things to talk about.

Beware of mystic formulae

In his lecture Feynman used the term 'mystic formulae' to describe some of the explanations used in science books to answer questions. In particular, he focused on the concept of friction and criticised the practice of using mystic formulae such as *'The soles of shoes wear out because of friction'* as scientific explanations. In his own words: 'Shoe leather wears out because it rubs against the sidewalk and the little notches and bumps on the sidewalk grab pieces and pull them off. To simply say it is because of friction is sad, because it's not science' (Feynman, 1999: 180).

Feynman's mini-narrative about how shoe leather wears out is the science behind the definition. Instead of labelling the wearing-out process as friction, he imagined the events which actually caused the shoes to wear out. To understand a concept, we can create in our minds a representation or mental model of it – a kind of story.

> ### Something to think about
>
> Richard Feynman describes scientific definitions as mystic formulae. Can you think of any mystic formulae that you have been required to learn? Ask yourself what images come into your mind when you think of friction. What words would you use to describe it?

Talking concepts into existence

If you were preparing to teach children about friction, how would you start? To relate the idea of friction to the child's experience, you might start by encouraging the children to feel the sole of a shoe or rub their fingers on floor surfaces. They could talk about which surfaces give good grip and which surfaces are slippery and try to explain why. Children could go on to talk about why they think shoes wear out. Can they explain why? What words would children use to describe how a shoe wears out? They might think of words such as rubbing or scratching – which are actions involving forces. The children could suggest which type of sole is likely to wear out more quickly and whether the shape and size of the sole affects how quickly they wear out. There are many things to talk about, and the more children talk about a concept and begin to see it as an everyday problem, the more likely they will be able to make sense of it.

Talking about how shoes wear out in this way enables children to construct meaningful pictures or images of the process in their minds. (These internal representations or mental models are discussed in more detail in Chapter 4.) Drawing pictures also helps children to create mental models of scientific concepts.

The key to developing children's understanding of friction is to help them see that all surfaces are uneven. Even the smoothest surfaces have irregularities which are not visible to the naked eye. An analogy using a familiar scenario, such as a car travelling over a rough road, can be useful. Children can visualise how the tyres collide with the bumps and holes in the road. Children need to be helped to visualise 'friction' – how the uneven surfaces rub up against each other – by employing a combination of drawings, analogies and figurative language until the most evocative images are constructed. Ultimately, the intention is to construct an explanation in words and pictures which describes how friction works.

This joint oral construction of understanding between teacher and children has the outcome of 'talking the concept into existence' (Ogborn et al., 1996). In this case, seeing the science means visualising how friction works and understanding how it applies to the practical situation. When we as teachers are able to 'see' the science, we are more able to manage the children's conceptual learning in ways which stimulate and maintain their interest (Asoko, 2000). (Helping to 'see' the science is the purpose of the teaching and learning framework set out in Chapter 3, and the examples of theme-based plans presented in Part 2 of the text.)

Something to think about

Talking a scientific concept into existence requires us to use words to create an image or representation of the concept in our mind. Think of a scientific concept which you can picture in your mind (friction, electricity, photosynthesis). What words would you encourage children to use to enable them to visualise the concept in their minds?

The pleasure of finding things out

It is not surprising to find that children may not enjoy memorising facts and learning how to spell complex scientific words. If we are to promote positive attitudes to science, the experiences which stimulate children's conceptual development must be rewarding both intellectually and emotionally. Feynman provides an elegant account of how, as a child, he first came to appreciate the value of scientific knowledge and the pleasure which can be gained from finding out that the world wasn't as he first perceived it to be. On regular walks in the countryside, the young Feynman would be tantalised by his father's questions about the animals and plants which they observed, and challenged to explain reasons for their behaviour (Feynman, 1999). Feynman describes one occasion when the conversation focused on the behaviour of a bird.

> **During the walks in the woods with my father, I learned a great deal. In the case of the birds, for example: Instead of naming them, my father would say, 'Look, notice that bird is always pecking in its feathers. It pecks a lot in its feathers. Why do you think it pecks the feathers?'**
>
> (Feynman, 1999: 181)

Feynman was encouraged by his father to suggest a hypothesis, offering what seemed to him to be a logical reason. His father would help him test if he was right. In this case he hypothesised that the bird was straightening its feathers because it had just landed. He was encouraged to test this idea by checking to see if other birds preened their feathers on landing.

Noting that this did not usually happen, they looked for another reason. Eventually his father introduced a new way of 'seeing' the event by suggesting that the preening bird could be removing parasites. The experience created a real opportunity to think together about the idea of *interdependency*:

> [H]e went on to say that in the world whenever there is any source of something that could be eaten to make life go, some form of life finds a way to make use of that source; and that each little bit of leftover stuff is eaten by something.
>
> (Feynman, 1999: 182)

Interdependence is a 'big idea' in science because it applies to a wide range of events and situations. It is a powerful idea which helps us understand how life on Earth has developed and how it is sustained.

Something to think about

Charles Darwin developed the concepts of adaptation and interdependence to explain how all living things in the world are related to each other. These ideas explain the origins of all living things on the Earth – they are 'big ideas'. What everyday examples of interdependence or adaptation are immediately available to the children in your class?

New ways of seeing the world

By considering the concept of parasites, Feynman was able to think of the events he had observed in a different way. Initially, he had been encouraged to explain his personal point of view but when the account proved unreliable there was a need to imagine, discover or find out about a new way of seeing the events. The explanation of a more scientific point of view, coupled with the pleasure he gained from being actively involved in the telling of a story, was very rewarding. For children, discovery involves creative thinking. Things that they have never realised and which are new to them require the exercise of creativity to imagine and understand – and 'finding out' can be very exciting.

> Now the point of this is that the result of observation, even if I were unable to come to an ultimate conclusion, was a wonderful piece of gold, with a marvellous result. It was something marvellous.
>
> (Feynman, 1999: 182)

The story of the birds reminds us that we can teach children by stimulating curiosity, asking interesting questions, and providing key information at the point it is required. An important purpose of science education is to share with children the amazing visions of the world that science has created. If it is shared through rational and evocative dialogue, children can experience the pleasure of learning science which comes from the wonder and awe of finding out that the world is not always as we first perceive it to be. In addition, children can learn that accurate scientific explanations 'hold water' when tested and questioned, which their own everyday descriptions of events might not. The child begins to realise that its developing knowledge is cumulative and can be put to use, whereas everyday understandings may not be sound or robust when tested.

Storytelling and science teaching

In his anecdote Feynman was reminiscing about an experience which was unique and very special to him. Producing similar rewarding intellectual and emotional experiences for a class of primary children may not be so easy. The more general and important point about the value of scientific knowledge is that the usefulness of science resides in its power to transform the way we see the world. To achieve this, learning has to be set in contexts which require the need for a scientific explanation. Contexts for science learning need to be familiar to children, yet hold the potential to produce dilemmas or problems which the development of conceptual understanding can help to resolve. Children commonly ask questions. In classrooms, they may find it harder to do so. A first step is to establish puzzles or encourage questions about the natural world. We can then organise science learning in meaningful stages so that children can have access to scientific ideas, can work through activities which help them to make meaning from experience and then go on to use their new understanding to solve problems and answer questions.

In Feynman's narrative, his father pointed out a puzzling event. He then took on the role of the expert to model the scientific skills of hypothesising, observation and investigation necessary to construct an explanation for the behaviour of the birds. Practising these scientific ways of thinking led to conflict between how Feynman initially visualised the event and the empirical evidence. This added tension and an imperative to consider alternative ideas. In effect, the puzzling event pushed Feynman's existing knowledge to its limit and created a desire to learn more. It stimulated his curiosity and fostered motivation to discuss ideas. The ensuing conversation enabled Feynman to re-describe aspects of nature in more scientific ways (Sutton, 1996). Eventually, his active participation was rewarded with a sense of pleasure and satisfaction as the puzzle was resolved. He was able to see the event in a new and more powerful way. The story ends with the child's heightened interest likely to create opportunities for more questions and stories. The pleasure of finding things out helps children want to go on to find out even more.

Something to think about

Think about a story which has had an influence on you – not necessarily to do with science. What did you like about it? Did it develop around some issues? If so, were these issues resolved? Did it help you resolve some personal issues? Did it make you think about the world in a different way? Would you describe it as an empowering story? Do you know any empowering scientific stories?

Storytellers arouse curiosity, create tension and provide the satisfaction of answered questions and an interesting resolution. Teachers can adopt this straightforward narrative sequence to help plan stimulating lessons. The difference between traditional storytelling and science teaching is that in the latter we want the audience (children) to take an active part in the storytelling. We want children to tell the story using their own voices, each with its own unique interpretation of the theme, but each based on sound science.

To facilitate a storytelling approach, science lessons need:

1. A theme which can be communicated to children in narrative form. *Feynman's narrative was developed from the theme of interdependency.*
2. A context which is relevant for the theme and also familiar to the children. *A woodland setting is an ideal place to observe the behaviour of birds.*
3. Events and/or activities which set the scene against which the narrative can unfold. *An adult set the scene by drawing attention to what the birds were doing.*
4. A 'hook' or puzzling event which arouses children's curiosity. *Why was the bird pecking its feathers? This was cast as a puzzling event which needed explanation.*
5. A complication which indicates there is more to the event than the children may imagine. *Feynman's initial suggestion proved incorrect and he was keen to find out what was really happening.*
6. A resolution with the help of a well-informed adult who can provide relevant guidance to help solve the dilemma. *Feynman's father introduced him to the idea of parasites. As a result, Feynman's understanding of the behaviour of birds changed and he learned to see the world in a new way.*
7. Opportunities for children to develop further understanding of the theme. *Feynman and his father went on to talk about the concept of interdependency, applying it to the behaviour of other living things in the woods.*

The way Feynman learnt science greatly influenced his love of the subject and influenced his thinking about what constitutes effective teaching. We suggest that primary science teachers can usefully draw on established storytelling techniques to create similar stimulating learning experiences for their children.

Summary

Teaching science as facts and definitions is unlikely to promote effective learning. Meaningful and memorable learning requires the children to be intellectually and emotionally stimulated. This is more likely to happen if we plan learning settings in which children can experience the pleasure of finding out things about the natural world which surprise them and satisfy their desire to know. We suggest it is possible to apply storytelling techniques to science teaching in order to arouse and satisfy children's natural curiosity about the world in which they live.

Chapter 3 presents a framework for organising children's learning based on a storytelling approach. The framework provides opportunities for children to express and test their own ideas before exploring the value of the scientific point of view.

Further reading

Read these books just for the pleasure of finding things out:

- Cox, B. and Cohen, A. (2013). *Wonders of Life,* London: Harper Collins.
- Cox, B. and Cohen, A. (2011). *Wonders of the Solar System*, London: Harper Collins.
- Feynman, R. (1999). *The Pleasure of Finding Things Out*, London: Penguin Books.
- Francis, G. (2015). *Adventures in Human Being*, London: Profile Books.
- Heiney, P. (2014). *Can Crocodiles Cry?* Stroud: The History Press.
- Roberts, A. (2015). *The Incredible Unlikeliness of Being: Evolution and the Making of Us*, London: Heron Books.
- Thompson, M. (2016). *A Space Traveller's Guide to the Solar System*, London: Transworld Publishers.

CHAPTER 2
VIEWS OF SCIENCE LEARNING

From personal discovery to storytelling

Words can have a power and influence quite out of proportion to their triviality as mere marks on paper or vibrations in the air. When circumstances are right they can excite people's minds and move their imaginations, in science as in any other area of human activity.

(Sutton, 1992)

The purpose of this chapter is to present the views on learning which have informed the practices set out throughout the book. The chapter begins by looking at the nature of children's own ideas and how they differ from established scientific ideas. A central theme of the chapter is the sociocultural nature of science teaching and learning. Effective science teaching is not as straightforward as simply telling children what they need to know. Scientific ideas are abstract things. No one can see an idea in someone else's mind. To communicate an idea, it has to be modelled using words, pictures and gestures. Talking together about a scientific idea is a good indication that children are starting to develop understanding. If we want to inspire children, stimulate their imaginations and extend their thinking, then we need to use teaching strategies which harness the learning power of talk.

Topics discussed in the chapter

- Overview of science learning
- Constructivism and enquiry learning
- The nature of scientific ideas
- Views on conceptual learning
- Sociocultural practices
- Communicating scientific ideas

Overview of science learning

Science education is a long-term process which involves learning to use the ideas of science to explore and explain how the natural world works (Asoko, 2002). Initially, children need to become familiar with the names and behaviour of the physical things which populate the natural world. They learn the names of common plants, animals and materials and gain first-hand experience of how they behave. As children become more familiar with the nature of living and non-living things, they can identify relationships between them and start to develop a bigger picture of how the natural world works.

Although first-hand experience is an important part of the science-learning process, there is a limit to what children can discover for themselves. For example, children could discover through enquiry methods that plants need water and light to survive. This is important foundational knowledge towards understanding how plants grow. However, explaining why plants cannot survive without light and water requires children to understand the process of photosynthesis, which is an established scientific idea. Science has a powerful set of established ideas which provide reliable information about how the natural world works. To develop their understanding of the natural world, children must learn to use scientific ideas as tools for explaining its behaviour.

Something to think about

What are your views about how children best learn science? How would you teach them that plants are living things? Could they discover this for themselves? If so, explain how.

Constructivism and enquiry learning

The constructivist view of learning is based on the belief that children make sense of the world by actively constructing their own knowledge and ways of understanding. From early in life children develop beliefs about how the world behaves, based on their experiences. They play with toys in water and, after a while, they are able to predict which will float and which will sink. They receive a new toy and, on the basis of previous experience, they are able to predict whether it is likely to float before they put it in water. Initially, the child's knowledge is restricted to the behaviour of a set of familiar objects, but, with intellectual development, the child may be able to make some connections between cause and effect. For example, a child may assume its own criteria for whether an object will float. In the child's mind, an object may be too big or even the wrong colour to float. By the time the child is old enough to be educated formally, it has already constructed a set of beliefs about floating and sinking. These personal ideas may not be fully formed or reliable but will be useful and sensible to the child. For these reasons, the child may be reluctant to change them, even when they conflict with the scientific view presented to them by their teacher (Roden, 2005).

Research into children's ideas

Over the past 30 years there has been extensive research into the nature of children's ideas. One influential project was called Primary Science Processes and Concept Exploration. It was run by

King's College London and Liverpool University. One of the aims of the project was to establish the ideas that young children hold in particular science concept areas and to develop teaching strategies to help them build their ideas into scientific ones. The SPACE approach, as it came to be known, was to develop scientific understanding by starting with the children's own ideas and modifying them by providing relevant practical-based experiences. The outcomes of the research can still be accessed through the Nuffield Foundation website.

Below are some examples of young children's (4–7 years) commonly held beliefs (Pine et al., 2001):

- Plants or trees cannot be living things because they do not move.
- Neither humans nor insects are animals.
- Plants die if they are not kept on a windowsill.
- The bigger the plant, the healthier it must be.
- A force comes out of the eye that makes one able to see.
- Rocks are dead and not natural.
- Steam and smoke are the same things.
- Small objects float and big objects sink.
- Heavy things sink and all light things float.
- Bigger things will be heavier.
- Large objects fall faster than small objects.
- The Moon is a source of light.
- The Earth stays still and the Sun moves around it.

Something to think about

Choose one of the children's beliefs. How does it differ from the accepted scientific view? Devise a teaching strategy to persuade children with similar beliefs to rethink their ideas so they are consistent with the scientific view.

Example: Alasdair's story

A group of 10-year-olds had been asked to draw what they thought might be inside a battery. After some discussion, one child remembered the mess a leaking battery had made of his bicycle light and so most of the children decided that inside was some form of corrosive chemical and tried to represent this in their pictures in some way. However, all of them had difficulty in visualising how this might result in electricity flowing from the battery once it was connected in a circuit. Alasdair, though, thought hard and then drew a picture of a hamster going round in a wheel. At first, the other children were perplexed until Alasdair explained that he had visited a local power station and seen the generators in the turbine hall. In the exhibition next door was an explanatory model of a generator with the steam turning the turbine which then turned a coil of wire within a magnetic field, so causing electricity to flow in the wire. Alasdair had realised that to make electricity all you needed to do was cause something to spin fast, and his hamster did that all night in the cage in the corner of his bedroom! So, although he admitted with a grin that he didn't really believe a hamster lurked in every battery, he had used existing knowledge to offer an analogy to solve the puzzle.

Educational theorist Jean Piaget saw children's learning as a process of personal intellectual construction arising from their interactions with the world. In the 1970s his views were adapted to inform a theory of science learning which recognised the influence children's existing ideas can have on their learning. Driver and Easley (1978) subsequently described children's personal ideas as 'interpretive models' and 'alternative frameworks' which endowed them with educational value and interest (Solomon, 1994). The focus on the status of children's ideas led to the description of children as young scientists with the potential to construct their own scientific explanations through the application of scientific enquiry skills. Constructing scientific knowledge through enquiry methods has proved to be a compelling and enduring vision of how children best learn science.

Children as scientists

The description of the 'child as a scientist' is commonly used in primary schools to justify an emphasis on enquiry learning. It is an attractive image which continues to be promoted by some educationalists and professional bodies. Enquiry methods enable children to gather reliable information about cause and effect relationships, such as the effects heating and cooling have on different materials and how the shape of an object influences its ability to float. Through enquiry practices, children become familiar with the behaviour of living and non-living objects which make up their world. For younger children, science learning is mainly to do with gaining first-hand experience of the world. Exploring their local environment provides essential knowledge which can be drawn on and further developed later in their education. The nature of enquiry learning is discussed later in the text (Chapter 6) and examples of relevant practice provided.

The nature of scientific ideas

In the view of Albert Einstein, scientific ideas are 'free creations of the human mind, and are not, however it may seem, uniquely determined by the external world' (Einstein and Infeld, 1961: 32). In other words, scientific ideas do not reside in nature, waiting to be discovered; they are images or models of the world made up by scientists. Take, for example, Darwin's ideas about evolution. An important part of his work was to study how the physical characteristics of animals and plants helped them to survive in their environment. He learnt a lot from first-hand experience, but his genius lay in his ability to create a credible 'story' or explanation for how they had acquired such beneficial characteristics. Darwin's theory of natural selection radically changed the way people perceived the natural world and their place in it. At the time, his ideas were controversial because they challenged religious beliefs about the genesis of life on Earth and, in particular, about the origins of the human race. Many people were outraged by the possibility that they were in some way related to apes. New scientific ideas are often controversial because they provide ways of seeing the world which can challenge long-established cultural and religious views.

Today, Darwin's ideas can help children make sense of their local environment. In early spring, children are likely to find the ground of the local woodland carpeted with bluebells, while the trees above are yet to grow leaves. Like all other plants, these small blue flowers need sunlight to grow. If they waited until summer came, the trees would have grown their leaves and blocked out the sunlight. Bluebells use food stored in their bulbs to grow rapidly, which enables them to flower before the trees come into leaf. They all flower together, increasing the chances of insect pollination and ensuring a new crop for the following year. By adapting to life under the dense canopies of deciduous trees, bluebells can avoid competition for growing space and are therefore more likely to survive and reproduce. Adaptation is a big scientific idea which can be used universally to explain why different types of animals and plants thrive in different environments. It is an example of a big scientific idea because it provides knowledge about the behaviour of all living things in the world. More information about adaptation is given later in the text (Chapter 15).

Something to think about

What do you think is the biggest idea in science? Discuss this with your colleagues and put together a list of the top ten big ideas.

Story about inventing the atom

The idea that things are made of atoms was first thought up in the time of the Ancient Greeks. Legend has it that a philosopher called Democritus was sitting at home when he caught the aroma of a loaf of bread being carried up the stairs by a servant. Democritus had a keen interest in the natural world and was rich enough to devote his time to finding out how it worked. The smell of the bread got him thinking. Perhaps he could smell the bread because it gave off tiny, invisible particles which travelled through the air. He then, through reasoned thinking, invented an explanation using cheese as an example. If you cut a bit of cheese in half, then half again, and so and so on, you finally arrive at something you cannot cut and this he called an atom (Mosley and Lynch, 1996). In this moment, Democritus created the concept of an atom; it could not be said that he discovered it. Since then, scientists have produced evidence that materials are made up of tiny particles, and the atom which Democritus invented has become part of established scientific knowledge.

Scientific ideas can be counter-intuitive

Scientific understanding is often counter-intuitive. Children often base their understanding of the natural world on their own behaviour. For example, they may think that bees have two eyes like themselves and are attracted to the flowers which have the most alluring colours. In fact, bees have five eyes which can detect ultraviolet light and hence see the world in a very different way than we do. (Pictures in Chapter 21 show how different a primrose looks, seen through the eyes of a bee.) From a honey bee's perspective, the reddish patterns provide 'landing strips' indicating where the pollen and nectar can be found. They are then able to use the position of the sun to navigate their way back to their nest. Honey bees do not waste energy randomly looking for food. Forager bees locate a food source and then perform a 'waggle dance' to tell others where to find it. A scientific understanding of the behaviour of bees reveals a fascinating story of cooperation and sacrifice for the survival of the colony. Bees provide intriguing studies because their amazing abilities are so different from what children would have imagined. This is not knowledge which they could discover from first-hand experience. It is a 'scientific story' which needs 'telling' and 'talking about', although it can be made more meaningful and further developed through first-hand and secondary sources of information. (Chapter 1 explores the relationship between storytelling and science teaching and focuses on the rewards which can be gained from learning scientific concepts.)

Something to think about

Think back to your own early science education. Which scientific ideas did you find to be counter-intuitive? Try to explain why.

Views on conceptual learning

One of the main concerns with enquiry learning since its inception is the ambiguous nature of how enquiry or process skills support children's learning of established scientific knowledge.

In the 1980s the Children's Learning in Science Project (CLIS) and the Science Processes and Concepts Exploration project (SPACE) carried out extensive research to find ways of applying constructivist principles to teaching scientific concepts (Warwick and Sparks Linfield, 2000). Each project provides an enquiry-based teaching sequence designed to structure the way children learn established scientific knowledge. Broadly, the sequences involve eliciting children's existing ideas, challenging their validity and providing experiences through which they can be persuaded to modify them in favour of the scientific view. For example, children commonly believe that seeds contain fully formed baby plants. It is useful to bear this in mind when teaching germination. Children's ideas can be challenged by asking them to draw what they think is inside a broad bean seed and then asking them to draw what they see inside after dissecting it. The difference between the drawings can provide a topic for discussion. An embryo inside a seed and a fully formed plant are different because they grow in different ways. The embryo will grow in the dark, whereas a fully formed plant needs light to grow. This is a puzzle which requires a scientific explanation.

Effective learning requires children to be provided with new ideas which are consistent with their experiences and which they recognise as useful (Posner et al., 1982). In this case, the teacher needs to provide a new way of visualising what is inside a seed and help the children imagine how it can be transformed into a plant. This involves the children making sense of the idea of germination and using it to explain how the embryo progressively turns into a fully formed broad bean plant. (Chapter 3 sets out a three-stage framework to help teachers organise the way children learn scientific concepts.)

Tools for conceptual learning

Interpretations of Lev Vygotsky's work have led educationalists to pay special attention to the role language plays in learning. Children's ability to talk about an idea is dependent on their understanding of it. When learning something new, children can at first find it difficult to put their ideas into words. Their talk is exploratory, hesitant and incomplete as they 'try out' ideas and modify them as they speak (Barnes, 2008). Trying out new ideas in their own words as expressions of thought is an important part of children's science learning (Sutton, 1996). (Chapters 4 and 5 provide detailed accounts of the role talk plays in learning science.)

Understanding scientific ideas requires children to construct representations or models of them in their minds (see Chapter 4). This involves interpreting the scientific ideas in accordance with knowledge they already possess. Barnes (2008) describes this process as 'working on understanding', which may require children to rethink and modify their existing ideas in order to accommodate the scientific ones. This is a powerful image because it not only reminds us that learning requires time and mental effort, but it also suggests the need for cognitive tools. Physical work often requires the skilful use of appropriate tools, such as hammers, saws and spades. For mental work, suitable tools include ways of talking such as explaining, persuading, negotiating, arguing and summarising, which can help children re-think and reshape existing ideas to accommodate new knowledge. In addition, creative writing, modelling through role-play, making physical models, thinking up analogies and drawing pictures are all strategies which can help visualise scientific ideas. (For more detail refer to Chapter 7.)

Whatever strategies are used, encouraging children to change their existing ideas is not straightforward and outcomes are never predictable. Children may cling tenaciously to their misconceptions, even when evidence and argument show them to be non-scientific. This is because ways of everyday thinking have proved to be useful in their daily lives. In fact, children may 'learn' the scientific view for use in the science classroom and continue to use their tried and trusted common sense view outside of school (Driver, 1983).

Something to think about

What teaching strategies would you use to help children visualise how seeds grow into plants?

Sociocultural practices

Children as apprentices

While Piaget was more interested in the part played by the actions of children in the learning process, Vygotsky focused on understanding the social and cultural influences. From a sociocultural perspective, science education can be perceived as a form of apprenticeship through which children learn by working alongside people who are more expert. Usually, the teacher takes on the role of the expert, but children can also learn from each other by working together in ways which enable them to share existing expertise. Chapter 5 describes how ground rules for talk can be used to guide the way children interact when learning together. Also, each subject knowledge chapter has a section called Talk Skills and Science Discussion which provides structured social contexts through which children can share ideas and learn from each other.

The apprenticeship model is a strong idea which can be used to help teachers understand their role in children's science learning. It is based on the premise that children's progress can be accelerated when the teacher participates in and guides the learning process.

> Unlike Piagetian theory, in which teachers often seem to be reduced to a largely peripheral role as the provider and manager of a suitable environment in which learning subsequently occurs, Vygotskian theory gives teachers a central role: leading children and students to new levels of conceptual and procedural understanding through social interactions mediated by language.
>
> (Hodson, 1999: 244)

Rogoff (1990) uses the term 'guided participation' while Tharp and Gallimore (1988) use the term 'assisted performance' as other ways to describe the apprenticeship model. Common to both approaches is the importance of modelling and joint participation of both teacher and children in learning and problem solving. A model of learning in which teachers and children set out together on a quest for knowledge is an appealing one. It involves sharing ideas and working collaboratively towards a common goal. A puzzling event or fascinating question can ignite children's curiosity and desire to find an answer. As the expert, the teacher takes a central role by organising learning tasks, modelling and demonstrating good practice and assisting the children to think, talk and act in ways which supports effective learning. The 'ideas for practice' in Part 2 of the text illustrate how children's learning of specific topics can be organised based on the sociocultural model of learning.

Modelling positive attitudes

> Modelling good practice includes displaying positive attitudes, such as excitement, interest and a sense of awe and wonder. How children feel about the scientific ideas, how they feel about themselves as learners, how they are influenced by their peers and their cultural beliefs can all have an impact on the quality of their learning. Clearly, feelings of wonder, delight, amusement, interest, disinterest, boredom and disgust will impact in different ways on a learning task – sometimes favourably, sometimes unfavourably.
>
> (Hodson, 1999: 243)

Chapter 1 describes how, as a child, Richard Feynman learnt science with his father. Feynman's father was not an expert scientist. He was fascinated by science and enjoyed finding out new ideas to share with his son. Feynman makes a point of how infectious his father's enthusiasm was for his own reading and learning about science. Often they would share the joy of finding things out by reading and discussing together things they found of interest in scientific books and magazines. The recognition that teachers do not have to know everything to begin with can be liberating for teachers. An infectious interest and enthusiasm for science could be more valuable.

Something to think about

Can you envisage any problems with a 'learning together' approach to science teaching? Do you think children need to be taught how to learn science, or is it the teacher's job to tell them what they need to know?

Modelling science learning

Chapter 4 exemplifies how classroom talk directed by the teacher can help children to re-think their ideas in ways which make them more consistent with the scientific view. The part entitled 'Learning to talk about the world in new ways' provides a useful picture of the difficulties children may have in joining in a scientific conversation with their teacher. At first, the new scientific words are foreign and the children may not be sure what the teacher is on about. They listen carefully to pick up familiar words to see if they strike a chord with their own ideas. As the words become more familiar, they are able to form mental pictures of what the teacher is talking about. At this point, they may feel confident enough to contribute to the conversation by asking questions and presenting points of view. If their ideas are well received, they are encouraged to take more risks; they become less hesitant and progressively take a more dialogically active role in their learning.

Robin Alexander (2006) describes dialogic teaching as teaching that leads to effective classroom discussions which stimulate and extend children's thinking. Chapter 5 addresses some of the important issues and provides guidance and ground rules to support different types of talk for science learning.

Research by Alexander (2001) into the nature of primary education in six countries highlights some differences in the way concepts were taught. In the UK and USA, teachers were likely to interact with the whole class at the same time, whereas in France and Russia they tended to focus on a small group while the rest of the class paid close attention to the arguments. This enabled the teacher to model ways of working on understanding with one group, while the rest of the class listened. Such conversation provides opportunities for children to try out scientific ideas under the guidance of the teacher.

Something to think about

What are the advantages and disadvantages of using a focus group of children to model scientific ways of talking? How would you organise it in the classroom?

Communicating scientific ideas

In his influential work, 'The scientific model as a form of speech', Clive Sutton sets out to re-describe science learning in terms of cultural and social processes. His work was intended to re-direct our attention away from the personal construction of knowledge to the re-interpretation and appreciation of science as someone else's point of view or story.

> Pupils who enter into the mental worlds that these (scientific) models offer could be said to be not so much 're-constructing' anything, as re-concerning what is going on, learning to talk in new ways, and appreciating that scientific ideas are an outcome of human effort.

> (Sutton, 1996: 146)

There is a story of invention behind every scientific idea which involves creative people using figurative language in new and powerful ways. A scientist may have a germ of a new idea in mind, but needs to be able to find the words and imagery to make sense of it and to communicate the idea to other people. Choosing the right words to communicate new ideas is a key part of developing understanding.

Example: Choosing the right words to communicate scientific ideas

When, in 1644, Evangelista Torricelli puzzled over the effects of the atmosphere, he described it in terms of depths of a fluid. He wrote that 'We live at the bottom of an ocean of air' (Sutton, 1996). Torricelli's new point of view changed the way people visualised the world and led to a whole series of experiments to test and develop the 'ocean of air' picture further.

Science is a social enterprise which involves scientists using language in new ways in order to communicate their point of view. Persuading other scientists to accept a new idea relies just as much on the imaginative use of language as it does on the collection of data. Importantly, the same can be said for science teaching. The use of stories, analogies and figurative language are powerful tools for helping children to work on their understanding of scientific ideas (Asoko and de Boo, 2001). (A range of strategies to help children make sense of the scientific view are discussed in Chapter 7.)

Something to think about

Because the scientific community have their own ways of acting and talking, science learning has been compared to learning a foreign language. How would this view influence the way you taught science?

Scientific stories

Communicating science in the form of narratives can make it more relevant and meaningful (Avraamidou and Osborne, 2009). Children love stories. They are fascinated by mysteries and eager to know how they are resolved. Science is about resolving nature's mysteries and its stories can be gripping as well as informative.

Example: Science story

It is raining DNA outside. On the bank of the Oxford canal at the bottom of my garden is a large willow tree, and it is pumping downy seeds into the air. There is no consistent air movement, and the seeds are drifting outward in all directions from the tree. Up and down the canal, as far as my binoculars can reach, the water is white with floating cottony flecks, and we can be sure that they have carpeted the ground to much the same radius in other directions too.

The cotton wool is mostly made of cellulose, and it dwarfs the tiny capsule that contains DNA, the genetic information. The DNA content must be a small proportion of the total, so why did I say it was raining DNA rather than cellulose? The answer is that it is the DNA that matters. The cellulose fluff, although bulkier, is just a parachute to be discarded. The whole performance, cotton, catkins, tree and all, is in aid of one thing and one thing only: the spreading of DNA around the countryside. Not just any DNA, but DNA whose coded characteristics spell out specific instructions for building willow trees that will shed a new generation of downy seeds. Those fluffy specks are, literally, spreading instructions for making themselves. They are there because their ancestors succeeded in doing the same. It is raining instructions out there; it's raining programs; it's raining tree-growing, fluff spreading algorithms. That's not a metaphor, it is the plain truth. It couldn't be any plainer if it were raining floppy disks.

(Dawkins, 1986: 111)

Dawkins' story is an evocative piece of writing designed to grab the reader's attention and to develop interest in the science. A hint of mystery is provided by the somewhat puzzling idea that it's raining DNA. A mystery or a puzzle is an essential part of a good story because it creates in the reader a 'need to know' what happens. Norris et al. (2005) use the term 'narrative appetite' to describe the desire a successful story provokes in the reader to find something out.

The unique and personal description of what is happening in Dawkin's back garden sets the scene for the science. The reader is drawn into a familiar world only to realise there are things going on which she has never before imagined. This opens up possibilities for a new way of looking at things. The language used presumes a certain level of prior knowledge; however, it is evocative and paints a new picture of the observable events which has the potential to change the way the reader perceives the world.

Writers endeavour to make the world look a little bit different. They set out to surprise, shock or delight the reader – or all three – with their ideas and imaginative use of language. As Carver (2005) points out, good writers make the world over according to their own specifications. This is what makes Dawkins' piece so appealing. What he has produced is a unique and personal view of the world which is consistent with the scientific perspective.

There is a wide range of science picture story books available for young children (up to the age of about 7 years) which are designed to communicate scientific knowledge. However, good science stories for older children (up to the age of 11 years) are harder to find. It is worth teachers investing the time to develop their own stories from information sources in order to whet children's appetites for scientific knowledge.

Teachers as storytellers

Primary teachers are often excellent storytellers and, with practice, can learn to communicate scientific knowledge in their own unique and creative ways. With imaginative use of language teachers can re-form information from newspapers, magazines, books and online sources into short stories or mini-narratives designed to stir children's curiosity in a topic. To grab children's attention, these narratives need to be precisely constructed. There should not be anything superficial and the dialogue needs to be focused on essential facts (Kubli, 2001). When developing a mini-narrative, teachers should carefully choose those ideas which are likely to appeal to the children. Teachers have the advantage of knowing their audience intimately and know what ideas will excite their children. It is often the things which are left out or implied which best stir children's curiosity and imagination. A key ingredient found in most successful short stories is the feeling that the author is holding something back, something hinted at which the reader really needs to know – the unheard-of something that only the author knows; the vital knowledge that gives the author control over both the characters and the readers (Casterton, 2005). Anticipating and ultimately finding out this vital knowledge provides the source of the children's pleasure.

Example of a mini-narrative: The Goldilocks Zone

You won't believe this, but Goldilocks is alive and well and living in outer space! Explain that if you can.

Did you know that scientists are trying to find out whether there are other planets like ours out in space? They are using very powerful telescopes to search the universe. And guess what! They found one in the Goldilocks Zone of a distant sun. Goldilocks Zone doesn't sound very scientific. I imagined the planet to be populated by bears eating porridge. What do you think?

Actually, when I found out what it meant, I was quite impressed. The conditions on planets which orbit their sun in the Goldilocks Zone are not too hot and not too cold to support life. Do you get it?

In fact, scientists think the surface temperature on this particular planet which they have named Kepler-22b is a lovely 22°C. A great place for a holiday! Problem is the planet is 600 light years from Earth. Even if it's inhabited, having a chat on the phone will be a bit frustrating. At that distance, a radio telephone message would not receive a reply for another 1,200 years.

Can you imagine what the sun called Kepler-22 could look like?

Comment

The above mini-narrative is based on information published in *The Guardian Online*. Much of the technical information from the original article has been left out. Only essential ideas which relate to the Goldilocks theme have been put in to stir children's interest in the search for habitable planets. The narrative style is informal and, by speaking directly to the children, it is able to communicate information and encourage discussion.

Together, children and their teacher can explore information sources to develop the narrative about the search for habitable planets out in space. In addition, children can work on their understanding of living things and use their knowledge to speculate about the kind of life which may be found on Kepler-22b.

Something to think about

Research up-to-date science articles in newspapers. Identify those which would make interesting stories to share with children. How could you rewrite one to create your own narrative? Use it in the classroom and/or share it with colleagues.

Children as storytellers

Children can be accomplished storytellers. Telling personal stories has traditionally been an important way for young children to communicate their ideas, feelings and experiences. They have a desire to communicate and actively seek to 'chat' with teachers and other caring adults (Davies and Howe, 2003).

Storytelling can be a useful tool for children as a means to communicate their understanding of scientific ideas. The re-telling of the scientific story from a personal perspective allows the lived experience of the child to interact with the scientific ideas (Avraamidou and Osborne, 2009). In effect, this makes the science more accessible by breaking down the boundaries between the 'hard' science (the adult conversation) and those 'softer' and more accessible spaces in which children are more able and willing to communicate (Levinson, 2008).

Example: My mystery mushroom

Given the chance, children are natural storytellers – as a trainee teacher found out when she took her class on an autumn walk in the local woodland. The purpose of the walk was to identify and record the seasonal changes to the woodland.

The children's attention was drawn to the various types of mushrooms, though they were told not to touch them because they could be poisonous. As it turned out, some of the children had been mushroom hunting with their parents and had stories to tell about how to recognise the poisonous ones. To further cultivate their curiosity, the teacher told them about the ink cap mushrooms that spring up overnight in her garden. 'It's a mystery where they all come from', she told them. Whether or not mushrooms are plants became a hot topic of conversion and the children wanted to know a lot more about mushrooms than the teacher had anticipated. The children took lots of photographs which could help them identify different plants and fungi when they got back to the classroom.

Back in school, the children agreed that mushrooms were indeed a bit of a mystery. Why do we rarely see them? Do they remain dormant like seeds? Where do they spring from? Why are they not classified as plants? They used their photographs to identify the mushrooms in the woodland and used secondary sources to construct their own stories entitled 'My mystery mushroom'. Each group told their story to the rest of the class.

Children's storytelling is a key part of learning science because it features the children's voices as opposed to the authoritative voice of the teacher. It enables children to talk about the science in their own words; hence, it can capture the nature of the children's understanding and reveal its influence on the way they think and feel. Children's stories can provide valuable formative assessment information which can inform the basis of peer and self-assessment and hence the children can have a say in what they need to do next.

Summary

Developing secure understanding of scientific concepts is a long-term process which involves the creative use of words as well as first-hand exploration of the living and non-living world. Practical work is an important part of science learning because it helps children become familiar with how the natural world behaves and brings to life the language and ideas of science. It is important to recognise the limitations of practical work with regard to conceptual learning. Scientific concepts are human creations and need to be communicated to children in ways which excite their imaginations and help them to create mental pictures (models) of them. Chapter 4 looks at the relationship between scientific understanding and mental models, and the crucial role language plays in their development.

Further reading

ASE journals:

- Primary Science 141 (Jan/Feb 2016). *Darwin's Doodles* by Robbie Kirkham.
- Primary Science 138 (May/June 2015). *Guided Science Activities Make a Big Impact* by Nicola Beverley and Craig Early.
- Primary Science 138 (May/June 2015). *Adventures on the Thames* by Sarah Parker.
- Primary Science 134 (Sept/Oct 2014). *Stories and Science: Stirring Children's Imagination* by Claire Seeley and Sarah Gallagher.

Books:

- Allen, M. (2014). *Misconceptions in Primary Science*, Maidenhead: Open University Press.
- Dunne, M. and Peacock, A. (eds) (2015). *Primary Science: A Guide to Teaching Practice,* London: Sage.
- Harlen, W. (ed) (2011). *ASE Guide to Primary Science Education*, Hatfield: ASE.

Peer-reviewed journals:

- McMahon, K. (2012). Case Studies of Interactive Whole-class Teaching in Primary Science: Communicative Approach and Pedagogic Purposes. *International Journal of Science Education,* 34(11): 1687–1708.
- Seimears, C.M., Graves, E., Schroyer, M.G. and Staver, J. (2012). How Constructivist-Based Teaching Influences Students Learning Science. *The Educational Forum,* 76(2): 265–271.
- Traianou, A. (2006). Understanding Teacher Expertise in Primary Science: A Sociocultural Approach. *Research Papers in Education*, 21(1): 63–78.

CHAPTER 3

ORGANISING HOW CHILDREN LEARN SCIENCE

The truth is, when all is said and done, one does not teach a subject, one teaches a student how to learn it.

(Barzun, 1991)

The close link between science and narrative can help us to stage the way that we teach science to children (Chapter 1). This chapter explains how we can usefully structure children's learning in stages so that they become engaged with a puzzle, work through relevant experiences to resolve it and, finally, apply their newly developed ideas.

Topics discussed in the chapter

- A three-stage framework for learning science
- An outline of the three-stage framework
- An example of how to stage children's conceptual understanding
- How the framework supports a storytelling approach

A three-stage framework for learning science

Children like stories. Stories have gripping openings, and then perhaps a complication or a puzzle; they involve characters actively engaged in a series of events to unravel the puzzle before finally coming to a satisfactory resolution. Science can be like this too. A question about the way the world works sets us off on a trail of enquiry; we generate a theory and test it; finally, we find a satisfactory explanation which helps us understand the world better.

The value of stories is not only in their ability to entertain but also in their power to persuade. For children, abstract scientific ideas can at first seem to have little relevance to how they usually visualise the world. Everyday experience stimulates children to develop their own ideas which they trust and are reluctant to change. For example, a child may visualise a battery as a container full of electricity which slowly empties out when connected to a circuit. This is not scientifically accurate but it is useful because it enables the child to explain why batteries go flat over time. It is consistent with the child's experiences and enables them to predict how a circuit will behave.

Because children place so much trust in their own intuitive ideas, they are often reluctant to engage meaningfully with more complex scientific ideas. Children need to be persuaded that the scientific ideas provide useful ways of visualising how the world works. As Clive Sutton points out:

> To involve someone else in your science is not just a matter of telling them what you have found; it involves persuading them of the usefulness and validity of the view you adopt, and the relevance of the evidence you present.
>
> (Sutton, 1996: 146)

Teachers can use a persuasive, narrative approach to help children visualise the world in more scientific ways. This chapter sets out a three-stage framework which is designed to help teachers to teach science in persuasive ways (Loxley, 2009).

Something to think about

What does Sutton mean when he says that teaching is not just a matter of telling children what they need to learn? Read Feynman's account of how he learnt about the concept of interdependence (Chapter 1). Would you describe the approach taken by his father as questioning or persuading?

The framework is built on firm foundations

During the 1980s, researchers at Leeds University developed a framework for science learning through the Children's Learning in Science (CLIS) project. The CLIS project was based on the constructivist view of learning which emphasised the way children construct their own understanding from their interactions with the physical world. The first step in the CLIS approach is called 'elicitation'. This involves providing opportunities for the children to make their own ideas explicit, exposing any misconceptions. Further stages involve activities which are designed to help children recognise the limitations of their everyday ideas when confronted with empirical evidence. Outcomes of the project suggest that children rarely completely abandon their initial ideas. They are more likely to construct hybrid ideas based on their own ideas and the parts of the scientific view which are most useful to them. (See Chapter 4.)

The use of empirical evidence in persuading children to adopt the scientific view as an alternative to their own ideas was an important part of science education research in the 1980s and early 1990s. Less emphasis was placed on the influence of context, culture and social interactions. In recent years, the focus on how children come to understand scientific concepts has changed. Rather than the emphasis being on children making sense of phenomena through practical enquiry, it has shifted to the types of cultural and social interactions which help children appreciate scientific ideas as someone else's point of view (Chapter 4). This sociocultural approach to learning focuses on persuasive ways of presenting and talking about established scientific ideas. To understand scientific ideas, children need to use their own cultural language to help create representations of the ideas in their minds (Loxley, 2009). By talking about abstract scientific ideas in interpretive ways, children can use their own words to give the ideas some physical reality. In other words, to talk them into existence (Chapter 1).

Something to think about

What do you think the authors mean when they refer to scientific ideas as someone else's point of view? Think of a topic of interest, not necessarily to do with science. How would you persuade another person that your point of view is valid and worth listening to? Is just telling them that you are right enough?

The process by which learners use language and other interpretive tools such as drawings, pictures and 3-D models to create images of scientific concepts in their minds is known as mental modelling. The three-stage framework set out below is designed to help teachers to organise the way children construct mental models of scientific ideas. (A more detailed account of the relationship between scientific understanding and mental modelling is provided in Chapter 4.)

An outline of the three-stage framework

1. **The exploratory stage** sets the scene for the children's learning by providing a puzzle or dilemma which they need to resolve. Activities in this stage should encourage children to share ideas and work collaboratively towards solving the puzzle. Complications help children recognise a need for a scientific explanation.

2. **The re-describing stage** encourages the children to rethink their ideas in the light of evidence and the scientific view. Coming to appreciate the usefulness of the scientific view is the goal of this stage. This involves talking about and interpreting the scientific ideas in ways which enable children to make sense of them and to see their value with regard to solving the puzzle or dilemma.

3. **The application stage** allows children to try out and experience the explanatory power of their newly acquired scientific ideas in other contexts. The more widely the children apply the scientific ideas, the more likely they will make them their own.

How progression is built into the three-stage framework

The purpose of the three-stage framework is to help children develop reliable and useful understanding of the topic and theme. This may involve modification of their initial ideas or simply an extension of what they already know. The diagram opposite, 'Progression in the three-stage frame-work', indicates the cyclic nature of the framework through which children's ideas are progressively developed into 'bigger ideas' which provide more explanatory power (Chapter 4). The term 're-describing stage' was first used by Sutton (1996) to emphasise the role language plays when a learner is developing a new way of visualising an event or phenomenon.

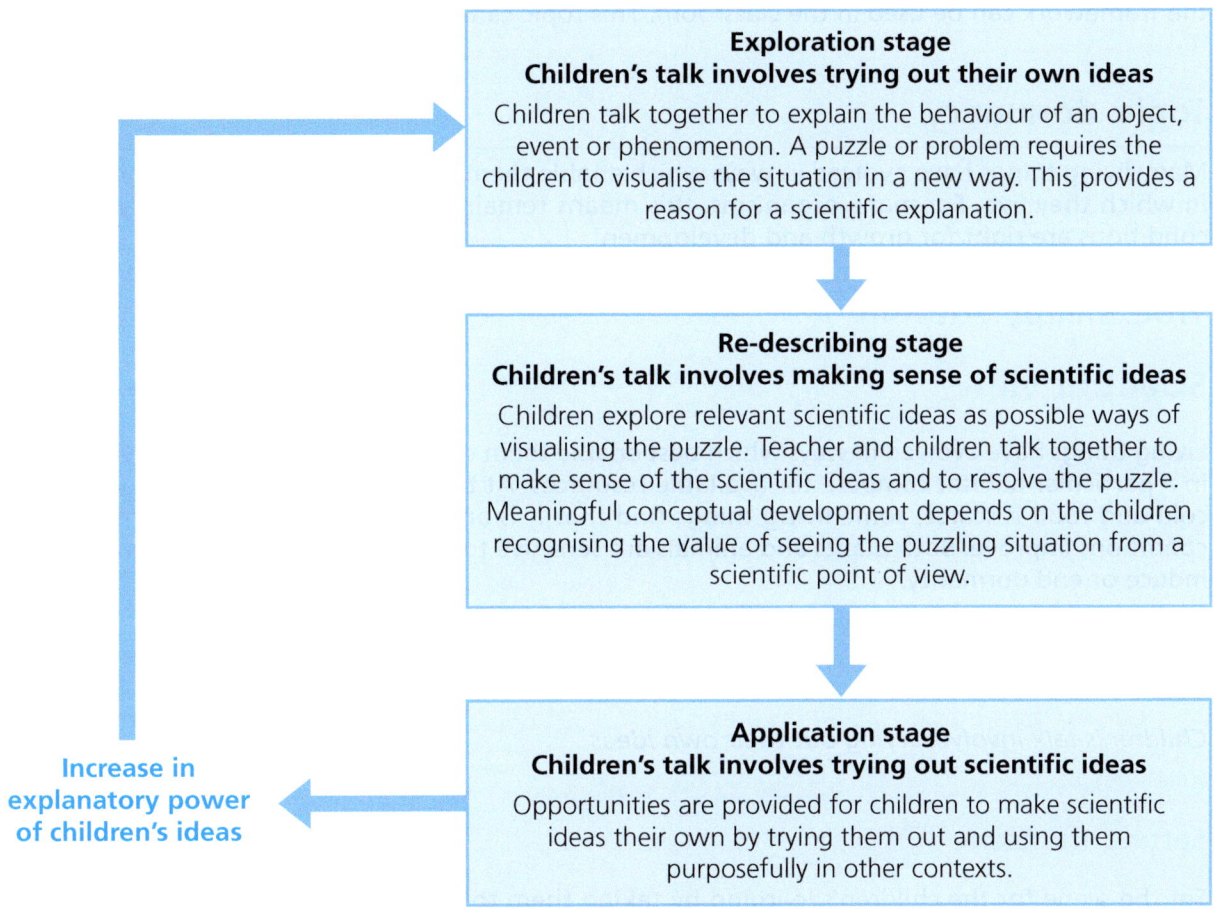

Exploration stage
Children's talk involves trying out their own ideas
Children talk together to explain the behaviour of an object, event or phenomenon. A puzzle or problem requires the children to visualise the situation in a new way. This provides a reason for a scientific explanation.

Re-describing stage
Children's talk involves making sense of scientific ideas
Children explore relevant scientific ideas as possible ways of visualising the puzzle. Teacher and children talk together to make sense of the scientific ideas and to resolve the puzzle. Meaningful conceptual development depends on the children recognising the value of seeing the puzzling situation from a scientific point of view.

Application stage
Children's talk involves trying out scientific ideas
Opportunities are provided for children to make scientific ideas their own by trying them out and using them purposefully in other contexts.

Increase in explanatory power of children's ideas

Progression in the three-stage framework.

Something to think about

The authors describe progression in children's science learning as developing children's existing ideas into bigger ideas with more explanatory power. What do you think they mean by explanatory power? Can you think of a big scientific idea which has explanatory power?

An example of how to stage children's conceptual understanding

This section provides an example of how to stage the development of children's understanding of the concept of dormancy. We do not provide a teaching plan but a brief outline to exemplify how the framework can be used in the classroom. This topic can be adapted for use with KS1 or KS2.

Topic: dormancy

Many living things have evolved in ways which enable them to make best use of the environment in which they live. For many organisms, this means remaining in a state of dormancy until the conditions are right for growth and development.

Title: sleepy autumn

Scientific view

Living things have evolved in ways which best enable them to survive and reproduce. Living things in a particular habitat compete for available resources. At times of the year when the weather is cold and food is scarce, some living things find that it is an advantage to remain dormant until conditions improve. Both plants and animals are sensitive to changes in temperature in ways that induce or end dormancy.

Exploratory stage

Children's talk involves trying out their own ideas

Setting the scene

Set the scene for the children's learning by taking them to a local park or woodland to find out what happens to plants in autumn. Before setting out, children can talk together about what they would expect to see on their walk. The following statements can be used as talking points. Ask children to discuss in groups whether they think these ideas are true, false or if their group is unsure. Admitting uncertainty should be highlighted as being very useful because it helps to establish what we need to find out. (For further information about talking points see Chapter 5.)

Talking points: true, false or not sure?

- We would expect to see lots of plants with flowers growing in autumn.
- In autumn, leaves turn brown because the trees die.
- In autumn, bushes create berries and seeds for birds to eat.

- In autumn, we would expect to see birds building their nests to keep warm in winter.
- There will be no insects or other small creatures in the wood.
- Discuss children's responses to the talking points. Examine the reasons for their answers and assess what the children know about woodlands during autumn.

Scientific enquiry

On the walk, collect a range of berries, seeds and different coloured leaves. Take tree/plant identification cards and find out names of trees which shed their leaves or produce seeds and fruits. Take photographs of a variety of trees, bushes and any animals which are around. Check under fallen wood and in leaf litter for evidence of animal life.

Things to talk about on the walk:

- Why are some trees losing their leaves? What could be happening to them?
- What is going to happen to the berries on the bushes? What is inside the berries?
- Why are there so many seeds on the ground? What's going to happen to them?
- What will the park/woodland look like later in the winter?
- How do the plants know it is autumn?

Back in the classroom, children can make autumn displays from their photographs and objects they collected on the walk. Children can talk together about what they saw on their walk. Compare with their responses to the talking points. Were children surprised by what they observed? Can they identify anything they have learned, or ask a question to share with other children?

Puzzle

What will happen to the woodland berries and seeds as the weather becomes colder in the winter? When will the seeds start to grow (germinate)? How can seeds tell when to germinate?

Scientific enquiry

Encourage the children to suggest solutions to the puzzle. Using fast-growing seeds such as bean sprouts or cress, test some questions and ideas in the classroom. Help children to identify key variables such as temperature and water availability. Encourage children to think how they can simulate winter, spring and summer temperatures. Children can establish through guided enquiry that seeds need water, air and a specific range of temperatures to germinate.

Formative assessment

Encourage the children to interpret the results of their enquiry in ways which can help solve the puzzle. Talk together about children's ideas and assess what they know about deciduous trees, and the concept of dormancy.

Something to think about

What do you think is the purpose of the 'talking points'? Can you think of any other talking points which you would want to add?

Re-describing stage

Children's talk involves making sense of scientific ideas

Use children's ideas as points for discussion. Solving the puzzle depends on children coming to understand that seeds can respond to changes in the world around them. Seeds are sensitive to changes in temperature in a way which determines when the conditions are right to grow. Different seeds need different conditions for germination and growth but most seedlings would not thrive in winter conditions of low temperature and little light. Introduce the scientific word 'dormant' to describe seeds which are living but inactive until the conditions are suitable for germination and growth. Help children to articulate their interpretation of the term. What words would they use to describe the inactivity of seeds during winter? What other living things exhibit dormancy? How does this advantage or disadvantage them?

Scientific enquiry

Children can use information sources to find out conditions which seeds in different parts of the world require to germinate. They can investigate the role that smoke and fire play in the germination of some types of seeds. Children can present findings in ways that help them to communicate their ideas and establish new questions that arise.

Assessment and further learning

Use the children's interpretation of dormancy and their presentations to assess their progress. What else would they like to find out? Children can raise and investigate their own questions.

Something to think about

Children may not use the word 'dormant' to explain the seeds' condition but they may use equivalent words. What other words could they use which would not represent misconceptions? Explain why.

Something to think about

The purpose of the re-describing stage is to help the children solve the puzzle by thinking about it from a scientific point of view. How would you organise and manage the children's learning in this stage?

Application stage

Children's talk involves trying out scientific ideas

Return to some of the original talking points

In autumn, the leaves of deciduous trees turn brown and fall. Encourage children to apply their understanding of dormancy to explain what they think is happening to the trees. What conditions will cause the trees to grow again? Why do some trees not lose their leaves in autumn/winter?

Exploring dormancy in common animals

Children can explore other types of living things which use dormancy as a survival strategy. Many cold-blooded animals such as snails and frogs hibernate over winter until spring brings a plentiful supply of food. Children can use a range of information sources to enquire into the behaviour of the animals in the local woodland which hibernate. They could present their findings in the form of a news report with a title such as, 'The mystery of the abandoned woodland: where have all the animals gone?'

Link to music and dance

Children can use music and dance to depict the coming of spring when the dormant animals and plants once again start to become active. Animals returning from warmer climates can be included. The performance could be entitled 'The awakening' and could be a whole class activity or performed in smaller groups.

> ### Something to think about
>
> Do you think understanding the scientific view could change the way children perceive autumn in the local woodland? Explain why. How would you assess their understanding of the topic?

How the framework supports a storytelling approach

Exploratory stage

Children's talk involves trying out their own ideas

The exploratory stage sets the scene for the children's learning. It is important that the context for science learning is both interesting and familiar and provides opportunities for the children to talk about the topic in their own words. During this stage, children consider ideas to the point where they begin to recognise a need for a scientific explanation. Observations on the walk can lead to questions about what happens to seeds during winter and what conditions encourage growth. Understanding the concept of dormancy will help children to solve the puzzle of what happens to the woodland in autumn.

It is useful to think of the exploratory stage as the opening chapter of a short story in which the scene is set for the action to come. The context, events and activities in this part are arranged to arouse children's curiosity in the topic and to introduce a dilemma that requires resolution. It is important when planning the exploration stage to choose contexts which enhance the significance of the scientific view. Both storytelling and science teaching are dependent on the skilful use of language and context. When talking about successful story writing, Carver (2005) points out the importance of providing unique ways of describing the world and finding the right contexts in which to express them.

> Some writers (teachers) have a bunch of talent; I don't know any writers (teachers) who are without it. But a unique and exact way of looking at things, and finding the right context for expressing that way of looking (understanding), that's something else.
>
> (Carver, 2005: 32; our brackets for emphasis)

Contexts play an important role in both storytelling and science learning because they add meaning to the events and ideas involved. When presented in inappropriate contexts, ideas can seem irrelevant and worthless. The same ideas, when used in another context, can appear insightful and inspirational. Choosing a context which has the potential to promote a scientific view of the world is an important part of planning a science lesson. Suitable contexts are those which are familiar enough for children to talk about from their own experiences, but also produce puzzling situations which scientific ideas can help to resolve. Activities in the exploration stage should focus on an event or phenomenon which is explored practically and discursively to the point where a scientific explanation is required to satisfy the children's curiosity.

Something to think about

Context plays an important role in children's science learning. Think how context has influenced your own science learning. Do you think an autumn walk in woodland is the right context in which to teach children about dormancy? Can you think of other contexts?

Re-describing stage: children's talk involves making sense of scientific ideas

In this stage, children explore scientific solutions to the dilemmas identified in the exploration stage. In the exploration stage, children have opportunities to use their personal ideas to explain the relevant events or phenomena. In the re-describing stage, they are encouraged to see and talk about the same events from a scientific perspective.

> A new scientific insight involves a re-description of the phenomenon which is being studied. Whatever the topic of interest, there is a problem in making sense of it, and then progress is made when someone starts to visualise it in a new way, drawing on language which has not been used in this context before. Taking words from some other area of experience, then try them out in the new context, and use them as an aid to figuring out what is going on.
>
> (Sutton, 1996: 144)

Something to think about

Sutton suggests that, when making sense of new phenomena, children need to draw on language from some other area of experience. What other areas of experience could children use to help them understand the concept of dormancy?

In our storytelling analogy, the re-describing stage is the part of the story when conflicts and disagreements are resolved. In the science class, this means revealing a scientific way of seeing the phenomenon or event which was the focus of discussion and enquiry in the exploration stage. The challenge for teachers is working out how to help children interpret this new vision in a way that will prove useful to them. Abstract ideas may be represented and communicated through words, symbols, gestures, actions, pictures, diagrams, physical models and mathematical formulae (Asoko and de Boo, 2001). These are mental modelling tools which children need to learn to use to make sense of scientific ideas (Chapter 4). In this stage, children may need to use a combination of different representations or modelling strategies to help them appreciate the scientific view.

When planning for conceptual development, the choice of modelling strategies needs to be carefully matched to the scientific ideas being taught and to the children's existing knowledge and experience. The key is to choose representations of scientific ideas which link to and enrich existing mental representations which children already hold. This is why analogies are important tools for science learning. Analogies enable children to use their existing understanding to make sense of a new way of visualising the world. (Strategies for modelling scientific ideas can be found in Chapter 7 and are part of 'Ideas for practice' presented in Part 2 of the text.)

Something to think about

In your own words, describe the purpose of the re-describing stage. What are the children re-describing? How should they be doing it? What should be the outcomes of the re-describing stage? How important is it that the children speak aloud; would writing achieve the same result?

Application stage

Children's talk involves trying out scientific ideas

To personalise scientific ideas, children need to be persuaded that they can be applied usefully in a range of situations. The more often children use new ideas and language in appropriate contexts, the more meaningful these ideas will become. The learning goal is for children to develop their own accurate and functional mental models of the relevant scientific concepts so that they can make use of them in other contexts. For example, if a child understands the concept of dormancy in seeds, they should be able to apply this knowledge to explain why some trees lose their leaves in autumn and why certain animals hibernate. The bigger the scientific idea, the more widely and extensively it can be used to make sense of how the world works. The concept of gravity is a big idea because it not only helps to explain why things fall to the ground but is also useful when explaining how the Solar System works and even how the universe was formed. Big ideas can change the way children visualise the world and provide much more powerful ways of interpreting events than their own intuitive models. The purpose of the application stage is to provide an opportunity for the children to apply their new knowledge in another context in order for them to experience and hence develop an appreciation of its explanatory power. In this stage, children use their new scientific knowledge to construct explanatory narratives about situations which they have not previously explored. The ability to apply ideas in different contexts is a measure of children's understanding; the application stage provides opportunities to assess children's progress.

> ### Something to think about
>
> What does the word 'functional' mean to you? How can scientific ideas be functional? Compare a scientific idea which you think is useful with one which has no use. Is functionality just about the idea or is it more to do with context? Could one idea be useful to one person and useless to someone else?

The application stage can be set in a wide range of contexts, both scientific and cross-curricular. Cross-curricular contexts need to be chosen carefully so that they help to promote the value of the scientific ideas (Chapter 10). The 'Ideas for practice' in Part 2 provide a range of examples of how scientific ideas can be used in cross-curricular settings.

Summary

Effective teaching involves persuading children of the value of the scientific ideas we want them to learn. This can be done by organising children's learning so that they become engaged with the resolution of a puzzle. To resolve the puzzle, children can work collaboratively to share ideas and make sense of the scientific view. Meaningful learning depends on the children appreciating the explanatory power of the scientific view and how it can provide them with useful ways of thinking and talking about the world.

Summary of stages

1. *Exploratory*: children are puzzled, intrigued and involved in a quest for understanding.
2. *Re-describing*: children explore ways of resolving the dilemma by developing an understanding of the situation from a scientific point of view.
3. *Application*: children are provided with opportunities to appreciate the usefulness of their new scientific understanding by applying it to other contexts.

The next chapter looks at the nature of understanding and why meaningful learning is dependent on children recognising the usefulness of the scientific ideas we teach them. The chapter emphasises the role language plays in teaching and learning science.

CHAPTER 4

SCIENTIFIC UNDERSTANDING AND MENTAL MODELS

The mind is not a vessel to be filled but a fire to be ignited.

(Plutarch, 45–120 CE)

Children learning science can usefully talk about things they already know and so find the limits of their understanding. Children's understandings, based on their everyday ideas of the world, may have limited power to explain how the world works. We can use science teaching to help children to see that a more scientific point of view offers the chance of more reliable explanations. The ways we think – our mental models – are bound up with the language in which they are expressed.

Topics discussed in the chapter

- The relationship between mental models and understanding
- How talk underpins mental modelling
- How science learning involves talking about the world in new ways
- Behind every concept is a fascinating story

The relationship between mental models and understanding

What do we mean by understanding?

A mental model represents one possibility – what seems to be true. For example, we see the Sun cross the sky; it is easy to deduce that the Earth is still and the Sun travels around or across this planet. This mental model was robust enough for centuries but was ultimately found to be flawed by careful further observation of the universe around us.

Our ability to talk about an object, event or phenomenon is dependent on our understanding of it (Borges and Gilbert, 1999). This may seem self-evident; but what do we actually mean by 'understanding'? Imagine what goes through your mind when on entering a room someone asks you to 'pull up a chair'. To understand this request, you need to have in your mind a picture or model of the state of affairs these words represent. You need to know what a chair looks like and how it is used. You also need to have a mental representation of the actions which relate to the word 'pull' within this context. That is, you can create a representation or simulation of how you are required to act in your mind (Greca and Moreira, 2000).

We have in our minds representations of a vast array of states of affairs, objects, sequences of events and processes which help us understand and make sense of how the world works. These 'mental models' help us to make predictions, to understand phenomena and events, to make decisions and control our actions, to talk about and explain an event or phenomenon. We use existing mental models as a basis for making sense of new situations. It may be quite difficult to relinquish mental models, but it is important to keep testing and revising them. For children, models may be hypothetical and fluid or quite entrenched; teaching involves eliciting the child's ideas and giving access to evidence which can help them to re-think and re-describe.

Example: A muddled mental model

A teacher was at the pond with three under-5s from the Reception class when this conversation took place with one of them.

T: Ducks. What do you think they are covered in, Cerelia?

C: Silk.

T: Silk, hmm. And how do they float?

C: They swim. But when they get out you can only see their back legs.

T: Back legs? How many legs do they have?

C: Four.

T: (*astonished but suddenly visualising all the ducks doing doggy-paddle*) Well! Only two really. They've turned their front legs into wings I think.

C: (*amused*) Hah!

Comment

The child had looked at the ducks' shape and, with little experience of birds (indeed maybe not knowing that ducks are birds), had imagined they had four legs like a cat or a dog. Confronted with the teacher's idea of two legs, she was not yet ready to change her mind. The child required further experience of how birds differ from other animals in order to develop a reliable mental model.

When it comes to understanding the natural world, children's mental models can be very imaginative but also limited and unreliable. The purpose of science learning is to help them develop mental representations of the natural world which are reliable and therefore more useful than their existing models.

> ### Something to think about
>
> Picture in your mind how electricity flows through wires. What do you imagine? Do you picture electricity as sparkly things in the wire or perhaps like a flash of lightning from the battery? Draw a picture of your mental model. Do you think your model is muddled or clear?

Children need to be persuaded of the usefulness of the scientific view

Children come to understand the world by constructing working representations of it in their minds (Johnson-Laird, 1983). These models may not be accurate or complete but are useful to the individual who uses them. A child may visualise a battery as a container full of electricity which slowly empties out when connected in a circuit. This is not scientifically accurate but it is useful because it enables the child to explain why some batteries light up bulbs more brightly than others and why a battery 'goes flat' (empties) over time. It is consistent with the child's experiences and enables them to predict accurately how a simple circuit will behave. This is why misconceptions are often so hard to redress. Children – and indeed adults – can be reluctant to replace a simple and trusted mental representation with a more complex model unless they can be persuaded that it is more useful or that their own model is untrustworthy.

The problem with simple intuitive models is that they can only adequately explain a small range of effects. For example, the model of the battery as a reservoir of electricity cannot fully explain why we need a circuit; why this must be connected to each battery terminal in order to light up a bulb. Why do we need a path in and out of the battery if the electricity is stored in the battery and used up in the bulb? For this model we only need one path for the electricity to flow along. Scientific concepts are representations of the natural world which can be relied on in a wide range of situations. In other words, they have more explanatory power than children's intuitive models. Teaching science involves promoting the usefulness of the conceptual models that science has produced and striving to show or persuade children that it is worth making the effort to understand them. Persuading children that scientific models are useful tools for interpreting, explaining and exploring events and phenomena in the natural world is an important part of effective science teaching.

> ### Something to think about
>
> What happens inside the filament of the bulb to cause it to glow? Can you use your mental model of electricity to explain this or is it starting to let you down? How functional is your mental model? How much explanatory power does it provide? Do you think you need to amend it?

How talk underpins mental modelling

A child's ability to talk about a concept is linked to their understanding of it. Therefore, talk should underpin conceptual learning in the classroom. To help children develop a useful way of visualising a concept we need to encourage them to say what they think and to listen to different points of view. For example, consider the transcript 'The pupil' below, a teaching episode in which a group of children are discussing how the pupil in the eye works.

Example: The pupil

A group of children discuss whether or not it is true that the pupil in the eye opens wider in the dark.

Alex: (*reading*) 'The pupil of the eye opens wide in the dark.' Hmm.

Bryn: Yes.

Alex: Opens wide (*using hands to show opening*) like, what opens wide, a door, your mouth …

Bryn: The pupil, what, what is…

Alex: The black round bit. That bit (*points to B's eyes*).

Bryn: Hey! mind out.

Alex: Shh, and so when it's dark, it opens, it says here, opens …

Samia: But look, I think untrue, because your eyelids open, not your eye …

Bryn: Yes (*blinks rapidly a few times*).

Samia: … and anyway you open your eyes in the day, not in the dark.

Bryn: Yes.

Samia: You shut them to sleep at night and open them in the morning.

Alex: Hmmm. The pupil. How can it open? (*Group are quiet for a few moments.*)

Samia: False then, we say.

Comment

As part of a topic on light, children were presented with the talking point 'The pupil of the eye opens wide in the dark' and were asked to discuss whether they thought it was true or false. The purpose of the discussion was to encourage the children to think together about how their eyes work in different light conditions. (See Chapter 5 for the uses of talking points and the nature of exploratory talk which they are designed to promote.)

Children's ideas

The children consider their understanding of how the pupil opens in comparison with that of their group mates. The word 'open' in this context causes some confusion. Alex's image of the pupil opening like a door on a hinge is misleading and cannot explain how the pupil works. Since opening and closing of the eyelids is more obvious, this is the focus for the children's talk. In the absence of a reliable model for how the pupil opens, the children conclude that the statement is false. This conversation helps the teacher to find out what the children need to know. They need further experience or explanation of the mechanism by which the pupil opens and closes and to think about reasons why it does so.

Helping children to re-describe how the pupil opens

In response to the children's ideas, the teacher intervened to help them rethink how the pupil could open and let in more light. The teacher encouraged all groups to share a wider range of ideas. She used a simulation to explain how the pupil allows light to enter the eye. She encouraged the children to continue talking about their understanding of the concept; could other vocabulary provide more useful representations? The teacher continued to prompt the children to critically reflect on their description of the pupil and encouraged them to provide alternative ideas. As the transcript 'I think, expand' indicates, she prompted the children to describe what they observed in their own words. This intervention was intended to help the children to choose words which provided clearer or more insightful ways of describing and talking about how the pupil works.

Example: I think, expand

Teacher intervenes to help children choose useful words to re-describe how the pupil opens wider in the dark.

Teacher: OK, let's try to use another word instead of 'pupil'. Now you've had a look, what other words could we use? Bryn?

Bryn: Well, it's the dark bit of the eye.

Alex: It's dark and round.

Samia: Like a dark hole.

Teacher: That's interesting, Samia. Why do you say it's a hole?

Samia: It looks like a hole.

Teacher: OK, a hole is a good way of thinking about it, a hole which lets light get into our eyes. But now do you think holes open and close? What other words?

Alex: Well, holes do open and close.

Bryn: Open wider.

Alex: I think, expand.

Teacher: OK, expand. We might be able to see if we can make it change … We could blindfold one of you and one of you could look at a book in bright light … What do you think?

Comment

When Samia described the pupil as a hole, the teacher reinforced this useful idea and used the same vocabulary to explain how light enters the eye. The description of the pupil as a hole enabled the children to imagine that it could get bigger and smaller – it could open wider or expand. This is a 'change of mind' from their earlier conception of a door opening and closing. The children went on to use mirrors and magnifiers to observe how the size of their own pupil changed in different light conditions. The conversation continued using the children's words to describe their observations. During the plenary discussion, the teacher introduced the scientific terms 'contraction' and 'dilation' to describe the changes that the children had observed.

This example highlights the crucial importance of spoken language as a mental modelling tool. In this case, the topic was taught over a series of lessons using a range of different strategies. The intended outcome of the lesson was to enable the children to visualise how the pupil controlled the amount of light entering the eye. Once the children had a useful mental model, the use of physical models, analogies and carefully explained vocabulary could develop deeper understanding.

Something to think about

In the transcript 'I think, expand' the teacher intervened to help the children choose useful words to describe how the pupil works. Why are these words effective? What difference did the discussion make to the children's developing ideas? Is it helpful to describe spoken language as a tool for mental modelling?

The differences between the children's initial ideas and the scientific view represent the changes that need to occur in the children's thinking if effective learning is to be achieved (Scott, 1998). In this case, conceptual development required the children to rethink their original understanding of how things can open. Once they were able to re-describe the concept in terms of widening or expanding, they were able to develop a useful mental model of how the pupil works.

Something to think about

In the preceding chapters, we point out the need for children to talk concepts into existence. What does this mean when we consider mental modelling? Can you explain or give an example to illustrate this idea: 'Children need to talk science concepts into mental models'?

Big ideas have more explanatory power

In a later activity, the children drew pictures to show how the pupil controls the amount of light entering the eye. This involved talking about how light travels in straight lines. The concept of light travelling in straight lines is a 'big idea' because it can be used to interpret and explain a wide range of phenomena. It can be used to explain how the behaviour of light enables us to see and locate objects. It can also be used to explain shadows and how images are formed in mirrors and lenses. Conceptual development involves providing children with progressively more explanatory power by helping them interpret and learn to use some of science's big ideas. Using newly acquired scientific ideas for different purposes helps children to become more familiar with such ideas and to adopt them for their personal use. Once scientific ideas are personalised as mental models, they can become part of the way children perceive the world.

Something to think about

Understanding that light travels in straight lines is a big idea because it offers much explanatory power. In other words, it can be used to explain the behaviour of light in a wide range of situations. What are the big ideas associated with sound? Which ideas have the most explanatory power?

How science learning involves talking about the world in new ways

The two transcripts exemplify the idea that an exploration of language is just as important for children's understanding of scientific concepts as is practical exploration. Science educator and philosopher Joan Solomon evocatively describes the process of science learning for children as similar to 'arriving on a foreign shore, or struggling with a conversation in an unknown language' (Solomon, 1994: 16). She describes science learning in terms of a child listening in on a family conversation and trying to make sense of what the adults are talking about.

> **Imagine an alternative picture of pupil learning. A young student sits outside a circle of disputing scholars picking up fragments of conversation and trying to piece them together. Once we were all that child, the family were the circle and we turned over phrases that we heard until they built up into an idea. We tried out the sense of it, and occasionally we were amusingly wrong. If we were lucky no one laughed. Then it was explained once more in helpful ways and with good games to go with the learning of it. When we tried again and the half-formed idea seemed to be accepted by others, it became stronger. Kindly adults encouraged us to use it in new ways: our understanding and pride in using it grew. The idea gradually became ours and, by the same token, we became a part of the privileged and knowing circle who uses it.**

(Solomon, 1994: 17)

Something to think about

What do you think of Solomon's description of science learning as 'struggling with a conversation in an unknown language'? Is this a useful analogy? What implications does it have for the way we teach science?

Children's language and scientific words

Solomon's description of science as an alien culture implies that children need to learn the language of science as they engage meaningfully in science activity. But learning how to speak a different language is not the same as simply learning words. A word becomes part of a child's language when they 'populate it with their own intent and adapt it for their own purposes' (Wertsch, 1991: 59). To make sense of a scientific word, children must use it in amongst their own language and ideas, creating a representation or model in their minds. Fostering this process in the classroom involves organising conversations in which children can put new ideas into their own words, trying out recently heard vocabulary. They need opportunities to engage with new thinking and to articulate their tentative understandings. Learning does not happen at the instant a new idea is encountered but is a cumulative process in which previous conceptions, vocabulary and images are tested and amended over time. The use of scientific vocabulary is important if a child is to gain confidence in their ability to express complex ideas with clarity and accuracy. The accumulation of a wide vocabulary requires chances to understand words in action and to use words with other learners. Such events as forgetting words or using them erroneously are invaluable experiences when they happen in supportive classroom contexts. Children may never hear particular words used in a scientific context anywhere else; we need to provide every opportunity for children to hear, speak, read, write, describe, explain and query unfamiliar words such as *photosynthesis*, *respiration* or *invertebrate*; or familiar words in unfamiliar contexts, such as *force*, *material* or *energy*.

Something to think about

What do you think Wertsch means when he says that a word becomes part of children's language when they 'populate it with their own intent and adapt it for their own purposes'? Consider the three-stage framework in the light of Wertsch's view. Does it provide opportunities for children to make sense of scientific words and then to adapt them and use them for other purposes?

Talking to develop a shared point of view

Scientific words have meanings linked to their origins. For example, the word 'pollen' is derived from the Greek word meaning 'fine flour'. This analogy was a useful way for the ancient Greeks to visualise and talk about the substance they found inside a wide range of flowers. Pollen, like flour, is a light and dusty material which can be dispersed by wind or animals. Children can observe and examine flour, pollen and other fine powders such as talc, and use their own words to describe them. They can think of different ways to describe or label pollen. They can share their individual ideas and evaluate which offers the most meaningful explanatory power: what is the best way to describe, explain and clarify the purpose of pollen. Children need opportunities to use spoken language to make their ideas explicit – to one another and to themselves. This type of classroom discourse is what Sutton (1996) describes as 'talking around a topic'.

> To persuade someone into your point of view requires talking around the topic until shared meanings are developed. The teacher's personal voice is important, but learners must also have freedom of re-expression. In order to be able to hear scientists' language as expressions of thought and not just 'description' of nature, they must understand language as an interpretive tool, and that means having experience of using it in that way themselves.

(Sutton, 1996: 147)

Behind every concept is a fascinating story

The German physician and botanist Rudolf Jakob Camerarius (1665–1721) is credited with describing sexual reproduction in plants. He identified stamens and pollen as the male parts and style, stigma and ovaries as the female parts. He described the mechanism of pollination. Charles Darwin interpreted pollination as 'acts of contrivances' between plants and animals, envisaging a profound and mysterious collaboration between plant and pollinator.

To these scientists, the act of pollination wasn't simply the transfer of pollen from the anther of one plant to the stigma of another: it was far more exciting and intriguing than that. Pollination can be explained as a story which describes the intricate and vital relationships between specific plants and animals. Such stories raise their own questions. How did the relationship develop? Why does it continue? What happens to the pollinator if the plant dies out and vice versa? Pollination is a real-life drama which children can narrate in their own words. But pollination is also a rather abstract scientific concept. In the classroom, it can be 'talked into existence' in ways that help children understand its explanatory power.

Words can have a power and influence quite out of proportion to their triviality as mere marks on paper or vibrations in the air. When circumstances are right they can excite people's minds and move their imaginations, in science as in any other area of human activity.

(Sutton, 1992: 1)

Something to think about

The 'Goldilocks Zone' is a term that present-day scientists use to describe extremely distant solar systems which could support life. The Goldilocks Zone contains planets which are not too hot or too cold to support life; they are just right! What is your favourite scientific term? Can you find out the story behind it?

Summary

Children create complex mental models which help them to talk about and explain their experiences. These can be unreliable when applied more widely. Scientific concepts offer more reliable ways of visualising how the natural world works. Effective science teaching helps children to make sense of the scientific view and learn to appreciate its explanatory power. Talk is the child's most powerful tool for understanding the scientific view. In the next chapter we examine the nature of classroom talk and look at how different kinds of talk can help children understand the world in scientific ways.

Further reading

ASE journals:

- Primary Science 138 (May/June 2015) *Thinking About Metacognition* by John Crossland.
- The Journal of Emergent Science (Summer 2016) *Helping Children to Express Their Ideas and Move Towards Justifying Them with Evidence. A developmental perspective* by Linda McGuigan.

Books:

- Harlen, W. and Qualter, A. (2014). *The Teaching of Science in Primary Schools*, London: Routledge. Chapter 11: Helping development of scientific understanding.
- Sutton, C. (1992). *Words, Science and Learning*, Buckingham: Open University Press.
- Sutton, C. (1996). *The Scientific Model as a Form of Speech,* in G. Welford, J. Osborne and P. Scott (eds), *Research in Science Education in Europe*, London: Falmer Press.

Peer-reviewed journals:

- Gillies, R.M., Nichols, K. and Khan, A. (2015). The Effects of Scientific Representations on Primary Students' Development of Scientific Discourse and Conceptual Understanding During Cooperative Contemporary Inquiry-science. *Cambridge Journal of Education*, 45 (4): 427–449.
- Kosso, P. (2002). The Omniscienter: Beauty and Scientific Understanding. *International Studies in the Philosophy of Science*, 16(1): 39–48.
- Newman, M. (2012). An Inferential Model of Scientific Understanding. *International Studies in the Philosophy of Science*, 26(1): 1–26.
- Rowell, P.M. and Ebbers, M. (2004). Constructing Explanations of Flight: A Study of Instructional Discourse in Primary Science. *Language and Education*, 18(3): 264–280.

CHAPTER 5

TALK FOR LEARNING IN SCIENCE

A great deal of education is to do with learning how to use language – to represent ideas, to interpret experiences, to formulate problems and to solve them.

(Mercer, 1995)

Why do we need to give speaking and listening – talk – special attention when we think about teaching science? And having focused on talk, what sort of talk is of most educational value? If we are convinced that talk is important for science learning, how can we ensure that children's talk is educationally effective? And finally, what are the implications for talk between ourselves as teachers, and the children we teach?

Topics discussed in the chapter

- The importance of talk for learning in science
- Exploratory talk and its ground rules
- Dialogic teaching and children's ideas
- Talking points: a strategy to promote effective talk

The importance of talk for learning in science

Piaget tells us that children learn through interacting with the world. Play and exploration start with children's curiosity and their (maybe unspoken) questions: 'What happens if I keep squashing this Plasticine?' 'What if I touch ice – how will it feel?' The chance to play provides the child with information from which they make meaning. The child adds newly gained experience to what they have already understood. If new experience doesn't fit, the child accommodates their new experience by changing what they think: that is, they learn from the experience. They develop a story or model that fits with what they 'know'. If new experience does not fit previous models, the child may rethink. For example, a child who has never played with jelly, seen a hamster or banged a drum will attend to the new input from their senses and find that it does not match with what they already know. This 'failure' to understand prompts the child to generate new ideas (such as, some red materials are sticky; small furry creatures are not all inanimate toys; if you hit round things they bang). Piaget envisaged the child encountering the world as a 'lone scientist', engaged in constant enquiry and continually faced with the puzzle of new experience and evidence which creates questions in the mind. The child engages in empirical enquiry; up against problems of understanding, they resolve these by reconsidering or, as Huxley puts it, by *giving up their preconceived notions*.

> **Sit down before fact as a little child, be prepared to give up every preconceived notion … or you shall learn nothing.**
>
> (Thomas H. Huxley, biologist, 1825–95)

But children are rarely alone and their experiences of the world are often shaped by the adults and children around them. As the child acquires language, they are offered the vocabulary to talk about what they experience; they are asked questions, and they share ideas about how things work and why things happen. The child's wish to communicate their experiences pushes the limits of language and enables development. Talk is the medium through which we consider the world and establish a scientific view of it. The Russian psychologist Lev Vygotsky recognised that the use of spoken language helps us to interpret experience, to explain and describe our ideas to one another and, in doing so, to learn from and with one another. The child's quest for meaning, at first carried out through sensory experience, is radically altered by speaking and listening. Children learn about the world through talk with others; simultaneously, they are developing their capacity to use the medium of language. In science classrooms we can organise particularly powerful ways to think and speak. Learning to talk like scientists provides children with a transferable learning tool with which to question, assert, explain, hypothesise, reflect … and more.

It is the link between speaking, listening, thinking and learning which makes talk so important in science classrooms. We can provide children with fascinating experiences and thoughtful resources; but unless we also provide them with opportunities to discuss what they are doing, their chance to learn is diminished. However, there is a problem for the classroom teacher. Learning depends on talk focused on the task in hand, and it is very easy for children to distract one another. What will drive the talk, the need to be social or the need to learn? Will children engage with one another's minds openly or will they fiercely defend their own ideas without really listening to other points of view? Will they withdraw and let others do the talking; or, while others talk, will their minds be entirely occupied by formulating their own next contribution? As teachers, we know how easy it is for children to lose concentration, and we can understand the importance of their continuous focus on social issues. But our concern about off-task talk should not mean that we silence children. It should remind us that children need help to understand the importance and purpose of their discussion and that we need to provide them with the language tools which will help them to think and learn through talk.

> ### Something to think about
>
> Are children aware of the value of discussing ideas? Do they understand how to provide their opinion with reasons and how to negotiate what they think with other children? What do they say when asked these things? Do they recognise the importance of talk for their own learning and that of their classmates? Can we teach them this?

Exploratory talk and its ground rules

What makes a good discussion? What are the features of the children's spoken interaction which will really help them to think and learn? Asked these questions, both teachers and children commonly agree that those taking part in a discussion should:

- listen attentively;
- include everyone in the discussion;
- ask questions;
- share all relevant information openly;
- challenge one another's ideas and opinions with respect;
- ask for and give reasons for ideas;
- seek to reach a group agreement before proceeding.

Science educator Douglas Barnes, listening to group work in science classrooms (Barnes, 1976), described hearing the sort of talk detailed above, in which children were hesitant in their thinking yet confident to speak out. Their views were aired and examined, and all seemed to be engaged in a joint quest for understanding. He described this as exploratory talk. Exploratory talk is talk in which everyone is invited to give their ideas and to challenge one another respectfully, share information and give and ask for reasons. Contributions may be hesitant or speculative, but children are confident to articulate their thinking. They understand the need for active listening and show interest in different points of view. Children are aware of the importance of the discussion and know that it is a strength to consider changing their mind in response to a challenge, a good reason or new line of thinking. Everyone seeks to reach a negotiated agreement.

Exploratory talk is educationally effective talk because it enables children to share their thinking and helps groups to do better than each child could have done alone. It is this sort of talk that we want to hear in science classrooms.

Class ground rules for exploratory talk

Classes benefit from devising a set of 'rules' which help everyone to remember that talk is crucial for learning and that the invaluable chance to discuss their science with each other can only happen in the special setting of the classroom. We can ask the children what rules they would use to ensure 'a good discussion'. Collect a short list of rules, making sure that these are positive, brief and embody the principles of exploratory talk (for example, 'We will all listen carefully' – and not, for example, 'Don't speak until you are asked'). Ask the class to sign up to using their rules during science. Have the rules visible and refer to them often. Ensure that they are used as learning intentions, that there is a chance within the lesson to talk about a relevant problem and that the use of talk is discussed in plenary sessions. Adapt the rules if they are not working for your class. Unless teachers help children to share these rules, they will talk to one another as if they were in a social setting. That is, talk will be dominated by the confident or opinionated. Some children will withdraw or become irrationally argumentative; children will see writing as 'real' work and talk as a waste of time; and learning will fall away. This is not because children are wilfully difficult but because each has a different understanding of what 'talk together' means.

Outcomes of teaching talk for learning

Children who have been directly taught how to discuss things with one another and who have an understanding of exploratory talk can be heard to make more use of such phrases as 'What do you think? Why do you think that?' The words 'think' and 'because' are more frequently used. They are more capable of collaborative work. Children in science classrooms need to be aware of their importance to one another – their responsibility for ensuring that time is spent on productive discussion. In science, we can teach children that spoken language is not just for giving information but for 'interthinking' (Mercer, 2000). Interthinking is the use of spoken language to support thinking together – collectively making sense of experience and solving problems. It enables the dynamic interaction of minds and is the best use of the social nature of human thinking. Talk is the child's tool for interthinking and every child can learn to use talk this way.

Dialogic teaching and children's ideas

So far, we have considered the child's discussion with their classmates. But much learning depends on whole-class sessions led by the teacher. How do the ideas of exploratory talk and interthinking fit with what happens in whole-class talk? Psychologist Jerome Bruner noticed that teachers provide learners with a special sort of help as they tackle a new task or idea. He described the help as 'scaffolding', a powerful metaphor to indicate the way that support could be provided and gradually withdrawn as a learner becomes more independent (Bruner, 1986). Scaffolding is part of a teacher's professional toolkit, constantly in use.

For example, a child may be able to read a thermometer but may not know what is being measured. The thermometer in a mix of ice and salt may read −8°C. The child may say, 'It's measuring the cold'. We, as teachers, can then see what it is that the child needs to know; we also know that to provide a lecture on thermodynamics would not help them at all. We know that small steps and a clear context for new vocabulary are a good way to proceed and that modelling a task can help. We know that talking the child through the process or concept means that at any stage the child can put to use the safety net of questioning. So this is what we do. As Bruner puts it, we reduce the degrees of freedom so that success is possible – whether in acquiring a skill or understanding a concept. This is scaffolding. We use scaffolding, through talk, to break down the task into achievable steps and move the child through them, then check if they are able to do the task alone.

The essence of the concept of scaffolding is the sensitive, supportive intervention of a teacher in the progress of a learner who is actively involved in some specific task, but who is not quite able to manage the task alone. […] A crucial quality of scaffolding is that it is the provision of guidance and support which is increased or withdrawn in response to the developing competence of the learner.

(Mercer, 1995: 74 and 75)

Exploratory talk tends to happen amongst groups of equals – it is symmetrical. Teacher-led discussion is *asymmetric*, in that the teacher is expected to organise and shape the talk. Whole-class dialogue between a teacher and class is like exploratory talk in that it may be grounded in children's experience, conducted with respect and show visible questioning and reasoning throughout. It is different from exploratory talk in that it has the teacher's idea of what children might accomplish built in. We can describe a particularly productive sort of talk between teachers and their classes as *dialogic teaching*. Dialogic teaching is particularly effective in science.

What is dialogic teaching?

Dialogic teaching harnesses the power of talk to engage children, stimulate and extend their thinking, and advance learning and understanding.

(Alexander, 2006: 27)

Dialogic teaching is described by educational researcher Robin Alexander as teaching that leads to effective classroom discussions and, ultimately, to deeper learning. Through dialogue, teachers find out what children think, engage with their developing ideas and help them to overcome misunderstandings. We can recognise dialogic teaching when we hear sustained contributions from children, with children listening and responding to their classmates. Another characteristic of a good dialogue is that the teacher helps children to express their ideas and generates a linked discussion. Children have time to think. They have access to one another's ideas in the same way as they might during exploratory talk, but the ideas are moved in a purposeful direction by the teacher's intervention.

In summary, by talking about their science in small groups or taking part in a whole-class dialogue, children can:

- articulate their everyday ideas;
- hear a range of alternative points of view;
- ask for and listen to reasons and evidence;
- create and elaborate on a science story;
- ask questions and express uncertainty;
- consider new ideas and change their mind.

The chance to hear children talking is an invaluable formative assessment opportunity.

Something to think about

What are the barriers that stop children from contributing to whole-class discussion? Do all children feel that they can say what they have found out, describe their confusion, elaborate on ideas or ask a question stimulated by their science activities? Are children directly taught how to do these things and, if not, why?

The transcript 'Thicker wire' is an example of a dialogue in a Year 6 classroom. The class had spent two sessions studying circuits including considering electrical resistance. The extract begins as the teacher, drawing a circuit on a flip chart, provides information and then checks for understanding of specific scientific vocabulary.

Example: Thicker wire

T: This is a kind of, um, virtually an electronic whiteboard here, you have to imagine … So when this current is going along a wire, there's a certain sort of, well, what do you think resistance means? Can you think of a good sentence with *'resistance'* in it that's *not* to do with electricity? What do you resist doing, Logan?

L: I resist tidying up my room.

T: Perfect example. There's some friction about it, you resist tidying your room, the wire resists the current – so a very thin wire like that, in a light bulb […] because it's resisting so much, it's giving out loads of light, and a bit of heat. OK, have a think about this; if you've got this *thin* wire here with a *high* resistance, what would we do to create a low resistance, if we want the current to flow easily? Beatrice?

B: Um, have a thicker wire.

T: We could have a thicker wire couldn't we? And we'd have a low resistance.

K: Why low?

T: Because it lets the current flow more easily. If, if you've got *low resistance* to tidying your bedroom, that means if your Mum says to you, 'I'll give you £20 if you tidy your bedroom' suddenly the resistance all goes away, doesn't it? 'Oh yes, I'll tidy my bedroom.' Thicker wire, lower resistance. Fletcher, in a minute I want to hear from you but not just now. We've got some thin wires and some thick wires over here, long wires and short wires. What difference do you think length will make? Daniel, what were you going to add?

D: I was just going to say we could, we could do some investigating on that.

T: You fancy having a go at trying out – investigating to see if you can see different resistances by looking at how well our bulbs light up. Right – is it important, Fletcher?

F: I know another example of resistance. Sam's resisting to learn.

T: Oh, Sam's good at that.

Comment

The teacher asks for children's everyday ideas about resistance, reminding them that she would like to hear their thoughts. K asks for clarification (the confidence to show uncertainty is a feature of good dialogue) and the teacher provides a direct answer, re-using the familiar context of tidying a room suggested earlier by a classmate. One child (D) anticipates the teacher's suggestion and is already thinking ahead about setting up an investigation while another takes the chance to make a joke about his friend. Knowing the child Sam to be both bright and hard-working, the teacher accepts this and moves on. Such dialogues, in which the class are relaxed but on task, commonly happen when a teacher and their class share an interest in science. In addition, the children know that their suggestions are highly valued by the teacher and by one another. This is not perfect dialogic talk; for example, no child takes an extended turn. But it is a dialogic episode, helping to develop the children's thinking and learning.

Talking points: a strategy to promote effective talk

Teachers have to create contexts which relate to children's everyday experience and simultaneously address learning intentions. Children need to be creative in the way they consider their own ideas and compare them with the ideas of others. Organising science in primary classrooms involves thinking about what resources are available.

Some resources usefully promote talk in science. These may be concrete resources like magnets or electrical circuits or snails, a particular piece of software, Concept Cartoons (Naylor and Keogh, 2000), science poems or stories (Rosen, 2000), non-fiction books or a classroom visitor such as a firefighter or dental nurse.

A particular resource which can promote talk in primary science is 'Talking points' (Dawes, 2008a; 2008b; 2012). These are discussion points generated by the teacher and maybe the class, which focus on the science topic in hand. Crucially, they are not questions but starters for sharing ideas. Talking points give children a chance to compare and contrast their own thinking with that of their classmates. In discussion, children can express ideas openly. They may share misconceptions enabling the teacher to plan relevant future experiences. They can consider the limits of their own understanding in a 'safe' forum where it is acceptable and even interesting to admit, 'I don't know...' Working in a small exploratory talk group allows every child to speak and means that the group can support one another during subsequent whole-class discussion.

Teachers can generate, or teach children how to generate, their own talking points. Below are two examples. Children (familiar with exploratory talk) are asked to talk to their group to decide if they agree or disagree with the ideas – or if they are unsure. Subsequent whole-class discussion orchestrated by the teacher helps everyone to consider a range of points of view, share their thinking, establish areas of uncertainty for further work and generally develop their vocabulary and ideas.

Talking points Example 1: Small creatures

What does your group think of these ideas? Are they true or false, and why do you think so?

- All creepy crawlies are insects.
- Insects eat plants.
- Spiders are insects.
- A woodlouse has more legs than a spider.
- Slugs are snails which are out of their shells.

- There is more than one sort of worm.
- Ladybirds lay eggs and tiny ladybirds hatch out in summer.
- Insects have six legs, so a caterpillar is not an insect.
- Dragonflies are carnivores.
- Some insects use camouflage to protect themselves.

Talking points Example 2: Force

Talk together to decide if these statements are true or false, or is your group unsure?

- A small object falls to the ground at the same speed as a large object.
- Things stop when they run out of force.
- A biro has a gravitational field and attracts other objects.
- There is no gravity above the Earth's atmosphere.
- The weight of an object measures how much stuff it's made up of.
- A larger object has more air resistance.
- A falling stone pulled by gravity is pushed up by air resistance.
- You can reduce pressure by spreading weight out over a larger area.
- The air is too light to be affected by the Earth's gravity.
- Steel ships float because they have air in them.

Summary

Children can use talk to explain their ideas, listen to others, ask questions and develop their thinking. By talking with a science focus, children can develop science concepts and, at the same time, practise ways of talking which will stand them in good stead in other contexts. By sharing ideas, asking for and giving reasons and keeping the talk on task, a group of children can make meaning from the experiences science exploration offers. Exploratory talk is educationally effective talk which enables interthinking. Teachers use talk to offer the careful support of scaffolding and to generate classroom dialogue. Dialogic teaching involves teachers taking the lead in orchestrating whole-class discussion, encouraging children to elaborate, explain and link their contributions and helping the whole group to attend and engage with ideas. By creating science stories and moving between a more authoritative, explanatory style and episodes of dialogue, teachers can engage children in thinking about their everyday ideas of science towards a more scientific point of view. Talking points are a particular resource which can help to generate exploratory talk and provide a useful basis for closing plenary dialogue.

Further reading

ASE journals:

- Primary Science 142 (March/April 2016). *Gardening Provides Valuable Time to Talk* by Margaret Boyd.
- Primary Science 142 (March/April 2016). *Learning to Talk* by Kirstin Greygoose.
- Primary Science 138 (May/June 2015). *Using Puppets to Provide Opportunities for Dialogue and Scientific Inquiry* by Maeve Liston.
- Primary Science 129 (Sept/Oct 2013). *Let the Children Talk: The Power of Talk in Promoting Understanding* by Keith Ross.

Books:

- Dawes, L. (2008). *The Essential Speaking and Listening: Talk for Learning at Key Stage 2*, London: Routledge.
- Dawes, L. (2012). *Talking Points: Discussion Activities in the Primary Classroom*, London: Routledge.
- Harlen, W. and Qualter, A. (2014). *The Teaching of Science in Primary Schools*, London: Routledge.
- Harlen, W. (ed) (2011). *ASE Guide to Primary Science Education*, Hatfield: ASE.
- Mercer, N. and Hodgkinson, S. (eds) (2008). *Exploring Talk in School*, London: Sage.

Peer-reviewed journals:

- Braund, M. (2009). Talk in Primary Science: A Method to Promote Productive and Contextualized Group Discourse. *Education 3–13*, 37(4): 387–397.
- Dawes, L. (2008). Encouraging Students' Contributions to Dialogue During Science. *School Science Review*, 90(331): 1–7.
- Mercer, N., Dawes, L. and Staarman, J.K. (2009). Dialogic Teaching in the Primary Science Classroom. *Language and Education*, 23(4): 353–369.
- Mercer, N., Dawes, L., Wegerif, R. and Sams, C. (2004). Reasoning as a Scientist: Ways of Helping Children to Use Language to Learn Science. *British Educational Research Journal*, 30(3): 359–377.

CHAPTER 6

SCIENTIFIC ENQUIRY AND THE PASSIONATELY CURIOUS

I have no special talents; I am only passionately curious.

(Albert Einstein)

Enquiry is at the heart of scientific activity. Very young children begin by using their senses to examine the world around them. Experience and observation give rise to questions as language skills develop. Finding out answers and generating new questions can help children to link what they already know to new experiences. Children are naturally curious – maybe even passionately curious – and we foster this in science. We can use practical activity, reasoning and narrative to help children develop their scientific understanding.

Topics discussed in the chapter

- Science and discovery: what can we expect of children?
- The outcomes of scientific enquiry
- Scientific enquiry and its link to narrative
- Scientific skills and attitudes
- Types of scientific enquiry
- Choosing contexts for scientific enquiry

Science and discovery: what can we expect of children?

Questioning and learning

Children's questions may challenge our ability to provide explanations. Questions such as 'Why is the sky blue?' or 'Why do rabbits have such big white tails?' require some thinking through. Children like to be taken seriously and benefit from straightforward explanations using clear language. But when children ask more speculative questions, 'What would happen if we left my ice lolly in the Sun?' or 'Which coat should I wear now it's raining?', they are asking questions that can be explored through scientific enquiry. Enquiry activities can provide contexts for learning which are both real and familiar to children. Enquiry can provide a resolution to some problem or puzzling observation. It is this resolution which offers the child greater scientific understanding. As the story 'Children exploring ice balloons' illustrates, scientific enquiries based on simple resources can catch children's imagination and enable them to see familiar events in new and exciting ways.

Example: Children exploring ice balloons

A class of 7- and 8-year-olds spent time exploring ice balloons, taking part in careful observational drawing, touching and listening. 'Why can I hear it crackle?' they asked. 'Why isn't it the same all the way through?' 'Will it melt?' 'Will a big ice balloon melt faster than lots of small ice cubes?' 'What does it weigh?' 'Why do my fingers stick to it?' Alistair wanted to know if the ice balloon would float. He suggested that although ice cubes float in fizzy drinks, the large ice balloon might be too heavy. A classmate remembered that icebergs float – was this the same thing? The children discussed what they knew about icebergs then tested their ideas by putting the ice balloon in a tank of water, where it floated. Watching this inspired Alistair to deeper thought. He noted that when he put the ice balloon in the water, the water level rose in the tank. His next question intrigued everyone: 'What will happen to the level of the water as the ice balloon melts?'

Comment

Alistair's engagement and need to know motivated him to spend the rest of the day exploring this puzzle. At intervals throughout the day, he marked the level of water in the tank as the balloon melted and, as he did so, he became more and more puzzled. More investigation would be needed to answer his new questions. Alistair was passionately curious.

Exploring ice balloons.
Source: Peter Loxley

Enquiries such as this provide opportunities to personalise children's learning. Raising their own questions increases children's engagement and stimulates curiosity. Children may not be able to discover the answers to every question from first-hand experience, but because the questions 'belong' to them, they are likely to be keen to search for answers using enquiry and information sources.

Can we expect children to discover scientific ideas for themselves?

Research suggests that experience and practical work cannot always lead children towards accepted scientific views (Asoko, 2002). But it is evident that learning through enquiry is greatly enhanced when children have a chance to talk about what is happening. Children talking together have the chance to work out a valid explanation for a puzzling observation. Sometimes, no amount of practical exploration and exploratory talk will resolve a dilemma or answer the question, '*Why* does this happen?' Resolution of the problem may require teacher-led discussion, research using all the resources at hand or even questioning an expert scientist.

The outcomes of scientific enquiry

The main purpose of scientific activity is to provide reliable knowledge about how the world works. As Feynman points out, the source of scientific knowledge is the interaction of experiment and the imagination of the experimenter.

> The principle of science, the definition, almost, is the following: The test of all knowledge is experiment. Experiment is the sole judge of scientific 'truth'. But what is the source of knowledge? Where do the laws that are to be tested come from? Experiment, itself, helps to produce these laws, in the sense that it gives us hints. But also needed is imagination to create from these hints the great generalizations, to guess at the wonderful, simple, but very strange patterns beneath them all, and then to experiment to check again whether we have made the right guess.

(Feynman, 1964)

That is, theories about how the world works can be tested by investigation, to which individual scientists (including children) contribute their own unique perspective and ideas. Children's conclusions based on the findings of an enquiry are likely to contain elements of their first-hand experience. Some everyday ideas are firmly held. However, some ideas are correspondingly rather woolly and, if children undertake a convincing enquiry, they may be very willing to 'change their mind'. The outcomes of scientific enquiry should move children towards a more robust scientific point of view which holds water when tested and applied.

By involving children in scientific enquiry, we can provide them with an understanding of the nature of science. Scientific enquiry enables children to think and behave like scientists. They seek out reliable knowledge by employing first-hand experience, discussion, secondary sources and, above all, imagination. Imagination helps children to create tentative explanations (hypotheses) and devise enquiries to test their ideas. If an explanation proves inconsistent, they can explore alternatives until they arrive at a more reliable account.

Outcomes of scientific enquiry should enable children to understand and talk about familiar objects and events in new and more reliable ways. As the story 'Paper clips' illustrates, children's curiosity can lead them to create imaginative explanations.

Example: Paper clips

Year 2 were finding out which objects floated and which sank. The teacher asked Ria if she could explain why some things sank and others floated. Ria thought carefully and said that heavy things sank. The teacher asked Ria to think about why a paper clip had sunk although it wasn't heavy. Ria spent some time observing and considering the objects on the bottom of the tank of water. After a little thought, she explained that there were scissors at the bottom of the tank and they were magnetic; paper clips were also magnetic, so the scissors must have attracted the paper clip and pulled it to the bottom.

Comment

Ria's explanation for why a paper clip sank was highly imaginative, and she was making sense of what she saw by drawing on prior learning. When encouraged to test her theory, she found that paper clips are not normally attracted to scissors. The evidence showed that Ria's explanation was unreliable and that she needed to look for other reasons why the paper clip sank. It was the teacher's pertinent question, and the chance to discuss it, that provoked her to think about what she knew in order to try to explain what she saw. Without this dialogue, it is likely that Ria would have persisted with her misconception. The teacher had gained insight into what experience of floating and sinking Ria would need to help develop her ideas.

Scientific enquiry and its link to narrative

It is useful when teaching through scientific enquiry to think of a hypothesis as a kind of narrative created by the children. Such tentative descriptions, or personal narratives, are rooted in the child's existing experience and draw on personal stories about how the world works. For example, the story 'Honey bees' illustrates the type of personal narrative or hypothesis children can construct to explain an event which is very familiar to them.

Example: Honey bees

A class of 5-year-olds watched bees visiting a lavender bush in the school grounds. When talking with her teacher about this, Sarah described bees collecting honey from flowers and taking it back to their hive. She explained that when people wanted honey they could open the hive and scoop it out with a spoon to put in jars.

Children draw on their everyday experience and their imagination to suggest what a bee does with nectar. This story made perfect sense to Sarah and matched her experience of the natural world as designed to meet the needs of humans. Subsequent discussion and teaching could focus attention on other insects that visit flowers but do not produce honey. The children could be asked to tell their own story about what the bee actually collects and what it does once it leaves a flower.

Their enquiry can be enriched by video, web resources and picture storybooks such as Eric Carle's *The Honeybee and the Robber* (1981) to challenge the reliability of the children's own stories. Research and carefully supported discussion can enable children to modify their 'everyday' stories towards a more scientific point of view; in this case, to offer a better understanding of the crucial role insects play in the life cycle of the plant and how plants attract pollinators.

A teacher sets the scene for a science narrative by focusing children's attention on a topic, encouraging close observation and inviting them to offer their thoughts and ideas. The teacher may offer a challenge or a puzzle or help the children to do so. The way children respond with ideas and explanations of what they observe will reflect their familiarity with how stories work. Younger children may suggest that things happen *because they do* ('that's the way things are'). More experienced children may devise a more complex storyline, either alone or through discussion following practical activity.

Children need to reach an understanding that they find believable but which also matches accepted scientific ideas. This achievement depends on activities and conversations that address the children's existing thinking and move the story on. It is the role of the teacher to provide new information, activities and guidance from which children can begin to build their own understanding. Children can usefully be encouraged to compare understanding by telling each other their stories before and after science activities.

Something to think about

Story books offer the chance to speculate, question and follow a narrative line of thinking from puzzle to resolution. Can children identify these aspects of the science topic they are studying? Do they enjoy speculating about how things work or asking 'What if?' or 'What might happen?' Do they want to think, talk and puzzle it out? Or are they more inclined to 'get it over with' and try to rush to a conclusion? Can we teach the capacity to be curious or is it something children bring along – and that we must foster?

Scientific skills and attitudes

What really makes scientists special is less their knowledge than their method of acquiring it.

(Dawkins, 1998)

Like Kipling's mongoose, Rikki-Tikki-Tavi, children are 'eaten up from nose to tail with curiosity' but this does not necessarily make them scientists. In order to behave like scientists, children must develop the enquiry skills that will enable them to collect reliable evidence to test the validity of their ideas. Children also need to recognise and manage any hazards associated with their practical work.

As the skills needed to carry out scientific enquiry are mastered, children become more independent in their learning. A scientific approach to enquiry relies on creative thinking to raise questions and form hypotheses, to make predictions and plan how to gather evidence using a range of techniques. Once evidence has been collected, it needs to be interpreted and conclusions drawn with reference to the original hypothesis. Finally, scientists must communicate their findings to a wider audience and be prepared to defend their assertions through careful evaluation of the reliability and validity of their enquiry process.

The development of positive scientific attitudes is also a crucial part of a child's science education. Attitudes that teachers can usefully foster include independence, perseverance, cooperation, respect for evidence, creativity and inventiveness, open-mindedness and respect for living things (de Boo, 2006). Attitudes are much more difficult to teach than skills: for example, a learning objective that says 'Today we are going to learn to persevere' may be somewhat optimistic. Teachers can model positive scientific attitudes, thinking aloud with the children and sharing enthusiasm for the work. Attitudes displayed by the teacher are crucial in shaping the quality of the learning experience for the children. Encouragingly, attitudes are flexible attributes, open to influence and dependent on experience and context. In science, we can create classroom contexts which help children experience strongly positive and socially useful attitudes.

Developing respect for evidence may be a particular challenge as children will arrive at school with a range of preconceptions about scientific concepts, e.g. 'Heavy things sink'. They also bring with them their own culture and experiences. In the story 'Child science investigators' a child exhibits an expectation of adult behaviour based on her experience, which underpins, and might interfere with, the interpretation of scientific data.

Example: Child science investigators

Year 5 children spent a day in their local University Science Education Department 'helping the police to solve a crime'. In the scenario, a lecturer had left her laptop containing her secret research on her desk and it had been stolen. The investigators urgently needed to find the culprit. Clues left at the scene of the crime included fingerprints, a footprint, a shopping list, fibres and some soil from the criminal's shoes.

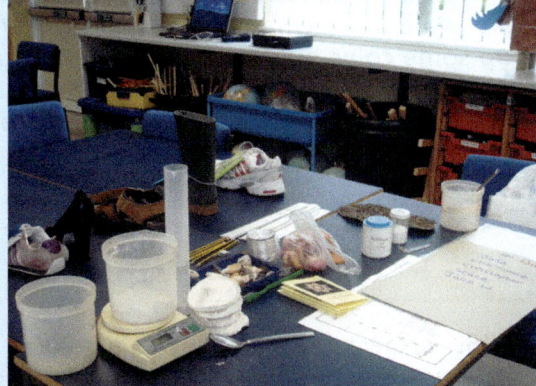

Five suspects had been identified – three women and two men – and the children were supplied with samples of their fingerprint, pens which might have been used to write the list, fibres, etc. The children tested the samples, matching findings against the clues and using their results as evidence to decide who was guilty of the crime.

At the end of the day, the investigators gathered to present their evidence. Several children identified the criminal and explained how the evidence supported their conclusion. Then Melanie began her presentation. 'Well, I knew straightaway it couldn't be one of the men,' she said, 'because one of the clues was a shopping list and men don't do the shopping.'

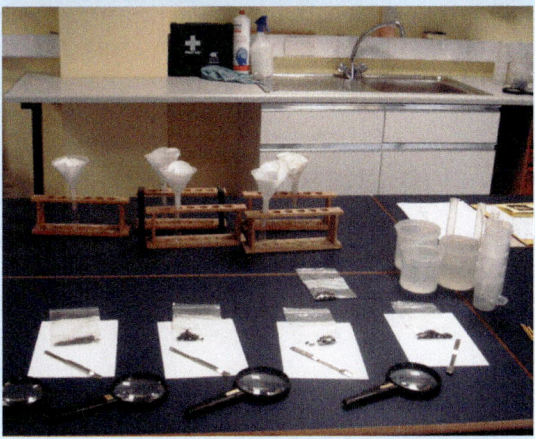

Crime scene investigations: (top) getting ready to match footprints found in the soil with types of shoes; (bottom) testing the type of soil found in the criminal's shoes.
Source: Peter Loxley

When children try to make sense of a situation, they bring their own culturally specific experience with them. In this scenario the 'criminal' actually was one of the women. It would have been interesting if it had been a man; how difficult would it have been for Melanie to acknowledge the evidence before her? Would this be a good chance to discuss attitudes or perhaps better to discuss the importance of using research evidence?

What do I need to know to teach scientific enquiry?

The basis of a good enquiry is a testable question, one which the children can answer by planning and carrying out an enquiry. For some children, asking the question is the most difficult part of the process. Questions sometimes arise through child-initiated activities but often they are the result of thoughtful teacher-planned explorations. The ice balloons story offers a good example of an exploration designed to stimulate questions.

One of the most important roles for the teacher is to manage the way children talk about the subject of their enquiry. Teacher-guided talk can help them to generate testable questions, create hypotheses, design investigations, interpret their observations and become active participants in the enquiry. Learning becomes more meaningful if children have opportunities to share what they have learnt with others and to use their new knowledge in other situations.

Good subject knowledge can enable teachers to feel confident in dealing with the unexpected when children are doing enquiries. Sometimes, children ask things which make it necessary to admit defeat; we all have limits to understanding! Why is the sky pink sometimes, how do sea-horses have babies, what are the blue bits in washing powder and why does a mobile phone pick up some coins but not others? Good questions cannot always be immediately answered. But such valuable learning opportunities can be encouraged and supported with curiosity fostered by setting up joint enquiry and research involving collaborative discussion amongst the class.

Types of scientific enquiry

The AKSIS project (Goldsworthy et al., 2000) identified six different forms of enquiry that can answer questions in classroom settings. These are: exploring, fair testing, pattern-seeking, classifying and identifying, investigating models, and technological enquiry. The project reported that 'fair testing' was perhaps overused in primary schools and encouraged the use of a wider range of enquiry strategies.

Exploring phenomena and seeking explanations

Exploration enquiries offer the opportunity to observe the behaviour of objects or natural events. Observations can ignite children's curiosity and give rise to questions that can be answered by further planned enquiries, as in the story 'The colour of bubbles'.

Example: The colour of bubbles

Children at a science fair were given the opportunity to play with bubbles. They put on gloves and caught the bubbles on their hands but when they took the gloves off and tried to catch them, the bubbles burst. They shone lights through the bubbles and were fascinated by the different colours they could see. The children asked a range of questions: 'Where did the colours come from?', 'Why do the colours seem to slide down the bubbles?' and 'Why do the bubbles burst?' They tried to predict the point at which the bubbles would burst. The answers to these puzzles needed further investigation and scientific explanations.

Investigating bubbles.
Source: Peter Loxley

A fair-test enquiry

Fair testing relies on observing and exploring relationships between variables. This involves changing one variable (the independent variable) and observing or measuring the effect it has on another (the dependent variable) whilst keeping all other factors the same (Goldsworthy et al., 2000). An example of a question suitable for a fair test is: 'When I change the height of the ramp, what will happen to the time it takes for a car to go down it?'

Learning the process of fair testing takes time and needs careful support. With younger children, fair-test enquiries may be initiated by the teacher, with structured recording formats to guide the children's work. Later, children can be encouraged to generate their own questions and to take increasing responsibility for demonstrating ways of working that characterise fair testing. The skills involved in questioning, setting up an enquiry, collecting and interpreting data and communicating conclusions require reinforcement and practice over some years.

Enquiries are sometimes labelled fair-test enquiries when they are not. For example, children might question if the length of a child's legs determines how far they can jump from a standing start. Whatever they do to ensure that all jumps are taken from the same point and the resulting distance accurately measured, it is impossible to control some variables which may have a direct impact on the outcomes – such as the strength of each child's muscles or an individual child's willingness to participate to their best ability. In this case, a pattern-seeking enquiry would produce more reliable results.

The nature of a pattern-seeking enquiry

These investigations involve children making observations and measurements and looking for patterns in their data. For example, if you did the jumping investigation described above with a class of 30 children, what sort of patterns would you expect if 'length of legs' did influence how far they could jump? This is the sort of investigation where the reliability of the result increases as you increase the size of the sample used. Pattern-seeking investigations provide opportunities for children to apply their measuring and mathematical skills and to critically defend their point of view in light of evidence. The story 'The baby's shape' is an example of how such enquiries can encourage children to use simple data to investigate an interesting question.

Example: The baby's shape

Baby Tom arrived to visit a Year 2 class with his mother. Sam noticed how big Tom's head looked in relation to his body and wondered if the same applied to himself and his classmates. Carefully measuring the baby, the children found that his head accounted for about a third of his body length. They then made measurements of their own heads and bodies and found that the same relationship (proportion) did not apply. They began to wonder when the proportions of their bodies had changed. Later, the class undertook a teacher-guided whole-school enquiry looking for patterns in the relationship between the two variables, height and length of head. This enquiry became wider and eventually involved all their families. The children discovered that this proportion altered for people aged 0 to 7 years but after that became fairly constant.

Classifying and identifying

Classifying the world around us helps us impose order on what might otherwise seem to be chaos. Classifying involves children in carefully and systematically collecting and grouping things on the basis of observational data. Their close observations can be used to encourage them to talk about and describe the similarities and differences in materials or objects. The resulting information may well provoke further questions that can be investigated in other ways. For example, a sorting activity looking at different types of paper might result in a fair-test investigation to explore which type of paper is best to wrap a parcel for sending in the post.

Example: The school wildlife pond

The school's wildlife pond offered opportunities to investigate the range of creatures that colonise its varied habitats at different points in the year. Children dipped the pond and each year group developed its own way of classifying and then identifying the animals discovered. Recording ranged from simple picture keys to branching databases. Digital photos and video recording enabled them to study physical characteristics and movement. Careful observation revealed how plants and animals were adapted to survive and thrive in the pond: for example, the pond-skater's ability to glide across the surface and the way the caddis fly larva builds itself a cocoon of stones and twigs to camouflage it from its prey.

The study of wildlife habitats, such as ponds, not only provides opportunities for classifying and identifying animals and plants, but also children can undertake pattern-seeking enquiries concerning populations. As a result of their observations at this pond, the children made models to find out how it was possible for pond-skaters to 'walk on water'.

Testing ideas by modelling

Models are used in science to simulate real-life conditions in a way that helps to try out ideas and explanations to see if they make sense. For example, children may think that the phases of the Moon are caused by shadows of the Earth cast on the Moon's surface. Using torches and relevant-sized balls, children can model the phases of the Moon in a way that matches their hypothesis. In this case, modelling is likely to show that the children's view is not reliable when tested against experience and that they need to rethink their ideas.

Example: Emperor penguins

A class of 10- and 11-year-olds were fascinated by a film showing colonies of emperor penguins huddling together to protect their chicks as they endured months of bitterly cold Antarctic weather. One group of children decided to find a way to investigate why penguins huddled in this way. They wondered about how to recreate Antarctic conditions until one child suggested they could make a model to simulate the penguins' behaviour. A simple model emerged; a large beaker was packed with successive rings of plastic test tubes, each containing a thermometer. The test tubes were then filled with hot water and the whole apparatus left in the fridge for an hour. An hour later, the thermometer readings confirmed that cooling was greatest in the outermost ring of test tubes.

The evidence the children collected helped them to think about what affects how quickly things cool. They concluded that temperature of the water fell more rapidly in the outermost test tubes because here the difference between the temperature of the water and the temperature in the fridge was greater than between the inner test tubes and the ones next to them.

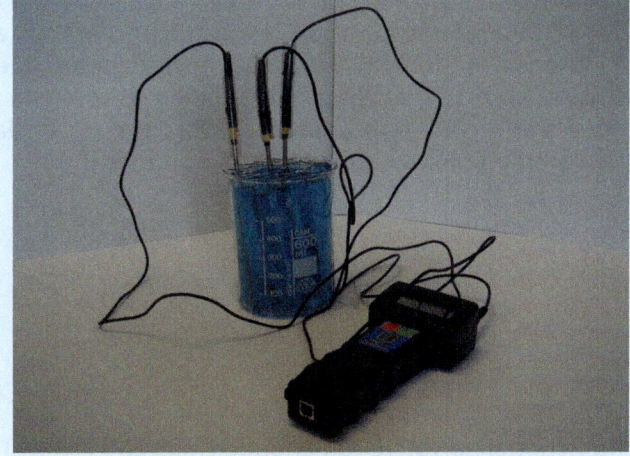

Modelling how huddling together helps keep penguins warm.
Source: Peter Loxley

Technological enquiry

Technological design may rely on the application of scientific skills and ideas. For example, the design of a sunhat depends on understanding the properties of the materials from which it is made. Children can test different fabrics to develop an understanding of their properties and then use this knowledge to inform the design. Another example is that of electric circuits. Once children understand that a circuit is needed for electrical current to flow, they can begin to explore the role of switches in interrupting the flow of electricity. They might then be set a challenge to design an intruder alarm that will sound when a door is opened or a circuit that will turn off the light when the fridge door is shut. This gives the children an opportunity to test their system and evaluate its fitness for purpose as well as demonstrating the strength of their understanding of the underlying concept.

Choosing contexts for scientific enquiry

The context in which an enquiry is carried out gives it purpose and meaning. Effective contexts are those which are already familiar to the children and make their enquiries personally significant. When enquiries are presented with little relevant context (for example: Which is the best insulator? Which is the most absorbent paper? Which sole has the best grip?), children's motivation may be decreased and their engagement diminished. If contexts for learning can be offered that make the children want to find out answers because they are interested and they can see the point of what they are doing, then motivation becomes intrinsic: 'When learning occurs for intrinsic reasons it has been shown time and again to be highly effective learning' (Falk and Dierking, 2000).

Genuine contexts make enquiry more real for the child. For example, 'My coffee keeps going cold when I am on break duty; how do you think I could keep it warm?' or 'We need to make a raincoat to keep teddy dry if it rains on our teddy bears' picnic. Which of these fabrics do you think will be best?'

Engaging cross-curricular contexts

The creative arts provide rich contexts to promote the development of process skills and conceptual understanding. Poetry, narrative, drama and art can all be used to engage children's interest and make them want to find out more. A short poem like Roger McGough's 'Snowman' haiku invites discussion about what the poet is saying before the class move on to considering the science of materials and change of state. It offers the potential for enquiry: Why do raindrops make the snowman melt? How could we stop him melting?

Snowman

Snowman in a field
listening to the raindrops
wishing him farewell

Roger McGough (1983)

Using fictional narrative can engage children's interest. A well-illustrated picture book or intriguing adventure can provide a range of contexts for investigation. For example, the story of Goldilocks sets the scene for children to learn about cooling and insulation. Children can investigate the reasons why the different bowls of porridge were different temperatures, and explore materials which can be used to keep the porridge warm. Work on forces and structures could be stimulated by the Three Pigs story and an exploration enquiry into life cycles and healthy eating could be inspired by *The Very Hungry Caterpillar* (Carle, 1994).

Making science into a drama and role-play can have a memorable effect

Drama can be motivating and can encourage creative approaches to communicating science ideas. For example, whilst studying invertebrates in the school grounds, children acted out their representation of an ant colony. They dressed as ants which brought food to the 'nest', attended the queen as she laid her eggs and relocated the nest when flood waters threatened. Such dramatisations are memorable and bring learning to life.

Children can also become active participants in creating models that explain a scientific concept; for example, a group of children can role-play the different components in an electrical circuit and show how electricity passes around the circuit. This could then lead into a practical enquiry of what happens when different components in the circuit are changed.

Art and science – a powerful combination

Art, like science, encourages children to observe closely. Collecting objects to draw, paint or to make into collages improves observational skills and at the same time encourages creativity in the representation of the objects. Painting flowers in the style of, for example, Aboriginal art can be a powerful way for children to interpret shape and colour and enable them to create personal representations of the structure of the flower. Studying the work of landscape artists such as Andy Goldsworthy can help children to look at familiar objects in a new way.

Observing the natural world can lead to questions that can be the basis of an enquiry. For example, when observing and drawing leaves, a Year 4 child noticed that when the veins on a leaf were opposite each other, the leaves on the twig were arranged alternately. But when the veins were arranged alternately, the leaves were opposite each other on the twig. This observation led into an enquiry to see if this rule applied more generally. Art offers the opportunity to take the children outside the classroom to learn about the natural world.

Learning outside the classroom

Although the majority of science lessons will take place in the classroom, there is much to be gained from learning outside the classroom. The phrase 'outside the classroom' covers both the nearby outdoors and visiting places of interest further away from the school, for example, a sewage works, a power station, a museum or an interactive science centre. Such visits can create a lifelong interest in a subject. However, such visits might provide only limited opportunities for science enquiry. Using the school playground or a neighbourhood site has a number of advantages and can encourage enquiry which goes on over several years. Carrying out enquiries that can be developed over a number of weeks or even months will help the children to see patterns in nature and to understand seasonal cycles. Observations on the school field throughout the year will help children to see the different stages of the life cycles of plants. For example, the yellow flower and the feathery 'clock' of the dandelion appear so unconnected that children may think they are different plants rather than different stages in the life cycle of the same plant. In learning about local plants and animals, children gain a basis for wider understanding.

A local church and churchyard can be a wonderful resource. As well as learning about plants and animals living in the churchyard, children can learn about materials, their properties and uses. Questions might be: Are all headstones the same? Why have some of the inscriptions on the headstones disappeared? Why is wood used to make the pews in church? How is stained glass made? Why are the carvings on one side of the church door more weathered than on the other side? Such queries necessitate several visits, each with a different focus, to enable children to take full advantage of the resources available. There are also many opportunities for cross-curricular learning.

Examples of children's art.
Source: Peter Loxley

Similarly, the local park and playground can provide opportunities to explore forces and motion. Children can start with questions such as, 'How can you make yourself go down the slide more slowly?' and 'How can you make the swing go higher?' These contexts have real relevance for the children and can lead into more scientific understanding.

If children become familiar with their local area, recognising its unique nature, they are more likely to value and to care for it. They will want to find out more about it and motivation to learn will become intrinsic; they become involved with their learning because they want to learn. This can promote citizenship and education for sustainable development.

It can help to begin or confirm an interest in science which lasts a lifetime.

Formative assessment and science enquiry

Children need to be actively involved in all stages of a science enquiry. In order to develop scientific skills, it is important for them to know which skills they will be focusing on in their particular enquiry. Where possible, teachers should involve the pupils in setting targets in order to develop these scientific skills. This can support teacher assessment and can help children to assess their own work, to monitor their own progress and to identify the next steps in their own learning.

Summary

Science enquiry is by its very nature creative. Enquiry offers children the opportunity to find answers to their own questions; to discover and think about new ideas for themselves for the very first time. Teachers have to be prepared for the unexpected. They act as models for a range of invaluable scientific attitudes, and can enable children to rethink everyday experience in new and exciting ways. Teachers may feel that their own science understanding is tested to its limits by the questions children raise. Such an effect holds no fears for the teacher who is aware that it is the process of thinking scientifically that is the most profound learning taking place. The chance to enquire, collect information and think with others to come up with answers to one another's questions is a powerful cycle in which every child can be involved. Teachers can offer stimulating and creative starting points, enabling children to remain, or even become, passionately curious about the natural world.

Further reading

ASE journals:

- Primary Science 142 (March/April 2016). *How the Fair Test Nearly Killed Enquiry* by Juliet Nickels.
- Primary Science 142 (March/April 2016). *'Curiouser and Curiouser': Supporting Children's Independent Enquiry Skills* by Debbie Myers, Maria McGrory and Cathy Westgate.
- Primary Science 142 (March/April 2016). *Concept Cartoons Conversations Lead to Inspiring Investigations* by Yanoula Constantinou.
- Primary Science 141 (Jan/Feb 2016). *How Can You Make the Most of Those 'Wow Moments'?* by Sally Hardman and Sue Luke.

- Primary Science Review 106 (Jan/Feb 2009). *'Science Enquiry'*. This issue is focused on scientific enquiry skills.

Books:

- Barnett, J. and Feasey, R. (2016). *Jumpstart Science Outdoors*, London: Routledge.
- Davies, D. (2011). *Teaching Science Creatively*, London: Routledge.
- Harlen, W. (ed) (2011). *ASE Guide to Primary Science Education*, Hatfield: ASE.
- Harlen, W. (2012). *The Fibonacci Booklet*, http://fibonacci.uni-bayreuth.de/resources/fibonacci-booklet.html.
- Harlen, W. and Qualter, A. (2014). *The Teaching of Science in Primary School*, London: Routledge.
- Turner, J. Keogh, B., Naylor, S. and Lawrence, L. (2011). *Is It Fair – or Is It Not?* Sandbach: Millgate House.

Website:

- Pri-sci-net (2017). *http://prisci.net/* – engaging children in science enquiry

Peer-reviewed journals:

- Dunlop, L., Crompton, K., Clarke, L. and McKelvey-Martin, V. (2015). Child-led Enquiry in Primary Science. *Education 3–13*: 43(5): 462–481.
- Zhai, J., Jocz, J.A. and Tan A. (2014). 'Am I Like a Scientist?': Primary Children's Images of Doing Science in School. *International Journal of Science Education*, 36(4): 553–576.

CHAPTER 7

PLANNING AND ASSESSING CHILDREN'S SCIENCE LEARNING

Do not train children to learning by force and harshness, but direct them to it by what amuses their minds, so that you may be better able to discover with accuracy the peculiar bent of the genius of each.

(Plato, 427–347 BCE)

Well-planned science lessons provide engaging learning opportunities. Planning involves deciding which strategies will best develop children's understanding. The ideas that children bring to the classroom are the basis for learning and can be assessed to inform planning. This chapter examines approaches to planning and assessment which can be integrated into the three-stage framework for organising science learning.

Topics discussed in the chapter

- The nature of formative assessment
- The nature of summative assessment
- Planning children's science learning
- Planning the exploratory stage
- Planning the re-describing stage
- Planning the application stage
- Across the stages

The nature of formative assessment

There are two purposes for assessment. The first is to check children's progress towards a learning goal and to evaluate what needs to be done to promote learning. This is assessment *for* learning or formative assessment. The second purpose of assessment is to create a snapshot or summary of children's progress at the end of a topic or over a period of time. This is assessment *of* learning, or summative assessment, used for formally reporting children's progress to parents and others.

The key characteristics of formative assessment are that it is ongoing, dynamic and progressive (Bell and Cowie, 2001). It also has to be responsive – something has to happen as a result of it. The following teacher's comment highlights the progressive and responsive nature of formative assessment:

> **If you do something to find out where they (children) are at, and then you do something from that to change your teaching or what you are doing, then it is formative (assessment).**
>
> (Bell and Cowie, 2001: 544)

Formative assessment may be informal, without written records being made, and can be used to inform teaching and learning in all stages of a lesson. In practice, it is often opportunistic, taking place as teachers listen to children's conversations and respond to their queries and comments. When planned, assessment activities may be carried out at the beginning of a lesson and again at the end to measure changes in understanding. Information can be used to inform what is taught in subsequent sessions.

Teachers and children can collaborate to ensure effective formative assessment. From the child's perspective, formative assessment can help them to understand what learning is possible and how it can be achieved. It should also clarify what they have done well and what they need to do to improve (Black and Harrison, 2000). Teachers often share their learning intentions with classes of children, usually towards the start of a lesson. By sharing learning intentions and deciding on indicators of children's progress (success criteria or 'steps to success'), children are better aware of the aims and purposes of their classroom activity (Clarke, 2008).

Although formative assessment can be carried out through different activities, it is by nature dialogic because it requires children to communicate their ideas. Questions such as: 'What do you imagine is going on here?', 'What do you think?', 'What do you mean by that?', 'Can you say a bit about …?', 'Can you explain more about …?', 'Why do you think that?' or 'What words would you use to explain …?' provide tools to mediate assessment activities and to probe more deeply into children's thinking. Having discovered what the child already knows, we can use the information to respond appropriately.

Something to think about

Is it always possible to plan for formative assessment? What formative assessment opportunities provide the sort of information that can be used to support planning?

Aspects of effective formative assessment

Learning needs: Essentially, the purpose of formative assessment is to gather information about children's ideas and to use it to help create new and appropriate learning opportunities. In science classrooms, development is dependent on finding out, and addressing, the difference between a child's existing ideas and a more scientific point of view. The ideas in question may concern understanding natural phenomena or events, or they may be to do with attitudes or ways of working scientifically. The difference between the children's way of thinking and ways of thinking from a scientific point of view can be defined as the 'learning needs' of the children (Leach and Scott, 2002). The concept of 'learning needs' helps us to target teaching strategies for different children, to identify next steps and to hold focused discussions with classes and individuals.

Teachers' questions: Teachers ask questions to stimulate discussion and help children to articulate their current ideas. Teachers' questions are meant to engage children by appealing to their personal memories and their willingness to contribute. They are used to ensure that all children are attending and to generate common knowledge. But some questions are more useful than others. Teachers may slip into asking questions to which children have to guess the right answer, that is, find out what the teacher wants them to say. For example:

T: OK, who can tell me what magnets do? Katy?

K: Stick to the fridge.

T: Um, yes, fridge magnets – but if you have two magnets, what happens?

And so on for many more turns until the class have come up with the required phrases, 'Like poles repel; unlike poles attract'. Teachers' questions require a lot of hand-waving on the part of the children and the teacher may have to manage some off-task behaviour created by boredom. This sort of interaction is the source of such phrases as: 'Listening ears on, everyone!', 'Let me see, who is sitting beautifully?', 'I can't ask you because you haven't got your hand up' or 'Can you repeat that, Josh? I couldn't hear because some people are just not listening' and so on. Episodes of inter-minable questions leave the class and the teacher quite baffled by one another and do not help children to understand anything. Less experienced teachers may copy this style from those who have had years of practice at handling children this way. Children, having little choice, rapidly learn the rules and then spend much of their time finding ways to subvert them.

In the story 'What seeds need', the teacher is starting a topic on growing plants with Year 5. Here the deadening impact of 'teachers' questions' is evident.

Example: What seeds need

T: Right. Now. What do seeds need to grow? *(hands go up)* Alice?

Alice.   Sunlight and […] water.

T: Hmm, sunlight and water, you think. What else? *(fewer hands)* Bryce?

Bryce: Earth.

Kieran: Compost.

T: Put your hand up. You might be chosen to talk if you put your hand up. *(Kieran puts up his hand.)* Hmmm, come on, someone different. Muj?

Muj: Something to grow in.

T: Yes, something to grow in, but what else? To grow?

Chloe: Blue pellets to keep away slugs.

T: That's not vital. What else does it have to have? What other vital things? We've got sunlight, water and soil.

Denes: Can worms help them grow? On my Gran's allotment, right, she has worms, they […]

T: *(dismissively)* Worms!

Denes: *(nodding)* Yes, she lets me pick them up, I can pick up worms.

Alice: Yes, in the soil, they make holes in the soil.

T: Um, yes, help the soil. Absolutely. Worms. Right, now I want you to put together a role-play for me …

Comment

The teacher had not decided whether to stick to talking about germination (seeds usually need water, air and some warmth) or to talk about plant growth (plants usually need light, water, air and some warmth and sometimes a growing medium such as soil). She asks six 'teachers' questions'. She accepts the children's suggestions, sunlight, water and soil – although not sounding too confident about it – but has another idea in mind and prompts the children to keep guessing what it is: possibly warmth or air. The interesting idea of slug pellets reminds Denes of soil creatures and he asks a question about worms, which is dismissed as nonsensical by the teacher but picked up by his classmate Alice. Alice's idea that worms make holes reminds the teacher that worms do help plants – which is what she asked – by aerating soil. But this is slightly too complex an idea to fit in the simpler narrative that plants need sun, water, soil and … air? Warmth? She covers up the slight muddle by rapidly moving on. This cannot happen to teachers who are asking genuine questions, which by their very nature indicate a quest for information or understanding. Teachers do better when they take up answers positively and make it clear what they do not know or what is new to them; clarifying their role as part of the enquiry rather than the complete solution.

The children have no chance to share what they genuinely know or understand. It is evident that Alice seems to understand what plants require, Denes has experience of allotments, Chloe has learned about keeping slugs at bay, Kieran offers the suggestion of compost as a different medium than soil and Muj may be summing up what soil and compost are or is aware that plants need a habitat, even if it's simply a plant pot. These ideas are not what the teacher wants. Each suggestion is taken as a slightly wrong end point rather than an opener to a wider discussion. But what is she trying to teach? The learning intention for this session was 'to be able to say what seeds need to grow into plants.' It would be more productive to hand out some seeds and ask the children to tell each other everything they can think of about how to help the seed grow into a big plant. The teacher can then invite children to share what they have heard or nominate a classmate who they think has something interesting to offer. Having listened to the children's ideas, the teacher can consider their 'learning needs' and then manage the next step in their learning accordingly.

The responses we get from children depend on the types of question we ask. From a question such as 'What will happen to the plant if we stop watering it?', the teacher may be expecting a factual answer: 'It will die'. The teacher is only interested in one answer. But if we show the children an unhealthy-looking plant and ask what they think is wrong with it, we are more likely to hear a range of views. To engage children in learning conversation, we need to ask questions which show an interest in their experience or require them to express a point of view, giving their reasons. In the three-stage framework, interesting questions or puzzles are introduced in the exploratory stage and this sets the scene for children's learning in the re-describing stage. Children's responses to puzzles and questions provide us with insight into their existing understanding. Planning questions and puzzles is crucial if we are to determine, and subsequently address, children's 'learning needs'.

The 'Blue Earth puzzle' provides an example of formative assessment in practice in a class of 8-year-old children:

Example: Blue Earth puzzle

Joe's class was shown a picture on the interactive whiteboard of the Earth taken from space. The children were asked to think about why the Earth looked blue from space.

Joe was convinced that the Earth looked blue because the sky was blue. He held firm views about the reasons for the colour and he was not ready to change them. He asserted that the picture from space was taken through the sky so it had to look blue.

When another child suggested that the Earth looked blue because of the seas and oceans that covered it, Joe became quite agitated. He walked up to the whiteboard and said that he was worried about this idea. He used his hands to explain that if the blue was water then the water on the sides and bottom of the Earth would run off and we would have no seas left. He knew that we have seas and oceans; he insisted that the only possible explanation was that the blue had to be the colour of the sky.

Comment

Joe's response revealed learning needs which the teacher had not expected. Here on Earth we constantly live with the effects of gravity, so that intuitively it makes sense that water would fall down and off the sides and bottom of the Earth. We need to recognise the explanatory power of Joe's reasoning. He has seen water running downwards. As teachers, we have to make the decision: in what way do we want Joe to change his understanding of the Earth and gravity? Once we decide this, we can plan and organise teaching strategies to help him to understand a more scientific point of view.

Something to think about

Read the 'Blue Earth puzzle' and assess Joe's learning needs. Think about how you might address them.

Self-assessment and peer assessment

Children can be involved in assessing their own progress. To do so, they need to be clear about what they should be able to do as a result of their learning, which they could not do before. Setting children a puzzle to solve provides them with an insight into what they are trying to achieve. Finding solutions to puzzling events brings not only measurable intellectual rewards but can also provide emotional satisfaction which can positively influence children's attitudes to further learning (Chapter 1).

Just as children need to be taught to talk and think together in scientific ways (Chapter 5), they need to be taught the assessment skills to monitor and manage their own learning. Children may need input in the language of judgement and assessment. For example, 'understanding' can mean being able to explain an idea clearly to someone else or being able to put an idea into practice or help solve a puzzle. Simple systems to record self-assessment include the use of 'traffic light' icons to signify whether children perceive they have achieved the learning goals, putting thumbs up or drawing smiley faces on work to show how confident individuals are in their learning.

Whatever strategies are used to promote self-assessment, children need to learn to question and reflect on their learning. Asking themselves particular questions can help shape children's thinking and understanding: What needs to be done next? How can I best find an answer to that question? Is there any other way to find an answer to that problem? Is there another way of looking at the problem or puzzle? Are there any other words I can use to explain my view more clearly? What reasons do I have for my belief? Do I really understand the meaning of that word?

These types of questions require children to reflect on the nature of their own learning and understanding. Children should be encouraged to communicate and justify their judgements to their peers and teacher, and make suggestions about how to proceed with their learning.

Peer assessment can usefully support self-assessment (Black et al., 2002). Strategies for peer assessment may not be immediately obvious to children. Asked to look at one another's work, they may take the stance of a very harsh and unyielding teacher! Effective ways to assess work and communicate helpful ideas really need to be made explicit. Exploratory talk (Chapter 5) between children has an important role to play in peer assessment. Learning takes place as children listen and respond to each other's ideas, and discussion can focus on how to achieve their learning goals collaboratively. Children need to be taught to offer supportive formative comments and suggestions, to query ideas and note what they have found new or interesting, and that it is not their role to make summative judgements about whether their classmates' ideas are right or wrong, 'good' or 'bad'.

In summary, a key purpose of formative assessment is to provide information for managing children's learning. It is also important for children's awareness of their own developing ideas, helping them to be better motivated by giving them a stake in their own learning. For teachers, the chance to talk to children about their understanding is always a source of interest, and one of the profoundly satisfying aspects of our role.

The nature of summative assessment

The purpose of summative assessment is to summarize children's achievements at particular points in time, such as at the end of topics or terms. Outcomes of summative assessment are recorded and used for various purposes including planning, reporting to children, reporting to parents and governors, and reporting to other teachers during transition from class to class or school to school. All forms of assessment should be used to improve learning. Whereas formative assessment is an ongoing and active process which influences children's learning as they learn, summative assessment involves the collection of a range of evidence from which judgements are made about their progress over time. For summative assessment to influence learning, it needs to be shared with the children and used to inform planning.

Traditionally, pencil-and-paper tests are used to collect evidence of what children have learnt over a period of time. Although these types of tests can be useful if well designed, they are often limited in scope by focusing on the recall of facts rather than eliciting children's points of view.

The Nuffield Foundation (2012) published a report which argues that there is no need for separate types of assessment for formative and summative purposes. It suggests that the rich and extensive descriptions of each child's achievements, which are provided by effective formative assessment practices, can be summarized and used to create a narrative-style annual report to parents. The report should indicate the child's progress regarding the learning outcomes for the year and indicate where support is being provided to ensure the expected learning can be achieved by the end of the key stage. The transfer from formative data to summative judgements at the end of each key stage should be subject to internal moderation and referenced to national exemplars.

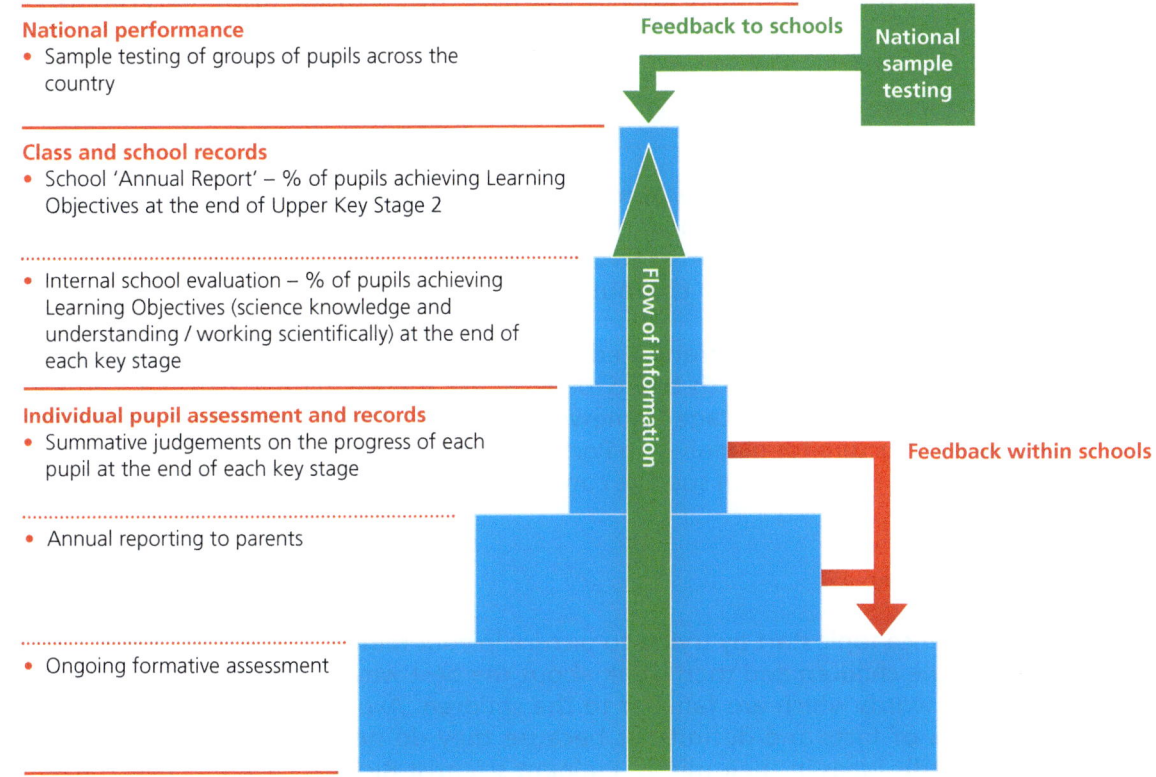

Individual, class and school assessment: A wide range of assessment processes provide a rich and extensive source of information on individual pupil's learning, which is used to report on achievement. Information on individual pupils is then summarised to provide summative judgements which can be collated at the level of class or whole school. Class and school level data can be used for internal reporting and the School Annual Report. Feedback from internal evaluation and summative judgements informs future improvements of teaching and learning.

National performance: Sample testing of groups of pupils across the country provides data on the national picture which in turn provides feedback to schools.

Figure of the flow of assessment data through the school published in the Nuffield Foundation report (2012).

Source: Nuffield Foundation, 2012. *Developing Policy, Principles and Practice in Primary School Science Assessment.* [Accessed June 2017]

The flow of assessment through school

The Nuffield Foundation produced a pyramid model (described above) which indicates how assessment information can flow from ongoing formative assessment in the classroom to whole school reporting. The Teacher Assessment in Primary Science (TAPS) project team worked with schools and other professional organizations to consider how the Nuffield model would work in practice. As a result, they produced a comprehensive model of school assessment with its foundations firmly embedded in shared understanding of good classroom practice. The model provides a structure containing examples from a wide range of schools, which can be used as a source of ideas for teachers or as a whole school self-evaluation tool to identify strengths and areas for development. The resource is especially rich in ideas which exemplify the many ways formative assessment practices can be integrated into the curriculum. The TAPS pyramid and reports are available for download from the Primary Science Teachers Trust website (https://pstt.org.uk/).

Planning children's science learning

Teachers manage the learning of large numbers of children with a diverse range of ethnic backgrounds, social behaviours, talents and interests. Sometimes, general teaching and learning theories do not easily translate into effective classroom practice (Lijnse, 2000; 2004). It can prove difficult for teachers to apply the outcomes of science education research in their classrooms.

In this book, educational theory is translated into classroom practice. The theory chapters in Part 1 provide examples of how research-based ideas can be applied in the classroom. These ideas are brought together into the three-stage framework which can help to organise science learning and which provides a structure for planning. In Part 2, 'Ideas for practice' exemplify how the three-stage framework can be used to teach specific concepts and skills.

The scientific view

When planning a science topic start by trying to picture in your mind the scientific view which you want to share with the children and then think about the best way of communicating that view. Take care to choose words which are familiar to the children. Avoid presenting scientific knowledge as a collection of facts and definitions because they do not help children create useful pictures of the scientific ideas in their minds. Eminent scientist Richard Feynman called scientific definitions 'mystic formulae' because for many children they are just empty, meaningless words (Chapter 1).

By starting with a clear view of the science in your own mind, you will be able to talk about and describe the key scientific ideas in language children will understand. A crucial part of teaching science is interpreting scientific ideas in ways which enable children to talk about and make sense of them. Children need opportunities to use spoken language to make ideas explicit and to appreciate their value. If we describe scientific ideas using everyday language, we can help children re-describe and re-think their experiences of the natural world from a scientific point of view.

When planning a topic think carefully about how you want to influence children's understanding of the world. The small ideas which we teach children can enable them to begin to see some of science's big ideas. For example, a topic on the feeding relationships in a garden, starting with a study of snails, can provide a way into grappling with big ideas such as interdependence and adaptation. Similarly, topics on light and sound provide opportunities not only to explore how we sense the world but also to find out how different animals and plants sense the world, providing a window on diversity and adaptation.

> ### Something to think about
>
> Reinterpret and expand the statement that 'light is reflected from surfaces' into a point of view accessible to children. What experiences could help children to think through the ideas?

Planning the exploratory stage: choosing strategies to elicit children's ideas

In the exploratory stage, activities should be planned to provide opportunities for children to communicate their ideas through appropriate means such as talking, drawing, modelling and writing. Bearing in mind the ideas and experience the children already have, decisions can then be made about what needs to happen in the children's minds to move their thinking towards the scientific view (Asoko, 2002).

Asking the right questions is the key to finding out what is going on inside children's minds. A 'big question' or 'puzzle' sets the scene for the children's learning and helps to stimulate curiosity and discussion (Chapter 1). Children's responses to the puzzle, and the information and questions which emerge from their discussion, provide feedback on children's existing understanding. In this way the puzzle is an important tool for formative assessment.

Examples of puzzles can be found in 'Ideas for practice' outlined in Part 2 of the text. Other strategies for eliciting children's ideas include the following.

Talking points

Talking points (Chapter 5) provide a focused stimulus for children to talk together and to raise their own questions. Talking points are statements relevant to the topic and the puzzle that provoke thinking and the exchange of ideas. Listening to others and offering their own ideas help children to establish their current thinking and to reflect on alternative ideas (Dawes, 2004). For example, we might offer children the following puzzle: 'What do you think of this idea: An acorn has an oak tree inside it?' Talk to your partner to decide whether this is true or false and why …' This is likely to bring out more ideas than holding up an acorn and asking questions such as: 'Who can tell me what this is? What has it got inside? What will it grow into?'

Concept Cartoons, created by Brenda Keogh and Stuart Naylor, provide stimulating talking points. Simple cartoon-style drawings present children with their own misconceptions and generate discussion and argument. They are remarkably easy to use in the classroom as a part of normal teaching. Concept Cartoons are available as a book or CD-ROM from Millgate House Publishers.

Unusual pictures and objects

The TAPS pyramid model (2015) provides a variety of activities for eliciting children's ideas. A stand-out activity is the use of pictures of 'challenging creatures'. Children can be asked what the unusual creature might be, where it could be found and how it is adapted to its habitat. Of course, the questions can be guided by the intended learning. It is important that children give reasons for their views hence providing a window into their thinking.

Example of a 'challenging creature' from the TAPS project.
Source: TAPS / Bath Spa

All kinds of thought-provoking pictures and photographs can be used in all areas of the curriculum. Interesting objects can be used in the same way. For example, small pieces of Moon rock and meteorites can be borrowed from the Science and Technology Facilities Council (STFC). More down-to-earth objects such as crystals, igneous rocks, fossils, unusual toys and even unfamiliar fruits and vegetables can stimulate curiosity and discussion. Many fascinating objects can be borrowed from museums.

Children's drawings

Annotated drawings can help to externalise what is going on inside children's minds. For example, we can ask them to draw how they think light enables them to see an object or what they think electricity looks like inside a wire. The diagram and, crucially, the child's written annotations are a resource for assessment.

The following example illustrates this. Thinking about the movement of particles of a gas, a Year 4 class were asked to sit very still. A perfume bottle was opened in a corner of the room. The class were asked to raise their hands when they could smell the perfume. After this activity, they were asked to draw a picture of the classroom, annotating it to show the movement of the scent and saying how they think that this movement happened.

Children's drawings can be compared and discussion focused on the reasons for the differences. Working collaboratively children can produce a drawing which they agree on and which represents their shared understanding.

Scientific enquiry

The value of practical enquiry is often seen as providing opportunities for children to develop scientific skills. In addition, enquiry creates puzzling events which arouse children's curiosity and provide contexts for discussion in which thinking is articulated, shared and clarified. For example, when enquiring into changes of state, children are often surprised to find that water expands when it freezes.

A puzzling event is the starting point on a quest for knowledge which begins with the sharing of children's ideas in the exploratory stage. Listening to children's ideas and responding to their questions provides insights into their *learning needs*, which can be addressed by looking at the puzzle from a scientific point of view in the re-describing stage.

Modelling through drama

Modelling through drama involves placing children in thought-provoking situations where they need to use their scientific understanding to decide how to act. The activities include: spontaneous role-play, hot seating, mind movies, miming movement, freeze frame, modelling concepts and phenomena, and acting out mini historical plays. The techniques are described in full in McGregor and Precious (2012; 2014).

Each of these activities requires children to act on their ideas and hence provide windows into their thinking. A teacher involved in a study of drama techniques reported:

> I think the benefits of using the drama – the techniques are easy to use, it's a very effective learning tool and I think it's an effective teaching tool because you can see how children are thinking, where they are in their learning. It's really good as an ongoing assessment tool.
>
> (McGregor and Precious, 2012: 13)

Storytelling

Children's storytelling is a key part of learning science because it features the children's voices as opposed to the authoritative voice of the teacher. It enables children to talk about the science in their own words; hence it can capture the nature of the children's understanding and reveal its influence on the way they think and feel. Children's stories can provide valuable formative assessment information which can inform the basis of self and peer assessment, so the children can have a say in what they need to do next.

Something to think about

What strategies have you seen or used in school to elicit children's ideas? Can you think of any strategies which are appropriate for particular science topics you may be planning to teach?

> # Planning the re-describing stage: choosing strategies to help children make sense of the scientific view

Scientific concepts are ideas which have been created over time by many people. Scientific ideas may be abstract and can be represented and communicated through words, symbols, gestures, actions, pictures, diagrams, physical models and mathematical formulae (Asoko and de Boo, 2001). They are often counter-intuitive and to make sense of them children need to be able to construct clear and useful mental models of them (Chapter 4). Below we provide some examples of strategies which teachers can use to help children visualise scientific concepts.

Analogies

Analogies can help children make sense of scientific ideas because they make the unfamiliar familiar (Treagust et al., 1992). Analogies work because they enable children to use familiar experience and existing knowledge to construct useful mental representations of the scientific concept. For example, when we ask children to imagine electricity in wires to be like water flowing through a pipe, we are helping them turn an abstract idea into something which they can visualise. Because electricity and water are not the same things and wires are not the same as pipes, this analogy has limitations and, pushed too far, will break down. All analogies have limited explanatory power. However, they can provide useful ways of seeing and talking about concepts which we want the children to learn. Asoko and de Boo (2001) is a good source of analogies for different topics. (Part 2 also provides examples of some useful analogies.)

Role-play

Children can model a concept through role-play. For example, during teaching about how simple electric circuits work, children can play the part of the current which transports the energy from the battery to the bulb. If they understand the model of the current as a transport system for energy, they can model what happens to the energy as the current travels through the filament in the bulb. They can role-play how difficult it is for current to pass through a filament wire. Role-play is based on analogy and hence has similar explanatory limitations.

Physical models

Physical models can be useful because they enable children to visualise a concept and to talk about how it works. Models provide children with something concrete to talk about. For example, in teaching about how we digest our food, it is not possible to have a real digestive system to explore. Physical models encourage children to hypothesise about what each part does. This is a form of scientific enquiry. The same applies to the use of models to make sense of more abstract concepts. For example, the motion of the balls inside a Lottery machine help children imagine the particle nature of a gas. The Lottery machine is both a three-dimensional model and an analogy.

Interactive models and simulations

Interactive simulations can be used to help children to investigate and make sense of scientific concepts. Simulations can be found on a variety of websites including the BBC Bitesize video clips. Popular ones include models for electric current, change of state, germination, photosynthesis and the Solar System. We need to be aware that children can interpret these models in ways which are different from what we may expect (Sutherland et al., 2004) and to make sense of the scientific ideas involved, children will need to talk about the simulations with each other and the teacher. Simulations that allow the children to alter variables, such as changing the shape or size of a parachute to see the effect on how it falls, can help children to explore possibilities and design investigations. Others can be used to speed up the impact of changing conditions, such as growth in plants, to support hypothesising. However, these virtual investigations are no substitute for hands-on practical work whenever possible.

Use of information sources

ICT in schools is used most often as an information source. Online illustrated texts, animations and videos can provide a rich source of information on science topics. Children enjoy finding things out for themselves and this can result in a change in the way that they perceive the world (Chapter 1). However, finding suitable websites can be difficult. Searching websites for information can be frustrating for children when most of the information has been written for an adult audience. Even websites designed for children can present ideas in ways which are complex and uninteresting for the intended age group. Time is well spent by teachers in building up a catalogue of the most interesting and useful websites for particular topics.

The BBC Bitesize websites are usually good starting points, while specialist websites such as 'The Space Place' and the 'NASA Kids' websites provide amazing imagery and up-to-date information. When it comes to wildlife projects, the 'Arkive Education' and the 'Woodland Trust' websites are full of useful information and when exploring the weather, the Met Office's 'Weather for Kids' website is the place to go.

A good science library stocked with both electronic and hard copy resources can play a vital part in children's learning. Multimedia products provide rich learning experiences for children. Footage from television programmes made by David Attenborough and Brian Cox for example, provide inspirational images of the natural world. Dorling Kindersley provides a wide range of science-based digital material including illustrated books for all ages. For young children, there is a series of big books covering science topics, which can be read by teachers and children together.

Links to relevant information and teaching resources are provided for each topic in the 'Ideas for practice' sections, in the second part of the book.

Something to think about

How would you decide which is the best way to represent a particular concept? Are there some criteria which you can use to help you? For example, would the Lottery machine model be useful when teaching 7- or 8-year-old children about evaporation? What model would you use to help them visualise what is happening? If we can't think of a suitable model, does this suggest that the ideas are too complex for the children?

> ## Planning the application stage: choosing strategies to promote the usefulness of the scientific view

Our ability to talk about and explain an event or phenomenon depends on the model of it we hold in our minds (Chapter 4). If the model is powerful and reliable, it can be used in a wide range of contexts and may even help us explain events we may not have previously experienced. Children need to experience the explanatory power of their newly acquired scientific ideas. In making purposeful use of a scientific point of view, they can appreciate its value and may be persuaded to assimilate it into their thinking (Chapter 4). Below we provide some examples of the types of activities which can provide opportunities for children to make use of scientific ideas. For details of specific activities, refer to the 'ideas for practice' sections.

STEM activities

Included in the application stage are activities designed to support the STEM agenda (Chapter 9), which aspires to making science more relevant to the children's lives. In these activities opportunities are provided for children to apply their scientific knowledge to solving problems in real-life situations and to involve them with science-based professions.

Redesigning nature

'Redesigning nature' is a creative problem-solving exercise in which children use their scientific understanding to design imaginary plants and animals which live in particular habitats. For example, after learning about pollination, children could design an imaginary flowering plant which is adapted to a habitat where there is little wind and no insects. The children have to work out how the plant will reproduce. Alternatively, after teaching about habitats, children could design an 'undiscovered' type of animal which lives deep inside the rainforest. It is important that children explain how their design has been informed by their scientific knowledge. As part of a D&T project, children can design and make moving models of their imaginary animals.

> ### Something to think about
>
> Imagine that you have just taught 6- and 7-year-old children about plants. What redesigning nature task could you give them?

Designing and making physical systems

Design and technology projects can provide opportunities for children to use their scientific skills and understanding to solve practical problems. For example, children can use their knowledge of electrical circuits when designing twin headlights for a model car (Chapter 19) or their understanding of friction and the properties of materials may prove useful when designing a pair of non-slip slippers (Chapter 20). The scientific ideas taught in science lessons are not necessarily useful for informing children's designing and decision-making. Research shows that if ideas are to be useful, they must be taught in ways which relate specifically to the D&T project (Layton, 1993).

Something to think about

List four D&T projects which would benefit from the application of scientific knowledge. Explain how the science underpins the projects.

Drama and debate

Children can play a part in a performance which involves the use of scientific ideas to inform a debate. For example, an environmental theme could be developed around a scenario where a company are seeking planning permission to build houses on a local wildlife area. Children can take on different roles to debate the relevant issues. Examples of other subjects for debate which can be informed by scientific knowledge include waste management, pollution and global warming.

Creative writing

Creative writing can provide children with opportunities to make use of their scientific knowledge in enjoyable and satisfying ways. Examples of creative writing include:

- science fiction stories based on contemporary science;
- writing and performing plays which involve famous scientists, past or present;
- writing science-based newspaper articles or blogs;
- creating poems based on scientific themes.

Painting and 3-D modelling

Children can depict scientific themes in painting, collage and by constructing 3-D models. For example, having learnt about the phases of the Moon, children can paint what they think the Earth looks like from the Moon and make 3-D models of the moon's surface.

A popular modelling activity is to make 3-D moving models of animals using programmable robots to control their movement. For example, working on the theme of adaptation, children paint pictures of camouflaged animals in their habitats. They then make 3-D models of their animals, which can be attached to programmable robots so they are able to move around in a model of their habitat.

Video modelling

Children can enjoy making animations using a digital camera or camcorder. Using simple materials such as Plasticine to make the objects, they can use stop motion techniques to create simulations of events such as plant growth, dissolving, electricity flowing in a circuit, the Earth moving around the Sun, how blood flows around the body and other scientific phenomena. Making animations based on scientific ideas requires children to have a clear understanding of the science and to be able to visualise how it applies to the model they want to create.

Scientific enquiry

Children can use their scientific understanding to raise questions and to make predictions about the behaviour of living or non-living things. For example, after learning about pollination, children plan an enquiry to find out whether bees are attracted to particular types of flowers. This can lead to other questions about whether it is the colour of a flower which attracts bees, or whether they are attracted to its fragrance.

Across the stages

1. *Safety*

   Risk assessments should be made for every lesson no matter what is being taught. They can be as simple as making sure all the furniture is safe, there are no obstacles in the classroom which children can fall over as well as focusing on the safe use of science equipment. The ASE publication *Be safe!* (2011) is a useful source of information to help assess risks associated with primary science activities.

2. *Organising talk*

   Since effective learning is linked to the ability to think and talk about the relevant ideas, we must provide children with opportunities to discuss and express their thoughts. Meaningful discussion can take place during small-group work or whole-class contexts. Children require clear guidelines to work collaboratively in both small-group and whole-class situations (Chapter 5). They should be aware that their talk together is an important part of their work and they need to be taught the strategies and skills which will help every child take an active part in exploratory talk.

3. *Worksheets*

   The choice of resources can have a profound effect on the quality of the children's learning and their attitudes to the topic. The disheartening phrase 'death by worksheet' describes the dull nature of the learning experiences which such resources may provide. But well-designed worksheets can be a very useful way of organising some activities. Worksheets should not be overused to the point where children's activity is just focused on 'filling them in'. Whatever resources are used, practical or otherwise, they need to provide the children with something interesting to talk about.

Summary

Assessment is used to inform planning, and planning should outline how assessment will be carried out. Lesson plans should include key questions that can help children to articulate their knowledge and understanding. Questions should help children to think and share experience and should not simply require children to guess facts. Children should be actively involved in the assessment process. Knowing the learning objectives and knowing the steps needed to achieve them can help children to engage with their learning, but the main motivating drive is children's curiosity. By helping children to ask their own questions and by ensuring they realise there is something interesting to discover, we can foster children's natural inquisitiveness and satisfy their wish to learn.

Further reading

ASE journals:

- Primary Science 140 (Nov/Dec 2015). *Introducing the TAPS Pyramid Model* by Sarah Earle.
- Primary Science 132 (March/April 2014). *Just Imagine: Using Drama to Support Science Learning with Older Primary Children* by Deb McGregor and Wendy Precious.
- Primary Science 123 (May/June 2012). *Dramatic Science: At Key Stage 1* by Deb McGregor and Wendy Precious.
- Primary Science 123 (May/June 2012). *Using Models to Promote Children's Scientific Understanding* by Jane Maloney and Sheila Curtis.
- Primary Science 123 (May/June 2012). *Making Movies* by Zoe Crompton and Emma Davies.

Books:

- Asoko, H. and de Boo, M. (2001). *Analogies and Illustrations: Presenting Ideas in Primary Science*, Hatfield: Association for Science Education.
- Association for Science Education (2011). *Be Safe! Health and Safety in School Science and Technology for Teachers of 3- to 12-Year Olds (4th edn)*, Hatfield: Association for Science Education.
- Clarke, S. (2008). *Unlocking Formative Assessment*, London: Hodder & Stoughton.
- Harlen, W. and Qualter, A. (2014). *The Teaching of Science in Primary Schools*, London: Routledge.
- Naylor, S., Keogh, B. and Goldworthy, A. (2004). *Active Assessment*, London: David Fulton.

Reports:

- Davies, D., Collier, C., Earle, S., Howe, A. and McMahon, K. (2014). *Approaches to Science Assessment in English Primary Schools*, Bristol: Primary Science Teaching Trust.
- Harlen, W. (2014). *Assessment, Standards and Quality of Learning in Primary Education*, York: Cambridge Primary Review Trust.
- Nuffield Foundation (2012). *Developing Policy, Principles and Practice in Primary School Science*. www.nuffieldfoundation.org/primary-science-assessment
- Primary Science Teachers Trust (2015). The Teacher Assessment in Primary Science (TAPS). https://pstt.org.uk/resources/curriculum-materials/assessment

Peer-reviewed journals:

- Earle, S. (2014). Formative and Summative Assessment of Science, in English Primary Schools: Evidence from the Primary Science Quality Mark, R*esearch in Science & Technology Education*, 32(2): 216–228.
- Loughland, T. and Kilpatrick, L. (2015). Formative Assessment in Primary Science, *Education 3–13*, 43(2): 128–141.

CHAPTER 8

LEARNING OUTSIDE THE CLASSROOM

Education is not something to keep in a box, even when the box is classroom-shaped. The habit of learning, an urge to find out more, is developed when we feel inspired. The world outside the school is richly inspiring, constantly re-energising what takes place within the classroom.

(RSPB, 2006)

Children can find learning science outside the classroom exciting, challenging and uplifting. Experiencing the world beyond the classroom not only helps to develop children's scientific skills and knowledge, it can also aid their personal development and promote positive attitudes to science. Children who sometimes struggle in the confines of the classroom can flourish in a context where they have greater freedom and have the opportunity to learn in different ways. Learning science outside may be the start of a lifelong interest in a subject.

Topics discussed in the chapter

- Home-initiated learning
- School-initiated outside learning
- Learning in the school grounds
- Exploring the local area
- Further away from home
- Preparing for learning outside the classroom

Home-initiated learning

Learning outside the classroom can be initiated by the home or the school. Home-initiated learning may be situated in the home such as watching television, using the internet or reading newspapers, magazines or books. It may also take place out of the home such as family visits to the seaside, nature reserves, museums and science centres. Children spend about two-thirds of their waking lives outside formal schooling, and perhaps we need to be more aware of how their out-of-school experiences influence their understanding of and attitudes to science (Braund and Reiss, 2004).

It is worth considering that the time children spend at home on information and communication technology is greater than they spend in school. Children now have access to sources of information of a wider and higher quality than they experience in school. Television and videos provide astonishing images of the natural world which can capture children's imaginations and substantially influence their attitudes to science. In recent years, the clichéd image of the crazy scientist in the white coat has been replaced with young enthusiastic and charismatic presenters whom children can aspire to emulate.

The nature of home and classroom learning is very different. At home, learning is voluntary, personal and individual. It is undirected and can quickly shift from one topic to another depending on the child's level of interest and mood. On the other hand, classroom learning is compulsory, teacher-led and collective. Conformity is at the heart of school learning and children are expected to learn whether they want to or not. The advancement of the quality of information and communication technology at home provides a conundrum for science education. While science on the television has never been more popular, science in school struggles to catch and maintain children's interest especially as they grow older (Braund and Reiss, 2004).

How home-initiated learning can be used to extend and improve children's science learning in school is not clear. Perhaps we should be asking how their school learning can be used to improve their home learning. What we can do is to engage with their personal interests by making space in the curriculum to talk about the science they have learnt at home.

Something to think about

What areas of science education could benefit from home-initiated learning? Could this become a regular feature of your teaching?

School-initiated outside learning

Benefits of outside learning

Children enjoy learning outside the classroom. They can get excited simply by the thought of doing something different. For younger children, going out to visit somewhere new is an adventure and they take great pleasure from anticipating the experience. From this perspective, the nature of learning in new locations is positive and stimulating. Learning outside the classroom offers diverse experiences that encourage active engagement with stimulating settings that will develop children's knowledge, understanding and skills in science. In addition to this, there is the added benefit of developing their general capabilities as learners.

Bianchi and Feasey (2011: 30) identify five 'personal capabilities' that could be addressed through taking children outside to learn. These are:

- Self-management – taking charge of your own learning
- Teamwork – working well in groups and teams
- Creativity – coming up with and sharing new or unusual ideas
- Problem solving – analysing problems and developing strategies and solutions
- Communication – speaking, listening and sharing feelings with meaning

These capabilities can also be developed in the classroom but, because of the physical constraints, the opportunities are not as great. The range of locations and experiences afforded by the outside classroom are far wider and more comprehensive than those available in the classroom. The outside classroom begins with the school grounds and then spreads out into the local area. With transport and perhaps accommodation, children can explore further locations around their home county and beyond.

Something to think about

Can you think of any additional benefits to those suggested by Bianchi and Feasey? Do you think outside learning would be of more benefit to children living in rural or urban communities?

Learning in the school grounds

Outdoor learning is considered to be a key aspect of a child's education in the early years. However, as children get older, they go outside to learn much less frequently. There are justifiable reasons, including the ever-increasing transport costs, issues relating to health and safety and lack of time to cover a prescribed curriculum. Children do not cease to benefit from outdoor experiences just because they are a few years older, and making good use of the school grounds is an easy and inexpensive way of making their science learning more relevant and exciting.

There are many benefits to using the school grounds:

- Children are in an environment they know and in which they are comfortable.
- They are able to make repeat visits and observations, which can help children to see patterns in nature such as the changes in the seasons.
- They can carry out investigations over a number of days and weeks.
- They can feel greater ownership of their own learning.
- From the teacher's perspective, accessing the school grounds is much less complicated than taking children away from the school.

Example: The school pond

After an unusually dry spring and warm July, the large school pond completely dried up towards the end of term. Looking at the base of the yellow flags and bulrushes where there was still some dampness, the children could only find a pond beetle or two but little evidence of the previously abundant pond life. By the time the children returned in the autumn, there was an inch or two of water at the bottom of the pond. When they dipped the muddy water, they found a few worms but no evidence of the larger pond creatures they were used to finding. Throughout the autumn term, a survey was undertaken by 10- and 11-year-old children to see if the pond life would reappear. Every week, they surveyed the pond, looking at depth of water, pH balance, temperature, weed cover and any other factors they thought might influence the health of the pond and support a more varied population. They also borrowed a dissolved oxygen meter from the local secondary school. This was a revelation, for they found that as the water cleared and the water plants re-appeared, the proportion of dissolved oxygen in the water increased. Gradually, their weekly dips began to yield the larger invertebrates such as the larvae of dragonflies and diving beetles. The children collated the data and were able to graph the improving water quality against the increasing variety and numbers of species found. Evidence gained by observation was also supported by research on the internet into the repopulation of dried-up or newly established ponds. By early spring, the pond was once again full and healthy and ready for the local frog population to conduct their mating rituals.

Comment

This example highlights the benefit of being able to carry out a biological survey of the same site throughout the school year. A one-off survey would not have helped the children to develop their knowledge and understanding of the impact of environmental change on the wildlife in their school pond. It is also a good example of the benefit of establishing good links with the local secondary school in order to enhance the learning of the children.

Something to think about

What health and safety issues do you need to address when children are working in the school grounds? Can you turn some of the precautions into science learning opportunities instead of just a list of do's and don'ts?

From bird boxes to composting

It is possible to make changes to develop the school grounds and this could be something as simple as putting in a bird table. Children can learn about the different birds in the area and the foods they like to eat. Bird boxes and bat boxes will also encourage wildlife to visit the school.

Growing plants is exciting and, if the plants produce a food crop, this is even better, as it can be harvested and eaten. Even if there is no garden in school, many plants can be grown in dump bags, large plant pots and grow-bags placed in a sunny spot in the playground. Dump bags (the kind builders use to deliver sand) make ideal mini-plots to grow fruit, herbs and vegetables. Increasing numbers of urban communities have set up food-growing schemes in which local schools play an important part.

Composting is an amazing process where waste plant material is broken down by bacteria, fungi, mites, worms, beetles and other beneficial organisms to produce humus. This can be used to improve the quality of the soil in the garden or growing area. Most children now have fruit as their mid-morning snack and they can put any waste from this into the composter. Many children are aware of the harmful effects of micro-organisms and composting can help them to start to understand some of their beneficial effects. Bacteria quickly populate any good composting environment. Other organisms become active as the conditions become favourable to them. All that needs to be done is to maintain the conditions that allow these organisms to thrive until the job is done.

The science of composting is fascinating. It brings alive the unfamiliar and hidden world of the microbes and the invertebrates involved. Magnified images of bacteria, fungi and mites are readily available in books and on the web. The invertebrates can be studied first-hand, using hand lenses and microscopes. It is worth bearing in mind that there are not only the micro-organisms and mini-beasts to learn about but also the changing properties of the materials and the role they play in plant growth. There is so much to talk about and so much science to be learnt.

Everyone likes a game of 'hide and seek'. Children can work in groups to design an animal to be hidden in some part of the school grounds. They start by surveying the grounds and choosing a habitat in which the animal would live. They can then design and make a cardboard model of the animal so that it would be hard for predators to find it. This is a great activity because it involves the development of all five capabilities listed above and raises lots of questions about the way animals adapt to their environment in order to survive.

Example: Multi-sensory garden

Children from a primary school collaborated with a group of multi-sensory impaired children to create, maintain and learn from a garden. Children's discussions of the design had to accommodate wheel-chair friendly paths, heights of beds and other practicalities. A local bank subsidised the make-over of an existing courtyard near the multi-sensory impaired (MSI) unit's class base. Parents, carers, bank employees and volunteers spent their weekends putting in the hard structure. Awareness of allergies, possible tactile defensiveness and sensory overload were all raised. Then it was over to the children. The focus began on the sense of touch. Each child from the MSI unit had a buddy. Together they explored the feeling of a variety of seeds and soils and chose their favourite seeds to plant. The buddies familiarised the children with the layout and materials of the garden. Through time spent in the garden, children could feel where the hottest and shadiest spots were. A visit to the garden centre provided different sensory experiences, including the smell of specific plants as well as their overall feel. Each child, including those without impairments, was able to choose their own favourite plant. The garden centre café provided a welcome experience for the sense of taste! The buddies were able to assist the children in the planting and nurturing of the chosen plants. They continued their own studies of life cycles, food webs and adaptation in the primary school. Meanwhile, they returned each week to measure the growth of the plants, helping each impaired child feel the increase in height or amount of buds, shoots or leaves the plants might may have put on. The specific shape of leaves and their veins led to the creation of an inventive tactile display. The herb area was cultivated for special sandwich and salad garnishes. These were shared at a memorable end-of-year picnic which re-united the bank employees and all the other volunteers – and, of course, children – who had contributed to the success of the garden. Plans for the creation of simple habitats such as a log colony and the growing of flowers from bulbs were already underway.

Comment

The long-term benefits of such collaboration reinforce communities and help children to develop personal capabilities. It can break down prejudices about disabilities and barriers to education. The sense of ownership, the pride in helping and nurturing, the sensitivities raised, all contribute to the development of engaged and caring citizens, into whose hands we deliver our planet.

Using technology in the school grounds

Many schools now have access to quite sophisticated technology and this can enhance learning outside the classroom. For example, putting a webcam near a bird table will enable the children to watch the birds remotely and to find out what happens when they are not at school.

Data-loggers are a convenient means of capturing data electronically. They can be used to take spot readings of temperature, light and sound in different areas of the school and the grounds. They can also be used to monitor these over time.

Example: Monitoring school grounds at night

A data-logger was left in the playground overnight to record the changes in light and sound. The next day, it was downloaded to the classroom computer and the 11-year-olds were able to see the information presented in the form of line graphs. From this, they were able to calculate how many hours of darkness there were and what time it started to get light again. By looking at the rise and fall of the sound levels, they were able to tell the 'sound story': when had children gone home from school? When had the site manager put the rubbish in the bins? When did the background noise of the traffic die down? When did the children come back in the next morning?

On another occasion, the data-logger was left for 24 hours to measure the changes in both the temperature of the pond and the land around it. This provided some revealing data for the children to compare, interpret and explain.

Comment

Without using data-loggers, it would be impossible to collect this sort of data. It also takes the focus away from data collection to data interpretation. This is one of the science process skills that is sometimes overlooked. It can take so long to tabulate and present the results of an enquiry that there is little time left in a lesson for the children to discuss what they have found out from doing their enquiry.

While data-loggers can record sound levels, they cannot record the nature of the sound. Simple devices such as *Easi-Speak* microphone recorders can be used by children of all ages to record the sounds they hear. They could be used for a sound treasure hunt – can you find a happy sound, a loud sound or a high-pitched sound?

Digital cameras are a very convenient way for children to record what they have seen on a visit outside the classroom. However, their use should not exclude opportunities for children to produce observational drawings. Close observation is a key scientific skill and helps children to see detail in an object that they might not notice when taking or looking at a photo.

> ### Something to think about
>
> Can you think of how to use other types of ICT equipment to support learning in the outside classroom?

Exploring the local area

Children play outside much less than they did a generation ago and some of them do not know their neighbourhoods well. Taking children into their own community helps them to find out more about where they live and creates links between learning at home and in school. Using the local area makes it easy for parents to become involved in their children's learning. It can also help them to value their local area more.

Teachers come from far and wide and do not necessarily know the area in which they teach. A walk around the neighbourhood with a colleague asking, 'Where is the science in this?', could open up many opportunities. It could be as simple as looking at all the different things beneath your feet. Is there a building site? Is there a church or park? Is there a river or canal? What about allotments, recycling points, car parks or interesting shops? It is worth auditing the expertise of members of the local community, starting with parents and school governors. What might they have to offer the children?

Example: Getting to know the local woodland

Over a two-year period, starting with 10-year-olds, children made regular visits to a small woodland area in the middle of their urban housing development. Although it was close to the school and very close to their homes, few children had visited it. They learnt about the plants and animals that could be found in the woods at different times of the year and, as importantly, they enjoyed their visits and started to recognise the wood as a valuable local resource. Local naturalists were invited to join the children on some of these visits to share their considerable expertise. But it was not a one-way process. When the children showed the curator from the natural history section of the local museum evidence of badger setts, he was delighted because, until that point, he had no knowledge of badgers living in this area. He was able to go back and alter the local natural history records. All of the work the children did was recorded and was used to start a local archive, which will hopefully be carried on into the future.

Through visiting this wood, the children developed their knowledge and understanding of life processes, but this was only one aspect of their learning. The school was in an area of social deprivation and the older children were aware of the poor reputation the area had in the town. In addition to this, many of the children had low self-esteem. When local naturalists – people from outside their neighbourhoods – talked to them about the value of this type of woodland, they started to think about their area differently. Talking to adults in a range of different contexts developed their social skills. Learning how to use technology to make video recordings and to set up their archive enhanced their skills and their self-esteem.

Visit to the local church

A visit to the local church need not be a 'grave' experience; it can be a lot of fun and provide opportunities for real-life problem solving as illustrated by the following example.

Example: Problem-solving at the local church

Heads on either side of the church entrance eroded to different extents.
Source: Peter Loxley

Children found that the two heads on either side of the arched entrance to a church were eroded to different extents. The question was: why has one weathered so much more than the other? There was no simple answer. There were a number of possible explanations which in this case generated a lot of diverse ideas and discussion amongst the children. This is a good example of a context in which the five capabilities listed on page 90 can be developed.

Back at school, the church experience led to more learning about erosion and the types of natural materials which are eroded by the weather. Through practical enquiry, children tested different materials for erosion and compared natural materials such as sandstone and limestone with manmade materials such as bricks and cement blocks.

Something to think about

Why do you think one head is eroded more than the other? How would you prepare children for a visit to the church in order to make the most of the learning opportunities?

Further away from home

Major national collections such as museums, interactive science centres, zoos and botanical gardens provide extensive learning opportunities. Their collections of real plants and animals, artefacts and simulations cannot be replicated in school. Combined with this, the expert knowledge of their staff can enhance learning considerably. Role-players, storytellers, explainers and specialist work-shops can all capture the children's imagination and increase the depth of engagement in their learning. Children get excited when they see things like an enormous diplodocus skeleton at the Natural History Museum or exotic animals such as snakes and crocodiles in a zoo.

Young 'explorers' at the Natural History Museum.
Source: Peter Loxley

Independent learners at the zoo.
Source: Peter Loxley

Many schools take children to a residential centre at some point in their primary education. This usually involves a change of scene, a new set of habitats or landscapes. Overnight stays widen learning in many ways. Apart from the personal development that results from being away from their families, children can learn about the night skies and nocturnal animals.

What is really exciting is the potential for children to develop an 'island of expertise' (Crowley and Jacobs 2002). The term describes a personal interest in a particular topic, animal or object which children pursue at home with the help of their parents. For instance, a child might become fascinated by meerkats during a school visit to a zoo. This might encourage the parents to go back to the zoo with the child to learn more about them; they might choose books about meerkats at the library, watch television programmes and talk about them together. This is a particularly rich form of learning because it is free choice learning that is led by the child's interest and enthusiasm. It involves learning together and developing the scientific literacy of the whole family.

> **Something to think about**
>
> How would you plan for children to share their 'island of expertise' with the rest of the school?

Forest schools

Highly stimulating experiences are offered by Forest Schools which are based on a Scandinavian approach to teaching young children. This approach was developed in the 1950s with the aim of enabling children to learn in and from nature. Initially, these schools were for children in the Early Years or Foundation Stage, but older children are now being offered the opportunity to visit them. The essence of forest schools is that whatever the weather, children make regular visits to a woodland area and these visits take place over a sustained period of time. Children are encouraged to learn using all of their senses, and they have the flexibility and freedom to learn and develop at their own pace.

Forest School sessions are usually run by teachers with specialist knowledge of the woodland and the learning possibilities it offers. They are skilled at allowing children to get messy and to take appropriate risks in order to develop their skills, knowledge and understanding. For example, the children might be taught to use a penknife to whittle a stick or they might be encouraged to climb a tree safely. While teachers plan the sessions, the children have the independence to engage in the learning in their own way.

Once the children have become comfortable with exploring and playing confidently in the area, learning linked to the curriculum may become an established part of the session. As they have repeated first-hand experiences, children's learning about the plants and animals in the wood is much deeper and richer than could be achieved through the use of books and ICT.

Preparing for learning outside the classroom

Preparation and planning for taking children outside school can be time-consuming and there can be anxieties about the risks involved. But the extra work is worth it. Children will remember the day that they found badger setts in the wood or when they dressed up as explorers for their visit to the Natural History Museum.

Risk assessment

All schools have a policy for the safe conduct of visits and most schools have a designated member of staff with responsibility for ensuring that all visits comply with this policy. Before starting to plan, it is important to read the policy. It is essential that a risk assessment is carried out, but doing it with another member of staff can cut down on the workload and save time. If all the paperwork for a visit is kept on file, it can be available for subsequent visits to the same or similar sites. However long the preparation takes, it is worth it in terms of the children's learning and their enthusiasm for the subject.

Costs

The costs of entry fees and transport to sites can be high and, for some families, this can make visits prohibitively expensive. There may be local solutions to this and subsidies are sometimes available. Using the school and the local neighbourhood will avoid this problem.

Organising science learning

The very nature of out-of-school learning is collaborative and its success depends on the children and teachers learning together. Teachers are not expected to know everything and it is good practice to find out things and help solve problems together with the children. For visits away from school, children are usually organised in small groups, each with a responsible adult who might be a teacher, teaching assistant or parent. Each of these adults must be very clear about their role in relation to the children's safety and well-being, but it is also important that they understand their role in the children's learning. It can be helpful to provide them with key questions and suggestions as to how they can help the children to engage with the experience. Many sites have an education officer who will help teachers to plan appropriate visits.

Something to think about

School trips are usually exclusively planned by adults. How could you incorporate the views and interests of your class?

Summary

Taking children outside the classroom will help them to learn new scientific concepts and skills, but they will learn much more. Learning in new contexts and in different ways can be fun and full of surprises, and it can make learning in the classroom more relevant and meaningful. Using resources that are not available in school may be inspiring and exciting, and meeting new people can help to develop social skills and improve self-esteem. Engaging with a wide range of new experiences can enhance children's attitude towards science and increase their motivation to learn.

Children's safety is paramount and it is essential that visits are carefully planned and thoroughly risk-assessed. To maximise learning, accompanying adults need to have a clear understanding of what they need to do to help the children to engage with the experiences on offer. Taking children away from school can be a time-consuming and costly business and it is a big responsibility to take on. However, in terms of the development of the whole child, it is worth it.

Further reading

ASE journals:

- Primary Science 137 (March/April 2015). *What Difference Does a More In-depth Programme Make to Learning?* by Athene Reiss.
- Primary Science 135 (Nov/Dec 2014). *Developing an APP-TITUDE for Learning in the Outdoors* by Emily Baker.
- Primary Science 132 (March/April 2014). *Outdoor Learning Can Help Children Flourish in Science and Across the Curriculum – The FSC Takes a Lead* by Hannah Rose and Anneke Kempton.
- Primary Science Review 91 (Jan/Feb 2006). *'Beyond the Classroom'*. This issue is focused on scientific enquiry outside the classroom.

Books:

- Bianchi, L. and Feasey, R. (2011). *Science Beyond the Classroom Boundaries for 3–7 Year Olds,* Maidenhead: OUP.
- Braund, M. and Reiss, M. (eds) (2004). *Learning Science Outside the Classroom,* Abingdon: Routledge Falmer.

- Crowley, K. and Jacobs, M. (2002). *Islands of Expertise and the Development of Family Scientific Literacy*, in G. Leinhardt, K. Crawley and K. Knutson (eds), *Learning Conversations in Museums*, Mahwah: Erlbaum.
- Cutting, R. and Kelly, O. (2015). *Creative Teaching in Primary Science,* London: Sage.
- Dunne, M. and Peacock, A. (eds) (2015). *Primary Science: A Guide to Teaching Practice,* London: Sage.
- Moggach, T. (2012). *The Urban Kitchen Gardener*, London: Kyle Books.
- RSPB (2006). *Out-of-Classroom Learning: Practical Information and Guidance for Schools and Teachers*, Sandy: RSPB.

Websites:

- Museums, Libraries & Archives Council. Inspiring Learning. *www. inspiringlearningforall.gov.uk* – includes a checklist for assessing all aspects of learning outside the classroom.
- TES. Teachers TV: Outdoor Learning with Forest Schools. *www.tes.co.uk/teaching-resource/ Teachers-TV-Outdoor-Learning-with-Forest-School-6046493/*

Peer-reviewed journals:

- Braund, M. and Reiss, M. (2006). Validity and Worth in the Science Curriculum: Learning School Science Outside the Laboratory. *The Curriculum Journal*, 17(3): 213–228.
- Passy, R. (2014). School Gardens: Teaching and Learning Outside the Front Door. *Education 3–13*, 42(1): 23–38.

CHAPTER 9

STEM EDUCATION:
ENRICHING THE PRIMARY SCHOOL EXPERIENCE

It is … not unreasonable to suppose that some portion of the neglect of science in England, may be attributed to the system of education we pursue.

Charles Babbage (1791–1871)

Developed and developing countries all over the world rely on people with expertise in Science, Technology, Engineering and Mathematics (STEM) to work in vital industries which underpin their economies. These industries are often referred to as the STEM sector.

STEM industries in many parts of the world find it difficult to recruit employees with the appropriate skills. Many pupils in secondary schools are not inspired enough to pursue the subjects beyond compulsory education. This chapter looks at young peoples' attitudes to the STEM subjects and discusses ways that STEM initiatives can be used in primary schools to enrich children's science learning and promote long-lasting interest in the subject.

Topics discussed in the chapter

- Attitudes to the STEM subjects
- STEM education
- STEM and primary science
- Organising real-world projects
- Outside the classroom
- Design and technology based projects
- STEM clubs and STEM days

Attitudes to the STEM subjects

Research carried out by the UK Government in 2014 used social media to analyse STEM in the context of informal conversations to find out what young people thought and the sort of career advice they gave each other. They found that attitudes were generally negative and those pupils who enjoyed the subjects in secondary schools were perceived as boring and socially inadequate. Words used on social media to describe pupils who were successful in the STEM subjects included 'nerd', 'geek', 'dork, 'social retards' and 'weirdos'.

The following tweet from a maths undergraduate about her mother's reaction to encountering 'maths geeks' on the train is enlightening.

> *How can Mum text saying 'sitting by maths geeks on the train argh'? She's a maths teacher and I'm doing a maths degree, we're maths geeks....*

Perhaps we should not read too much into this tweet, but it is hard not to be struck by the irony. It is also a reminder that the stereotypical views about the STEM subjects are so deeply ingrained in societal attitudes that they are very difficult to dispel.

Something to think about

How important is it for primary teachers to have positive attitudes to science learning? Should teachers discuss attitudes to science with their children? How can science teachers promote positive attitudes?

STEM subjects are difficult, boring and useless

Attitudes which dominated the conversations on social media were that STEM subjects were boring, difficult and useless. Few pupils described the subjects as fun, creative, useful or enjoyable, apart from design and technology which was thought to be hands-on and creative, as well as being the easiest subject. On the whole, pupils in the study preferred to choose subjects which they felt gave them a better chance of success in examinations.

The pervading view was that science and mathematics were too difficult and were the choice of the smart kids. Many pupils were reluctant to study them because they were hard work and because they conceived the subjects to be 'useless' in the real world. The point was made by the following tweet from a 15-year-old boy:

> *Unless your (sic) a scientist or a doctor your (sic) never going to use science when you leave school, so what's the point?*

Some of the girls' comments were amongst the most hard-hitting:

> *No one should do a maths degree, it makes you stupid at all the useful things in life.*

Another girl commented:

A level physics are (sic) for dumb people, I done (sic) English because that's actually useful in real life.

As the UK Government report points out, this is not a new problem. Young people have long been disaffected with science and mathematics. Although many pupils enjoy science when they are younger, evidence shows that engagement with the subject decreases throughout secondary education as they conceive it to be difficult and leading to limited career opportunities. Full details of the Government report, entitled *Project STEM: Book of insights,* are published online.

Something to think about

How would you describe your attitudes to science? Discuss the following talking points with your peers and see if you can come to some agreement. Remember to justify your responses.

Talking points: true, false or not sure?

- Science is boring.
- Biology is fun but chemistry is for geeks.
- Physics makes you stupid.
- Science is just learning facts or playing with equipment.
- I don't like science because my teachers were boring.
- I could have done better at science with better teachers.
- I love science, I think it is fascinating.
- Science has nothing to do with real life.
- Progress depends on science.
- Only bright people like science.
- Physics is for boys.

Add some talking points of your own. Reflect on your attitudes to science and think about how you will present yourself as a positive role model for the children you teach.

STEM education

In schools around the world the term STEM education is used as a call to action to make the subjects more relevant to pupils' lives and to open them up as career options. In many schools in the UK, STEM education involves extracurricular initiatives designed to inspire interest in the subjects. Rather than teach the subjects independently, STEM initiatives aspire to integrate them within real-world contexts to bring the subjects alive and help pupils appreciate their social and economic value.

STEM education is often project-based and with a strong emphasis placed on collaboration, enquiry based learning, problem-solving and innovation. Rather than being spoon-fed information by their teachers, STEM courses promote active learning where pupils acquire knowledge with real-life purposes in mind. Underpinning STEM education is the belief that success in today's highly complex and competitive world is not so much driven by *what you know* but by *what you can do with what you know*.

> ### Something to think about
>
> Discuss with your peers whether you agree that it is not 'what you know' that is important in life but 'what you can do with what you know'. Does this mean that learning knowledge for the pleasure of knowing is misguided and a waste of time?

STEM and primary science

Developing long lasting positive attitudes to science is a central theme of STEM education and is also centre stage throughout this book. Chapter 1 tells the story of Richard Feynman's early experiences of science which led to his life-long enthusiasm for the subject. The chapter highlights the value of adopting a puzzle-solving model for science learning which arouses children's curiosity and rewards their learning with feelings of satisfaction and achievement.

STEM projects often use problem-solving scenarios as starting points for science learning because they promote and contextualise active learning. Professor Ainissa Ramirez from Yale University makes the point that learners today need to be able to think expansively and solve problems resourcefully (Ramirez, 2013). Good problem-solvers work collaboratively, which involves listening to each other, challenging one another's ideas in respectful ways, presenting reasons for their ideas and seeking to reach agreement before making decisions. Chapter 5 describes how children can be taught to collaborate effectively and provides ground rules for effective group discussion. Active collaboration is underpinned by exploratory talk which enables children to think critically and share their thinking. Exploratory talk helps groups to do better than each child could have done alone.

Problem-solving, critical thinking and collaboration are STEM skills that are considered necessary for people to participate successfully in our 21st century global society. Regardless of their future occupations children will need to acquire levels of STEM literacy which will enable them to make informed decisions about their everyday lives. STEM literacy is underpinned by the development of a capacity for life-long learning. As adults, children will be required to continually update their knowledge and skills to keep pace with new technological developments. In a fast-changing world they will need to adapt and accept new technologies and find creative solutions to problems which today are unimaginable (Zollman, 2012).

> ### Something to think about
>
> Reflect on the content of the primary science curriculum. How do you think the curriculum supports the aims of STEM education? Do you think the skills and knowledge it sets out are suitable for children growing up in the 21st century?

STEM can enrich primary science teaching

Many of the skills which STEM promote are fundamental parts of contemporary primary science practice. Collaboration, communication, creativity, critical thinking, curiosity and problem solving are all elements of effective science learning in today's primary schools. STEM initiatives can enrich the primary science curriculum through the inclusion of projects which enable the application of scientific ideas and skills to solve problems in the world outside the classroom.

Applying ideas learnt in the classroom to solve problems in real-life contexts is not as straightforward as it may seem. Much of the elementary scientific knowledge set out in the National Curriculum serves as the basis for more complex learning in later years, and cannot be applied easily to situations outside the classroom. To enable children to make use of their embryonic scientific knowledge we need to teach science with a purpose in mind. Therefore, planning starts by identifying those scientific ideas which can be linked to a specific issue, profession or technology. These ideas will then need to be restructured and enriched to make them suitable for a specific purpose.

Take for example ideas concerning the growth of plants. The National Curriculum for England states that children should be taught to explore the requirements of plants for life and growth (air, light, water, nutrients from soil, and room to grow) and how they vary from plant to plant. What plants require to grow is clearly of some interest to the agricultural industry. The use of fertilizers is a big issue in the industry both in the developed and developing world. For effective STEM learning, children will need to know something about the science of fertilizers, what chemicals they contain and how they help to produce healthy crops. When planning the project, the teacher should identify the science the children need to know, structure it in a form that will be meaningful to them and teach it as part of the project. Often this will require the enrichment and expansion of the requirements of the science curriculum.

Organising real-world projects

An interesting project concerning agriculture in the developing world can be found on the STEM Centre website. Every year vast areas of Bangladesh are flooded. These floods are likely to get worse due to climate change. When the flood waters recede, the land next to rivers (called the char lands) is left covered with deposits of sand and silt which do not contain sufficient nutrients to grow crops. Practical Action is an aid organisation which supports families to grow pumpkins on these lands by digging pits, adding compost and then planting pumpkin seeds. Some pumpkins are then eaten by the family; others are sold at market to provide an income.

Chapter 3 offers a three-stage framework for learning involving exploring current understanding, re-describing ideas in a more robust scientific way then applying this new knowledge to further problems. Using this approach as a guide, children can start by enquiring into the problems people face in Bangladesh when trying to grow crops in sand. In the exploration stage they work collaboratively to discover the extent of the problem. Why is sand a poor medium for growing crops? What else do crops need to grow other than light and water? In the re-describing stage children can learn about the science of composting and the production of chemical fertilizers. They can investigate growing pumpkin seeds (and other vegetables) in conditions faced by people of Bangladesh. They can also investigate different ways of adding nutrients to the sand to discover the most efficient way for growing the crops. Cost and availability are factors which will need to be considered before solutions can be found. In the application stage children can use their knowledge of plant growth and fertilizers in a different context. They can explore how fertilizers are used by farmers in the developed world and have a critical look at the advantages and disadvantages of organic farming.

Topics like this one take time, but are valuable because they can have long lasting effects on children's attitudes to science. They are often multidisciplinary; this one involves elements of science, mathematics, technology and geography and could be extended to investigate other aspects of Bangladeshi life, history and culture.

Something to think about

Starting with the statutory knowledge requirements for the primary science curriculum, identify scientific ideas which could help children make decisions or solve problems in real-life situations. For example, dissolving is a useful idea to help understand the soft drinks industry. Plan a project which involves the use of these ideas. You may need to adapt or extend the ideas to suit the project.

Skill-based projects

Some real-world projects do not require children to have in-depth scientific knowledge and can be addressed principally with the application of scientific skills. For example, the STEM Centre presents a project for children aged 9 to 11 years which requires them to investigate the properties of materials and decide which would be suitable for use on board a spacecraft. A PowerPoint presentation, which includes an introduction from a space scientist, sets the real world context for their challenge. Children then investigate eleven materials, looking at mass, magnetic attraction, impact tests, electrical and thermal conductivity. They plan tests, record their findings and draw their own conclusions. Finally, they report back on which materials they think are most suitable for the satellite and why. The project can be adapted to meet the needs and resources of specific schools.

Environmental projects

The STEM Centre have published a book called *Biology loves technology* on its website, filled with examples of how scientists are combining Computing and Biology. One of the examples explains how conservationists use the way the search engine Google operates to help them know which species need protection. Google ranks a web page's importance partially by looking at how many other pages link to it. Biologists have tried the same approach to rank the importance of species in an ecosystem by looking at how species depend on each other for food. Using this approach, the scientists can suggest more accurately which ones are the most crucial for other species' survival.

As part of their work on food webs children can survey a local area which has a diversity of flora and fauna. In the city this may be a local park or even the school grounds. The area being studied can be mapped and divided into sections. (Different groups can explore different sections.) In each section all living things both above and below the ground should be recorded. Each group can display the feeding relations in their section on a chart, and then the information combined with other groups on an 'eco-chart,' to determine which species are most important to the survival of the ecosystem. Children can use internet sources to explore the work done by conservationists in the UK and around the world.

Media headlines

Media headlines can be used as starting points for projects through which children explore the issues and examine the scientific evidence. Perhaps the biggest environmental issue of our age is climate change. Articles appear regularly in the media warning us of the impending consequences for the planet. For example, a headline published on the BBC News website – 'ARCTIC ICE MELTING AT 'AMAZING' SPEED, SCIENTISTS FIND' – is indicative of the urgent nature of the debate.

'Ideas for practice', in Chapter 17, exemplifies how the above headline can be used to set children a challenge to discover whether melting ice in the arctic regions could lead to rising sea levels. The project involves planning their own enquiries to find out whether icebergs contribute to rising sea levels, exploring the work of polar scientists and designing accommodation for use in arctic conditions.

Outside the classroom

Wherever a school is situated, be it near the coast, in a rural village or in the middle of a large city, it is worth getting out of the classroom and making use of scientific knowledge to provide children with stimulating new ways of seeing their environment. We all get excited when we see programmes on the television about magnificent animals like blue whales, which we are told are bigger than dinosaurs. But what about the animals that live in our gardens, parks and woodlands? Bees have six eyes, beetles can lift 850 times their own weight and butterflies taste food with their feet and we walk past these wonderful creatures every day. Now that's something worth knowing, just for the sheer pleasure of finding out the world isn't quite how we imagine it to be!

Something to think about

Can you imagine what weight a beetle could lift if it were the size of a horse? Work it out.

Chapter 8 provides a wide range of ideas for outdoor projects which include designing a multi-sensory garden, problem-solving in the graveyard and the use of forest schools. Planning a wildlife garden, no matter how small, makes a really worthwhile project. Children can discover the right plants to grow and find out how to provide for the needs of the animals which they want to attract. They can also look at real-life dilemmas like what to do about snails and slugs and whether to use insecticides and chemical fertilizers.

Children will find real-world issues to address and problems to solve when teaching is taken out of the classroom. For example, Chapter 2 tells the story of how an autumn trip to a local woodland to observe seasonal changes turned into a project about mushrooms. Children were fascinated to know how the mushrooms got there and were especially intrigued by the way they just pop straight out of the ground.

Of course, mushrooms are not plants; they are a form of fungi which feed off rotting vegetation in the ground. The mushrooms we see are only the fruiting part of the organism. Fungi come in all shapes and sizes and are important parts of the ecosystem and our everyday lives. Children know about edible fungi such as mushrooms, but what do they know about other types of fungi which are widely used in the medical, food, brewing, agricultural and recycling industries? Alexander Fleming discovered a bacteria-destroying fungus in 1928, which he called penicillin.

Since then penicillin has saved countless lives. However, today its effectiveness is in question due to bacterial adaptation.

This example shows how real-life learning can start with a visit to a local woodland. The direction of science learning is then preceded by questions and problem-solving. As children explore issues regarding fungi and its uses, the trail eventually leads to a major real-life dilemma. Why are bacteria becoming resistant to penicillin, and what can we do about it?

The rewards for children are the pleasure and satisfaction they get from working together to solve significant problems, which could herald the start of a life-long fascination with science and the natural world.

> ### Something to think about
>
> Explore the life and work of Alexander Fleming. Decide whether his discovery of penicillin was a lucky accident or was there more to it than that? Does luck have any part to play in the advancement of scientific knowledge?

Design and technology based projects

Design and technology projects can also provide opportunities for children to work collaboratively in order to solve problems. Science topics which link well with design and technology include: electricity, energy, materials and structures, forces and motion, and food and nutrition. This book provides a range of examples indicating how science can be linked to D&T in the 'Ideas for practice' sections. There are many more projects on the STEM Centre website.

Chapter 20 describes a D&T project to design and make non-slip slippers, which is part of a topic for 7–9-year-olds on friction. The science involves testing the properties of different materials to find the most comfortable and hard wearing. Designing the slippers does not require detailed knowledge of friction but does involve the application of scientific and technological skills. Costing, sizing, measuring and marketing the slippers which involve the use of mathematics and communication skills would make the project more STEM-inclusive.

The slipper project is indicative of the relationship between D&T and primary science. It may be argued that children could make slippers without knowing anything about friction. When we buy slippers from a shop the concept of friction does not necessarily cross our minds, although we may wonder whether the soles are likely to be slippery or not. Everyday understanding of properties of materials is enough for children to choose suitable materials for the slippers. It is often not so much their scientific knowledge that is crucial when children are designing and making as the scientific attitude of 'let's find out' which is most useful (Banks and Barlex, 2014). Problem-solving, evaluation of evidence and making sense of information in D&T contexts can help children see the value of these essential 21st century skills.

> ### Something to think about
>
> Design and technology is a popular subject and relates directly to the world in which we live. Do you think, from a STEM point of view, D&T should take a high priority like English and Mathematics in our education system?

Get involved in 'real' science and engineering projects.

Tim Peake's mission aboard the International Space Station in 2015/16 created a buzz of excitement in many schools, especially those which got involved in the many projects published by organisations such as *The European Space Education Resource Office*. The support and resources for teachers enabled them to use the space mission to inspire their children. Now that Tim is back on the ground, teachers need to look for ways of keeping that enthusiasm going.

There is a wide range of national and international organizations involved with science and engineering which provide support and teaching resources related to their work. For example, Chapter 20 focuses on the work of engineers involved in *The Bloodhound Project*, which is an attempt to build a car which can travel at 1000 mph. *The Bloodhound Project* website contains a range of teaching resources associated with the project. There are also opportunities for children to post questions for the project team, and to arrange for a STEM ambassador to visit the school.

Organisations such as NASA, ESA, MET office and National Geographic have websites especially designed for children. BP Educational Services, Practical Action, Association of the British Pharmaceutical Industry (ABPI), Royal Horticultural Society (RHS), the Royal Academy of Engineering and the Woodland Trust are just a few of the organisations which provide teaching resources associated with their field.

STEM clubs and STEM days

A STEM club is any out-of-timetable session that gives children opportunities to explore aspects of science, technology, engineering and mathematics away from the constraints of the school curriculum. The aim of STEM clubs is to increase children's levels of engagement and confidence with the STEM subjects and to provide opportunities for children to gain practical, teamwork and leadership skills. Because of their informal nature, STEM clubs can improve relationships between children and their teachers, and boost children's motivation for the subjects.

STEM club activities can focus on specific disciplines such as science or explore topics which go across the STEM subjects. They normally meet during lunchtime, after school or in some cases at the weekend. The topics they choose are diverse ranging from cookery to robotics. The following list is just a small sample of the range of clubs held throughout the UK. A fuller list can be found on the STEMNET website.

Types of STEM clubs

Animal Clubs, Astronomy Clubs, Baking Clubs, Butterfly Clubs, Café Science Clubs, Construction Clubs, Crystal Growing Clubs, Gardening Clubs, Fashion and Textile Clubs, Film Production Clubs, Fossil Clubs, Photograph Clubs, Young Engineers Clubs.

Periodically, some schools run STEM days for the whole school or year groups. These days can be linked to national initiatives and awards. Details can be found on the STEMNET and STEM Centre websites.

Something to think about

Discuss with your peers what you think is the value of STEM clubs. Do you think the freedom they provide for children to work on projects and follow their own interests is an approach to learning that could be integrated into the normal curriculum?

Visiting experts

In the UK, STEM clubs are coordinated by STEMNET. They are supported by a network of national learning centres which provide resources and professional development for teachers working with students aged 5 to 19. The schools' STEM Advisory Network provides a free advisory service to schools and teachers to help increase the quality of STEM education.

One of their key services is the STEM ambassador programme. Over 25,000 volunteers from industry and universities give their time to promote and help teach the STEM subjects in schools.

Visiting experts are an important part of STEM education as they provide role models to which children can aspire. Children look forward to having visitors, who often bring with them exciting new resources, experiences and ideas. STEM ambassadors have been trained to actively support the teaching of the subjects in schools in normal classroom situations, on STEM days and in STEM clubs. STEM ambassadors cross all ages and backgrounds, representing thousands of different employers across the UK. Information about STEM ambassadors can be found on the STEMNET website.

Apart from the STEM ambassadors, every neighbourhood has its local industries and people with STEM skills. These include the local doctor, vet, farmer, engineering company, energy company, college, university or gardener. There are people in local communities that can help bring science and the other STEM subjects alive for children. Professionals can open children's minds to a world of opportunities and possibilities which come from pursuing STEM subjects and careers.

Summary

In schools around the world the term STEM education is used as a call to action to make science, technology, engineering and mathematics more relevant to pupils' lives and to open the subjects up as career options. Primary science has an important part to play by promoting long-lasting positive attitudes and helping children develop the knowledge and skills that they will need to participate successfully in our 21st century global society. A STEM approach involves active learning with a strong emphasis placed on collaboration, enquiry based learning, problem-solving and innovation. Underpinning STEM education is the belief that success in today's highly complex and competitive world is not so much driven by *what you know* but by *what you can do with what you know*.

Further reading

ASE journals:

- Primary Science 139 (Sept/Oct 2015). *Integrating STEM into the Primary School Curriculum* by Asima Qureshi.
- Primary Science 139 (Sept/Oct 2015). *STEMing the Growth of Primary Science* by Kelly Dockerty.
- Primary Science 133 (May/June 2014). *Young 'Science Ambassadors' Raise the Profile of Science* by Katie Ridley.
- Primary Science 132 (March/April 2014). *Learning About the Weather Through an Integrated STEM Approach* by Gokhan Serin.
- Primary Science 130 (Nov/Dec 2013). *Interconnecting with VIPS* by Robert Collins.

Books:

- Banks, F. and Barlex, D. (2014). *Teaching STEM in the Secondary School*, London: Routledge.
- Howard, S. and Scott, L. (2014). *Success with STEM: Ideas for the Classroom and Beyond,* London: Routledge.
- Johnson, C., Peters-Burton, E. and Moore T. (2016). *STEM Road Map,* New York: Routledge.

Reports:

- Campaign for Science and Engineering (2014). *CaSE Report – Improving Diversity in STEM*, www.sciencecampaign.org.uk/resource/ImprovingDiversityinSTEM2014.html
- National Foundation for Educational Research (2013). *Improving Young People's Engagement with Science, Technology, Engineering and Mathematics (STEM)*, www.nfer.ac.uk/publications/99927/99927.pdf
- Department for Business Innovation and Skills (2014). *Project STEM: Book of Insights*, www.gov.uk/government/uploads/system/uploads/attachment_data/file/351433/BIS-14-899-STEM-book-of-insights.pdf
- Science and Engineering Education Advisory Group (2012). *Supporting Scotland's STEM Education and Culture*, www.gov.scot/resource/0038/00388616.pdf
- Confederation of British Industries (2015). *Tomorrow's World: Inspiring Primary Scientists*, www.cbi.org.uk/tomorrows-world/assets/download.pdf

Websites:

- STEM Learning. *www.stem.org.uk*
- STEM Ambassadors (2017). *www.stemnet.org.uk*
- STEM Clubs (2016). *www.stemclubs.net*
- The Royal Society (2014). Vision for Science and Mathematics Education. *https://royalsociety.org/topics-policy/projects/vision/*

Peer-reviewed journals:

- DeCoito, I. (2016). STEM Education in Canada: A Knowledge Synthesis. *Canadian Journal of Science, Mathematics and Technology Education,* 16(2): 114–128.
- Silver, A. and Rushton, B.S. (2008). Primary-school Children's Attitudes Towards Science, Engineering and Technology and Their Images of Scientists and Engineers. *Education 3–13,* 36(1): 51–67.
- Woods-Townsend, K., Christodoulou, A., Rietdijk, W., Byrne, J.B., Griffiths and Grace, M.M. (2016). Meet the Scientist: The Value of Short Interactions Between Scientists and Students. *International Journal of Science Education,* Part B, 6(1):89–119.

CHAPTER 10

THE ORIGINS OF SCIENTIFIC KNOWLEDGE

At the heart of science is an essential balance between two seemingly contradictory attitudes – an openness to new ideas, no matter how bizarre or counterintuitive they may be, and the most ruthless skeptical scrutiny of all ideas, old and new. This is how deep truths are winnowed from deep nonsense.

(Sagan, 1997)

This chapter looks at the origins of science to show how it has changed the way we understand and feel about the natural world. We focus on the development of science from the time of the ancient Greeks. It may be argued that science was going on before this time and in other parts of the world, but it is widely accepted that what we call science today can be clearly traced back to the work of the ancient Greek philosophers.

We have included this chapter to help teachers recognise the unique nature of scientific knowledge. In Chapter 1, Richard Feynman describes scientific knowledge as 'wonderful pieces of gold' which can change the way we think and feel about the world. In his best-selling book *Unweaving the Rainbow*, Richard Dawkins compares the feelings of awe and wonder which science can inspire to the aesthetic passion stirred by the finest music and poetry. How we feel about science will influence how we teach it. If we believe it to be an amazing human achievement comparable with the greatest works of art, we are likely to inspire those same feelings in our children.

Topics discussed in the chapter

- The nature of scientific knowledge
- Early scientific theories
- Christianity's influence on the development of science
- Galileo's influence on the development of science
- The new age of science

The nature of scientific knowledge

Scientific knowledge is knowledge, not fact – a gallery of pictures painted by scientists to portray in some simplified, comprehensible way the (seemingly) infinite complexity of nature. The pictures are put up and taken down, cleaned, replaced, and destroyed. Any account of scientific knowledge is therefore … an account of unfinished business.

(Holden, cited in Rogers and Wenham, 1980)

The purpose of a scientific theory is to enable us to picture how nature works. For example, Sir Isaac Newton's theory of gravitation enables us to construct the most remarkable images (mental and physical) of how our Solar System works. Not only that, the same theory enables us to visualise how the whole universe was formed (Chapter 11). Some scientific theories, like Newton's, are masterpieces of science in the same way as great paintings or poems are thought of as masterpieces of art.

Science masterpieces, however, are never completely finished. Whereas works of art are often unique and subjective visions of the world, works of science are mainly collaborative and objective representations. When one generation of scientists stops working on a theory, the following generation continues the work. Scientific theories are therefore unfinished pictures of the natural world which scientists constantly struggle to improve. New generations of scientists evaluate, investigate and apply their own imaginations to the representations of their predecessors.

Something to think about

Why do the authors compare scientific theories to pictures? What point are they trying to make about the nature of scientific knowledge?

Behind every scientific idea there is a fascinating story which often involves exceptional people challenging the conventional wisdom of their time. The history of science involves stories about the lives of real people with human frailties as well as exceptional abilities. Many scientists in the past endured hardship and sacrifice in their pursuit of scientific knowledge. In this respect, science and art are very similar. Both of these cultures owe a debt to the tenacity and genius of a relatively small number of extraordinary people.

Why is scientific knowledge unique?

To understand the unique nature of scientific thinking, we must first reflect on the way people explained their world before the emergence of science. Traditionally, different civilisations have developed their own mythological stories to explain where they came from, to interpret the origins of natural phenomena and to underpin their social customs. These forms of knowledge integrate everyday experiences and metaphysical imaginings into a coherent and powerful belief system which satisfies intellectual, social and psychological needs. All mythologies have in common accounts of how the actions of supernatural powers cause things to happen in the natural world.

For example, Australian Aboriginals developed a comprehensive resource of oral literature. Prior to colonisation by the Europeans in 1788, there were about 300,000 Aboriginals living in small tribes throughout Australia. Each tribe had its own traditional 'dreamtime' stories which gave the tribe both its spiritual identity and an understanding of the nature of the world in which they lived.

Dreamtime stories relate to the time of the Dreaming before humans populated the land. The Dreaming is a time of creation when the eternal ancestors wandered the Earth, creating new life forms and sculpting the landscape. *The Dreamtime* represents an aboriginal account of how life was created.

The Dreamtime: An Australian Aboriginal creation myth

In the beginning the Earth was a bare plain. All was dark. There was no life, no death. The Sun, the Moon, and the stars slept beneath the Earth. All the eternal ancestors slept there, too. But at last the eternal ancestors woke themselves out of their eternity and broke through to the surface of the Earth. This was Dreamtime. Now the ancestors arose and they wandered the Earth. Some were in animal form, as kangaroos, or emus, or lizards. Some were in human shape. And some were part animal, part human, part plant. Two of the ancestors were Ungambikula. As they wandered across the world, they found half-made human beings. These beings were made of animals and plants, but they were shapeless, bundled up, vague and unfinished. With their great stone knives, the Ungambikula carved heads, bodies, legs and arms out of the bundles. They made the faces, hands and feet. At last the human beings were finished. So every person was created from nature and owes allegiance to the

animal or plant that made the bundle from which it was created; such as the plum tree, the grass seed, the lizard, the parakeet or the rat. When this work was done the ancestors went back to sleep. Some returned underground, while others became rocks and trees. The trails they walked in Dreamtime are holy trails. Everywhere they went they left sacred traces of their presence – a rock, a waterhole, a tree. And so the Dreamtime does not just lie in the distant past; the Dreamtime is the eternal Now. Between heartbeat and heartbeat the Dreamtime can come again.

(Livesey Museum for Children)

Charlie Allungoy (Numbulmoore), *Wanalirri Wanjina*, 1970 Natural pigments on bark, Australia.

Wanalirri is the ancestral Wanjina central to Ngarinyin law; the people were drowned by the Wanjina Wanalirri's ability to evoke floods to create justice to punish people for disobeying the law. Governed by a commitment to repaint the Wanjina's impression on the rock, repainting ensures rejuvenation, keeping nature 'alive' whilst continuing to honour the eternal ancestors' presence.

Every Aboriginal tribe had it own ceremonies in which their Laws of the time of the Dreaming were told and interpreted in ways which informed the life of the people.

> **For the Ngarinyin language group their Law was governed by the Wanjina who is the creator spirit who formed the land, the animals and the people, creating the Law for Aboriginal people in Australia to live by. Their image is found in the rock art sites to remind people of how the law started. The Wanjina spirit of the Ngarinyin creates all life; the babies, water, green grass, bush food, yams, all our food, they are all governed by the Wanjina's law. Senior Law people today still live their lives and teach their younger generations these laws.**
>
> (Interview with Mr Paddy Neowarra, Chairman of Ngarinyin and Wilinggin Aboriginal Corporations. Interview and translation by Heather Winter [Melbourne University] on the 2 November 2009 in Derby, Western Australia.)

The Laws for Aboriginal people have traditionally had a profound spiritual and psychological influence on the Aboriginal people and have underpinned their cultural knowledge and customs for many thousands of years. Dreamtime stories informed every aspect of aboriginal life from the time of conception to the moment of death. Underpinning Aboriginal culture is the belief that the eternal ancestors live amongst them in numerous forms including parts of the landscape such as rocks, hills and mountains. The belief that these spiritual ancestors exist as features in the landscape has created a powerful spiritual bond between the Aboriginal people and the land on which they live. For Aboriginal tribes, different features in the landscape provide iconic representations of their spiritual beliefs. Aboriginal people think of themselves as custodians of the spiritual landscape in which they live.

Something to think about

Pandora's Box is one of the ancient Greeks' most well-known and powerful myths. It is a story of desire and deceit which depicts some of our worst traits and fears. Research the story on the web. Why are stories like this so memorable? Can they influence the way people think and behave? Can science have a similar impact on people?

Most cultures have their own traditional ways of understanding the world. Great civilisations of the past, such as those of the ancient Greeks, Romans and Aztecs, believed that phenomena such as thunder and lightning, droughts, earthquakes and pestilence were caused by the actions of malevolent gods. As a result, sacrifices were offered to persuade the gods not to wreak havoc on the world. Today, people's religious beliefs are based on the interpretation of ancient texts such as the Jewish Torah, the Christian Bible and the Muslim Qur'an (Koran).

How is scientific knowledge different from religious knowledge?

Science began when people first imagined that phenomena such as thunder and lightning might not have anything to do with the action of gods. Underpinning scientific knowledge is the belief that there are natural explanations for how the world works, which people can discover for themselves.

Scientific ways of understanding the world can be traced back to the time of the ancient Greeks. Like most other civilisations, the ancient Greeks explained the behaviour of their world in terms of the actions of supernatural beings. Explanations for phenomena such as rain, thunder, lightning and disease were attributed to the action of capricious gods. Human fallibilities were imposed on these gods, so at times they might be happy and content but at other times angry or jealous. It was believed that their moods affected their behaviour in ways which had consequences for the people. For example, angry gods could cause earthquakes or storms, and while in a more benevolent mood, the gods could prevent famine and disease.

Greek society at this time was affluent enough for some privileged people to have the time and confidence to challenge contemporary beliefs. There was tolerance of a wide range of religious views and, as a result, there emerged a group of radical thinkers who found pleasure and intellectual satisfaction in challenging the authority and even the existence of the gods. The theologian Xenophanes (520 BCE) was one of the earliest philosophers to challenge the validity of the traditional myths. He claimed that the gods as described in the traditional tales were not real but a fabric of people's imagination. He argued that it was no coincidence that in every culture the gods took on the appearance and behaviours of the local people.

> Homer and Hesiod have ascribed to the gods all those things which are shameful and reproachful among men: theft, adultery and deceiving each other … Mortals believe that the gods are born, and that they have clothes, speech and bodies similar to their own … If cattle, horses and lions had hands, and could draw with those hands and accomplish the works of men, horses would draw the forms of gods as like horses, and cattle like cattle, and each would make their bodies as each had themselves … The Ethiopians claim their gods are snub-nosed and black, while the Thracians claim theirs have blue eyes and red hair.
>
> (Gregory, 2003: 11)

Something to think about

The philosopher-scientists of ancient Greece did not, as a rule, do experiments to help them discover knowledge. Most of their time was spent in thinking, reading, reasoning and arguing. They were mainly concerned with persuading each other that their views made most sense. Do you think we should do more reasoning, arguing and persuading in our science lessons?

Who were the first scientists?

The term 'scientist' is relatively modern and was first used in the nineteenth century. However, to avoid confusion, we use the term in this chapter to describe those ancient philosophers who sought out natural explanations for the behaviour of the physical world.

Many of the first scientists came from Miletus in Asia Minor, which is now part of Turkey. This was an important cosmopolitan trading centre which had strong links with eastern cultures. Exposure to these other cultures and their mythologies caused philosophers like Xenophanes to reflect on the nature of their own knowledge. For example, if other cultures had their own creation stories which differed in essential ways from the Greeks', which accounts were to be believed? After all, how many different ways could the Sun and stars be created? Surely only one account could be true. It seems that once sown, these seeds of doubt grew into radically new ways of thinking. The rejection of mythological explanations was a liberating act which enabled the Greeks to search for new ways to understand the world.

Around 600 BCE, philosophers started to develop the first scientific theories. They considered the world to be an ordered system in which events such as rain and earthquakes had natural causes. The word *cosmos* is a Greek word which means a sense of good order or a well-ordered place (an ordered, harmonious whole). The scientists believed that everything that happened within the *cosmos* could be explained by the way it was structured. Therefore, phenomena such as drought, lightning and disease were not caused by the whim of unpredictable gods but happened for natural and predictable reasons which were the result of the way the physical world was organised. The origins of scientific thinking can be traced back to the philosophers such as Thales of Miletus (624–565 BCE) who thought all the materials on the Earth were made of water and Anaximenes of Miletus (*c*. 570 BCE) who thought everything was made of air. Heraclitus of Ephesus (535–475 BCE) believed that the causes of events in the natural world would be comprehensible to humans once they had discovered its fundamental structure, which clearly demonstrates the ancient Greeks' commitment to natural, rather than supernatural explanations. This type of thinking led to the development of the first scientific models of the universe.

Early scientific theories

Believing that everything in the physical world was part of a well-ordered system, the first scientists put their minds to creating representations of the universe which would help them explain how it worked. Thales was one of the first to provide a systematic way of explaining the world. He thought the Earth was a big flat island surrounded by sea. He imagined the planets, stars, Sun and Moon to be fixed to a sphere spinning around the stationary sea and Earth every twenty-four hours. This model of the universe enabled him to explain day and night and to provide reasons for the movement of the objects in the heavens. However, if we observe the Moon and planets on different nights, we find that they have moved their position relative to the stars that surround them. The Moon and the planets seem to wander amongst the stars as well as rotate around the Earth. How could this be possible if they were all firmly fixed to the same spinning sphere? What does this tell us about the reliability of Thales' model?

Flat Earth model of the universe showing the Sun and stars attached to a spinning sphere.

In later years, Thales' simple model was replaced by more complex models. Observations of ships disappearing and reappearing over the horizon convinced the ancient Greeks that the Earth must be round. The separate motions of the Moon and planets were accounted for by adding extra spheres. After much modification, the models started to become very complex. Some had over fifty spheres moving in different ways and still could not precisely account for the movement of the planets. Aristotle's (384–322 BCE) model shows a simplified version of the multi-spheres model.

Something to think about

Scientists today describe the best theories or models as 'beautiful' and 'elegant'. Do you think this description applies to Thales' and Aristotle's models of the universe? Explain why.

According to Aristotle, the universe consisted of a terrestrial region, which was subject to change, and a celestial region, which was unchanging. This division was convenient because it allowed Aristotle to provide different types of explanation for the movement of objects in the different regions. In the celestial region, the Moon, Sun, planets and stars were all attached to solid, transparent spheres and moved in perfect circles around the Earth. Aristotle considered circular motion to be superior to other forms of motion and the heavens to be perfect and unchanging.

The terrestrial region was far from perfect and things in it were subject to change. According to Aristotle, everything in this region was made from a combination of four elements: earth, water, air and fire. Each element had its natural place in the *cosmos* and always strove to return to it. Therefore, a rock when released would fall to the ground because it was made of earth and wanted to return to its natural place. The concept of the four elements was a very powerful scientific model and could be used to explain why things in the terrestrial world were able to change their form. For example, phenomena such as burning could be explained by the separation of wood into its basic elements. If we believe wood to be made from earth, water, air and fire, then burning can be explained as a process through which these elements are released. When wood burns, we see fire being released along with the other three elements.

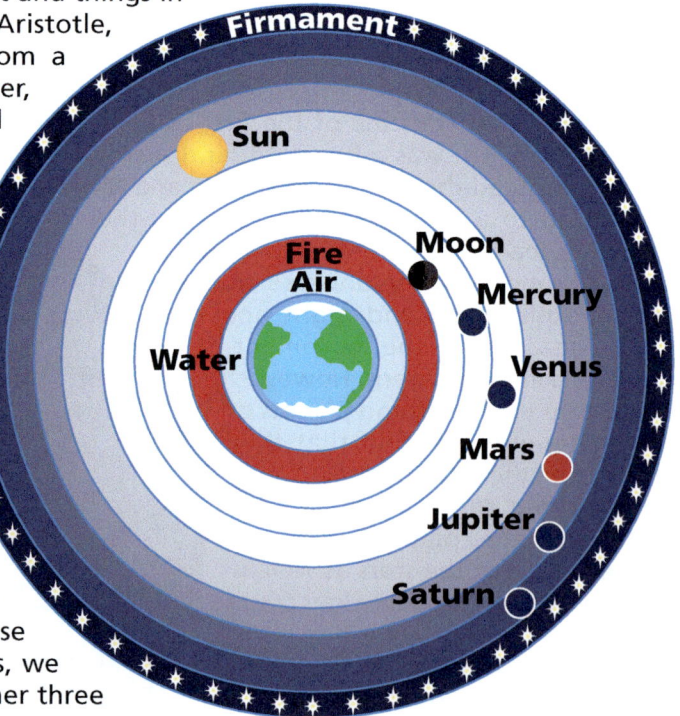

Aristotle's geocentric model of the universe.

Was the geocentric theory ever challenged?

The geocentric (Earth-centred) model of the universe continued to be accepted for over two thousand years. Ironically, the heliocentric (Sun-centred) model which later replaced it in the seventeenth century had been suggested by an ancient Greek called Aristarchus in the third century BCE. Aristarchus audaciously proposed that, rather than the Sun moving around the Earth, the Earth may in fact be moving around the Sun. He suggested that the movement of the heavens was an illusion caused by the rotation of the Earth. To persuade other scholars to believe in his model, he had to persuade them that the Earth was moving. This is not an easy thing to prove because we do not sense its movement.

Aristarchus could not prove that the Earth was spinning and the Sun was stationary. Other philosopher-scientists argued against him. If the Earth was moving, then it would create a continuous wind as it moved through the air. (Why don't we feel this wind?) With the physical evidence pointing against a moving Earth, it was not possible for Aristarchus and his supporters to persuade the early scientists to reject the geocentric model.

School of Athens by Raphael (1483–1520). Painted between 1510 and 1511, this picture depicts the great Greek philosophers and other ancient scientists. Plato and Aristotle are the two central figures.
Source: iStock

In the development of the early theories we can see how the philosopher-scientists used their imaginations to create representations of the world and tested them against observable evidence. The ancient Greeks observed that the Sun, Moon, planets and stars revolve, day and night, around what seemed to be a stationary Earth. The model of a geocentric universe was the obvious explanation, yet they were aware that it did not properly fit with all their observations. For this reason, the ancient Greeks were never firmly convinced that the geocentric model truly represented the physical world. They realised that their conceptual portrait was unfinished and more work was required.

Christianity's influence on the development of science

The ancient Greeks were never able to complete their scientific masterpiece of the structure of the universe. By 200 BCE, the Greek empire was on the wane as the Romans became the dominant military and political force around the Mediterranean. Under the influence of the Romans, science began to languish. The Romans were more interested in the social implications and practical application of Greek scientific knowledge than continuing with its development.

With the emergence of Christianity and the fragmentation of the Roman Empire, people started to look once again towards the spiritual rather than the physical to help them understand their world. As the power and influence of the Christian Church grew, scientific thinking was discouraged and scholars were expected to look instead to religious texts as the only true source of knowledge.

In 390 CE, Augustine wrote:

> What has Athens to do with Jerusalem, the Academy to do with the Church, the heretic to do with the Christian? … We have no need for curiosity after Jesus Christ, and no need of investigation after the gospel. Firstly we believe this, that there is nothing else that we need to believe.

(Gregory, 2003: 154)

From Augustine, we get a sense of the antagonism that the early Christian Church held towards the development of scientific thinking. As far as the Church was concerned, people should be more concerned with understanding their relationship to God than seeking new knowledge about the physical world. Understanding God was the way to attaining salvation in the spiritual world after death. Science had no part to play in the saving of souls.

How science was kept alive in the Muslim world

During the seventh to the thirteenth centuries the ideas of the Greek philosophers were kept alive in the Muslim world. The works of Plato, Aristotle, Euclid, Archimedes, Hero, Ptolemy, Galen and Hippocrates were translated into Arabic and stored in great libraries. These works were studied by Islamic scholars who produced critiques of them and commentaries, which presented the ideas in ways which non-specialists could understand. In this way Greek science continued to flourish at the heart of Islamic intellectual life.

For a thousand years there was virtually no science studied in Western Europe. During this time, learning focused on the interpretation of religious texts and, hence, monasteries developed into the main centres of education. It wasn't until the eleventh century, when universities began to be established, that Western Europe's interest in science was reignited. By 1200 CE universities were flourishing in Bologna, Paris and Oxford.

With the advent of universities, Western scholars began to take an interest in the classical works of the ancient Greeks. Key works were translated from Arabic or Greek into Latin. Demand fuelled supply and soon translations of ancient Greek texts – and especially commentaries by Islamic and Greek scholars – were being distributed throughout Europe. The most popular works were those of Aristotle and Galen. Aristotle's works on natural philosophy, interpreted by Islamic commentators, formed the framework on which medieval science came to be constructed.

Science plays a subservient role in the Christian world

Medieval scholars spent much time interpreting Aristotle's manuscripts and comparing them with religious texts. Where there were inconsistencies, the Greek teachings were regarded as erroneous. The Church demanded that such 'errors' be amended. Perhaps the biggest clash concerned the origins of the physical world. Christian belief was based on the biblical account in the book of Genesis in which God created the world. But according to Aristotle the world was eternal and had no beginning. This was a difficult dilemma and led to much debate between the followers of Aristotle and the theologians. Theologians maintained that *revelation* was superior to all other forms of knowledge. Natural philosophy – science – was built on reason, not revelation, and so was considered to be less reliable than theology.

Science was subservient to theology until the sixteenth century. Aristotle's natural philosophy was useful to Christianity because, on the whole, it was consistent with scripture and consequently enhanced doctrine. Dante Alighieri's (1265–1321) model of the medieval universe demonstrates how the Church integrated Greek cosmology into its doctrine.

Dante's model of the medieval universe (historical image).
Source: © British Library Board / Bridgeman Art Library Ltd.

All the celestial objects (Sun, Moon, planets and stars) above the Earth were thought to be perfect and unchanging. Each was attached to a solid translucent sphere which rotated, through the love of God, around the Earth. Beyond the ninth outer sphere is the tenth Heaven. This is the eternal and infinite realm of God, of which people can have no knowledge. In contrast, earthly things within the terrestrial region were within the realm of human understanding. Within the terrestrial region the Church was happy to adopt Aristotle's natural (scientific) explanations. When clashes between science and doctrine arose, such conflict was attributed to errors in the interpretation of Aristotle's works. For medieval scholars in Western civilisation, an understanding of how the world works was a mixture of theology and ancient Greek science. This provided a coherent and acceptable way of thinking in which scientific knowledge and religious belief combined to serve useful social and spiritual purposes for many centuries.

Something to think about

Do you think religious and scientific views can be compatible? Compare examples of religious thinking and scientific thinking to justify your answer.

Galileo's influence on the development of science

There are periods in history when the time is right to challenge the established worldview. For example, it became possible for Greek philosopher-scientists to challenge the mythological beliefs of their society and develop a natural way of explaining their world. This once new and radical natural philosophy endured for over two thousand years and eventually became established knowledge throughout the Western world. Once the powerful Christian Church integrated Greek cosmology into its own teachings, the authority of Greek philosophers such as Aristotle became as absolute as the doctrine derived from the holy texts. Scholars who dared to challenge Aristotle could be accused of heresy as they were, in effect, challenging the teachings of the Church. This was the situation in 1543 when a Polish monk, Nicolaus Copernicus, published his book *On the Revolution of the Heavens* in which he argued for a Sun-centred model of the universe.

The importance of Copernicus' book was that he was able to show that a Sun-centric universe was a possibility. His model was too complex to be popular at the time and for 50 years it was regarded as little more than a moderately useful academic text. However, Copernicus had sown seeds of doubt in Aristotle's natural philosophy. Other scientists were starting to question its infallibility. The astronomer Tycho Brahe published a detailed account of an unusual star which first appeared in the sky in 1572; it shone brightly for about two years then disappeared again. This was evidence that change could occur in the heavens, contrary to the teachings of both Aristotle and the Church. In 1577, Brahe observed the great comet pass through the sky and argued that it must have been travelling beyond the Moon and hence through the celestial spheres. According to Aristotle's cosmology, the spheres were solid; nothing could travel through them. Both Brahe and Aristotle could not be right.

The time was right to begin new work on Aristotle's masterpiece. What was needed was a powerful advocate who was prepared to argue and publicise the case against Aristotle and to persuade the Church that it was time to think again about the Earth's place in the cosmos.

Galileo challenges accepted beliefs

That powerful advocate was Galileo Galilei (1564–1642) who, with the help of the newly invented telescope, set out to prove that Aristotle's cosmology was wrong. When Galileo turned his telescope towards the heavens, he was able to observe things that were impossible to see with the naked eye. For example, he observed the moons of Jupiter orbiting around the planet. He also used his telescope to show that the Sun had spots which moved across its surface and that the Moon's surface seemed mountainous. He discovered that the planet Venus had phases which were very similar to the phases of the Moon. The world seen through Galileo's telescope was a very different world from the unblemished, unchanging one described by Aristotle. Galileo published his observations in easy-to-read books, which became very popular with the educated elite all over Europe. The books sparked people's interest in science and awakened them to the possibility that there was more to know about the world than was contained in ancient Greek texts.

Something to think about

The telescope is an example of how new technologies have played a crucial role in the advancement of science. What is the difference between science and technology? Provide an example of how science has aided the development of a new technology.

Galileo.
Source: iStock

Type of telescope used by Galileo.
Source: SSPL / Getty Images

Galileo's popularity made him less sensitive to the views of other scholars. At times he could be scornful and arrogant. His often rude dismissal of other people's views made him unpopular with some of his fellow academics, especially those who remained firm believers in Aristotle's science. His arrogance and contempt for some of his peers can be witnessed in his letter to Johannes Kepler (1571–1630):

> I wish, my dear Kepler that we could have a good laugh together at the extraordinary stupidity of the mob. What do you think of the foremost philosophers of this University? In spite of my oft-repeated efforts and invitations, they have refused, with the obstinacy of a glutted adder, to look at the planets or Moon or my telescope.
>
> (University of St. Andrews, 2013)

At the time Galileo wrote his letter to Kepler, he was determined to publicly refute Aristotle's Earth-centred theory in favour of Copernicus' Sun-centric model. The response of the Church was to try to reason with Galileo and they asked him not to directly promote the Copernican model until he had conclusive proof. After all, they had the proof of their own senses that the Earth was stationary. The same old arguments that were used in ancient times for believing in a stationary Earth were used against Galileo. They had endured so long because they were very difficult to dispute. We cannot feel the motion of the Earth, so how can we ever really know whether it is moving? Followers of Aristotle preferred to be led by their common sense rather than by the arrogant Galileo.

The Church runs out of patience with Galileo

For some years, theologians were very patient with Galileo and allowed him to speak his mind in public as long as he did not say anything that was explicitly contrary to the teachings of the Church. Church doctrine recognised Copernicus' model as a mathematical theory, which could be useful for calculating the motion of the planets; they did not accept that it described the physical reality. The notion that we lived on a moving Earth, which rotated and at the same time orbited the Sun, was considered by the Church to be both philosophically incredible and theologically heretical. A Church report on the possibility of a Sun-centred cosmos concluded it to be:

> [F]oolish and absurd, philosophically and formally heretical inasmuch as it expressly contradicts the doctrine of Holy Scripture in many passages, both in their literal meaning and according to the general interpretation of the Fathers and Doctors.
>
> (Poole, 1990: 44)

Galileo was eventually warned to abandon his support for the doctrine of Copernicus. Threatened by imprisonment, Galileo reluctantly agreed, but he later published a book called *Dialogue Concerning the Two Chief World Systems,* which was designed to refute and even ridicule Aristotle's ideas and at the same time to promote the Copernican theory.

Some influential theologians saw his book as a direct attack on the teachings of the Church. This was the last straw and Galileo was arrested and put on trial for heresy. It was no ordinary trial. Galileo had been a friend of the Pope for many years and was a popular public figure. Although the Pope felt humiliated and betrayed by Galileo, he still dealt with him leniently. Galileo was guilty of heresy and could have been executed. As it was, he was sentenced to house arrest; he was 70 years old and lived another nine years.

Although the theologians managed to silence Galileo, interest in science had been rapidly growing throughout Europe. Scientists no longer had to rely solely on their senses to collect data; they now had access to a range of powerful instruments. Telescopes, microscopes, thermometers, prisms, pendulum clocks and barometers were becoming widely available. Galileo and his contemporaries had seriously discredited some of the old science of ancient Greece and had started to replace it. This sparked a renaissance in scientific thinking, which spread throughout Europe.

The new age of science

By the time Galileo died in 1642, some scholars were still holding on to the ancient cosmology because they lacked alternative explanations. What made the Sun, Moon and Earth move? What held them in orbit? These were questions which scientific scholars in the middle of the seventeenth century could not answer. The British scientist Robert Hooke thought there must be some force of attraction between the heavenly objects which kept them in orbit. The French philosopher-scientist René Descartes imagined that objects could naturally move without being pushed along by a force. Therefore, the planets did not require a divine driving force to keep them moving. These ideas represent the type of thinking of the scientific community at the time. There were many ideas, but no one had managed to put them together in a way which would explain how a heliocentric *cosmos* would work. That is, until Isaac Newton published the *Principia* in 1687, which explained how the force of gravity could control the movement of the heavens. Newton's great achievement was to realise that gravitation is a universal force, which not only applies to objects on the Earth, such as apples falling from trees, but also to objects in the heavens, such as the Moon, Sun and planets. Newton's theory of universal gravitation turned the Copernican model into a physical possibility by explaining how the natural force of **gravity** could control the movement of objects in the heavens.

Newton's model of the universe held together by a force so powerful that it controls not only the movement of the Moon but all the distant planets that move around the Sun is one of the most enduring masterpieces of scientific thinking. It is an awe-inspiring vision, which owed as much to the power of his imagination as it did to the power of his reason and his dogged determination to once and for all solve the problem of the spheres. After 1,500 years of scholars exploring ancient texts for scientific explanations, Newton had firmly established the possibility of progressing beyond the conventional knowledge of the ancient Greeks.

In more recent times, the work of scientists has enabled more complex conceptual portraits of the universe to be constructed. Science has now produced a truly awe-inspiring theory called the **Big Bang**, which not only explains how the universe could have been formed but also completely transforms how we visualise its nature. Newton's theory of universal gravitation is so powerful that it remains an important part of this latest masterpiece.

Women in science

Social conditions until the late 1960s meant that women found it either impossible or very difficult to work in investigative science; their achievements until recently were necessarily informal or simply went unrecorded. Women now have better opportunities to work as scientists. We need to discuss such issues with children. They should be aware that, despite changing times, stereotypes are doggedly persistent. A 'scientist' in the print media is often a male with wild hair and a manic grin, wearing a white coat and flourishing a foaming test tube; or a whiskery Victorian gentleman. We need to talk about the history of science and the reasons why we see no women contributing. We need to provide inspiring examples of role models for all children.

Something to think about

Find out about the lives and work of scientists such as Marie Curie (1867–1934), Rosalind Franklin (1920–1958), Dorothy Hodgkin (1910–1994), Barbara McClintock (1902–1992) and Christiane Nüsslein-Volhard (1942–present day).

Summary

The origins of science can be traced back to the time of the ancient Greeks when a small number of radical thinking people began to seek natural, rather than supernatural, explanations for how the physical world works. These first scientists developed new knowledge from experience and reasoned argumentation. The theories developed by the ancient Greeks endured for 2,000 years until many of them proved to be unreliable when rigorously tested in the sixteenth century. Out of this period emerged a new scientific age with more rigorous methodology and greater freedom for people to express their ideas. From that time onwards, our understanding of how the natural world works has developed at an ever-increasing rate.

Further reading

Books:

- Brown, H. (1994). *The Wisdom of Science: Its Relevance to Culture and Religion*, Cambridge: Cambridge University Press.
- Crump, T. (2002). *Science: As Seen Through the Development of Scientific Instruments*, London: Constable and Robinson Ltd.
- Fara, P. (2010). *Science: A Four Thousand Year History*, Oxford: Oxford University Press.
- Fortey, J. (2007). *Eyewitness Great Scientists*, London: Dorling Kindersley Ltd.
- Gregory, A. (2003). *Eureka: The Birth of Science*, Cambridge: Icon Books.
- Reed, A.W. (1993). *Aboriginal Myths, Legends and Fables* [compiled by A.W. Reed], Chatswood: N.S.W.
- Sobel, D. (1999). *Galileo's Daughter: A Drama of Science, Faith and Love*, London: Fourth Estate.
- Weinberg, S. (2015). To Explain the World: The Discovery of Modern Science, London: Penguin Books.
- Wootton, D. (2015). *The Invention of Science: A New History of the Scientific Revolution*, New York: Harper Collins.

PART 2

SUBJECT KNOWLEDGE AND IDEAS FOR PRACTICE

Overview

This part provides 'Subject knowledge' and 'Ideas for practice' for the following themes:

- The Earth and beyond
- Energy and the well-being of the planet
- Interdependence
- Diversity
- Adaptation and evolution
- Health and well-being

- The particle nature of materials
- Changing materials
- Electricity and magnetism
- Forces and motion
- Light
- Sound

Subject knowledge

'Subject knowledge' sections begin with a brief historical context to introduce some of the key scientists who contributed to the development of the knowledge presented in the chapter. We would encourage you to find out more about the lives and work of these great scientists. Within each theme are 'Something to think about' scenarios for reflection and personal learning. These are designed to make you think creatively about key ideas in a different context or to encourage you to extend and develop your understanding. If you need further support with your subject knowledge you can refer to the texts listed in Appendix A.

Ideas for practice

'Ideas for practice' sections are based on the three-stage framework for science learning (introduced in Chapter 3). The 'Ideas for practice' are not designed as specific teaching programmes or lesson plans to be followed step by step in the classroom. Their purpose is to exemplify how a range of topics can be taught using the three-stage framework. It is envisaged that teachers will adapt and extend the activities to meet the needs of their children and to suit their own way of working.

In each stage, terms such as *talk together* or *work collaboratively* are written in italics to emphasise the key role that classroom talk plays in children's science learning. Children need to be made aware of the importance of discussion, and their learning will benefit from devising 'ground rules', which serve to guide their interactions. Characteristics of a good discussion and ideas for devising 'ground rules' for working collaboratively are examined in Chapter 5.

For each chapter, 'Ideas for practice' are presented for two suggested age groups. Topics for each age group are consistent with the requirements of the primary school science curricula in the UK, including England, Wales, Scotland and Northern Ireland. They are also applicable to the curriculum in The Republic of Ireland.

'Ideas for practice' are based on the following outline structure:

- *Introduction:* Provides a brief outline of the nature of the intended learning, including activities in the application stage.
- *Scientific view*: Provides a description of the scientific ideas which the children are expected to learn.
- *Working scientifically*: Outlines the enquiry skills children require to find answers to questions.
- *Exploration stage*: Presents a range of teaching and learning strategies designed to support collaborative learning and to enable children to voice their ideas.
- *Re-describing stage*: Presents a range of teaching and learning strategies, which can be used to help children make sense of the scientific view.
- *Application stage*: Presents opportunities for children to make use of their newly acquired scientific knowledge for specific purposes. Where appropriate, the activities link children's science learning to real-world issues, but other contexts are also used, including design and technology, storytelling and drama.

Assessing learning needs

Children's *learning needs* are the differences between their everyday thinking and the scientific view which we want them to adopt (Chapter 7). Opportunities to identify *learning needs* arise whenever children engage in written or oral discussion about scientific ideas. Well-judged questions enable teachers to probe children's thinking and assess their understanding of the scientific view.

Strategies which promote talk for learning and provide assessment opportunities are discussed in Chapter 7. Strategies used in the 'Ideas for practice' sections include puzzles, talking points, children's drawings, scientific enquiry, modelling through drama and storytelling. Listening to children's talk, challenging their ideas and probing the reasons for their thinking enables teachers to identify their learning needs and assess their understanding of the scientific ideas. *Talk for learning* (Chapter 5) is a key part of the 'Ideas for practice' because it can capture the nature of the children's understanding and reveal its influence on the way they think and feel.

The role of digital technology

The book does not have a chapter dedicated to the use of digital technology. This is because we see the use of digital devices as integral to science lessons and hence make reference to them in the 'Ideas for practice' sections when required. Tablet devices, such as iPads, provide access to a wide range of apps which can be used to research information, audio-record discussion, record video, take photographs, measure sound and light levels, and collate and present data.

Information and teaching resources

As part of each topic, web links and references to relevant information and teaching resources are provided. Some web links give access to video clips which can be used to help teach key scientific ideas, others provide access to teaching resources which can be used to extend and enrich the 'Ideas for practice'. The references feature articles published in the ASE journal 'Primary Science', which present wide ranging views on effective ways of teaching science. Further resources can be found in Appendix A.

Health and safety

When teaching topics in part 2 of the book, it remains a teacher's duty to assess classroom management, hygiene and hazard risks. The most commonly used publication for assessing risk is the ASE's *Be safe!* CLEAPPS and SSERC can also be consulted. Teachers should also take account of school policies. Technology and the internet are useful classroom tools but they can be open to abuse and place children in danger. Teachers should be aware of the potential problems and should follow their school guidance.

Companion book

Routledge have published a companion book to this text which was written by Peter Loxley, entitled *Practical Ideas for Teaching Primary Science: Inspiring Learning and Enjoyment* (2018). The companion book presents a wider range of 'Ideas for practice' than can be accommodated in this book and is supported by the same learning theory and subject knowledge.

Each chapter in the companion book provides theme-based ideas for practice at three age-related levels: key stage 1 (5–7 years), lower key stage 2 (7–9 years) and upper key stage 2 (9–11 years). Consistent with the approach taken in this book, the 'Ideas for practice' support teaching styles which value collaboration, communication, creativity, critical thinking, curiosity and problem solving as important elements of science learning. References are made at the end of each subject knowledge chapter to additional teaching resources in the companion book. The contents of the companion book are set out in Appendix B.

CHAPTER 11

THE EARTH AND BEYOND

Over the past few decades, scientists have sent many missions out into the Solar System to discover its secrets. Space probes have sent back pictures and made discoveries, which have enabled us to understand the structure of our Solar System in great detail. In addition to the information gained by spacecraft, new and more powerful telescopes have enabled scientists to see beyond our Solar System to gain understanding of the faraway objects which populate the universe.

This chapter presents a scientific view of how the universe was first created and how the Solar System was formed. It explains the causes of common phenomena such as day and night, the seasons and the phases of the Moon.

Topics discussed in the chapter

- Historical context
- A close-up view of the stars
- How the universe was created
- The structure of the Solar System
- Experiences related to the Earth, Moon and Sun

Part 1: Subject knowledge

Historical context

Our present-day understanding of the structure of the Solar System dates back to the sixteenth century when a Polish monk called Nicolaus Copernicus (1473–1543) suggested that the Earth may revolve around the Sun. Before this time, it was generally accepted that the Earth was at the centre of the universe with the Sun, Moon, planets and stars orbiting around it. Copernicus challenged this view and presented a radically new model, which placed the Sun at the centre of the cosmos. For many people, the idea of a heliocentric universe contradicted Christian doctrine. However, by the start of the seventeenth century, a small but influential number of scientists believed Copernicus was probably right.

The most significant of these scientists was Galileo Galilei (1564–1642). With the help of the newly invented telescope, Galileo was able to provide a persuasive argument against the established view and in favour of Copernicus' heliocentric universe. Galileo established the possibility of challenging and improving traditional views. This was the birth of modern science (see Chapter 10).

A close-up view of the stars

Viewed from Earth, the stars appear to be specks of light hanging in the sky. They create interesting patterns, but don't seem to be doing anything spectacular. However, close-up, things are very different. We need to take a closer look to find out what makes them shine.

Something to think about

What would you expect to see if you could get closer to a star? What would it look like? Are all stars the same? What do you imagine they are made from?

Our nearest star

From Earth, our nearest star is the Sun. The Sun is a relatively small star but enormous compared to the Earth. A total of 109 Earths would be required to fit across the Sun's disk, and its interior could hold over 1.3 million Earths. Of course, it looks quite small in the sky because it is 150 million kilometres away. The Sun's outer visible layer is called the **photosphere** and has a temperature of 6,000°C. Although the Sun appears to be calm and unchanging, it is in fact a raging nuclear furnace. **Solar energy** is created deep within its core where the temperature is 15,000,000°C. Every second, the Sun releases 5 million tonnes of pure energy. If you visited the Sun, you might be amazed by the spectacular solar flares, which dance across its surface.

Solar flares.
Source: AFP / Getty Images

Scientists think the Sun has been burning for 4.6 billion years. At the end of its life, it will begin to swell up, ultimately growing so large that it will swallow the Earth. Fortunately, the Sun has enough fuel for another five billion years or so.

Out into the Milky Way and beyond

The universe is full of stars like the Sun. All the stars we see in the night sky are nuclear furnaces emitting vast amounts of energy. Many of them are much bigger than the Sun but appear so small because they are much further away. Most of the stars we see from Earth belong to the Milky Way **galaxy**, in which the Solar System is situated. More than 200 billion stars make up the galaxy. With the naked eye we can only see approximately 2,000 stars at any one time.

A galaxy is a huge collection of stars, dust and gas. The Milky Way is a spiral galaxy. If viewed from the 'top', it would look like a slowly spinning pinwheel. The Sun is located on one of the spiral arms. The Milky Way gets its name from a Greek myth about the goddess Hera, who sprayed milk across the sky. In China, the band of stars across the night sky is called the *Silver River*, and in the Kalahari Desert in Southern Africa it is described as the *Backbone of Night*. Even if we could travel at the speed of light (300,000 km per second), the galaxy is so immense it would take about 25,000 years to reach the middle. Since time travel is not yet possible, scientists rely on very powerful telescopes to explore the Milky Way.

Something to think about

What would the sky look like if we could see all the stars in the Milky Way from Earth?

Stargazing through the Hubble Telescope

Four hundred years ago, Galileo was the first scientist to use a telescope to explore the night sky. Through the telescope he observed that Saturn had rings and Jupiter had moons. He also saw that the hazy patch across the centre of the sky, called the Milky Way, was not a cloud but an assortment of innumerable stars. The telescope changed forever our understanding of the nature of the universe and has enabled scientists to take some amazing images of the stars.

Something to think about

What can we find out about the universe by looking at pictures taken by telescopes such as Hubble? What do these remarkable images tell us about the nature of the universe? You can view pictures taken by the Hubble Telescope at http://hubblesite.org/gallery/.

We now have telescopes which can see into the depths of the known universe. The Hubble Telescope is the most powerful optical telescope ever made. It was launched into orbit around the Earth in 1990 to provide an unobstructed view of the universe. Hubble is so powerful that it enables us to see objects in space which are 1.5 billion times fainter than can be seen with the naked eye. Since its launch the Hubble Telescope has taken the most astonishing photographs, which show the universe to be a dynamic and beautiful place in which new stars are constantly being born in stunning stellar nurseries and old stars meet their end in spectacular explosions.

Outside the Milky Way galaxy, the universe may contain over 100 billion galaxies, each of which on average contains 100 billion stars. A universe which contains over 10,000 billion, billion stars is unimaginable; we can only be in awe of the magnitude of the universe around us.

How the universe was created

The biggest question of all

The big question for scientists is where all these galaxies and stars came from. Have they always been there, or have they developed from something else? The ancient Greek scientists believed that the heavens were unchanging and had always existed as we see them today. In the seventeenth century, the Christian Church calculated 4004 BCE to be the date of the creation of the universe. Apparently this figure was worked out by adding up the ages of the people in the Old Testament.

Big Bang theory

The debate about whether or not the universe had a beginning was only resolved relatively recently. Discoveries by Edwin Hubble in 1929 and by Arno Penzias and Robert Wilson in 1964 provided evidence for an expanding universe and the possibility that something happened, which caused the universe to be formed. The event, which caused the creation of the universe, is commonly known as the *Big Bang*.

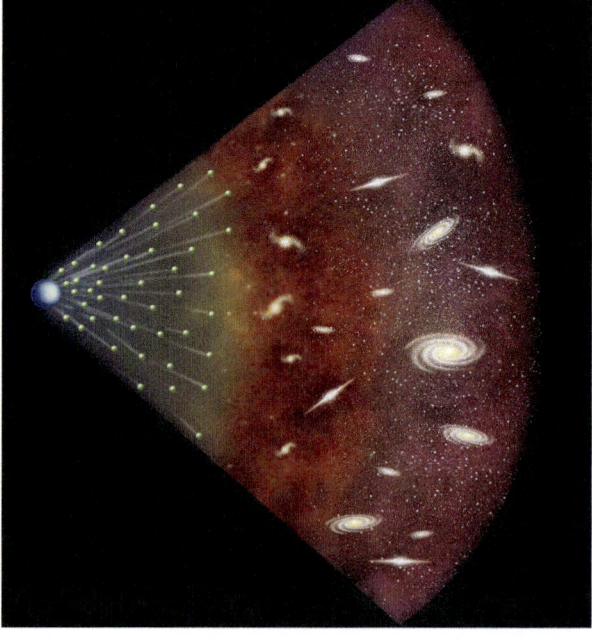

Understanding what happened in the Big Bang continues to be a major challenge for the scientific community. What seems to be agreed is that an indescribably large explosion sent subatomic particles of matter hurtling out into space. Over the first 300,000 years these particles combined to form **atoms** of hydrogen and helium. Over the next billion years, hydrogen and helium gas were drawn together by the force of gravity into huge dense clouds from which the first stars and galaxies were formed.

Hubble telescope.
Source: James Benet / E+ / Getty Images

An early version of the Big Bang Theory according to the scientist Georges Lamaitre (1894–1966). Find out about his work and why he didn't receive the recognition he arguably deserved.
Source: Universal Images Group / Getty Images

The structure of the Solar System

How was the Solar System created?

The universe was already over 11 billion years old when our Solar System was created from the embers of dead stars. As stars get older, they manufacture a range of different materials within their nuclear furnace. In addition to helium, they produce other materials such as iron, silicon, oxygen and carbon. Towards the end of their lives, very large stars become unstable and can explode, throwing out all these materials into space. These exploding stars are called **supernovas**. The different materials created from supernova explosions form clouds of dusty and gaseous debris called nebulae.

Nebulae are places in which Solar Systems are created. The force of gravity acts to draw together the materials thrown out into space by the supernova. The illustration shows how gravity fashioned our Solar System within a swirling cloud of dust and gas about 4.6 billion years ago.

Towards the centre of the cloud, materials including hydrogen were drawn together. As more and more mass accumulated at the centre, the temperature increased dramatically. Eventually, there was enough energy to set off nuclear reactions. Hydrogen atoms fused to form helium, releasing enormous amounts of energy. This marked the birth of the Sun.

The planets were created from particles of iron, silica, nitrogen, oxygen and other materials that made up the cooler dust and gas that spun around the hot centre. Gravity slowly gathered these particles together into clumps that became asteroids and small planets called planetesimals. These objects repeatedly smashed into each other and gradually got bigger. After about 100 million years the planets had formed.

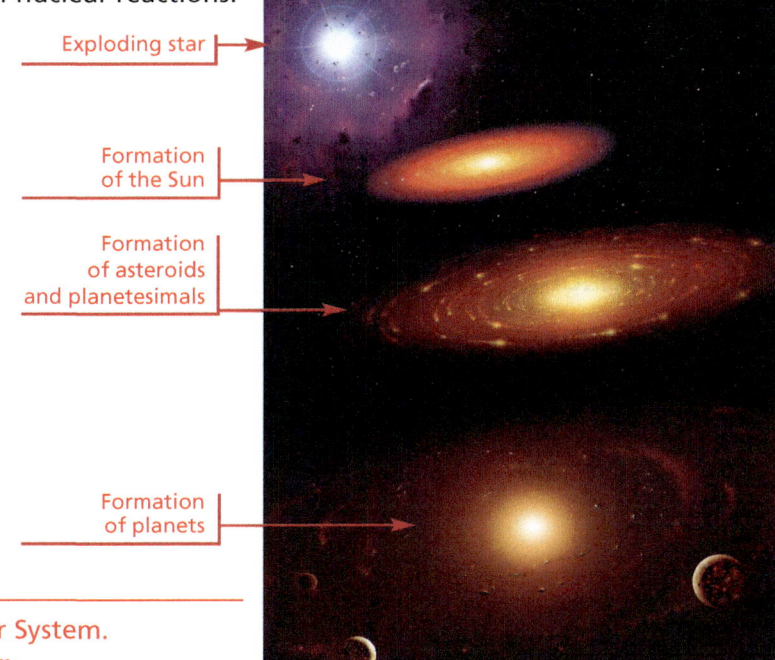

Exploding star

Formation of the Sun

Formation of asteroids and planetesimals

Formation of planets

Steps in the formation of the Solar System.
Source: © Mark A. Garlick / markgarlick.com

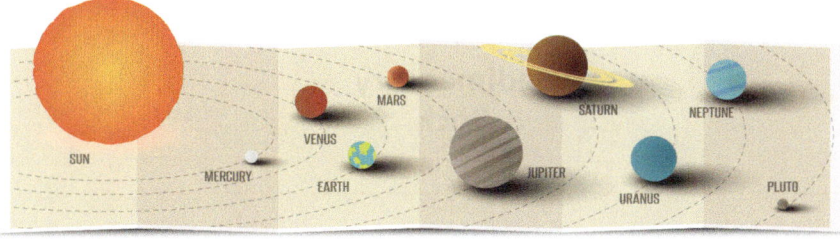

The structure of the Solar System (not to scale).
Source: iStock

How different types of rocks were formed on Earth

The oldest rocks on Earth were formed as the early Earth cooled; these are **igneous rocks** such as granite, which are hard and often contain crystals. Over time these rocks were eroded by rain and the action of the wind and ice. Particles of rock were washed into streams and rivers and laid down in layers on the sea bed; successive layers built up and new **sedimentary rocks** such as limestone were formed. These rocks are layered and often porous and may contain fossils. Movements in the Earth's crust cause both sedimentary and igneous rocks to uplift or be pulled down towards the Earth's core where heat and pressure transform them into **metamorphic rocks**. These are rocks such as slate and marble which were originally sedimentary rocks or gneiss and schist which may once have been granite. Weathering and erosion of rocks produce one of the constituents of soil.

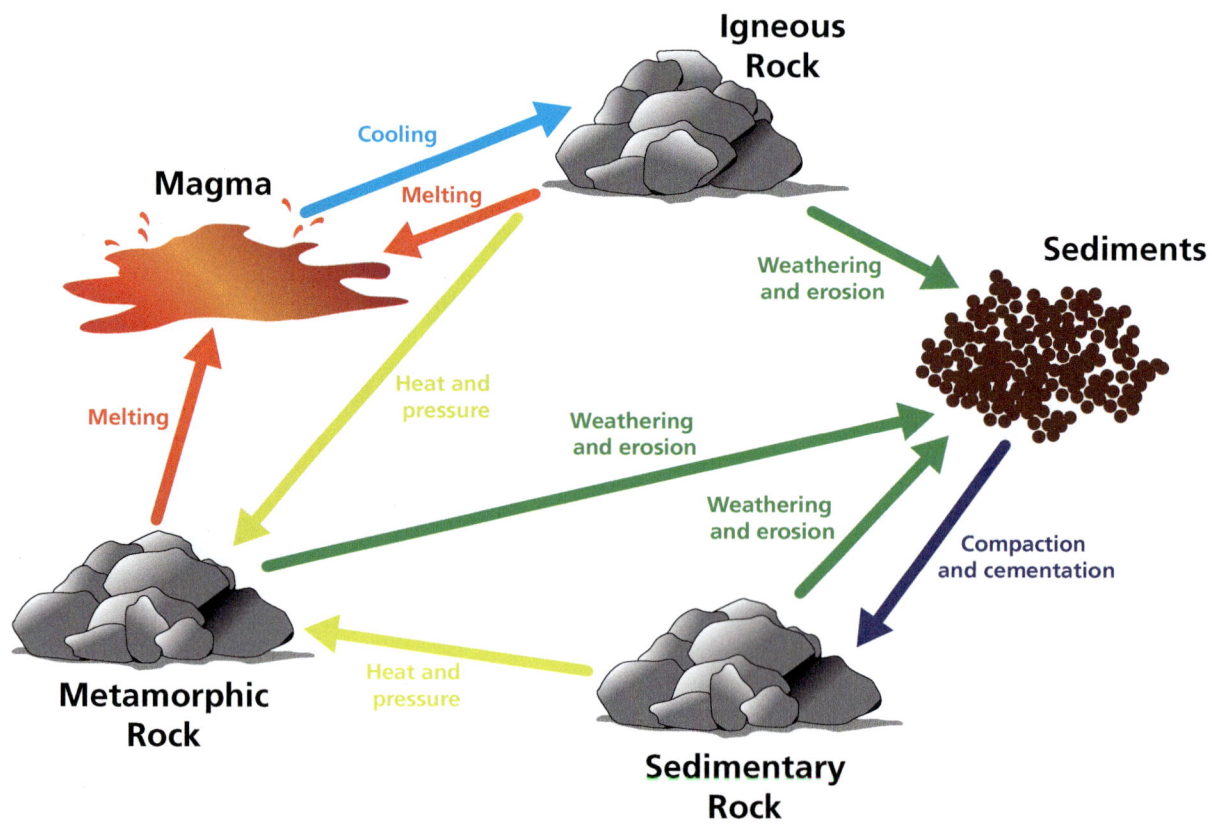

The rock cycle.

Planets: celestial wanderers

People have been studying the movement of the planets since before the time of the ancient Greeks. The planets are things of interest and fascination because they do not appear to behave like the myriad other stars in the sky. When viewed from Earth, they do not maintain a fixed position within the star patterns; they seem to wander about from one **constellation** to another. The planets are named after Roman gods. For example, Venus is the Roman name for the goddess of love. The Romans thought Venus to be the brightest and most beautiful object in the heavens.

Table 11.1 Information about the major planets

Planet	Structure	Size (diameter)	No. of moons	Icy/rocky rings
Mercury	rock and metal	4,878 km	0	0
Venus	rock and metal	12,103 km	0	0
Earth	rock and metal	12,756 km	1	0
Mars	rock and metal	6,786 km	2	0
Jupiter	gas	142,984 km	16	3
Saturn	gas	120,536 km	18	7
Uranus	gas	51,118 km	17	10
Neptune	gas	49,528 km	8	6

The planets are not stars because they do not emit their own light. Planets orbit a sun and can be seen because they reflect the Sun's light. The four inner planets in our Solar System (Mercury, Venus, Earth and Mars) are quite different from the outer planets (Jupiter, Saturn, Uranus and Neptune). The inner planets are relatively small and made mostly of rock, whereas the outer planets are quite enormous and mostly gaseous. All the planets are held in their orbits by the gravitational force of the Sun.

Caught in space

A moon is an object which orbits a planet. The force of gravity of the planet pulls the moon around in its orbit as if it were attached by an invisible string. The small inner planets have few or no moons orbiting them, while the bigger outer planets, which have far more gravity, have captured lots of moons. Some also have rings of ice and rock orbiting around them.

Something to think about

Gravity controls the movement of all the planets in the Solar System. How does it do it? What would happen if gravity could be turned off?

Why is Pluto no longer a major planet?

There used to be nine designated planets in our Solar System. However, in 2003 a new object in the depth of our Solar System was discovered using a powerful telescope based at the Palomar Observatory in the USA. The object was at first considered to be a tenth planet and was named Eris after the Greek goddess of conflict. This was an apt name as its discovery caused a heated debate amongst the scientists about whether or not it was big enough to be a planet. Eris is one of the most distant objects that scientists have discovered in the Solar System, being more than three times farther from the Sun than Pluto. It is also bigger than Pluto, which is why there was so much debate about whether or not it should be classified as a planet. With the prospect of other small planets being discovered in the future, the International Astronomical Union designated Eris as a dwarf planet. This meant Pluto had to be downgraded to a dwarf planet, and hence we consider that there are now only eight major planets.

> ### Something to think about
>
> Imagine what it would be like to travel to the edge of the Solar System. What would the Sun look like from out there? How warm would it be on Eris?

Space debris: meteors, asteroids and comets

There are huge amounts of rock and ice speeding around the Solar System. This space debris ranges in size from specks of dust to massive chunks of rock hundreds of kilometres wide. We can observe the fiery trail of small fragments of space rocks when they plunge into the Earth's atmosphere and burn up. We see them as shooting stars or **meteors**. Sometimes the Earth passes through areas of space which have a high concentration of ice and dust and which can create a spectacular shower of meteors. Each year, between 13 and 21 November, large numbers of meteors rain down on the Earth. This is the Leonid meteor shower, first discovered in 1833. In that year, it was estimated that up to a thousand meteors per minute lit up the sky. Astonishingly, over 4.5 million tonnes of space rock bombard the Earth every year. Most of these rocks (meteoroids) are very small and burn up in the Earth's atmosphere; however, larger rocks have crashed into the Earth's surface, creating craters.

What do we know about the asteroid belt?

Asteroids are the name we give to the space debris which orbits the Sun in a region between Mars and Jupiter. This region is called the asteroid belt. Asteroids are irregularly shaped rocky objects which vary in size from tiny pebbles to about 930 km in diameter. The biggest asteroid (Ceres) has recently been classified as a dwarf planet. Sixteen of the 3,000 known asteroids are over 240 km in diameter and some even have orbiting moons. Scientists think that Jupiter's strong gravity may have prevented the asteroids from building up into a planet-sized body. Another explanation could be that all the rocky debris in this part of the Solar System may have once been a planet that was destroyed by a collision with a large **comet**. There is enough material in the asteroid belt to form a planet about half the size of our Moon.

Even if Jupiter prevented the creation of another planet billions of years ago, we need to be grateful that its strong gravitational force prevents the asteroids from soaring towards the inner

An impression of the asteroid belt against the Sun.
Source: iStock.com / johan63

planets. Many objects have struck our Earth in the past. It is thought that an impact with a huge piece of space debris about 65 million years ago caused mass extinction of life, including the loss of the dinosaurs. Other theories suggest that the building blocks of life and much of the water we have on Earth arrived on the multitude of asteroids and comets that bombarded our planet in its infancy. We have good reason to fear another collision with even a relatively small asteroid. On 30 June 1908, an asteroid about 100 m in diameter struck the Earth and devastated more than half a million acres of forest in the remote region of Tunguska in Siberia.

Imagine the effect if it had landed on one of the Earth's largest cities. The scariest event of recent times happened on 23 March 1989, when an asteroid 400 m wide very nearly struck the Earth. Scientists estimated that Earth and the 50-million-tonne asteroid had been in the same position in space but, fortunately, a vital six hours apart.

Where do comets come from?

Comets are huge dusty snowballs which normally reside in the freezing outer regions of the Solar System. The dark, cold area of the Solar System where comets can be found is called the Oort cloud, which is 100,000 times further away from the Sun than is the Earth. The cloud is made up of about six trillion comets which surround the solar system. Just like the planets and the asteroids, the comets are held in orbit around the Sun by its powerful gravitational force. Sometimes a comet drifts away from the Oort cloud and travels through the inner Solar System. When this happens, the comet starts to warm up as it gets closer to the Sun. The energy from the Sun causes some of the ice to thaw and to change into a gas which streams out to form a long tail. This gives the comet the distinctive shape which we see from Earth. Lit by the Sun, the comet glows as brightly as a planet.

A comet with its distinctive tail.
Source: Photodisc / Getty Images

Throughout history, comets have been perceived as omens heralding disaster or great events. Records of comets exist from before the time of the ancient Greeks. The following account of a comet was found in an ancient text in 1140 BCE:

> A star arose whose body was bright like the day, while from its luminous body a tail extended, like the tail of a scorpion.
>
> (Brady, 1982)

It is possible that this comet could be the same one which was named after the English astronomer Edmond Halley. Halley's Comet was recorded many times in history before Halley predicted its return in 1705. Many people, both ancient and modern, have seen this comet. It is very bright and a regular visitor, orbiting the Sun every 76 years. It was last seen in 1986 and is predicted to return in 2061. Halley will never return to its original home in the Oort cloud. It is now trapped by the Sun's gravity in a smaller orbit, which takes it just beyond Neptune before heading back towards the Sun.

The Earth viewed from the Moon.
Source: iStock

Experiences related to the Earth, Moon and Sun

The spinning Earth

From Earth, the most easily recognisable objects in our Solar System are the Sun and the Moon. By watching the movement of the Sun, it is easy to think that it travels around the Earth. In fact, the movement of the Sun is an illusion caused by the spin of the Earth. When we watch the Sun rising in the morning and setting in the evening, we rarely imagine how these events are caused by the rotation of the Earth.

Something to think about

Have you ever thought how fast we are moving on the surface of the Earth as it spins around on its axis? Standing on the equator you would be speeding along at about 1000 mph. Why don't we sense this movement? Shouldn't we expect the movement of the Earth to create gale-force winds as it cuts through the air?

What do we know about the Moon?

At 384,400 km away, the Moon is our closest neighbour in space. This may seem a long way away compared to the distances we travel on Earth, but, compared to the overall size of the Solar System, the Moon is very close. Some scientists think that the Moon may have been created when an object the size of Mars smashed into the Earth billions of years ago, throwing huge amounts of rocky material into space. Over a long time, gravity fashioned this material into the Moon we see today. If we look at the Moon with binoculars, we can see that its surface is covered with craters caused by impacts with space debris.

Phases of the Moon

As we move through a month in time – a twelfth of our journey around the Sun – the Moon appears to change shape. A full moon happens when the whole surface of the moon facing us is lit up by the Sun. As the Moon orbits the Earth, the proportion of its surface facing us which is lit by the Sun decreases (wanes) and, consequently, we see reducing fractions or phases of the moon. The Moon appears to change shape progressively until we can see no part of it at all. At this stage the side of the Moon facing away from us is fully lit by the Sun, leaving our side in darkness. As the Moon continues its orbit around the Earth, the proportion of its surface reflecting sunlight towards the Earth steadily increases (waxes) until once again the side facing us is fully lit.

Something to think about

The illustration on page 143 shows the Moon partially lit by the Sun as it moves around the Earth. Imagine what the Earth would look like if viewed from the Moon. Would the Earth have similar phases or would it be in the Moon's shadow?

The faces of the Earth and Moon to the left are lit by the sun. The faces to the right are in shadow – that is, completely dark because there is no nearby light source.
Source: iStock

Why do we have seasons?

Owing to the **tilt of the Earth's** axis relative to the sun, the intensity of sunlight received by the northern and southern hemispheres changes throughout the year. Different areas of the Earth receive different amounts of sunlight depending on the Earth's position around the Sun. When the northern hemisphere is angled towards the Sun, rays of sunlight shine directly onto this part of the world, creating a hot summer climate. As the Earth continues around the Sun, the situation changes until the northern hemisphere is angled away from the Sun. This creates cooler, winter conditions in the north because of the reduced amount of sunlight it receives. Because the direction of the Earth's tilt always remains the same, the southern hemisphere experiences opposite seasons to the north.

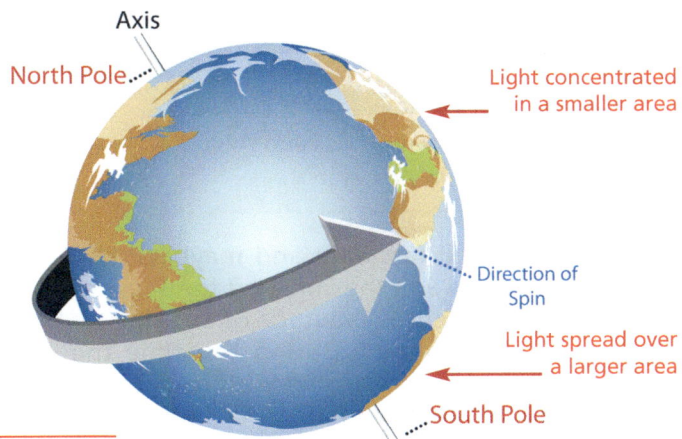

Intensity of light varies due to the tilt of the Earth.
Source: iStock

Solar eclipse

The ancient Chinese thought that during an **eclipse** the Sun was being eaten by a dragon or demon. They would yell and shout and bang on pots and drums to frighten it away. The Incas had similar beliefs. The ancient Greeks thought that an eclipse was a sign that the Sun, which they considered to be a god, was abandoning them. The word 'eclipse' comes from the Greek word meaning 'abandonment'.

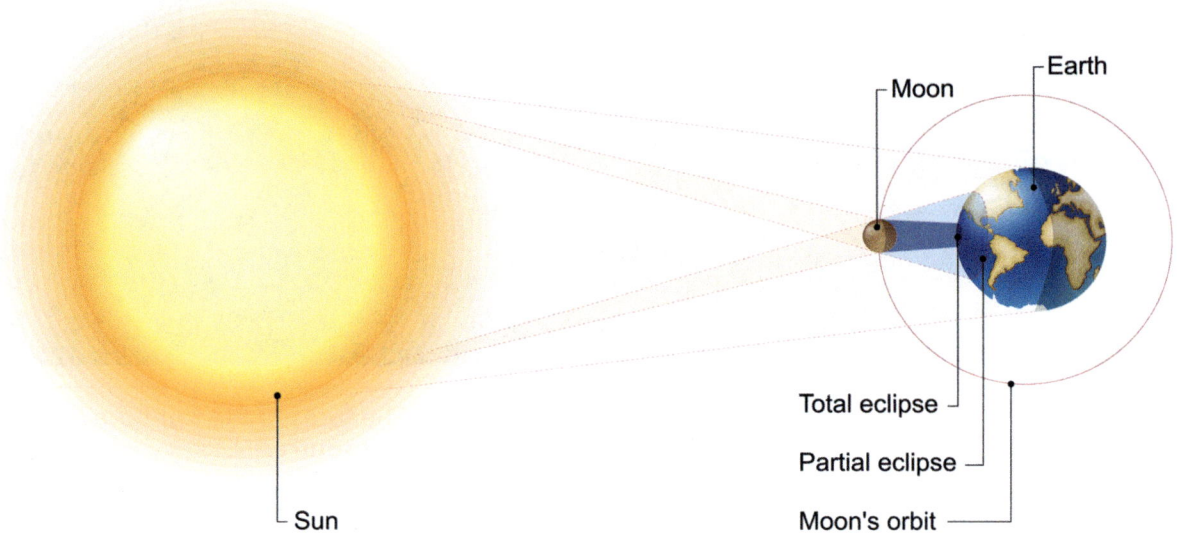

Solar eclipse.
Source: iStock

Something to think about

Find out about the equinoxes and solstices. Use a globe (Earth) and a torch (Sun) to model the spring equinox and the winter solstice.

Today, eclipses still fascinate and maybe frighten us. During a solar eclipse the Moon moves between the Earth and the Sun, and for a few minutes the Sun seems to disappear, which can be an alarming experience. The stage of an eclipse when the Moon completely covers and blocks out the Sun is called *totality*. During this time the glow of the Sun's outer atmosphere with its spectacular solar flares becomes visible. Although total solar eclipses are quite frequent, about two every three years, relatively few people witness them because the shadow cast by the Moon onto the Earth is very narrow. It is often less than 100 km across. Only people who view the eclipse from within the shadow will see its totality.

Something to think about

What would an eclipse of the Sun look like if the Moon was either bigger or smaller? What would we see if the Moon was further away from the Earth? Would a solar eclipse still be such a spectacular event if the relative sizes and distances of the Moon and the Sun from the Earth were different?

Why lunar eclipses are more common

Lunar eclipses are more commonly observed because at any one time they can be seen from a huge area of the Earth. Lunar eclipses occur when the Moon travels into the shadow cast by the Earth. The Earth casts a huge shadow which can take up to four hours to cross the face of the Moon. Anyone standing on the night side of the Earth can witness the lunar eclipse. Surprisingly, the Moon often turns red when it is eclipsed. This is because the Earth's atmosphere acts like a prism and separates the sunlight into its different colours. Of the colours of the **spectrum**, red light is refracted the most and becomes directed onto the face of the Moon. The Moon reflects this red light back to the Earth.

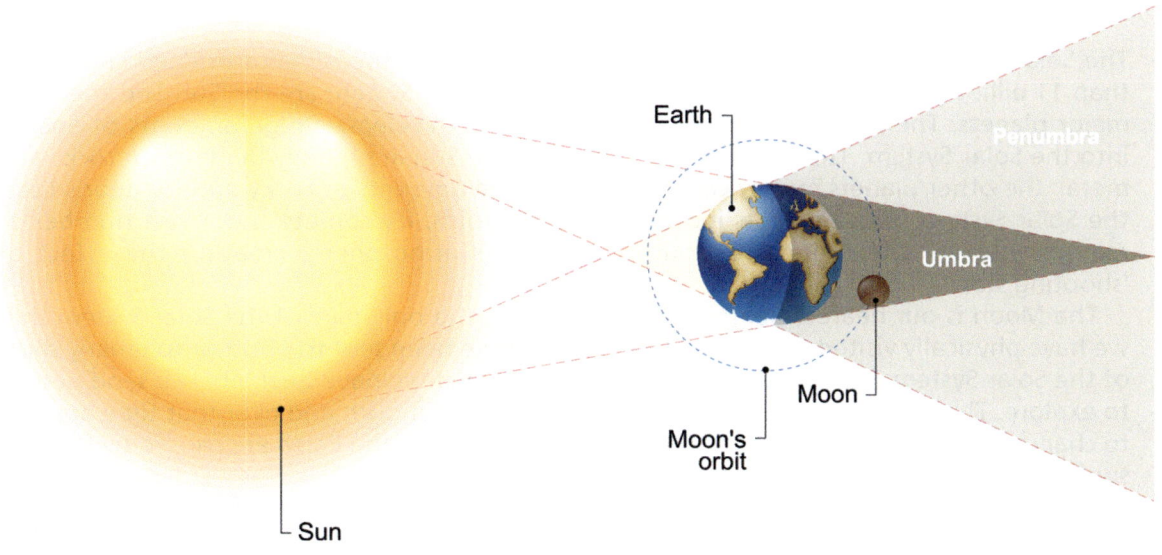

Lunar eclipse.
Source: iStock

Global dimensions: Artificial satellites and the role they play

Whilst the Moon is our only natural satellite, estimates vary as to the number of artificial satellites currently orbiting the Earth. Since the launch of Sputnik 1 by the Soviet Union in October 1957, over 20,000 satellites have been put into orbit. Of these, only about a thousand are still active and in their correct orbits. Sputnik was about as big as a beach ball and weighed 83kg. Present-day satellites range in size from the largest, the International Space Station, to communications satellites or the Hubble Space Telescope (both of which are about the size of a bus), to mini satellites that are used for research or to test new technologies.

Artificial satellites support our global communication systems – from everyday telephone calls to distributing television transmission. We are all now familiar with images of Earth from satellite or the Global Positioning Satellite network that enables us to navigate our road systems with such accuracy. Weather satellites are increasingly useful to track and predict weather patterns and warn of adverse conditions or impending storms. Their images show areas of destruction of habitat and map the extent of flooding or fire damage. GPS systems are now being developed to monitor disturbances of the sea floor and so predict tsunamis and map the movement of shoals of fish to aid fishermen. See:

- http://satellites.spacesim.org/english/index.html
- www.howstuffworks.com/satellite.htm
- www.youtube.com/watch?v=ydbbd-4oEds
- http://earthobservatory.nasa.gov/Features/OrbitsCatalog/

Summary

The Solar System was formed by the force of gravity from the remains of dead stars more than 11 billion years ago. The largest objects in the Solar System are the Sun and the eight major planets. The Sun is a fiery nuclear furnace which releases huge amounts of energy into the Solar System. The four planets closest to the Sun are mainly made from rocks and metal; the other planets mainly consist of gas. Large amounts of rocky and icy debris litter the Solar System. These objects include rocky asteroids, icy comets and a vast number of meteors, which often plunge through the Earth's atmosphere, creating the effect of 'shooting stars'.

The Moon is our nearest neighbour in space. It is the only part of the Solar System that we have physically visited. Unmanned spaceships have been sent to photograph many parts of the Solar System, but the Moon is the only place that we have been able to send people to explore. The Moon orbits around the Earth once each month and over that time appears to change shape progressively. The phases we observe from the Earth are caused by the way sunlight is reflected from the surface of the Moon.

At any one time the Sun's light shines on one side of the Earth, leaving the other side in darkness. As the Earth spins around on its axis, different parts of the Earth move from light into shadow, causing the phenomena we call day and night. The seasons are caused by the angle of tilt of the Earth.

Part 2: Ideas for practice

Topic: Moon craters

Age group: 7–9 years

Introduction

This topic provides opportunities for children to explore the structure of the Moon's surface and to answer questions concerning how its craters were formed. In the application stage, children take on the role of NASA engineers to design a Moon Base, which according to NASA sources could be up and running by the year 2031.

Scientific view

The Moon is a barren and lifeless place. Unlike the Earth, it has no air to breathe, no rivers or seas to swim in and there are no sounds to listen to. Its mountainous surface is a silent desert peppered with craters created by meteoroids (space rocks) smashing into its surface.

Working scientifically

In these activities children will:

- ask questions and use scientific enquiry to answer them;
- set up practical enquiries, make systematic observations and take accurate measurements;
- test ideas using evidence from observation and measurement;
- record findings using scientific language and photographs, draw conclusions and make predictions;
- use first-hand experience and information sources to answer questions.

Exploration stage

Children's talk involves trying out their own ideas

Setting the scene

Read this poem with the class.

> **The Moon**
> **The Moon out**
> **There.**
> **The Sun out**
> **There.**
> **The whole galaxy out**
> **There**
> **and me stuck in my bedroom**
>
> Ki Ellwood-Friery, aged 8 years old (1996)

Talk about children's responses to the poem. What do they think about when they look up at the Moon? Do they think the Moon is special? What do they think it is made from? Would they like to visit the Moon? If they could see it close up, what would it look like? Find out if any of the children have viewed the Moon through binoculars or a telescope and ask them to describe what they could see. There are lots of interesting websites which provide photographs of the Moon, such as the NASA website for children.

Scientific enquiry

Working in small groups, children explore video clips and images of the Moon. Talk to the children about the nature of the lunar landscape and encourage them to interpret the images in their own words. Compare the surface of the Moon to a desert. Make children aware that the Moon is more barren than any desert on Earth because there is no air to breathe and hence there is no life. Children record their findings by producing paintings of the lunar landscape. They could also write poems describing 'a walk on the Moon'. Children can extend their enquiry to find out about the Apollo Missions when astronauts travelled to the Moon.

Children's work can be used to create a display. *Talk together* about their pictures and poems. Focus on their representations of the Moon's craters. What other words would they use to describe them?

Puzzle

What are craters? How were the ones on the Moon created?

In groups, children discuss how they think the craters have been formed. Encourage the children to *work collaboratively*. Provide groups with the opportunity to present their ideas to the rest of the class and see if any consensus emerges.

Formative assessment

Provide opportunities for children to voice what they have learnt in the exploratory stage. Use evidence from their responses to the puzzle and other activities to assess differences between children's ideas and the scientific view. Plan how you will use the re-describing stage to help the children address their *learning needs.* You may want to modify the activities depending on the shared and individual needs of the children.

Information and teaching resources

- National Aeronautics and Space Administration (2017). NASA Kids' Club. *www.nasa.gov/audience/forkids/kidsclub/flash/index.html*
- ESA Kids. *www.esa.int/esaKIDSen*
- NASA Goddard (2012). Tour of the Moon. *www.youtube.com/watch?v=2iSZMv64wuU*
- Tvinsider4 (2007). NASA Apollo 11 Moon Mission Original Footage. *www.youtube.com/watch?v=LNm1LVJTJ2k*

Re-describing stage

Children's talk involves making sense of scientific ideas

Teacher-led discussion

Start by showing children pictures and video footage of the Apollo astronauts on the Moon. The video clip entitled 'Moon' is a good starting point. Talk about how the astronauts travelled to the Moon, and why they need to wear spacesuits.

Storytelling

Ask children to imagine they were a modern day astronaut on a mission to discover whether it was feasible to build a station to live in on the Moon. Part of the mission was to find a suitable place to build the station which meant travelling around the place in a moon buggy. Another part of their job was to post a daily blog about their mission. *Working collaboratively* children create blog entries for three consecutive days describing their experiences including what the weather was like, what they ate, where they slept, what they did, what they discovered and how the experience made them feel. Children use information sources to make sure their stories are consistent with what is known about the Moon.

Scientific enquiry

Whether travelling to the Moon or the Space Station astronauts need to be fit and healthy, which means eating the right food and doing physical training. The website 'Mission X' uses the context of astronaut training to help children explore how to keep fit and to understand the need for a healthy diet. The activities are appropriate for both science and physical education lessons. Children can plan their own training regime in preparation for a trip to the Moon.

Teacher-led discussion

Return to the puzzle. Provide children with pictures of asteroids, meteoroids and comets, and talk about how these space rocks can be found speeding around the Solar System. Could space rocks like these have created the craters on the Moon? Are there any other possible causes? Discuss children ideas and address misconceptions.

Modelling

Children speculate about the types of objects which could have created the huge impact craters on the Moon. They can use the *Impact Calculator* on the Down2Earth website to simulate the size of craters produced by different types of terrestrial objects, travelling at different speeds and trajectories.

Scientific enquiry

Children test the space rock hypothesis by dropping a variety of rocks into trays filled with silver sand or flour. Flour is best but messy. They can use video cameras to capture the impact and record the size and shape of the craters produced.
Encourage groups to make predictions about questions such as:

- Will bigger space rocks make bigger craters?
- Does the shape of the crater depend on the shape of the space rock?
- Does the size of the crater depend on how fast the space rock is travelling?

Talk together about the reasons for the children's predictions and use the sand tray to test them out. Provide opportunities for the children to compare images of their craters with photographs of craters on the Moon and to talk about the similarities and differences. Do their video images support the scientific explanation that space rocks caused the craters on the Moon? If so, which types of space rocks? Encourage children to justify their conclusions and assess their progress. Address any outstanding *learning needs*. Children can raise their own questions for further learning.

Information and teaching resources

BBC Bitesize:

- BBC (2007). The Moon. *www.bbc.co.uk/education/clips/zvw8q6f*
- BBC (2007). Earth, Sun and Moon. *www.bbc.co.uk/education/clips/zf4g9j6*
- BBC (2000). What Does the Moon Look Like and Why? *www.bbc.co.uk/education/clips/zqbvr82*

Other websites:

- Mission X: Train Like an Astronaut (2017). About Mission X. *https://trainlikeanastronaut. org/about*
- Impact Calculator. *www.down2earth.eu/impact_calculator/*

Exploring craters.
Source: Peter Loxley

Application stage

Children's talk involves trying out scientific ideas

Design a Moon Station

Setting up a permanent base to live on the Moon has been the aspirational dream of scientists and engineers for decades. Many think it is a feasible project and NASA has predicted that a base could be built by the year 2031.

The thing about designing something as exceptional as a Moon Base is that there is no precedent. At present, the International Space Station is the only existing manned structure, which can be used as a model for a Moon Station. Scientists have learnt a lot from the ISS project about living in space, which could be applied to the design of a Moon Station. With this in mind, children can take on the role of NASA engineers to design a Moon Base to be built by the year 2031. As part of the project, groups explore NASA websites to discover where the best place would be to build the base and some of the basic functions it would serve. Children build models of their base and present their designs as part of a class conference entitled 'Moon Base 2031'.

Information and teaching resources

- Jeff Quitney (2012). Building a Moon Base from Lunar Materials. *www.youtube.com/watch?v=EgOg0mzqGAM*
- Stevebd1 (2010). Living on the Moon clip 3. *www.youtube.com/watch?v=jhJgR6QhNPU*

- NASA Goddard (2010). NASA Best: Living on the Moon. *www.youtube.com/watch?v=TN rhADcTNBk*
- National Aeronautics and Space Administration (2017). International Space Station. *www.nasa. gov/mission_pages/station/main/index.html*

Topic: Our Solar System

Age group: 9–11 years

Introduction

In this topic children explore ways of modelling the phases of the Moon, and describe the movement of the Earth and other planets relative to the Sun. They also use fruit to create a scale model of the Solar System. In the application stage children create their own science fiction stories about a journey to Mars based on up-to-date science and technology.

Scientific view

The Moon is our closest neighbour and the brightest object in the night sky. Although it shines so brightly, it has no light of its own. We can see the Moon because it is lit up by the light of the Sun. It appears to change shape because as it moves around the Earth we see different proportions of light and shadow. The Earth and the Moon are just two of many objects which orbit the Sun, which include other planets and their moons.

Working scientifically

In these activities children will:

- plan scientific enquiries to answer questions;
- use results to make predictions and create models;
- report and present findings orally, in written form and in the form of models;
- use information sources to support and refute ideas;
- present and communicate ideas creatively.

Exploration stage

Children's talk involves trying out their own ideas

Setting the scene

Read this poem with the children

> **The Moon**
> The moon is just a big potato floating in the sky
> And little men from outer space are often passing by.
> If they're feeling hungry they eat a bit for dinner.
> That's why the moon is sometimes fat, and other times it's thinner.
>
> Kjartan Poskitt (1991)

Discuss children's responses to the poem. Have they noticed how the Moon changes shape? Do they know why?

Puzzle

Why does the Moon change shape? Is there a pattern in its behaviour or are the changes unpredictable?

Scientific enquiry

Children *work collaboratively* to draw pictures of the Moon's phases starting with a full Moon. They then use information sources to check the accuracy of their drawings and make modifications. Each group should hypothesise about why the Moon changes shape and how long it takes to complete all its phases.

Modelling

In groups, children use globes (Earth), tennis balls (Moon) and torches (Sun) to model the phases of the Moon. Encourage *collaborative* ways of working in which ideas are shared and reasons for their views given. Discuss what children think they know and what they need to find out. A common misconception is that the phases of the Moon are caused by shadows of the Earth. At this stage, children's misconceptions can be challenged by asking them to develop a reasoned argument for why their ideas make sense. Inconsistencies in their arguments can become the focus of discussion.

Children modelling the phases of the Moon.
Source: Peter Loxley

Formative assessment

Provide opportunities for children to voice what they have learnt in the exploratory stage. Use evidence from their responses to the puzzle and other activities to assess differences between children's ideas and the scientific view. Plan how you will use the re-describing stage to help the children address their *learning needs.* You may want to modify the activities depending on the shared and individual needs of the children.

Earth rising as viewed from the Moon.
Source: iStock

Re-describing stage

Children's talk involves making sense of scientific ideas

Teacher-led discussion

Start this stage by addressing children's misconceptions using video clips, which model how light from the Sun causes the phases of the Moon. Discuss how the Sun's light shines on part of the Moon, leaving the other part in shadow.

Modelling

Ask the children to review the way they modelled the phases of the Moon in the light of the previous discussion. Each group can present and explain their models, which can then be compared. Children need to persuade each other that their models best explain what we actually observe happening to the shape of the Moon. Encourage them to use language such as waxing and waning, full Moon, new Moon, crescent Moon and gibbous Moon.

Organise a whole-class model with children standing holding hands in a circle, facing out to represent the Earth. Use a big white ball to represent the Moon and a powerful torch for the Sun. Make the room as dark as possible. Turn out the lights and ask the children in the circle to explain what they can see. Shine the torch on to the Earth. Which children are in the dark and which are lit up by the Sun's light? Relate to day and night. The circle of children (Earth) now rotate so that each moves from night to day and back again. Now introduce the Moon and demonstrate how its movement around the Earth creates the phases. Compare with the children's models. Reinforce the point that the phases of the Moon are caused by the way sunlight is reflected off its surface. Question the children during modelling to assess their levels of understanding. Address outstanding *learning needs*. What else would they like to find out? Can the children model the phases of the Earth viewed from the Moon?

Children practise modelling the phases of the Moon for the camera. The activity is best done in a darkened room.
Source: Peter Loxley

Scientific enquiry

The Institute of Physics website contains some useful ideas for teaching the Solar System. One of their ideas is to use fruit to build a scale-model of the Solar System. Rather than just show children what to do, let them discover for themselves which sized fruits to use to build a scale model. Using information sources children can collect data about each planet and compare their sizes. They can then choose appropriate sized fruits to represent each planet. Provide a wide variety of fruit to choose from including cherries, plums, grapes, watermelons, coconuts, apples, oranges and peas.

Modelling

Groups create models which represent the relative sizes of the planets. How big would the Sun need to be on their scale? Children should explain their models and provide reasons for their choices of fruit. Challenge the children to include relative distances from the Sun as part of their model. They will need a large space for this, at least 12 metres long. Compare children's models with the one published on the IOP website.

Information and teaching resources

BBC Bitesize:

- BBC (2007). The Moon and Its Orbit Around the Earth. *www.bbc.co.uk/education/clips/z3jd7ty*

Other websites:

- Makemegenius (2013). Phases of the Moon Explained for Kids. *https://www.youtube.com/watch?v=bWeaQctUp1c*
- Moon phases demonstration. *https://www.youtube.com/watch?v=wz01pTvuMa0*
- Learning about the Moon and its phases. *https://www.youtube.com/watch?v=UhhSmpFtg7k*
- Modelling the Solar System with fruit. *www.supportingphysicsteaching.net/Es03TA.html#TA1*

Application stage

Children's talk involves trying out scientific ideas

Journey to Mars

We probably know more about Mars than any other planet in the Solar System (except the Earth). Like the Moon, its surface is covered by craters created by collisions with space rocks. Children can use a range of sources to compare the surface of Mars with that of the Moon.

An imaginary journey to Mars can provide a stimulating and creative context for storytelling, as well as providing opportunities for children to develop their understanding of our neighbour in space. Tell children that events in the story can be fictional, but descriptions of the journey to

Mars, of the Martian landscape and how they live and move around on the surface must be scientifically and technically accurate. Children start planning their stories by visiting NASA and other relevant websites to learn about the science and technology essential to their plots.

Is there anyone out there? This could be an evocative title for their stories. It is also the title of a STEM Centre teaching resource funded by the UK Space Agency in which children take on the role of space scientists or space engineers on a quest to discover whether life ever existed on Mars. The resource provides images, ideas and data which children could incorporate into their stories. Organise a school 'story festival', a bit like a book festival, where the 'authors' read and talk about their science fiction stories to small groups of children, parents and teachers.

Information and teaching resources

- Mars exploration. *http://mars.nasa.gov/*
- Curiosity rover. *http://mars.nasa.gov/msl/*
- Participate. *http://mars.nasa.gov/participate/*
- Mars for kids. *http://mars.nasa.gov/participate/funzone/*
- Solar System missions. *www.nasa.gov/content/solar-missions-list*
- Is there anyone out there? *www.stem.org.uk/elibrary/resource/30199/is-there-anyone-out-there*

Talk skills and science discussion: Talk for learning

Ask groups to discuss and research a topic such as:

- The dwarf planet Pluto
- Neil Armstrong
- Tim Peake
- Designing a colony on the Moon

Organise a session in which groups present their ideas to the class. Discuss in groups, and then as a whole class, how scientific knowledge is accumulated and changes over time. Ask children to evaluate the value of discussion for thinking and learning. Bring out any difficulties experienced in group work and talk through ideas which can help to establish effective talk sessions. Establish the idea that effective groups can achieve more than individuals and that the achievement of individuals depends on the achievement of the group. Every child should feel that they can both contribute and learn.

Ask the class to suggest why scientists mostly work in groups or teams.

Additional information and teaching resources

Companion book:

- Loxley, P.M. (2018). *Practical Ideas for Teaching Primary Science: Inspiring Learning and Enjoyment,* Abingdon: Routledge, Chapter 5: Rocks and Fossils and Chapter 11: Earth and Space.

Websites:

- Animations of phases of the Moon. *www.childrensuniversity.manchester.ac.uk/interactives/science/earthandbeyond/phases/*
- ESA kids. *www.esa.int/esaKIDSen/index.html*
- ESERO website. *www.stem.org.uk/esero*
- Hubble Telescope. *http://hubblesite.org/gallery/*

ASE journals:

- Primary Science 138 (May/June 2015). *Creative and Tactile Astronomy: Exploring the Universe Using All the Senses* by Isabel Borges, Linda Canas, Alison Alexander and Ruth Wiltsher.
- Primary Science 136 (Jan/Feb 2015). *Using Space to Inspire and Engage Children* by Allan Clements.
- Primary Science Review 108 (May/June 2009). *Journeys into Space.* This issue is dedicated to topics related to the Earth and beyond.
- Primary Science Review 88 (May/June 2005). *Watching the Moon from Tenerife* by Baruch, Machell and Norris.

CHAPTER 12

ENERGY AND THE WELL-BEING OF THE PLANET

Energy makes things happen. It is used every day to heat and light our houses, to run our cars and to make electronic gadgets work. It is used for transport and today we travel in ways that previous generations would never have thought possible. Industry uses large amounts of energy in manufacturing processes. However, concerns about the amount of energy we use and the depletion of fossil fuels feature regularly in the news and on television.

Topics discussed in the chapter

- Historical context
- Understanding energy
- Types of energy
- Energy sources

Part 1: Subject knowledge

Historical context

Gottfried Leibnitz, a seventeenth-century German scientist, was one of the first people to study energy. In the late seventeenth century, he proposed the theory of *vis viva,* which means 'living force'. Leibnitz believed that moving objects needed this 'living force' to move and he developed a mathematical formula to calculate it. He thought that *vis viva* could not be lost or destroyed.

Antoine Lavoisier (1743–1794) had explained heat in terms of the 'caloric theory', which suggested that heat consisted of a fluid called caloric which could be transferred from one body to another to warm it. Count Rumford (1753–1814) proposed a different theory. He observed that when cannons were being bored, the metal became hot and he suggested that mechanical *vis viva* was converted to heat *vis viva.* Rumford's views were not accepted for a number of years. Thomas Young (1773–1829), a British physician and physicist, introduced the term 'energy' instead of *vis viva.*

Throughout the nineteenth century, scientists continued to develop their understanding of the nature of **energy**. James Joule (1818–1889), who gave his name to the unit of energy, suggested that there was a relationship between electricity, heat and mechanical work. He thought the energy needed to do work was contained in **molecules**. Lord Kelvin (1824–1907), together with William Rankine (1820–1872), developed the first two laws of **thermodynamics**. In Greek, *thermo* means heat and *dynamics* means power. These laws state that energy cannot be created or destroyed and that it is converted from one form to another.

Understanding energy

Technology enables us to use energy purposefully

Throughout history people have exploited energy through the use of technology. They have used the heat and light energy that the Sun has always provided. Once people had learnt how to make fires with wood, they had an energy source that enabled them to heat and light their homes and to cook. Some 5,000 years ago, the ancient Egyptians harnessed energy from the wind to make their sailing boats travel faster, and they may have even used kites to help lift the heavy stones they used to make their temples and pyramids. The ancient Greeks built their homes to take advantage of the natural light and heat from the Sun. Hot water from natural **geothermal** springs was used by ancient Romans for bathing, and at the same period the Chinese burnt oil in lamps to heat and light their homes. The Persians built the first windmills which were used to grind grain, and in the Middle Ages windmills and watermills were used widely in Europe to grind corn and to pump water.

What is energy?

Energy can be defined as the ability to do work or to make things happen. We cannot see energy, but whenever something moves, heats or cools, energy is involved. When sound or light is produced, energy is involved. In everyday language, the word 'energy' is often applied only to living things and relates to enthusiasm or motivation – for example, 'The politician spoke with energy' or 'I haven't got the energy to go to the gym'. In science, the word is used differently and it is not confined to living things. Matter is the 'stuff' that everything is made of, and all matter has energy in the bonds between the particles in its atoms and between atoms and molecules. The unit of energy is the joule.

All the energy which we use today was released billions of years ago as the result of the 'Big Bang', which is considered to be the origin of our universe. Since then, no energy has been created and none has been destroyed. All the energy that existed at that time still exists.

Much of the energy we use on Earth comes directly or indirectly from the Sun. Plants store the Sun's energy by the process of **photosynthesis**. Animals, including ourselves, gain access to this energy by eating plants or eating other animals which have eaten plants. We can then make use of the Sun's energy to move, make sounds and to heat our bodies. **Fossil fuels** such as coal and oil are made from dead plants and animals and provide us with other ways to harness the Sun's energy. We use machines to transfer the energy stored in fossil fuels into other types of energy, which we can use to do work and make things happen. For example, we manufacture petrol from oil and use it to run our cars and other vehicles. We burn fossil fuels in power stations to produce electricity and burn natural gas in our homes to keep us warm and cook our food.

Toys such as a jack-in-the-box also indirectly depend on energy from the Sun to work. To push 'jack' into the box we need to do some work in order to compress the spring. The energy to do this work comes from the energy stored in our food – the Sun's energy. This energy is then stored in the compressed spring. When the box is opened, the spring releases and it pushes 'jack' upwards, creating movement. As a result, the stored energy is transferred into movement or kinetic energy of the puppet.

Jack-in-the-box.
Source: iStock

Something to think about

Can other sources of energy be traced back to the Sun? Does wind get its energy from the Sun?

Types of energy

It can be useful to categorise energy as **kinetic (movement) energy** and **potential (stored) energy**. Potential energy is stored energy which can be transferred into other forms of energy when the conditions are appropriate. The chemical energy in petrol is stored until the car is started. It is then transferred by the engine into kinetic energy and sound energy. A boulder balanced at the top of a hill has potential energy because of its position. When it is released, the force of gravity causes it to move downhill and its stored energy is transferred into movement energy.

Although energy is described as having different forms, it can be helpful to think of it as the same energy behaving differently. For example, in an electric circuit, the chemical energy in the battery is transferred to electrical energy in the circuit. This is the same energy behaving in two different ways.

Table 12.1 Types of energy

Kinetic or movement energy	Potential or stored energy
Moving objects have **kinetic energy (KE)** which is dependent on their mass and their speed. The larger the mass and the greater the speed, the more KE they have.	**Elastic or spring energy** is energy stored because of tension or strain forces acting on an object. For example, in a compressed or stretched spring or a stretched rubber band.
Heat energy is internal energy associated with the movement of atoms and molecules in matter.	**Chemical energy** is energy stored in the spring-like bonds between atoms and molecules, which hold the particles together.
Electrical energy is associated with the movement of charged particles in an electrical circuit.	**Gravitational energy** is associated with the position of an object: the higher above the ground it has been raised, the more energy is stored.
Light energy is an example of electromagnetic energy that travels in waves.	
Sound energy is associated with the movement of vibrating objects.	

Something to think about

Think about a woman and the multiple roles she has in her life. She might be a daughter, a mother, a wife, a voter, a washer of kitchen floors or a university professor. In all roles she is the same woman but in each role she takes part in different types of activities; she behaves differently and her impact is seen differently. Can you make useful comparisons with energy?

The transfer of energy can make things happen

When energy is transferred, something happens. In a candle, chemical energy is stored in the wax but it is of no practical use until the candle is lit and the wax starts to melt and burn. Burning results in the chemical energy in the wax being transferred to heat energy and light energy, which can be useful.

Here are two everyday examples of how energy transfers make things happen:

1. A battery-operated toy works when the chemical energy stored in the battery is transferred into electrical energy and then into movement and sound energy.

2. A cyclist needs to do work to turn the bicycle's pedals and to make it move. The energy to do the work comes from the cyclist's food and it is transferred into movement energy.

In both cases, energy has been transferred and something has happened.

Something to think about

A lottery winner wins a large amount of money. It can be saved under the mattress until the winner is ready to spend it and at this point a lot of things can happen. Can you make useful comparisons with the transfer of energy?

Can energy be used up?

Energy cannot be created or destroyed, but it can be transferred in ways that mean that some of it is no longer useful. Consider a small room being heated by a coal fire; the room is warm and cosy. If the door to the hall is opened, the fire is now heating a much larger area of the house and the room becomes less warm. If we open the windows and the fire is heating air outside the house, the room is even less warm. The heat has not disappeared, but it is now so spread out it is no longer useful. The energy has been dissipated.

Whenever there are transfers of energy, some of the transfers will not be useful. When mowing the lawn, unwanted sound energy will spread into the surrounding air and may well irritate the neighbours. Unwanted heat energy that results from the friction of moving parts in the mower will transfer to air particles and warm them slightly. Neither of these transfers is useful.

Something to think about

Imagine that you are using an electrical vacuum cleaner. Think of all the energy transfers that are taking place. Which of these are useful transfers? Which transfers are not useful?

Energy sources

What is the difference between energy and energy sources?

The news media sometimes suggest that we are running out of energy when, in fact, we are running out of sources of energy. Energy cannot be created or destroyed. Some energy sources, on the other hand, can be destroyed. Fuels are sources of energy and fossil fuels are examples of **non-renewable energy** sources. There are concerns that supplies of fuels are running out. Before this happens, it is important that we find alternative means of heating and lighting houses and alternative energy sources for running our cars.

Which energy sources are non-renewable?

Much of the energy we use comes from the fossil fuels: coal, oil and natural gas. Millions of years ago, plants used light energy from the Sun to make their **biomass** through the process of photosynthesis (see Chapter 13). When plants died, many decayed, but some did not. Instead, they were preserved in shallow marshes and lagoons. Similarly, when tiny marine plants and animals died, their remains were covered by sediments and preserved on the seabed. The energy from the sunlight was locked up in the cells of these plants and animals. Over hundreds of millions of years, as a result of heat and pressure, the plant remains were fossilised and converted to coal, and the animal remains were fossilised and converted to oil and gas – hence the term 'fossil fuels'.

Fossil fuels are burnt to generate electricity and to heat our buildings. Oil is also used to make fuels for vehicles and to make plastics and other chemicals. Although fossil fuels took millions of years to create, they can be burnt in a matter of minutes. They are still a major source of energy but the supply is running out.

Problems with fossil fuels

There are relatively small amounts of carbon dioxide in the atmosphere. However, when fossil fuels are burnt, carbon which has been locked inside the fuels for millions of years is released in the form of carbon dioxide, causing the amount of this gas in the atmosphere to increase significantly. Carbon dioxide is described as a **greenhouse gas** because it can absorb large amounts of heat and it acts like a blanket surrounding the Earth. Although the Sun's rays are able to pass through it to reach the Earth, the heat becomes trapped. This is thought to be one of the causes of excessive **global warming** and the resultant changes in our climate.

The Earth has always benefited from the 'greenhouse effect' of its atmosphere and this is what has created the conditions for life on the planet. It is *excessive* global warming due to high concentrations of gases such as carbon dioxide that is causing problems for life on Earth.

The need to turn to renewable energy sources

As the Earth's fossil fuels continue to be depleted, much attention is being given to using **nuclear energy** and **renewable energy** sources for generating electricity, for heating and for producing fuels. Using renewable energy sources may reduce the amount of greenhouse gases being released into the atmosphere. Governments have met in a series of World Summits to discuss ways of reducing consumption of energy sources and of making more use of renewable energy sources. Renewable energy sources have two major advantages over fossil fuels: they cannot be used up and most do not produce greenhouse gases. At the moment, the technology associated with some of these energy sources is expensive and this can be a barrier to their more widespread use.

What are the advantages of solar energy?

Solar energy provides both heat and light energy to the Earth. It can be used to heat water in pipes and tanks directly. It can shine directly into houses to heat them. This is called passive heating. Light energy from the sun can be transferred to electricity in a **photovoltaic cell**. These cells have

Greenhouse effect: human activity adds to greenhouse gases such as carbon dioxide, methane and water vapour, which trap the Sun's energy.
Source: iStock

been available for many years and we are familiar with their use as an alternative to batteries in, for example, calculators. Groups of photovoltaic cells – solar panels – have been used on houses to supply domestic electricity since the middle of the twentieth century, but until now these panels have been very expensive and their use has been limited. As the technology improves, it is hoped that solar panels will become more economically viable.

Solar energy in action

It is easy to understand the potential of using solar energy to produce electricity in hot countries but even in temperate countries light energy can be useful. Builders of a new eco housing development in England are installing photovoltaic tiles (solar panels) on the roofs of the houses. As well as providing electricity to individual households, excess electricity can be sold to the National Grid. Some houses are also able to heat their water by installing solar water heaters on roofs. In addition to this, all houses have thick layers of insulation to minimise heat loss, thus reducing the consumption of electricity and gas for heating the house.

Recent research has led to the production of very thin photovoltaic tiles, which can be manufactured at half the cost of traditional units. It is hoped that in future this will make the installation of such tiles economically possible for many more people.

The rooftops of energy-saving houses – two sides of the same rooftop: the green roof slows down the run-off of rain water and reduces the potential for localised flooding. The solar water heaters at the top of the roof provide some of the hot water for the houses, and the photovoltaic tiles and wind turbine generate electricity.
Source: Linda Nicholls

Is wind energy a feasible option?

When the Sun heats the atmosphere, air moves and creates winds. Wind turbines use the energy in the wind to generate electricity. The electricity they generate is described as 'clean' because no fossil fuels were burnt in the process. Although they provide clean energy, wind farms are controversial. They may spoil the aesthetic appeal of some of the most beautiful areas of the country; local residents may find them noisy. The current state of technology means that wind turbines can only produce a fraction of the electricity we require.

Wind energy in action

Dabancheng is a six-mile-wide plain between the mountains in Xinjiang Province in eastern China. The plain acts like a natural tunnel for the winds that blow between the mountains. It used to be part of the Silk Road, but now 118 giant wind turbines, which generate electricity for the provincial capital, Urumqi, are sited there. China is a rapidly growing industrial economy and the emissions from its factories and power stations are adding significantly to atmospheric pollution. At the same time, some of China's oilfields are starting to become unproductive and coal prices are increasing. There is an urgent need to find alternative energy sources for its population of a thousand million people. Wind energy is becoming increasingly important. The country's wind generation capacity has increased rapidly and more large wind farms are planned.

A wind farm: as the wind causes the blades to rotate, they turn a turbine, which generates electricity.
Source: iStock

Is water the answer to the problem?

The energy in moving water can be exploited in a number of ways.

● *Hydroelectricity*
The energy from falling water has been used for hundreds of years to turn waterwheels to operate machines such as flour mills. Hydroelectric dams enable people to generate electricity on a large scale. Water is held back by the dam and when it is released into sloping pipes it turns a turbine which generates electricity. Most of Norway's electricity is generated by hydroelectric means.

● *Tidal energy*
Tidal movement is created by the gravitational pull of the Moon on the oceans. Tidal energy is associated with the rise and fall of the water. Using turbines, the movement energy of the tide can be transferred into electrical energy. This form of energy is little used at the moment because of the cost and the need for a high tidal movement.

The Severn Estuary, situated between south Wales and the West Country, has the second-highest tidal rise and fall in the world and is considered to be a possible site for turbines to generate electricity.

A hydroelectric dam: as the falling water rushes through the pipe, the blades of the turbine rotate and this generates electricity.
Source: iStock

Supporters of the project say that using tidal energy produces no greenhouse gases, that it is a clean source of energy and it could provide about five per cent of the electricity used in the UK. However, there are concerns about the environmental impact of such a project. Conservationists point out that the barrage, which will disrupt the tidal flow, will lead to the disappearance of mudflats and saltwater marshes. This will mean a loss of habitat for numerous plants and animals, including the tens of thousands of wading birds that feed on the invertebrates in the estuary mudflats.

- *Wave energy*

   Waves are formed when wind passes over the seas. The movement energy of the waves can be used to generate electricity but, as with other alternative energy sources, it can be expensive. However, recent advances in technology have resulted in the development of the 'anaconda' generator, a cheap and robust wave-power machine. This device is a long snake-like tube made of fabric and rubber, which is filled with water and sealed at both ends. It is tethered to the seabed and sits under the surface of the water, facing the waves head-on. The motion of waves causes the water in the tube to travel in pulses towards its tail where there is a turbine. The electricity generated by the movement of the turbine is fed to shore via a cable (Farley and Rainey, 2006).

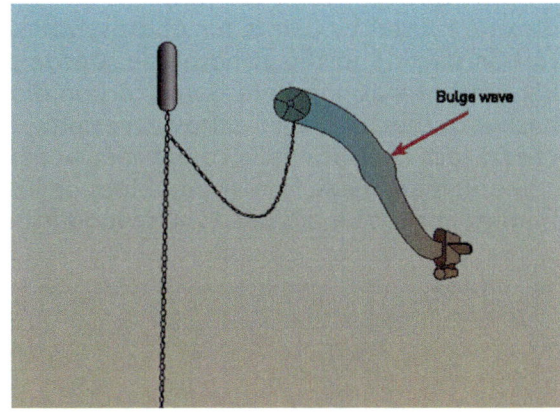

An 'anaconda' generator – a simulation of the anaconda: the bulge wave moves towards the tail and turns a turbine. It is expected that, when fully developed, the 'snake' will be 200m long with a diameter of 7m. It will be tethered 40–100m under the sea.

How can we use geothermal energy?

Geothermal (from the Greek *geo* = earth; thermal = heat) energy comes from the Earth itself. The temperature of the Earth's core is thousands of degrees Celsius and, throughout the year, the top three metres of the Earth's crust have a temperature between 10 and 16 degrees Celsius. This heat energy can be harnessed to provide domestic heating.

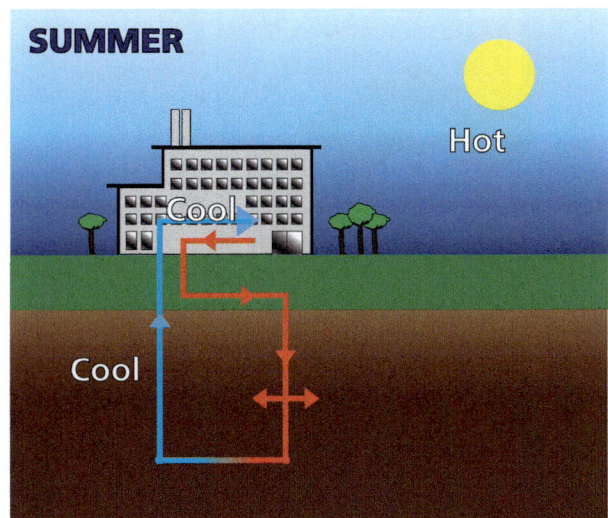
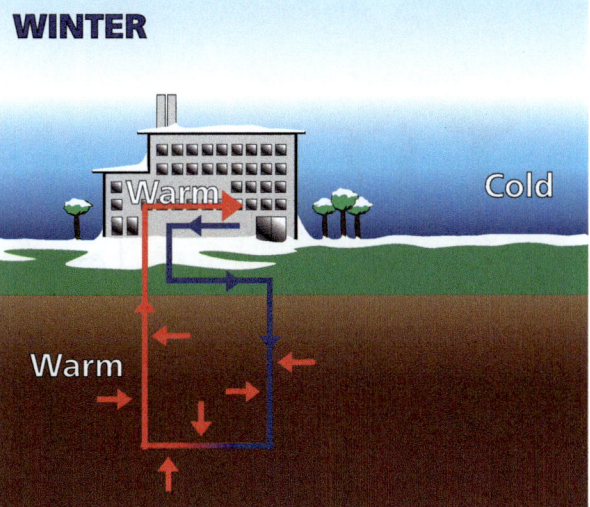

A geothermal pump.

Geothermal pumps work in a similar way to the cooling system in a refrigerator, transferring heat from one area to another. Fluid is pumped through pipes, which run either horizontally or vertically down into the ground. The fluid absorbs the ground's heat and transfers it to the house where it is concentrated by a special pump and used to provide underfloor heating or to heat the domestic water supply. In the summer, when the ground is cooler than the buildings, the pump transfers heat from the house back to the ground, cooling the house as it does so.

The debate about using biofuels

When considering the debate about the use of **biofuels**, it may be helpful to think about the carbon cycle.

Some carbon is removed from the air for relatively short periods of time. For example, carbon dioxide is used by plants for photosynthesis, but when plants and animals respire they return carbon dioxide to the atmosphere. **Decomposers** release carbon from dead plants and animals back into the atmosphere. Some carbon dioxide is absorbed by the seas but this can be released back into the atmosphere. However, some carbon that has been removed from the atmosphere can be locked up for millions of years, as in the case of fossil fuels.

Biofuels are made from living things or, in the case of biogas, from animal waste products; wood is an example of a biofuel. When wood is burnt, it provides heat and light energy and it releases

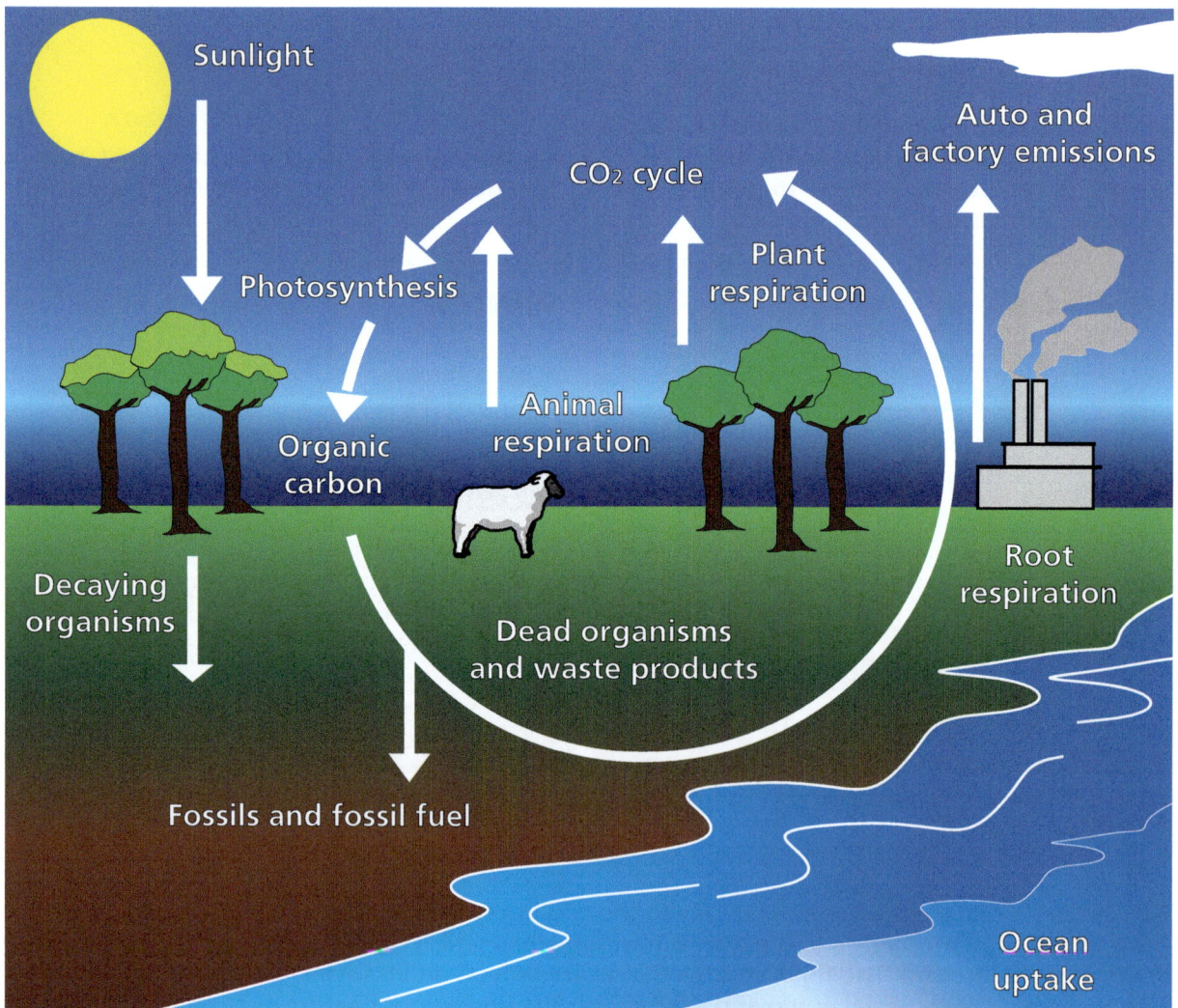

The carbon cycle: some carbon is locked in rocks and fossil fuels for millions of years.

carbon dioxide, a greenhouse gas, into the atmosphere. Burning biofuels is considered by some to be more environmentally friendly than burning fossil fuels, because when fossil fuels are burnt the carbon that was removed from the atmosphere millions of years ago and 'locked' underground in the form of oil, coal and gas is released back into the atmosphere at a much faster rate than it can be removed. This is adding to the total amount of carbon dioxide in the atmosphere. When trees are burnt, they release the amount of carbon dioxide that they have taken from the atmosphere during their growing phase (see Chapter 13). If wood fuels come from a sustainable source, where replanting matches harvesting, there should not be a net increase in carbon dioxide in the atmosphere (Centre for Alternative Technology). Opponents would argue that large areas of woodland would be needed to provide this extra wood and, if they are not managed in a sustainable way, there will be a net increase in atmospheric carbon dioxide. There is also concern that other gases released when wood is burnt can pollute the atmosphere and contribute to global warming.

Plants such as corn and sugar cane are being used to manufacture bio-ethanol and bio-diesel, which are being used as alternatives to petrol and diesel. As with wood, the emission of carbon dioxide from these fuels is less than from fossil fuels, but there are hidden costs. Fuel is needed to produce the fertilisers used on the fields and for the machinery used in farming and processing the crops. This may make biofuels just as polluting as petrol and diesel. In addition to this, people still need to be fed and, to find the extra land needed to grow crops for biofuels, some governments are considering cutting down forests or clearing ancient peat-based land, which contains stored carbon dioxide. This would result in a significant increase in the level of atmospheric carbon dioxide.

To produce biofuels, farmers are planting large areas of land with one type of crop. This is known as monoculture. This results in reduction of habitats for animals and native plants, leading to an overall reduction in biodiversity.

Nuclear energy is a controversial option

Nuclear energy can make a significant contribution to meeting people's needs for energy but its use is controversial. A full discussion is outside the scope of this chapter but, briefly, the benefit of this type of energy is that it does not result in the release of greenhouse gases. Increasing provision of nuclear energy will enable governments to meet their targets for fighting global warming. Opponents argue that nuclear plants are hugely expensive to build. There are extreme risks to health because of the possibility of accidental leakage of radioactive particles, and there is also the possible danger of attack by terrorists who want nuclear material to make weapons. Added to this, nuclear waste remains radioactive for many years and safe storage is a very expensive long-term problem.

Global dimensions: Using solar energy to help people and the planet

Energy from the sun is a free and abundant resource and, in many cases, can be used simply and efficiently without the need to release energy by burning scarce trees, despoiling landscapes by extracting fossil fuels or polluting the environment. Making clever use of simple technologies can free isolated or rural communities from a reliance on wood as a prime source of cooking, heating and lighting. For example, in many rural communities in the developing world, cooking is done over wood or charcoal fires. Women and girls usually have to collect the wood and make or buy charcoal. The use of solar ovens can significantly reduce the work of women and also help to conserve trees in the area.

Among other things, lack of electricity means lack of refrigeration, which can make storage of fresh food in hot countries particularly problematic. Food is wasted and poor food safety can result in health problems. As an alternative, 'two-pot' fridges have been developed, which need no electricity. Damp sand is placed between two porous pots, one of which sits inside the other and a damp towel is placed over the pots. As the water evaporates from the sand and the towel, the temperature of the inner pot drops. Stored in these pots, food will keep for longer and this in turn leads to health and other social benefits.

Two-pot refrigerators:

http://practicalaction.org/docs/agroprocessing/FC29_34.pdf

www.youtube.com/watch?v=ZNKifJHqScc&feature=related www.solarcookers.org/basics/how.html

Parabolic solar power stations:

www.youtube.com/watch?v=klPT4ktnXYc

www.nrel.gov/docs/fy03osti/34186.pdf

Something to think about

Governments need policies relating to the provision of energy. How should they be providing electrical and heat energy for domestic and industrial use? Should they introduce transport policies to reduce the amount of oil we are using? Can renewable energy sources provide what we need? Do the benefits of using renewable energy sources outweigh the disadvantages? What about nuclear energy? Do we need to alter our behaviour in the way we use our resources, including reducing the amount of energy we use in our homes and the amount we travel?

Summary

Energy can be explained as the ability to make things happen and it can be described in different ways. Energy becomes useful to humans when it is changed from one form to another. Energy cannot be created or destroyed but it can become dissipated and less useful to us. Most energy transfers can be traced back to the Sun, one of our main sources of energy.

Sources of energy can be classified into two main groups. Non-renewable sources of energy, such as oil, coal and gas, are used to provide heat, electricity and to power vehicles. When they are burnt, carbon which has been locked up in them for millions of years is released into the atmosphere as carbon dioxide at a faster rate than it can be removed. This causes a net increase in the amount of atmospheric carbon dioxide and this is part of the cause of excessive global warming. Renewable sources of energy are used to provide heat, electricity and to power vehicles. Solar energy, wind energy and water energy are described as clean sources of energy because they release no carbon dioxide into the atmosphere. Biofuels release carbon dioxide but they only return to the atmosphere the amount of carbon dioxide they absorbed during photosynthesis. This may then be used by other plants in the process of photosynthesis. At the moment, alternative energy sources are expensive and cannot provide the energy we need to maintain our present way of life.

The future well-being of our planet will be affected by decisions made by governments around the world and the lifestyle choices made by the people.

Part 2: Ideas for practice

Topic: Solving Zak's flooding problem

Age group: 5–9 years

Introduction

This topic provides opportunities for children to use enquiry skills to solve a problem. As part of the problem-solving they will explore the properties of various materials and discover how the shape of an object affects its ability to float. In the application stage children design a house boat, and have the option to make a working model.

Scientific view

Some objects sink and others float depending on the material from which they are made and on their shape. Boats are objects which are designed to float.

Working scientifically

In these activities children will:

- ask questions which can be answered through scientific enquiry;
- perform simple tests;
- identify and classify common materials;
- make simple comparisons;
- use first-hand experience to answer questions;
- communicate their findings to an audience.

Exploration stage

Children's talk involves trying out their own ideas

Setting the scene

Puppets can be used to develop contexts which stimulate children's interest and promote scientific ways of working. In our story, the puppet Zak is an alien from a faraway planet. Zak has a problem and he has been told that the children may be able to help him. Recently, the climate has changed on Zak's planet and now it is windy and rainy nearly every day. Everywhere is flooded, and people can only live in houses built on the top of hills. Zak has promised his people that he will come to Earth and find out how to build homes which can float on water. Zak's people are only small, so the homes don't need to be very big.

Zak inside his spaceship.
Source: Linda Nicholls

Puzzle

What materials can Zak use to build floating homes?

Storytelling

Children discuss the puzzle and make suggestions about suitable materials based on their experiences. Listen to their stories and find out what they know about boats.

Scientific enquiries

Which materials float best?
Children test different materials to find out which float and which sink. Use materials including wood, metal, rock, rubber, polystyrene and plastic. They can also decide which materials float best.

1.   Does the shape of an object help it float?

     Children test different shaped objects to see if they float. Amongst other things, they can test plastic bottles, cups and trays, metal tins, trays and pans, rubber balloons which are deflated and inflated, and cardboard boxes.

2.   Does changing the shape of a material help it float?

     Provide children with aluminum foil, Plasticine or play dough and paper, which can be folded into different shapes. Children produce a variety of 3-D shapes out of each material and test whether they float.

Children use demonstrations, drawings and photographs to communicate the results of their enquiries to Zak. They should explain to Zak how their tests are scientific and why he can trust the results. Discuss children's reasoning.

Formative assessment

Provide opportunities for children to voice what they have learnt in the exploratory stage. Use evidence from their responses to the puzzle and other activities to assess differences between children's ideas and the scientific view. Plan how you will use the re-describing stage to help the children address their *learning needs*. You may need to modify the activities depending on the shared and individual needs of your children.

Re-describing stage

Children's talk involves making sense of scientific ideas

Teacher-led discussion

Summarize children's results and explain to Zak that boats may be a solution to his problem. People can live in them, and they float on water. Small boats are traditionally made of wood but can be made of a wide range of materials. Show Zak and the children video clips and photographs of various types of boats. Children discuss which type of material would be best for Zak to use. What types of materials does he have on his planet?

Storytelling

Children use their imaginations to picture the planet where Zak comes from. Children tell stories in words and pictures of what it might be like on Zak's planet and what materials may be available to make house boats. They can also describe how he travelled all the way to Earth. Create a display which tells Zak's story.

Application stage

Children's talk involves trying out scientific ideas

Design and make a boat for Zak

Children use videos and pictures of boats designed for people to live on. They could include cruise boats, yachts, canal boats and house boats from around the world. Which do they think Zak would like best? Groups choose a design and use it to draw a picture of a house boat, which Zak could take back to his people. They should also supply a list of materials Zak will need to make the boat. Children can make simple models of the boat, which Zak can photograph. As the product of their work, children present a folio of designs including drawings and photographs which Zak can take home with him. Children's work can be added to Zak's display, showing how they helped solve his problem. Use the children's drawings and models to assess their progress. Address outstanding *learning needs* and explore what else Zak would like to know!

The project can be extended to include the design of a powered boat. Depending on the age and abilities of the children, they can design and make a working model of a wind-powered boat or a model of a paddle boat powered by an elastic band. Older children could use an electric motor to drive a paddle wheel. Choose materials, tools and glues appropriate to the maturity, experience and any special needs of the children. Follow ASE guidance (*Be safe!* 2011) for making things.

Information and teaching resources

Useful websites:

- TES. KS1/2 Materials and Forces: Build and Test a Sail Boat. *www.tes.com/teaching-resource/ks1-2-materials-and-forces-build-and-test-a-sailboat-6307338*
- Things That Go TV! (2013). Canal Boats. *www.youtube.com/watch?v=UbRBF9sH_tA*
- Things That Go TV! (2014). Cruise Ship. *www.youtube.com/watch?v=_FbYuYPhQjw*

Topic: Climate change

Age group: 9–11 years

Introduction

Activities in this topic focus children's attention on the possible reasons for climate change. In the exploration stage they explore the difference between climate and weather, and look for evidence that climate change is happening. In the application stage children look at alternative forms of energy in order to reduce carbon dioxide emissions, and design and make model flood-proof homes to help solve flooding problems.

Scientific view

Our world is getting warmer. Records show that over the last 100 years the average global surface temperature has risen by about 0.74C, and since 1995 we have experienced 11 of the 12 hottest years ever recorded. According to the Intergovernmental Panel on Climate Change (IPCC), it is "very likely" that the rising level of carbon dioxide in the atmosphere is the cause of climate change. The burning of fossil fuels is the main cause of the increase in levels of carbon dioxide which acts like a blanket around the Earth, slowing down the rate at which it can cool.

Working scientifically

In these activities children will:

- plan scientific enquiries including controlling variables to answer questions;
- make systematic observations and measurements including the use of data-loggings;
- record data and use test results to make predictions;
- use information sources to answer a question;
- communicate their findings to an audience;
- use established scientific knowledge and evidence to support and refute ideas and arguments.

Exploration stage

Children's talk involves trying out their own ideas

Setting the scene

'Floods Caused By Global Warming, Says Minister'

'CLIMATE CHANGE STRONGLY LINKED TO UK FLOODING'

'UK FLOODS AND EXTREME GLOBAL WEATHER LINKED TO CLIMATE CHANGE'

'Scientists Predict Huge Sea Level Rise Even If We Limit Climate Change'

The above headlines appeared in UK newspapers during 2015, which was the warmest year since records began in 1880. Discuss the headlines with the children and *talk together* about global warming.

Puzzle

Is climate change really happening or are we just experiencing natural variations in the weather? What evidence is there for climate change?

Storytelling

Children use information sources to compare different views on climate change. To solve the puzzle, they will need to have a clear understanding about the difference between climate and weather. The big question is whether the extreme weather experienced in the UK in 2015 was an isolated, unpredictable event or part of a long-term global trend? Were people affected by flooding unlucky, or do they and others who live in flood risk areas need to expect it to be a regular problem? Children should use their own words to report their findings in the style of a newspaper article entitled, 'Is climate change really happening?' The article should include descriptions of both the possible causes and predicted effects of climate change.

Talking points: true, false or not sure?

- Global warming is caused by climate change.
- The weather is always changing.
- The climate changes throughout the year.
- The Arctic is cold because it is full of ice.
- Global warming occurs naturally.
- Global warming is a good thing.

Groups' responses to the talking points, and their stories, can be used to create a class debate on climate change. Listen to the arguments and probe children's reasoning. Discuss the difference between climate and weather.

Formative assessment

Provide opportunities for children to voice what they have learnt in the exploratory stage. Use evidence from their responses to the puzzle, talking points and debate to assess differences between children's ideas and the scientific view. Plan how you will use the re-describing stage to help the children address their *learning needs.* You may need to modify the activities depending on the shared and individual needs of the children.

Information and teaching resources

ASE journals:

- Primary Science 126 (Sept/Oct 2013) *Now Here's the Weather Forecast …* by Mathew Richardson.
- Primary Science 132 (March/April 2014) *Learning About the Weather Through an Integrated STEM Approach* by Gokhan Serin.

Re-describing stage

Children's talk involves making sense of scientific ideas

Teacher-led discussion

Recap children's responses to the puzzle and discuss the nature of climate change with the help of video clips. There is a wide range to choose from on the web. Focus on the causes of global warming and discuss how burning fossil fuels contributes to the greenhouse effect.

Scientific enquiries

1. Which cools quickest, land or sea?

   Model the Earth as a big radiator constantly emitting heat, just like the radiators in our houses. At the same time as the Sun warms up the Earth, the Earth emits heat back into the atmosphere. Ask children to imagine what the climate would be like if the Earth stored all the heat it gets from the Sun? Does the land or the sea cool down quickest at night? Children can set up their own fair-test models to answer this question. The safest way of doing it is to put equal masses of salt water and sand at room temperature in the cool section of a fridge. Use identical containers and take temperature readings of the water and sand at regular intervals. Children record and compare the results. Take them out and test which returns to room temperature the quickest. Discuss how differences between land and sea temperatures influence the weather.

2. The greenhouse effect

   Children can model the greenhouse effect using thermometers and small plastic bottles. Avoid using mercury-filled thermometers. Each group of children will need one clear plastic bottle and two thermometers. One of the thermometers should be fixed with its bulb inside the bottle. They seal around the neck of the bottle so that air cannot escape and, on a warm day, lay the bottle on its side in a sunny position. Children use the other thermometer to measure the air temperature. At intervals in the day, they measure the temperature inside the bottle and the corresponding air temperature. With data loggers, children could continue taking readings well into the evening. They record the results graphically and compare the changes in temperature.

Groups interpret the results to help explain the greenhouse effect. They can apply this knowledge to make sense of how polluting the atmosphere with ever more greenhouse gases, such as carbon dioxide, serves to trap the heat emitted by the land and sea by preventing it escaping into space. As the layers of greenhouse gases get denser, less heat escapes and the average temperature of the Earth increases. Children discuss what they have learnt about global warming and what else they would like to find out. They can raise and investigate their own questions. Address outstanding *learning needs* before moving on to the application stage.

Information and teaching resources

BBC Bitesize:

- Global warming and the effect it has on the planet. *www.bbc.co.uk/education/clips/z8jmdmn*
- How environmental issues are impacting on our planet. *www.bbc.co.uk/education/clips/ztwjcwx*
- Why is Antarctica so important in measuring climate change? *www.bbc.co.uk/education/clips/zgq8v4j*

Other websites:

- Vengencefrom1979 (2011). Global Warming: A Video by NASA. *www.youtube.com/watch?v=ab6jV4VBWZE*
- Practical Action (2016). Climate Change. *http://practicalaction.org/climate-change-resources*

Application stage

Children's talk involves trying out scientific ideas

Alternative forms of energy

Using alternative sources of energy can reduce the amount of fossil fuels we need and limit the amount of carbon dioxide deposited in the atmosphere. Children use information sources to explore the viability of alternative forms of energy in your part of the country. They can present their findings and recommendations as part of a class forum entitled, 'What to do about climate change?' Presentations should include PowerPoints with embedded hyperlinks to relevant websites. Recommendations should be based on evidence and reasoned arguments. Groups also design and make working models of their preferred method of power generation such as wind-powered or water-powered turbines or the use of solar cells. The *Practical Action* website has a variety of ideas and useful resources which could be adapted for this project.

Solar toys: solar-powered toys are fitted with small photovoltaic tiles. They work in strong artificial light but they work much more efficiently in sunlight.
Source: Peter Loxley

Beat the Flood

As flooding becomes more predictable due to climate change, vulnerable communities around the world need to take action to protect themselves and their properties. 'Beat the Flood' is a project which can be found on the *Practical Action* website. Set on the fictitious island of Watu, children set to work to help communities to be better prepared for flooding. The challenge is for teams to design and make a model of a home able to withstand the effects of flooding and then test it in 'extreme weather conditions'. This entails standing it in water and blasting it with a hose pipe. Good luck with that one! Full details and teaching resources can be found on the website.

Information and teaching resources

BBC Bitesize:

- Flood defence - embankments in Bangladesh. *www.bbc.co.uk/education/clips/zt9q6sg*
- Rainfall and flooding around the world. *www.bbc.co.uk/education/clips/zkwxn39*
- The causes and effects of flooding in Britain. *www.bbc.co.uk/education/clips/zfnb9j6*

Other websites:

- Practical Action (2016). Beat the Flood Challenge. *http://practicalaction.org/beattheflood*
- Practical Action (2016). Wind Power Challenge. *http://practicalaction.org/wind-power-challenge-stem*

Talk skills and science discussion: Good group work

Ask groups to research information and ideas about energy sources such as wind, waves, water, sunlight, coal, oil and gas.

Children discuss in groups, and then as a whole class, the benefits and problems associated with different methods of producing electrical energy.

Ask children to say what was positive and helpful about their group work – who shared information, asked sensible questions, helped with reading, found resources and so on. Bring out the importance of group work and collaboration. Help children to see that a group can do better than any one individual alone when working cooperatively. Link this to the achievements of groups of scientists.

Additional information and teaching resources

Companion book:

- Loxley, P. (2018). *Practical Ideas for Teaching Primary Science: Inspiring Learning and Enjoyment,* Abingdon: Routledge, Chapter 9: The Material World and Chapter 12: Electricity.

BBC Bitesize:

- BBC (2013). Green Issues in Poland. *www.bbc.co.uk/education/clips/z823r82*
- BBC (2017). Human Impact on the Environment. *www.bbc.co.uk/education/clips/zcb3hv4*

Websites:

- National Geographic (2007). Global Warming 101. *www.youtube.com/watch?v=oJAbATJCugs*
- NASA Goddard (2015). NASA Long-term Global Warming. *www.youtube.com/watch?v=WtPkFBbJLMg*
- The Royal Society (2017). Energy, Environment and Climate. *http://royalsociety.org/policy/climate-change* - up-to-date information from The Royal Society.
- Carbon Detectives. *www.carbondetectives.org.uk/*

- The Children's University of Manchester (2012). Energy and the Environment. *www.children-suniversity.manchester.ac.uk/interactives/science/energy/*

ASE journals:

- Primary Science 129 (Sept/Oct 2013). *Tackling Weather and Climate Change Creatively in Science* by Murray Dale.
- Primary Science 132 (March/April 2014). *Using Science and Much More to Beat the Flood* by Claire Seeley.
- Primary Science Review 100 (Nov/2007). *Harnessing Wind and Sun: Using Energy Wisely* (editorial).

CHAPTER 13
INTERDEPENDENCE

Plants and animals in the same habitat depend on each other for their mutual benefit and survival. Feeding relationships, showing the transfer of energy through the food chain, are one means of exploring this interdependence. This chapter looks at how plants store the Sun's energy as food and how animals are able to access a share of this energy. We will look at feeding relationships as cycles, as well as chains and webs, recognising the essential role of the decomposers in these cycles.

Topics discussed in the chapter

- Historical context
- Growth in green plants
- Feeding relationships
- Decomposers – nature's recyclers

Part 1: Subject knowledge

Historical context

How our understanding of photosynthesis was developed

For many centuries, people accepted Aristotle's (384–322 CE) ideas that plants grew in the soil and were fed by soil. It was not until the middle of the seventeenth century that Jan Baptista van Helmont (1580–1644) questioned and rejected this idea. He grew a willow tree in a pot for five years. At the end of this time, the mass of the tree had increased by 74 kilogrammes but the mass of the soil had hardly changed. He thought the increase in mass was due to the water absorbed by the plant over the years.

Puzzling observations

In about 1754, Charles Bonnet (1720–1793) observed that a brightly lit leaf under water gave off bubbles of gas. Almost twenty years later, Joseph Priestley (1733–1804) carried out a famous experiment, which would now be considered unethical. He put a mouse in a closed jar and timed how long it took before it collapsed. He found that, if he added a green plant to the jar, the mouse survived for much longer. In a similar and somewhat more ethical experiment, he put a lighted candle in a jar with a plant. It burnt for some time before it went out. Twenty-seven days later, Priestley focused light onto the wick of the candle using a magnifying glass and found that it re-ignited. From this he proposed that plants return to the air whatever it was that the breathing animals and the burning candles remove. We now know that this gas is oxygen.

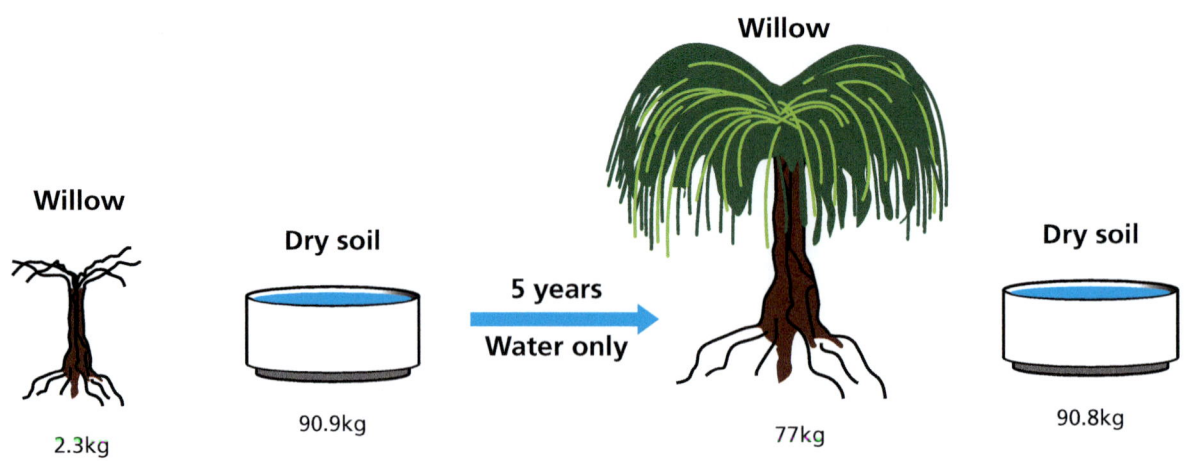

Van Helmont's experiment: Van Helmont had added only water to his plant. There was no change in the weight of the soil after five years, so where had the extra weight of the plant come from?

Puzzle solved

Over the next two centuries, scientists continued to develop their knowledge of this process. They found that **chlorophyll** is needed for a reaction to occur and that this is contained in chloroplasts, found mainly in leaves. Carbon dioxide is absorbed by the leaves and this reacts with water to produce glucose and oxygen. Sunlight is needed for the reaction to occur. The term 'photosynthesis' (light-making) was introduced in 1893 by Charles Barnes.

Major research was carried out by Melvin Calvin (1911–1997) and his team of scientists in the middle of the twentieth century. They discovered that photosynthesis was a two-stage process. In the first stage, the light phase, energy from sunlight is transferred to chlorophyll to fuel the chemical reactions that occur in photosynthesis. In this phase, the hydrogen and oxygen in water that had been absorbed by the plant are split and the oxygen is released into the atmosphere. In the second stage, the dark phase, the hydrogen made available in the light phase combines with carbon dioxide to make **glucose**. The energy from the sunlight is transferred to the chemical bonds in the glucose. They also showed that the 'dark reactions' of photosynthesis do not need light. This sequence of reactions is called the Calvin Cycle. Calvin received the Nobel Prize for this work in 1961.

Growth in green plants

Something to think about

Imagine you are standing near a 500-year-old oak tree. How tall is the tree? How many people do you think you would need to make a circle around the trunk? Remembering the proverb 'Great big oaks from little acorns grow', think about the acorn that this giant oak grew from. What was inside it? Where do you think all the wood in this tree came from?

More about photosynthesis

Green plants produce sugars during the process of photosynthesis. Plants do not take in food from the soil. As Calvin explained, the raw materials for photosynthesis are carbon dioxide, which enters the leaves through pores called stomata on the underside of the leaf, and water, which is absorbed by the roots and travels through xylem tubes to get to the leaves. Plants do take water and minerals such as magnesium and sodium from the soil.

Green plants are green because they contain the pigment chlorophyll, which is stored in chloroplasts. This pigment appears green because, when light falls on it, it absorbs the blue and red light and reflects or scatters green light. In the chloroplasts, carbon dioxide and water are converted to glucose using the energy from the blue and red light. The by-product of photosynthesis is oxygen, which passes out through the pores on the underside of the leaf into the air. This oxygen supports life on Earth.

A person is dwarfed by an oak tree that has been growing for hundreds of years.
Source: Linda Nicholls

Photosynthesis can be described using equations:

carbon dioxide + water + light energy $\longrightarrow$ glucose + oxygen

light energy

$$6CO_2 + 6H_2O \longrightarrow C_6H_{12}O_6 + 6O_2$$

Plants cannot store large amounts of glucose and what is not used immediately is changed into other chemicals. Some is converted into other sugars, which are transported from the leaves to all the other parts of the plant through a set of pipe-like structures called the **phloem**. Some is converted into starch, a complex energy-rich **carbohydrate**, which can be stored in different parts of the plant. Some is converted into **cellulose** and used to make the cell walls of the plants. Glucose is also a building block for making proteins and fats.

This means that most of the 'stuff' that a plant is made of comes from carbon dioxide in the air and water. If van Helmont had realised this in 1650, he would have been able to explain why his tree had gained 74 kilogrammes when there was no change in the mass of the soil.

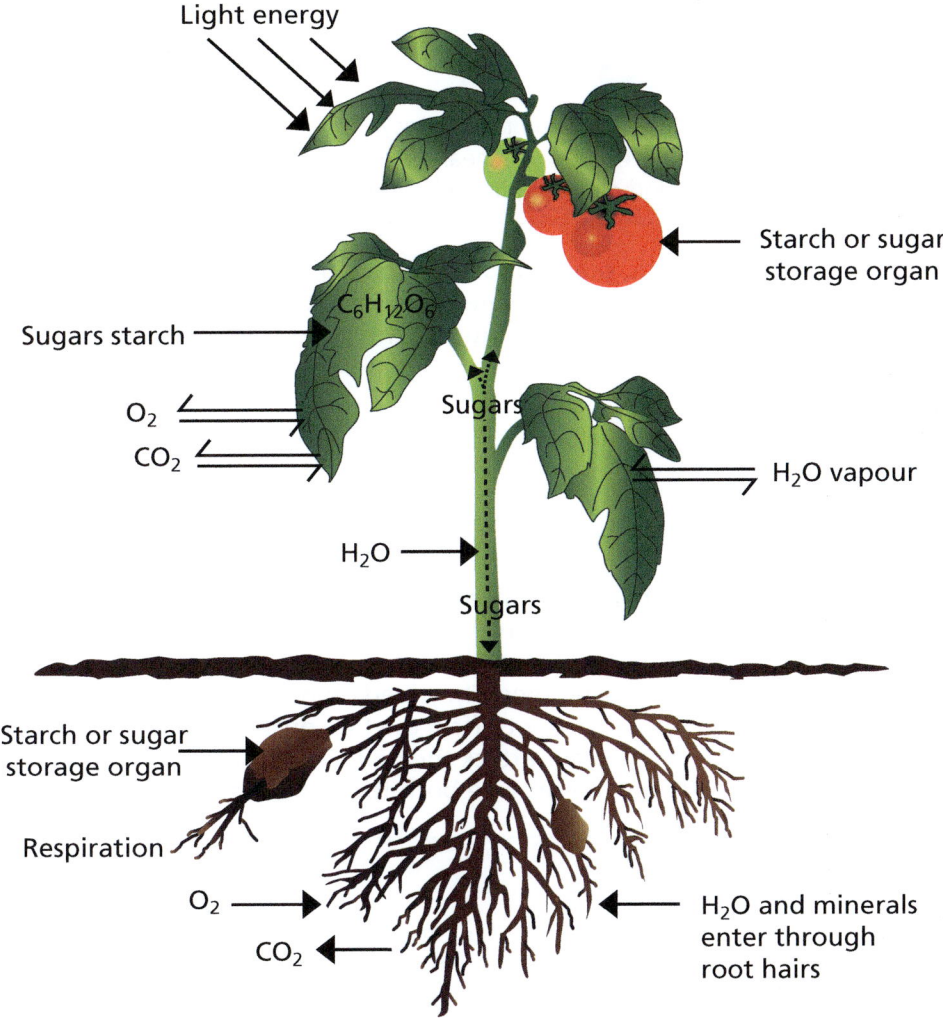

Photosynthesis and the storage of sugar and starches.

Why do we 'feed' plants?

If plants make their own food, why does a Venus flytrap eat insects? And why are there shelves full of 'plant foods' at the garden centre?

The answer to both questions is the same. Flies and 'plant foods' both provide nutrients or minerals. Even though plants make their own food through photosynthesis, they need these nutrients in order to maintain their health. The Venus flytrap is found growing in poor soil conditions which do not provide enough nutrients. It extracts and absorbs the minerals from the fly's body. Soil and plant foods provide plants with minerals such as potassium, magnesium, phosphorus and nitrogen. These minerals can be compared with the minerals and vitamins that animals need to stay healthy. They are not a source of energy but without them we fail to thrive.

Something to think about

Imagine you are standing inside a leaf, observing photosynthesis. It is daytime. Can you describe what is happening? What can you see? Can you hear anything? How is the water getting into the leaf? How are the carbon dioxide and oxygen getting in and out? What will happen overnight?

As well as carrying out photosynthesis, plants also need to respire. They use carbon dioxide during photosynthesis and oxygen during **respiration**. Respiration takes place throughout the day and night and any excess carbon dioxide produced during the process escapes through the stomata (see Chapter 16).

Feeding relationships

Animals and plants depend on each other

Living organisms depend on each other in a number of ways for their survival. Animals help plants by acting as **pollinators** or agents of seed dispersal. Some animals and plants have developed very close relationships and provide mutual benefits for each other. For example, African acacia ants live in the base of swollen thorns on acacia trees. They feed on nectar and special **protein** particles found in the tips of the leaves. In return, the ant offers the tree protection by attacking leaf-eating insects and other **herbivores**. The ants do not attack the pollinators which visit the acacia's flowers, allowing the tree to reproduce. Plants can provide both food and shelter for animals.

Something to think about

Think again about the 500-year-old oak tree. What animals and plants live in its branches, on its trunk and in the ground underneath it? What are they getting from the tree? What is the tree getting from them?

How do animals obtain energy?

Plants make their own food during photosynthesis; they are considered to be self-sufficient. They are **producers** or **autotrophs**. Most of the energy they capture through photosynthesis is used for growing and living, but some of it is stored in the plant and this becomes an important source of energy for animals. Animals are not self-sufficient as they cannot make their own food. They get their energy by eating plants or other animals which have eaten plants. **Food chains** demonstrate how energy is transferred from one organism to another.

Here is an example of a simple food chain:

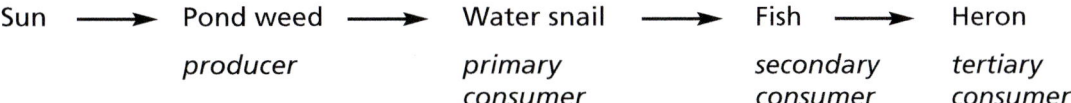

The arrows show the direction of energy flow. The pond weed can photosynthesise and is the producer. The **primary consumer** eats the plant. If an animal eats only plants it is called an herbivore; the water snail is an herbivore. Animals that eat only other animals are **carnivores**. A carnivore can also be described as a **predator**. The animal eaten by the predator is called the **prey**. **Secondary** and **tertiary** consumers are usually carnivores. However, a few animals are **omnivores**: they eat both plants and animals. Bears are omnivores because they eat fruit, berries and fish. Some humans choose to be vegan and eat only food that comes from plants, but most humans are omnivores.

Interdependence – an oak tree ecosystem.
Source: De Agostini Picture Library / Getty Images

Energy transfer in food chain

Animals get their energy from food and they use about 90 per cent of this energy to carry out life processes. Any energy that is not used in this way is stored in their bodies. Similarly, plants use about 90 per cent of the energy from the sugars they make to carry out life processes and they store any unused energy. It is this stored energy that is available to the next animal in the food chain. Let us use the pond food chain as an example. If 100 units of energy from the Sun are used by the pond weed to make sugars, 10 units are available for the snails, 1 unit for the fish and 0.1 unit for the herons. Only a fraction of the original energy stored in a plant is available to the tertiary consumer, the heron.

Draw a food web for a pond which includes the common frog.
Source: iStock

The representation of the food chain in a pond offers a very simple model of how energy is transferred. In reality, most animals feed on a range of plants and other animals. As well as eating pond weed, snails will eat other plants in the pond. As well as eating snails, the fish will eat other small invertebrates and so on. A **food web** can show the complexity of feeding relationships.

There are usually a large number of plants at the base of the food web. The number of primary consumers is usually fewer than the number of plants. The number of secondary consumers is fewer than the number of primary consumers. At the 'top' of the food chain, the organisms are very small in number compared to the base of the food chain. This can be represented by a pyramid of numbers.

Something to think about

Consider again the 500-year-old oak tree. What do you think happens to all the leaves that fall off it every autumn? What do you think happened to the bodies of the birds and squirrels that lived in its branches when they died? Imagine what the countryside would look like if all the leaves that had fallen off the tree in the past 500 years were still lying around it. Where has all the energy gone?

A woodland pyramid: a pyramid showing the decrease in the numbers of organisms at each level in the food chain. This also reflects the amount of energy available at each level of the food chain.

Decomposers – nature's recyclers

Decomposers play a crucial role in food chains and webs and without them **ecosystems** would not function. **Fungi** and bacteria are decomposers. They break down proteins, **starches** and other organic matter in dead and decaying animals and plants by secreting **enzymes** onto them. This decomposes the organic matter into liquids, which the **bacteria** and fungi absorb. A group of animals that have a very similar role are the **detritivores**. Detritivores are more complex organisms than fungi and bacteria. They have mouth parts and they eat small amounts of dead and decaying organisms. Earthworms, slugs and snails are detritivores and, although there are some differences, detritivores can be considered to be decomposers.

Decomposers recycle materials

As well as getting the energy they need by breaking down organic matter, decomposers play a vital role in that they recycle nutrients from the dead and decaying organisms back into the soil, making them available to growing plants. Instead of thinking of food webs and chains as linear, we can think of them as part of a food cycle.

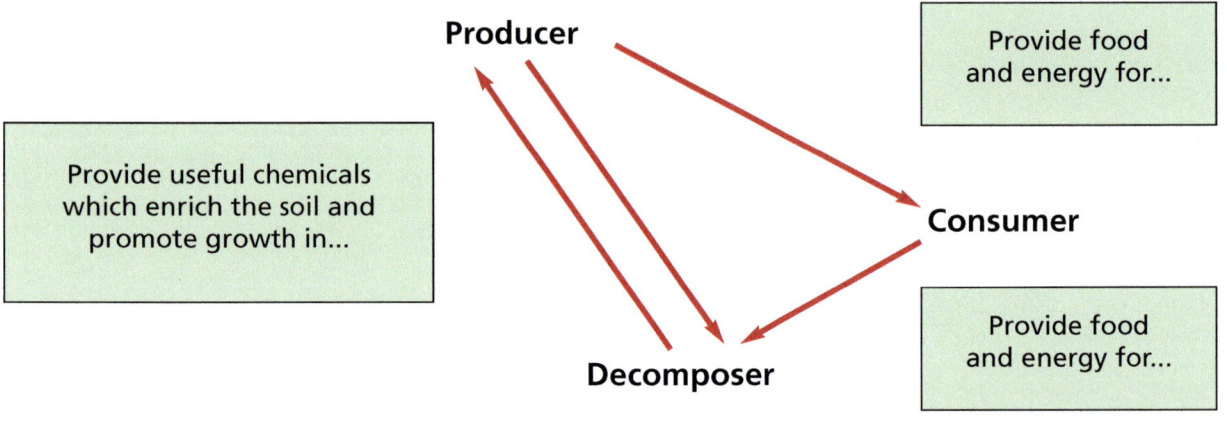

Food cycle.

Magnificent maggots

In the natural world, maggots are often found inside the bodies of dead animals, eating the decaying flesh, breaking down the tissues and returning the minerals to the soil. However, they can also be used to help in a different way. In the First World War, an American doctor, William Baer, found that when soldiers were injured on the battlefield and their wounds became infected with maggots, the wounds often healed much more quickly than those of the soldiers who had been cared for using traditional treatments at the military hospital. When he returned to the United States, Dr Baer carried on using maggots to help heal infected wounds. Antibiotics had not yet been discovered. When antibiotics became available in the 1940s and 1950s, the use of maggots died out because doctors now had a more pleasant way of combating infections.

However, in the last decade, there has been a resurgence of interest in the use of maggots for healing infected wounds such as leg ulcers, which are difficult to treat with conventional treatments. The maggots used for this are specially bred and are only about 2 millimetres long. They clean the wound by eating away the dead tissue. They do this by squirting enzymes onto the tissue. This turns the cells into a liquid which the maggots can then suck up. The maggots are very well adapted to do this because they breathe through tubes that have openings near their bottom end, which means they never have to stop eating to take a breath! The maggots, which do not eat healthy tissue, are left on the wounds for three days, during which time they triple their body size and leave the wounds clean and healthy and able to heal.

Why should children learn about decomposers?

By teaching children about a practical application of decomposers such as composting or using worm farms to break down organic waste, we are helping them to learn about how they can make an active contribution to their community. We can offer them the opportunity to reflect on the way in which society uses its resources and to think about other ways in which their own families can reduce the amount of waste they throw out every week in their wheelie bins or black sacks. Learning about decomposers is therefore very relevant.

Our generation is the first to knowingly degrade the environment at the expense of children now and in the future – a fact that challenges much of our rhetoric about the importance of children in society. Evidence provided by the Sustainable Development Commission suggests that it may not be possible to deliver a socially responsible curriculum unless the environment becomes one of its leading considerations. Sustainable development is not an optional extra for children's policy and services; it is a necessary part of building a society that cares for its children (SDC, 2007).

Earthworms at work in a composter.
Source: Linda Nicholls

Global dimensions: Rabbits in Australia

Whether we consider a small British woodland, the Amazonian rainforest or the harsh environment of the Polar regions, animals and plants occupy their own particular niches in an ecosystem. They are well adapted to the conditions there and they depend on each other for their survival. The introduction of new species to an ecosystem can upset this interdependence and have a dramatic effect on native species.

In the nineteenth century, rabbits were introduced to Australia as a ready source of meat for settlers. The rabbits bred quickly and, as their numbers increased, large tracts of vegetation were destroyed and many plant species became extinct. This loss of vegetation led to soil erosion as the exposed soil was either blown or washed away. The resulting lack of nutrients in the remaining soil hampered the development of new plants. This destruction of habitat has contributed to the reduction in numbers of some native animals that depended on these crops. Rabbits also compete with domestic livestock, especially in periods of drought, for available grazing. The rabbit problem in Australia costs the country hundreds of millions of dollars and extensive control measures have had to be put in place to try to minimise the damage caused.

www.animalcontrol.com.au/rabbit.htm

www.youtube.com/watch?v=pgPhn4tYxJQ

http://webarchive.nationalarchives.gov.uk/20140605100108/

www.naturalengland.org.uk/ourwork/conservation/biodiversity/threats/default.aspxnonna-tivespecies.aspx

http://assets.wwf.org.uk/downloads/web_of_life.pdf

www.rspb.org.uk/ourwork/policy/species/nonnative/index.aspx

Summary

Animals and plants in the same **habitat** depend on each other for their survival. Plants provide food and shelter to animals. Plants are self-sufficient and make their own food. Photosynthesis, which takes place in the green parts of the plant, is the process by which plants make this food. They use the light energy from the Sun to convert carbon dioxide from the air and water into glucose. The Sun's energy is locked up in the glucose and this energy enables the plant to carry out all the life processes. Some of the glucose is converted into other carbohydrates, proteins and fats, which are stored in the plant. These are the building blocks of the plant's cells and are responsible for the increase in mass of the plant.

Animals are not self-sufficient and they have to eat plants or other animals in order to gain the energy they need. Feeding relationships in a habitat can be described using food chains or food webs. When plants and animals die, their remains are broken down by decomposers or detritivores. This returns important chemicals to the soil. These chemicals promote healthy growth in plants.

Part 2: Ideas for practice

Topic: Food chains

Age group: 5–7 years

Introduction

This topic provides opportunities for children to closely observe the behaviour of snails. Habitats and food chains are the key ideas for children to explore. In the application stage, children use their knowledge to make sense of feeding relationships in habitats close to school.

Scientific view

A habitat is the home of a variety of animals and plants which depend on each other to survive. Plants in a habitat provide food and shelter for the animals. Some animals only eat the plants, while others hunt and consume other animals. Plants are an essential part of the food chain in a habitat because without them the animals could not exist.

Working scientifically

In these activities children will:

- try to find answers to questions;
- observe closely using simple equipment;
- perform simple tests;
- identify and classify;
- use their observations and ideas to suggest answers to questions;
- gather and record data to help in answering questions.

Exploration stage

Children's talk involves trying out their own ideas

Setting the scene

Bring in some snails. Let the children observe them closely using magnifiers. Put the snails on sheets of clear Perspex so that children can see them move from underneath. Children can role model how they move. How do they think snails climb up the sides of a container? Focus discussion on their shells, and encourage children to observe the shapes and patterns. Can they work out the purpose of the shell? When handling snails, children should use protective gloves and take due care of the animals. Refer to guidance on keeping animals in the ASE publication *Be safe!*

Show the children Matisse's picture. Ask them to imagine what it could be. Does it remind them of an animal? Establish that it was Matisse's way of picturing a snail. Do they think it looks like a snail? How is it similar? What are the differences?

The Snail by Matisse.
© Succession Henri Matisse / DACS, London 2009.
Photo: Tate Picture Library

Scientific enquiry

Children draw and paint their own pictures of a snail. Encourage them to describe their pictures in words and justify them with regard to what they have observed. Encourage the children to observe the live snails and compare them with their pictures. Explore their knowledge and understanding by discussing how the snail sees where it is going and what it might be looking for. Children can *talk together* about what snails like to eat and where they find their food. Do they know of any animals that eat snails? How does the snail keep safe?

Children can explore which types of food snails prefer by setting up an investigation. Snails can be kept safely in tanks in the classroom (see ASE, *Be safe!* 2011). Foods such as cucumber, apple, soft fruits and different leaves can be put into the tanks and children can observe which the snails prefer. Any snails taken from their natural environment for study should be returned as soon as possible.

Puzzle

Show the children an empty snail shell. Tell them you found it in your garden and were wondering why it was empty. Do they know what might have happened to the snail? The talking points provide some ideas for children to consider.

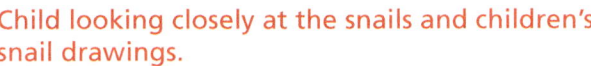

Child looking closely at the snails and children's snail drawings.
Source: Babs Dore and Linda Nicholls

Talking points: true, false or not sure?

- The snail shed its shell because it found a new one.
- The shell was too heavy for the snail.
- The snail shed its shell because it turned into a slug.
- The snail must have been eaten.

Discuss the talking points with the children and probe their thinking. Which animals do they think may have eaten the snail?

Formative assessment

Provide opportunities for children to voice what they have learnt in the exploratory stage. Use evidence from their responses to the puzzle, talking points and other activities to assess differences between children's ideas and the scientific view. Plan how you will use the re-describing stage to help the children address their *learning needs.* You may want to modify the activities depending on the shared and individual needs of the children.

Re-describing stage

Children's talk involves making sense of scientific ideas

Teacher-led discussion

Focus on the idea of food chains. Start by discussing children's responses to the puzzle. Establish the types of animals which may have eaten the snail, possibly a bird.

Discuss the idea of feeding relationships and establish a simple food chain which includes snails:

plants   ⟶   snails   ⟶   thrush

Talk about how animals, directly or indirectly, depend on plants for their food. What would happen to the birds if there were no plants for the snails to eat? Do other animals eat the birds? Extend the food chain:

plants   ⟶   snails   ⟶   thrush   ⟶   fox

Start to introduce some scientific vocabulary. Do snails eat only plants? What do we call animals that eat only plants? What other things do birds eat? What do we call animals that eat both plants and other animals? What other things do foxes eat? What do we call animals that eat only other animals? Explore scientific vocabulary such as *herbivore*, *carnivore* and *omnivore*.

Use video clips to promote discussion and illustrate the scientific ideas. Introduce the term habitat as a place where a variety of plants and animals live. Children can construct food chains from habitats and events depicted by the video clips. Probe children's thinking behind their food chains and address any outstanding *learning needs*.

Information and teaching resources

BBC Bitesize:

- BBC (2017). What Is a Food Chain? *www.bbc.co.uk/guides/z3c2xnb*
- BBC (2007). Food Chains. *www.bbc.co.uk/education/clips/z8hxpv4*
- BBC (2017). What Types of Food Do Animals Eat? *www.bbc.co.uk/education/clips/zqvjxsg*
- BBC (2017). What Is a Woodland Habitat? *www.bbc.co.uk/guides/zc42xnb*
- BBC (2007). The Life Cycle and Inhabitants of an Oak Tree. *www.bbc.co.uk/education/clips/zx3ygk7*

Application stage

Children's talk involves trying out scientific ideas

Outside the classroom

Take the children into the school garden or the local park. When assessing risk, refer to *Be safe!* (2011) for advice concerning good hygiene. Examine leaves for damage and look for small animals which may have caused it. Observe animals that visit flowering plants and look under stones and logs for animals which live there. Talk about what the different animals eat and hypothesize about possible food chains. If you can find a spider's web, ask the children to think about why the spider spins its web. Can they see anything caught in the web? Can they create a food chain that includes a spider? You can sometimes encourage a spider to appear by gently spraying water on the web. This mimics the movement of the web that occurs when a small insect is captured.

Children take photographs of the plants and animals to create food chains back in the classroom. *Talk together* about what would happen if certain animals were missing from the food chain. Listen to children's use of scientific language, assess and address their understanding of the scientific ideas.

Food chain song

Teach the children the traditional song 'There was an old woman who swallowed a fly'. Compare real food chains with this imaginary one. Children could make up their own scientific song based on their knowledge of actual food chains. They could also use musical instruments to add sound effects to their song, such as the sound of a snail sliding across the ground or the sound of a bird swooping down to catch its prey.

Topic: 'Nature's ploughs'

Age group: 7–9 years

Introduction

This topic provides opportunities for children to closely observe the behaviour of earthworms and learn about how they help recycle dead material. They also explore the work Darwin did on earthworms. In the application stage, children discover the purpose of worm farms and experiment with composting as a way of studying invertebrates.

Scientific view

Worms are invertebrates which play an important part in the food cycle. Darwin discovered that worms aerate soil and mix in decomposing materials. Worms also break down rotting materials and mix it into the soil. As a consequence, they improve the soil for plant growth. Invertebrates such as worms which feed on rotting materials are called detritivores, which also include woodlice, millipedes and types of beetles.

Working scientifically

In these activities children will:

- plan scientific enquiries to answer questions;
- make systematic observations and use drawings and diaries to record in a systematic manner;
- use observations to draw conclusions;
- identify scientific evidence from information sources to extend and justify their scientific ideas.

Health and safety issues

Activities in this topic involve studying animals in the classroom, composting and working outside the classroom. Earthworms are a suitable animal to study in the classroom but should be returned as soon as possible to their natural habitat. Assess health and safety issues for all activities in this topic in the ASE publication *Be safe!*

Exploration stage

Children's talk involves trying out their own ideas

Setting the scene

Bring in some earthworms or show video footage of worms. *Talk together* about what the children know about earthworms. Why can they be classified as invertebrates? *Working collaboratively*, children can imagine they are worms living underground. What would they do all day? What would they eat? What eats them? How could they see where they are going? What type of soil would be best to live in? What makes worms come to the surface? Could they live in a sandy desert? What danger would they be in when it rained? How would they keep safe?

Scientific enquiry

Children investigate where earthworms like to live. On an area of lawn or soil, they look out for worm-casts or leaves sticking out of the ground. Listen to children's ideas about how the casts were formed and why the leaves are half-buried in the ground. They can try to induce worms to rise to the surface using a range of strategies. They can try stamping on the surface or watering the surface. Soapy water may irritate worms and make them leave their burrows; they must then be rinsed in fresh water if collected in this way. Children collect worms and set up a wormery in the classroom. Note that worms must be kept out of ultra-violet light and given food and water. Children should wear protective gloves when collecting worms and handling soil. They should also wash their hands thoroughly after this activity.

Puzzle

Charles Darwin was very interested in worms, especially how they produced worm-casts. His work led to worms becoming known as 'Nature's ploughs'. What did he mean by this? Does this name provide a clue to how worm-casts are produced? Children *work collaboratively* to resolve the puzzle. Probe the thinking behind their responses.

Formative assessment

Provide opportunities for children to voice what they have learnt in the exploratory stage. Use evidence from their responses to the puzzle, talking points and other activities to assess differences between children's ideas and the scientific view. Plan how you will use the re-describing stage to help the children address their *learning needs.* You may want to modify the activities depending on the shared and individual needs of the children.

Re-describing stage

Children's talk involves making sense of scientific ideas

Teacher-led discussion

In this stage children can solve the puzzle by working on their understanding of the earthworm as a detritivore. Set the scene by talking about why farmers plough the soil. They use ploughs to break up the soil and to mix organic materials into it. Ploughing breaks up the soil and compost into smaller pieces and mixes them together. It also allows air to mix with the soil and excess water to drain away. Generally, plants grow better in soil which has been ploughed. Show children pictures of farmers ploughing the land.

Scientific enquiry

Children enquire into the way worms 'plough' the soil. They use a combination of information sources and practical enquiry to find a solution to the puzzle. Observe the behaviour of worms in the wormery and note what they are doing in each layer of the soil. Observe what is happening to the organic layer and to any leaves on the surface. Children should keep a diary of their observations with diagrams and explanations for the behaviour of the earthworms.

Teacher-led discussion

Listen to children's accounts of how worms 'plough' the soil. Discuss evidence children recorded in their diaries. Summarize the key ideas, including how earthworms tunnel through the soil, turning it over and creating passages, which help to aerate the soil and provide drainage for rainwater. The roots of plants use these worm tunnels to spread out and find water. Darwin realized that earthworms dragged decaying plant matter underground to eat. In doing so, they also turned the soil over. What was left after

A wormery: children can observe worms moving through different types of soil in a wormery. The wormery should be kept out of sunlight and it should be kept moist.
Source: Tim Ridley / © Dorling Kindersley / Getty Images

digestion was worm-casts, which act as a very rich natural fertiliser for the soil. The earthworm is a detritivore because it helps to break down dead and decaying plants, turning them into compost and returning important minerals to the soil. Without detritivores, plant and animal remains would not be recycled. Use video clips to illustrate how worms help 'plough' the soil and recycle organic material for use by plants.

Storytelling

Charles Darwin's book of 1881, which reported his study of earthworms, was his last scientific book and published just before his death. Children can use information sources to explore his experiments and discover what he found out. In their own words, they can tell the story of the last part of his life. They could also carry out some of his experiments, such as ones to test whether earthworms could hear sound and whether they react to vibrations. Details of these experiments and other ideas can be found on the Darwin Correspondence Project website.

Information and teaching resources

- The Long Wriggly Earthworm. *www.youtube.com/watch?v=opu9QqK6SCk*
- Worms Are Wonderful. *www.youtube.com/watch?v=l-zc_1vjLnl*
- Darwin Correspondence Project (2017). Earthworms. *www.darwinproject.ac.uk/earthworms*
- Darwin Correspondence Project (2017). Earthworms: Experiment. *www.darwinproject.ac.uk/earthworms#experiment*

Application Stage

Children's talk involves trying out scientific ideas

Worm farms

There is currently much interest in the use of worm farms as a means of composting waste food and other plant matter. Some children might have a worm farm at home and they will be able to share what they know. Children can research online how to make a worm farm. They should use red worms or red wigglers which you can order from a commercial worm farm. Setting up a worm farm in the school garden would be an excellent opportunity for children to become actively involved in making a contribution towards waste management. They can also research how worms are used to clean up soil that is contaminated with industrial waste. These activities would provide purposeful cross-curricular links with citizenship and sustainable development.

Children could also set up a normal compost heap which will attract other types of detritivores as well as worms. Remember not to compost dairy, egg or meat products and to use protective gloves when sorting the compost. Refer to *Be safe!* to identify health and safety issues.

At intervals throughout the year children can explore the different detritivores and other invertebrates which inhabit the compost. These may include snails, slugs, earthworms, millipedes, beetles and centipedes. Children use information sources to identify and classify the animals as primary or secondary consumers and create food chains. They can also survey how the populations of the different types of invertebrates change over time. They will need to work out how to estimate the numbers of different creatures in the compost heap/bin. Children can present written scientific reports on how the populations of invertebrates in the compost heap change throughout the year. Discussion of the reports can be used to identify misconceptions and any outstanding *learning needs*.

Waste management

The work could be extended to include different forms of waste management. This could lead to a debate about how to reduce waste and what to do with it in the future.

Information and teaching resources

- Worm Composting Basics. *http://compost.css.cornell.edu/worms/basics.html*
- Invertebrates of the Compost Pile. *http://compost.css.cornell.edu/invertebrates.html*

Talk skills and science discussion: Asking others for ideas

Ask groups to question one another to find out how much everyone in the group knows about specific, or generalised, topics to do with interdependence. They could consider earthworms, woodlice, fungi, animals in a woodland, bacteria, owls, pond life and others.

Ask the group to think of three questions to ask others and to write them down.

Discuss in groups, then as a whole class, topics or information that children have found out from one another. Encourage the children to ask their questions, take responses and chain ideas together.

Emphasise the importance of questioning, and the idea that everyone has something to contribute if they ask with respect. Ask the class to devise a list of questions which can be taken home and used to ask parents or carers about a topic under discussion. Ensure that those who answer the questions are thanked both in class and at home.

Additional information and teaching resources

Companion book:

- Loxley, P. (2018). *Practical Ideas for Teaching Primary Science: Inspiring Learning and Enjoyment,* Abingdon: Routledge, Chapter 2: Growing Plants, Chapter 4: Woodland Habitats and Chapter 7: Decomposers.

BBC Bitesize:

- BBC (2013). Wildlife in Our Gardens. *www.bbc.co.uk/education/clips/zxw8q6f*
- Features of spiders. *www.bbc.co.uk/education/clips/zg7w2hv*

Websites:

- Study.com (2017). Detritivores: Definition and Examples. *http://study.com/academy/lesson/detritivores-definition-examples.html*
- Study.com (2017). What are Detritivores? *http://study.com/academy/lesson/what-are-detrivores-definition-examples-quiz.html*
- Natural History Museum. *www.nhm.ac.uk/nature-online/index.html/*
- The Great Plant Hunt. *www.greatplanthunt.org/*

ASE journal:

- Primary Science Review 101 (Jan/Feb 2008). *More Than Just Mushroom* by Liz Holden.

CHAPTER 14
DIVERSITY

Evidence suggests that life on Earth has existed for about 3.7 billion years. As far as we know, life is unique to our planet. Why is this so? What is life? There is no absolute reason why we should be able to answer these questions, but we are an inquisitive species and like to get to the bottom of things. Scientists have looked at living things in a systematic way and have provided some answers to these big questions. For example, we now know what living things have in common and what conditions are essential to support life. This chapter looks at life on Earth from the chemicals needed to build living things to the great diversity of life forms that colonise almost any habitat available on the planet.

Topics discussed in the chapter

- Historical context
- Characteristics shared by all living things
- Life cycles of plants and animals
- Why there is variation in the same species
- How classification helps make sense of a complex world

Part 1: Subject knowledge

Historical context

Where did life come from? World religions answer this question by designating a god, or gods, who created life. The charming but discredited Theory of Spontaneous Generation says that if you put ears of wheat and an old cloth in a box, after about a month you will miraculously find that the box now contains a nest of mice. People noted that frogs appear from mud and maggots from meat; they reasoned that living things arise from non-living things. However, in the 1800s, French chemist Louis Pasteur showed that bacteria do not come from nowhere but exist around us and are introduced into food, water and ourselves in ways we cannot see.

In 1952, American scientist Stanley Miller demonstrated that if you mix basic chemicals such as water, methane (which contains carbon), ammonia (which contains nitrogen) and hydrogen, warm them and run electric currents through them, you can synthesise amino acids. Amino acids are some of the complex chemicals from which living things are built. More recently, scientists and entrepreneurs have deciphered the genetic code, which can generate and organise living cells. Scientists can now synthesise sequences of the code. This knowledge potentially gives people the capacity to build a life form from non-living materials. We may see such activity as a Doctor Frankenstein project or a benevolent attempt to help those with genetic problems. How the scientific knowledge is applied, who by and what for, is for societies to consider and decide.

Characteristics shared by all living things

What are living things made from?

All known life on Earth is built around carbon and carbon-based compounds. Living things use energy to organise these chemicals into complex molecules from which cells, tissues, organs and entire bodies are built. All living things require an energy source – that is, they feed if they are animals, or absorb sunlight if plants. The ability to make complex materials from basic chemicals enables living things to reproduce and grow.

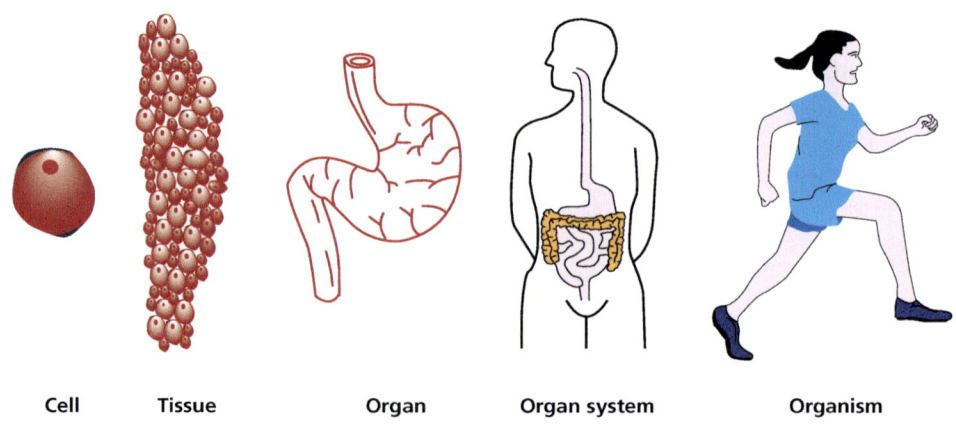

| Cell | Tissue | Organ | Organ system | Organism |

How cells combine to make a human being: the cell is the building block of all organisms.

Cells are the most basic units of living things. Organisms such as bacteria and yeast are made from single cells. In more complex organisms such as humans, cells combine to make tissue, organs and organ systems.

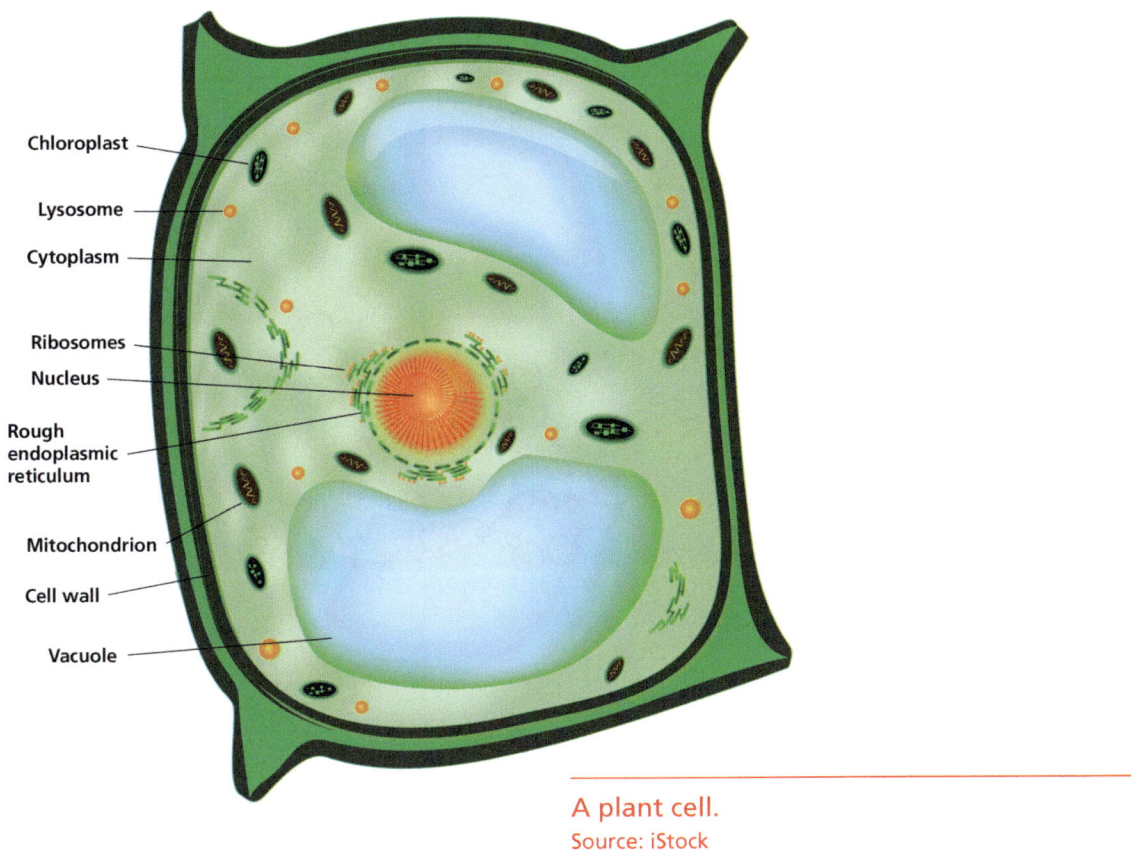

Chloroplast

Lysosome

Cytoplasm

Ribosomes

Nucleus

Rough endoplasmic reticulum

Mitochondrion

Cell wall

Vacuole

A plant cell.
Source: iStock

How does a living organism behave?

We can decide whether something is living or non-living by examining its behaviour. Non-living things have never been alive. Dead things used to be living organisms. The key characteristics of living organisms are movement, **reproduction**, sensitivity, growth, **respiration**, **excretion** and nutrition. Non-living things can share some of the same characteristics but not all them. For example, a car can move, its alarm system can sense vibrations and it excretes waste products such as carbon dioxide and water. However, it cannot grow and reproduce in the way living things do.

Something to think about

Fire moves, grows and throws off sparks to start new fires; it uses up oxygen, makes waste products – carbon dioxide and soot – and is sensitive to water. Does this mean that fire is alive?

Food provides the basic materials to maintain life

Carbon compounds containing hydrogen, oxygen and nitrogen are known as organic chemicals; they are the chemicals of life.

Food that we (and other animals) take in every day provides us with the materials to make the different kinds of organic chemicals our bodies need for energy, growth and repair. For example, starch, found in rice, potatoes, maize and flour, is a long chain of glucose molecules containing carbon, hydrogen and oxygen. The chemical bonds within a glucose molecule contain energy which can be released for use if the bonds are broken. That is what happens in cells during respiration to provide the energy for the processes of life.

Proteins found in milk, fish, meat and eggs are long chains of amino acids. Amino acids always contain nitrogen along with carbon, hydrogen and oxygen. Different amino acids combine to form different proteins. Some proteins act as enzymes, which help reactions to take place in cells.

Glucose unit

A starch molecule is a complex carbohydrate.

Life cycles of plants and animals

Plants

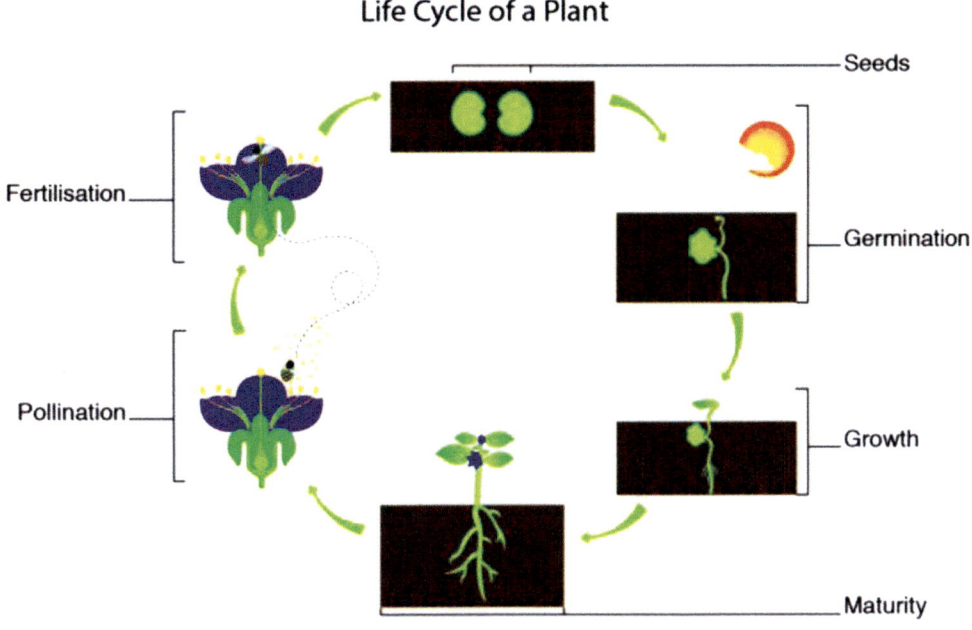

Life cycle of a plant.

A flowering plant is built from organic chemicals. Seeds contain a store of starch to fuel the growth of the embryo plant. When water enters the seed, the process of breaking down starch into sugar begins. Sugar molecules release the energy they contain and this is put to use to build the new root and stem. This early stage of root and stem development is known as **germination**. The developing roots provide more water. Once the first leaves emerge above the soil, the plant can produce its own food through photosynthesis (see Chapter 13). It can make glucose from simple inorganic materials and use this to grow and develop.

Pollination is the process whereby pollen is transferred from an anther, where it is produced, to a stigma, the female part of a flower. If the pollen is transferred to the stigma of the same flower, it is called self-pollination. If it is transferred to the stigma of a different flower of the same species it is called cross-pollination. Pollination happens in two main ways – by wind and by animals, such as insects and birds. These animals are called pollinators. Flowers that rely on pollinators produce nectar and they are usually brightly coloured and scented in order to attract the pollinators (see Chapter 15). Flowers that are wind pollinated do not need to attract pollinators. They are usually small and insignificant. Their anthers and feathery stigmas hang outside the flower. This allows the wind to blow pollen from the anther and puts the stigma in a position to catch the pollen that is floating in the air. When the pollen lands on the stigma a pollen tube goes down the style. When it meets the ovules, fertilization takes place.

After **fertilisation**, a fruit is formed. Inside the fruit is at least one seed which contains a combination of genetic information from two parent plants. This sharing of genetic information creates greater variety, which enables a species to adapt to changes in environmental conditions.

Hazel pollen frequently triggers hay fever and asthma during springtime.
Source: Erik Tham / Corbis Documentary / Getty Images

As the butterfly drinks the nectar, pollen sticks to its body and can be transferred to the next flower it lands on.
Source: Linda Nicholls

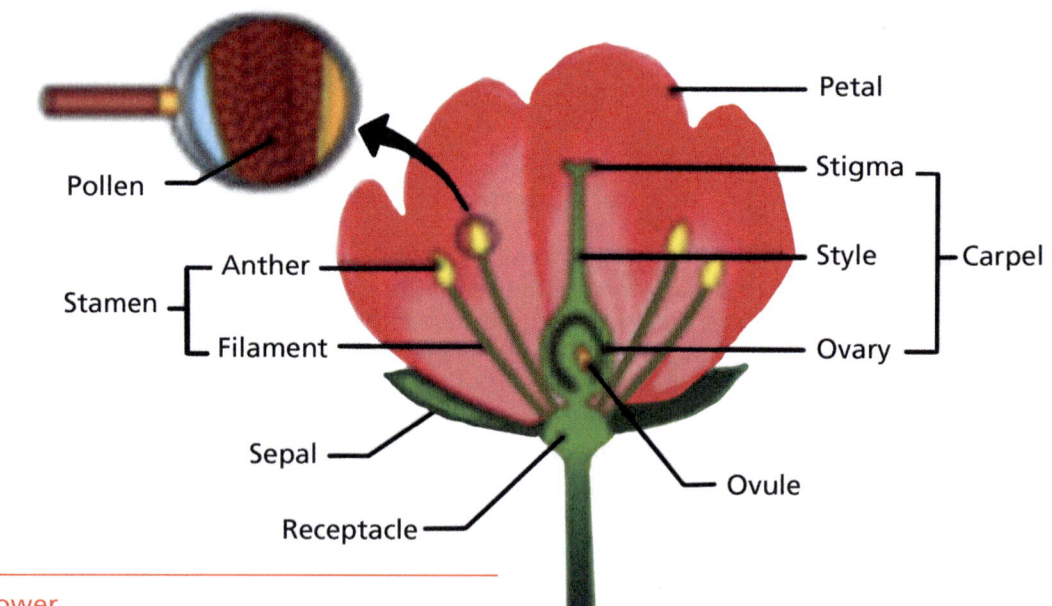

Parts of a flower.

Plants disperse their seeds to prevent over-crowding. They do this in a range of different ways, depending on the habitats to which they have adapted. Animals play an important role in seed dispersal. Some plants, such as a burdock, produce fruits with hooks. These hooks can stick to a passing animal's fur and drop off in a different place. Animals may eat fruits and the seeds, which can pass through the animal's digestive system undamaged, can be widely dispersed. Seeds such as peas are dispersed when the ripe pod 'explodes' shooting the seeds away from the plant. Some fruits, such as the horse chestnut, simply drop off the tree and roll away from the parent plant. When the conditions are right, dispersed seeds are able to germinate.

Seed dispersal.

Source: iStock

Different stages in the life cycle of a dandelion.
Source: Linda Nicholls

> ## Something to think about
>
> Some plants do not have flowers. How do they reproduce?

Animals

Animals exchange or transfer genetic material through special cells called gametes. Gametes fuse to form an **embryo,** which develops into an immature form and, eventually, an adult. The young of some animals undergo complete transformation or **metamorphosis** as they develop. The immature stage of the animal looks completely different from the adult stage. For example, a frog lays eggs which develop into tadpoles, which then change into froglets and frogs.

Some animals spend much time and care on rearing their young. For example, in the 14 days or so that blue tit chicks are in the nest, the parents will bring at least a thousand caterpillars for them. Even humble creatures like earwigs are ferocious in defence of their eggs. Many mammals will defend their young at all costs. The young are the creature's genetic investment in the future; unless the young survive, the creature's genes will be lost to the gene pool of the **species.** For creatures like elephants and humans, things become even more complicated by the development of emotional bonds. Protective care may well be extended to unrelated young.

> ## Something to think about
>
> Why do you think a herd of elephants will risk their own safety to defend an orphaned calf against a pride of lions?

What influences how animals behave?

Development is associated with physical growth but also involves the emergence of the adult body from the juvenile. Generally, adults are able to reproduce, whereas juveniles cannot. Maturing over time can enable creatures to learn. Learning influences behaviour; learning over time can help the creature to work out how to behave if it is to have the best chance of survival.

Behaviour is a mix of what the creature does because of its instincts and the impact of what it has learned throughout its life. Some creatures rely almost entirely on instinct to govern their behavior – that is, behaviour is 'hard-wired' into their **genetic code.** How such a creature acts is dictated by the interaction of the environment with its genes. For example, the way that magpies build nests is not based on any previous experience; it is instinct. Learning takes place as a result of the experience a creature gains as it goes about its life. Magpies scavenging a dead rabbit on a busy road quickly learn to time their retreat as traffic goes by. Those that cannot learn do not survive to pass on their genes to the next generation.

Learning has no impact unless it is put to use – that is, unless it influences behaviour or is communicated in some way. Human learning is powerfully coupled with our ability to use language to communicate. We are not confined to what we know and have learned as individuals but can draw on the understanding of others and can make decisions about behaviour with others, to our mutual benefit.

Animals may act as individuals, groups or colonies. They relate to one another by instinct and can accept retribution if they step out of line. A hungry young wolf will defer to older members of the pack when there is food; if it does not, it will be bitten and so it will learn. Generally, survival is the strongest driving force for much animal behaviour. If a creature does not survive to breed or does not succeed in raising young, its genes are lost. It can create no future creatures. Learning held within individuals is lost on death, but learning distributed amongst social groups is still available when individuals die. Individuals learn by various mechanisms such as habituation, conditioning or emulating others. So it is that we, as teachers and parents, exert a very powerful influence on children and, equally powerfully, children influence one another.

Why there is variation in the same species

Members of an animal species can interbreed, producing young that are capable of reproduction themselves. Animals cannot breed with members of another species. There are some strange 'mixes' created by human intervention, such as mules, which have a male donkey and a female horse as parents. However, these are usually sterile and are not a viable species.

Genetic variation

Each animal is a distinct representative of its own species, carrying an individual genetic code. A wide variety of creatures may all belong to the same species. A dog show is a good place to witness variation; the dogs look and behave very differently but as a species are still capable of interbreeding. This ability to interbreed is used in the development of new varieties, for example, crossing a Labrador with a poodle results in a labradoodle. Variation within a species has great advantages if the species is to survive. A particular habitat might require that a dog has long legs or a thick coat or be camouflaged by being brown or be able to discern scent over a distance; each aspect of variation has its own advantages in survival terms. Some aspects of a variety may be disadvantageous. If we think of the Canadian winter, a variety of dog with a thick coat and the ability to run tirelessly over long distances will be advantaged. If, however, the variety of dog fitting this description also has a weak sense of smell and poor hearing, the balance of its likelihood to survive alters.

Environmental variation

Variation within a species can also be due to environmental conditions. Well-fed wolves with healthy teeth and bones are stronger than malnourished, parasite-ridden individuals and therefore more likely to survive. But this sort of variation is not transmitted through the generations. A wolf can inherit keen eyesight and can pass this advantage on to its offspring. But a wolf cannot inherit being well fed.

Variation within a species is important because those creatures which have a combination of attributes which help them do well will survive to breed. They will pass on the distinctive genes, which are their variation of the species' blueprint to another generation. Conversely, those variations which disadvantage a creature make it less likely to breed successfully. The creature which best fits its environment will survive – as Charles Darwin recorded (Chapter 15).

Variation in dogs.
Source: iStock

How classification helps make sense of a complex world

Classification of living things allows us to group similar species and distinguish them from others. Living things are classified by identifying similarities and differences between them. Classification puts the huge range of animals and plants on our planet into some sort of order so that we can make better sense of it. Similarities between creatures indicate that, in the past, they may have been a single species in which variation became just too great to allow breeding. Starting with the features of the creatures themselves, a scientific system of classification helps us to discern genetic relationships and better understand how they, and we, fit into the natural order.

> ### Something to think about
>
> Carl Linnaeus is sometimes called the father of classification. What can you find out about his work?

Diversity helps maintain life on Earth

The Earth has always been a changeable place, and the capacity of a particular life form to survive depends on what sort of circumstances it finds itself in. Living things have colonised even the most inhospitable of environments on Earth. In the struggle for survival, the small advantages conferred by being a particular *variety* can be the difference between life and death – and between breeding success and failure. Varieties of a species separated by land, food supply or water may become so different that they can no longer interbreed and go on to become different species. This process, **evolution**, has produced an impressive diversity of animals and plants.

Diversity benefits not just a particular species but life on Earth generally. The great variety of life on Earth makes it much more likely that, even if some species are lost, others will remain. We humans have gained much control over our own environment, and our behaviour affects the environments of other living things on the planet. This does not mean that we are exempt from feeling the adverse effects of such problems as climate chaos, rising sea levels and pollution of air and sea. Like the dinosaurs, we are vulnerable to changes in our environment and completely dispensable in cosmic terms. Whatever fate has in store for us, it is likely that the diversity of living things will ensure the survival of life itself.

Basic classification of living things

Classification of living things.
Source: iStock

Global dimensions: Diversity in the seas and oceans

Fish and other sea creatures provide protein for us as part of our diet, but their popularity is having an adverse impact on their numbers and diversity in many parts of the world.

Fish and chips is a favourite meal in the United Kingdom, but this has led to over-fishing of cod in the waters around the British Isles. Modern trawlers and dredgers scrape the sea floor clean, leaving the fishing grounds almost barren. The east coast of Scotland was once famed for its herring catch – the 'silver darlings' as they were known – but they have disappeared and, with them, the rich fishing culture they supported. As the stocks of cod and many other fish in the northern hemisphere become depleted, large factory trawlers are moving further south and over-fishing the waters off the coast of Africa and other areas of the developing world.

The use of very large nets leads to large catches of fish and those that are not commercially useful are thrown back to die. Not only is this causing a decrease in biodiversity but it is having an adverse effect on the livelihood of local fisherman throughout the world.

www.school-of-fish.co.uk/index.php

www.guardian.co.uk/global-development/2012/apr/02/senegal-fishingcommunity-act-foreign-fleets

http://ocean.nationalgeographic.com/ocean/global-fish-crisis-article/

http://ocean.nationalgeographic.com/ocean/take-action/impact-of-seafood/#/ intro-video/

Summary

The quest to understand the origin and nature of life on Earth continues, but we can now say what chemicals living things are made from and what properties of complex molecules like proteins, carbohydrates or enzymes enable living things to function. Science has established the links between living things: physical links, such as similarities or differences of body form, and ecological links, such as food webs and chains. The dynamic interaction of the creatures in a habitat with each other and their environment can lead to such changes as the increase of some types of creature at the expense of others or the extinction of whole groups. We know that small differences between individuals can affect whether they survive or not, and that such differences are transmitted to offspring in the genetic code of parents. Those that survive are, in effect, copied to produce the next generation. They are the ones that best fit the environment.

By looking at similarities between living things, we can discern groups that are related as families. Classifying living things in this way helps us to understand and appreciate the diversity of life on Earth. In destroying habitats, we are at risk of losing the diversity of life that characterises Earth. Individual creatures, or even whole species, may seem insignificant, but a balance of plants, animals and bacteria is essential for human existence. Our aim as teachers must be to ensure that children value the diversity of life on Earth.

Part 2: Ideas for practice

Topic: Growing plants

Age group: 5–7 years

Introduction

This topic provides children with opportunities to explore diversity in plants including differences in structure and variations in how they grow. The activities also explore how the seasons affect plant growth and enquire into the conditions required for bulbs and seeds to grow into mature plants. In the application stage children have opportunities to tell their own 'gardening stories' and produce a simple gardening manual which offers advice on how to grow seeds.

Scientific view

Our world is full of different types of plants of various shapes and colours. Often plants grow from seeds or bulbs. Most plants prefer warm, sunny weather. Some plants shed their leaves and fruit in autumn so they can rest throughout the winter. In spring when the weather is warm enough, they grow new leaves and flowers. Bulbs and seeds planted outside in autumn remain dormant throughout the winter, waiting for the soil to warm up in spring.

Working scientifically

In these activities children will:

- ask and try to find answers to questions;
- observe closely using simple equipment;
- identify and classify;
- use their observations and ideas to answer questions;
- communicate what happened through speech and drawings.

Exploration stage

Children's talk involves trying out their own ideas

Setting the scene

Start this topic in autumn, in time to plant bulbs that grow in spring. Begin by reading 'The Little Gardener' by Emily Hughes. Read the book with the children, taking time to marvel at the great variety of plants which inhabit the garden. Talk about the different colours and shapes of the leaves, flowers and stems. Have fun spotting the insects, and discuss children's responses to the cola can. Children can imagine who may be responsible for littering the garden. My bet, it wasn't the Little Gardener! Ask the children whether they would like to do some gardening?

Storytelling

Talk together about gardening. Do children think they could do better than the 'The Little Gardener'? Listen to the children's stories and encourage them to describe the colours, shapes and sizes of plants they would grow in their garden. Children draw pictures to show what they imagine their gardens would look like.

Scientific enquiry

Tell children that autumn is a good time to start a garden and fortunately you happen to have lots of bulbs to grow in it. *Working collaboratively*, children compare different types of bulbs. They can group them according to characteristic such as shape, colour and size. Help children identify the bulbs. What common characteristics do all the bulbs have? Help them dissect a bulb so they can use magnifiers to look inside and see the parts waiting to grow. Children should wear protective gloves when handling the bulbs, and warn them that they should not put bulbs in their mouths. Refer to the ASE publication *Be safe!* when planning these activities.

Talking points: true, false or not sure?

- A bulb is not a plant.
- A bulb is not alive.
- A bulb is a baby plant.
- A bulb is a plant waiting to wake up.

Children discuss the talking points and decide whether a bulb is a plant and hence a living thing. Help them decide by pointing out what living things are able to do. Focus on the fact that growth is a characteristic of a living thing. Children can draw pictures showing how they think the bulb will grow into a mature plant. Discuss drawings and explore their reasoning.

Scientific enquiry

Bulbs can be grown in containers or in a small garden plot in the school grounds. Plant according to instructions on the packages. Children should have a hand in preparing the ground and planting the bulbs. Now, like the Little Gardener they need to be patient and wait for spring. For H&S advice on gardening and handling bulbs refer to *Be safe!* (2011).

Puzzle

Why do we have to wait until spring for the bulbs to grow? Why do most not grow in autumn? Discuss children's ideas and find out what they know about how the seasons influence plant growth.

Scientific enquiry

To help solve the puzzle arrange for a visit to a local park or woodland in the autumn. Take cameras to record the different types of plants. Help children identify the diversity of plants by comparing the different colours, textures and the shapes of the leaves, fruits and seeds. Allow them to collect fallen leaves, conkers, acorns and any other fruits and seeds they find.

Warn children against picking plants and fungi. Children should wear protective gloves and use appropriate equipment to collect samples. Refer to the ASE publication *Be safe!* when planning these activities.

Storytelling

In words and pictures children tell their stories about their visit to the park or woodland in autumn. Explore their ideas. What do they think was happening to the trees, which were shedding their leaves? Children make displays which present 'plants in autumn' using photographs and some of the things they collected.

Formative assessment

Provide opportunities for children to voice what they have learnt in the exploratory stage. Use evidence from their responses to the puzzle, talking points and other activities to assess differences between children's ideas and the scientific view. Plan how you will use the re-describing stage to help the children address their *learning needs.* You may want to modify the activities depending on the shared and individual needs of the children.

Re-describing stage

Children's talk involves making sense of scientific ideas

Teacher-led discussion

Discuss the puzzle and address children's ideas. Use video clips to illustrate how the weather changes from season to season. Focus on how deciduous trees prepare for winter by shedding their fruit and leaves. *Talk together* about how plants remain dormant (rest) throughout the winter because it is not sunny or warm enough for them to grow. When the weather turns warm in spring they grow again, and produce leaves and flowers. Can children now resolve the puzzle? Why do they have to wait until spring for their bulbs to grow? Listen to children's ideas and probe their thinking.

Scientific enquiry

Focus children's attention on the seeds they collected in the exploratory stage. Compare them with the bulbs they planted. Use video clips to show children how seeds grow into mature plants. There is information on the web which describes how to grow acorns, conkers and seeds from other trees. Working with the help of an adult children plant some of their seeds, which they expect to germinate in the spring. Follow H&S guidance provided by *Be safe!* (2011).

Back in the classroom, children draw pictures showing how they expect their seeds to grow. Probe children's thinking behind their pictures and address any outstanding *leaning needs.*

Information and teaching resources

BBC Bitesize:

- BBC (2017). What Are the Seasons? *www.bbc.co.uk/guides/zcx3gk7*
- BBC (2013). The Changing Seasons. *www.bbc.co.uk/education/clips/zrjd7ty*

- BBC (2007). How the Changing Seasons Affects Apple Trees. *www.bbc.co.uk/education/clips/ zf62tfr*
- BBC (2017). What Is the Lifecycle of a Plant? *www.bbc.co.uk/guides/z2vdjxs*

Other websites:

- The National Forestry Company. Grow a Tree from a Seed. *www.nationalforest.org/document/ involved/tree_from_seed.pdf*

Application Stage

Children's talk involves trying out scientific ideas

This stage should be started in spring.

Spring growth

Children monitor the growth of the bulbs and the seeds they planted in autumn. They can take photographs of the bulbs at different stages, for example when they produce shoots, leaves, buds and flowers. The bulbs need to be kept well-watered and in a sunny position. After flowering feed the plants with liquid fertilizer to enable them to create healthy bulbs for next year.

Seedlings from acorns or conkers can be planted out in the school grounds and children can monitor their progress for years to come. During dry spells in summer the saplings will need to be watered.

Sowing seeds in spring

Spring is a good time for children to grow flowering plants from seeds. They can use information sources to explore the diversity of flowering plants available to gardeners.

Choose an assortment of fast growing seeds, which children can germinate in seed trays or yogurt pots. As a non-variable use a standard seed compost. Help children plan investigations to find out the conditions in which the seeds grow best. Encourage children to maintain good hygiene throughout (refer to *Be safe!* 2011). Once they have germinated, some of the healthy seedlings can be potted on into bigger containers or planted out in the garden. Children monitor the plants until they flower and produce their own seeds. Children can design and produce their own gardening manual, which provides advice on how to grow plants from seeds.

The Little Gardener

Through words and pictures, children tell their own stories of the 'The Little Gardener' who worked from autumn to summer to bring the garden alive by growing a wonderful diversity of plants. Probe children's thinking behind their ideas and assess their understanding of plant growth.

Information and teaching resources

BBC Bitesize:

- BBC (2017). What Does a Plant Need to Grow? *www.bbc.co.uk/guides/zxxsyrd*

Topic: Diversity amongst vertebrates

Age group: 9–11 years

Introduction

The topic provides opportunities for children to identify and compare the life cycles of different type of vertebrates and to explore how their methods of reproduction are adapted to their habitats. In the application stage children look at the problems caused by poachers to elephant populations due to their slow rate of reproduction.

Scientific view

Animals with an internal skeleton are called vertebrates. The five vertebrate groups of animals are mammals, birds, reptiles, amphibians and fish. Numerically, vertebrates represent only a very small percentage of the living things in the world. But their size, mobility and intellect often allow them to dominate their environment. There is a large diversity of different species of vertebrates. Each has adapted to its environment in ways which enable it to survive.

Working scientifically

In these activities children will:

- plan enquiries to find answers to questions;
- use a range of information sources to answer a question;
- present their findings in various ways including multimedia format;
- use established scientific knowledge to explain their findings;
- review their work and the work of others.

Exploration stage

Children's talk involves trying out their own ideas

Setting the scene

Bring in photographs of yourself at different ages. If you judge it to be okay, children can do the same with permission from home. Children in stepfamilies and those who are adopted may be sensitive about this. Also check school policy regarding the use of photographs. *Talk together* about how people change. Display photographs and ask children to put them in order from youngest to oldest. Discuss the children's reasoning. Explain that humans are vertebrates and discuss some functions of the skeleton. Find out if the children can suggest other animals that are vertebrates and if they can describe how vertebrates grow and change.

Storytelling

Divide the class into five groups and assign a different vertebrate to each group of children:

1.   Frog (amphibian)
2.   Snake (reptile)
3.   Robin (bird)
4.   Elephant (mammal)
5.   Salmon (fish)

Ask the children to consider the changes that happen in 'their' animal as it grows into an adult. Their task is to use information resources to explore growth and development and present their ideas in documentary form to the rest of the class. They should focus on the problems a creature might have at different stages of growth and talk about its characteristics which help it to survive. Children should not present a list of facts. Ask them to tell stories about real events using pictures and video clips taken from the web.

Puzzle

Why do some animals lay eggs and others give birth to live young? Children discuss the following talking points as the first step in solving the puzzle.

Talking points: true, false or not sure?

- Elephants don't lay eggs because they can't make nests.
- Birds would be more successful if they had live young.
- Elephants don't lay eggs because baby elephants take too long to hatch.
- Having live young makes life easier for mammals.
- Bird chicks and elephant calves need the same amount of help to survive.
- Elephants don't lay eggs because they are clumsy and would break them.
- Elephants don't lay eggs because baby elephants are too big.
- Elephants don't lay eggs because they couldn't keep them safe from predators.

Working collaboratively in groups, children try to reach agreement on their responses to the talking points. Then, as a whole class activity, groups compare their responses and share their reasoning. Probe children's thinking and discuss their ideas.

Formative assessment

Provide opportunities for children to voice what they have learnt in the exploratory stage. Use evidence from their responses to the puzzle, talking points and other activities to assess differences between children's ideas and the scientific view. Plan how you will use the re-describing stage to help the children address their *learning needs.* You may want to modify the activities depending on the shared and individual needs of the children.

Eggs come in all shapes and sizes. Whose eggs are these? Which other animals lay eggs?
Source: iStock

Re-describing stage

Children's talk involves making sense of scientific ideas

Teacher-led discussion

Ask children to name types of animals that give birth to live young and those which lay eggs. Is it only mammals that give birth to live young? Together with the children, search the web for an answer to this question. Address the puzzle and discuss reasons why some animals lay eggs and others give birth to live young. Talk about how long it takes for the chicks to form and grow inside the egg (in chickens this is 21 days). Compare this with how long it takes for a baby elephant to grow inside its mother (22 months). This means elephants would have to keep their eggs warm and safe for nearly two years before they hatched. Discuss the implications of this for adult elephants as well as their offspring. Elephants are constantly on the move in search of food. They need to eat enormous amounts of vegetation. How would they keep their eggs safe? Does it make more sense to carry their young inside their bodies until they are able to walk?

Can children think of the advantages birds gain from laying eggs? What would be the problems caused by giving birth to live young? Children use information sources to compare the eggs of amphibians, reptiles and birds. Would amphibians and reptiles be better off giving birth to live young? Ask children to relate the structure of different eggs to the environment in which the animal lives. Ask children how different methods of reproduction can be explained by the big idea of adaptation.

Modelling and storytelling

Children imagine that they are scientists studying a remote environment. They can choose if this is very cold, hot, wet, dry, dark, sunny, seawater, freshwater, a cave, a desert, a jungle, snowy and so on. The scientists come across an egg. They study it over a year to see how it grows and develops. The task is to make the egg out of clay or modelling clay, then to make the imaginary creature that emerges and classify it in a vertebrate group. Finally, the children can make a model of what it changes into as an adult. The group must decide why the changes take place and what conditions are necessary to sustain the life of the creature. They must consider the creature's need for shelter and food and its predator–prey relationships, and design it accordingly.

Acting as scientists, children present an academic paper on what they have learnt about the creature to other interested scientists (the rest of the class). Explain that scientists communicate with one another in this way at conferences. Prepare the class to ask the presenters questions about the creature's growth, development and behaviour. To assess their understanding of the topic, ask the children to provide positive feedback on the work of other groups and discuss the models. Help them to address any outstanding *learning needs* identified in the exploratory stage.

Information and teaching resources

BBC Bitesize:

- BBC (2007). Animals that Lay Eggs. *www.bbc.co.uk/education/clips/z72w2hv*

- BBC (2015). Birds, Reptiles and Mammals. *www.bbc.co.uk/education/clips/zyh7v4j*
- BBC (2017). Classification of Organisms. *www.bbc.co.uk/education/clips/zwgp7hv*
- BBC (2009). How Ostriches Care for Their Young. *www.bbc.co.uk/education/clips/zk84d2p*

Application stage

Children's talk involves trying out scientific ideas

Elephant conservation

Humans provide the greatest danger to the survival of many vertebrate species, especially elephants. Poachers kill elephants for their ivory, which is then sold and made into anything from jewellery to religious objects.

Elephants have longer pregnancies than almost any other mammal. They carry their calves for 22 months, and cows usually only bear one calf every two to four years. Because of their slow rate of reproduction, elephant populations can be devastated by poachers.

Children research the problems caused by poaching and what is being done by different trusts and foundations to protect elephant populations. Much information can be found on the web about different elephant conservation projects in both Africa and Asia. These sites provide teaching resources, fascinating video footage and stories of the lives of elephants and the people who are trying to protect them. The 'International Elephant Foundation' publish an eNewsletter in which conservationists explain their work in their own words. As a result of their research, children can produce their own eNewsletter on the topic of elephant conservation.

Information and teaching resources

- African Wildlife Foundation. Elephant. *www.awf.org/wildlife-conservation/elephant*
- Daphne Sheldrick (1992). The Elephant Debate. *www.sheldrickwildlifetrust.org/html/debate. html*
- Wildlife Conservation Network. Elephant. *http://wildnet.org/wildlife-programs/elephant*
- World Wildlife Fund (2017). Elephant. *www.worldwildlife.org/species/elephant*
- International Elephant Foundation (2016). *https://elephantconservation.org/*
- Five Films (2016). Uganda's Elephants: The Real Story. *https://vimeo.com/150885498*
- International Elephant Foundation (2016). Interview with Conservationist Dr. Michele Millar. *https://elephantconservation.org/interview-dr-michele-miller/*
- BBC (2017). Human Impact on the Environment. *www.bbc.co.uk/education/clips/z3fsmnb*
- International Elephant Foundation (2016). Just for Kids. *https://elephantconservation.org/stay-informed/just-for-kids/*

Talk skills and science discussion: Giving ideas with reasons

Provide children with a simple diagram for classifying vertebrates into the five groups – mammal, bird, fish, reptile and amphibian – with basic information about each group.

Provide them with pictures of a variety of creatures to classify. Make sure that children know that they are expected to ask one another, 'What do you think?' and 'Why do you think that?' in order to elicit ideas and reasons and make a group decision. Explain that, in science settings, reasons should be based on evidence. The nature of evidence is another topic for discussion.

Pictures can include dinosaur, crocodile, duck-billed platypus, emu, penguin, woodlouse, whale, toad, porpoise and so on or can relate to environmental topics (e.g. rainforest, pond study, oak tree study, etc.).

Ask children to evaluate the quality of their discussion by saying what reasons were given and how this helped the group to think together. Ask them to identify the importance of reasons and evidence in scientific discussion.

Additional information and teaching resources

Companion book:

- Loxley, P. (2018). *Practical Ideas for Teaching Primary Science: Inspiring Learning and Enjoyment,* Abingdon: Routledge, Chapter 2: Growing Plants, Chapter 3: Flowering Plants and Chapter 6: Living Things.

Websites:

- Science and Plants for Schools (2017). Having Fun Growing Plants. *www.saps.org.uk/primary/ teaching-resources/199-having-fun-growing-plants*
- BBC (2017). What Plants Can You Find Outside? *www.bbc.co.uk/guides/zw2y34j*

ASE journals:

- Primary Science 138 (May/June 2015). *'Animals Don't Grow Feathers When They Want To …'* by Terry Russell and Linda McGuigan.
- Primary Science 131 (Jan/Feb 2014). *Evolution in Action* by Mike Dennis, Adrienne Duggan and Deb McGregor.
- Primary Science 129 (Sept/Oct 2013). *Let the Children Talk: The Power of Talk in Promoting Understanding* by Keith Ross.
- Primary Science Review 101 (January/February 2008). *Teaching Life Process (Wobbly Corner)* by Leigh Hoath.

CHAPTER 15

ADAPTATION AND EVOLUTION

This chapter discusses the key ideas about adaptation and evolution. Starting with Charles Darwin's work, we look at how he arrived at his theory of natural selection and then provide case studies to exemplify how his theory applies to both plants and animals. The chapter concludes by looking at the problems that rapid environmental change presents for many animals and plants.

Topics discussed in the chapter

- Darwin's theory of natural selection
- Survival of the fittest and adaptation
- Adaptation in flowering plants
- Adaptation in animals
- The effects of changing habitats

Part 1: Subject knowledge

Darwin's theory of natural selection

Who was Charles Darwin?

Charles Darwin was born in 1809, at a time when the Industrial Revolution had just begun in England. The big northern cities were starting to develop, but most of the country was still very rural. The Church was responsible for spiritual and pastoral care, education and spiritual guidance. A Christian view of the natural world was that God had created every species of animal and plant and these species were immutable. They could not change.

Darwin was born into a middle-class and privileged family who were interested in the natural world. His father Robert was a country doctor. His grandfather Erasmus was a surgeon, naturalist and poet who had published his own ideas about the nature of evolution in a book called *Zoonomia*. As a child, Darwin was fascinated by nature and he collected animals and plants. He was unhappy at school, where he was considered idle and ordinary. There was no indication of his creative mind and the contribution he was going to make to science in the future.

How Darwin developed a passion for biology

Robert Darwin was determined that his son should follow in the family footsteps and become a doctor. At the age of 16, Darwin was sent to Edinburgh University to study medicine. Unfortunately, he did not share his family's enthusiasm for medicine. When he saw an operation being performed without anaesthetic on a child, he was deeply upset and refused to continue his studies. But through his childhood interest in collecting insects and shells, he met a Scottish zoologist – Robert Grant. They went out regularly collecting together. Darwin also met a freed Guyanan slave called John Edmonstone, who made his living by teaching taxidermy – the art of preparing, stuffing and mounting the skins of animals, including birds. Darwin became one of Edmonstone's pupils, and the skills he learnt were to become very useful on his future voyage to South America.

Since it was clear that Darwin was not going to become a doctor, his father decided he should become a clergyman and he was sent to Cambridge to study theology. Darwin once again had little enthusiasm for his studies. He was introduced to the Reverend John Henslow, a professor of botany, and started to accompany him on field trips. He attended Henslow's lectures and his interest in the natural world developed into a passion. Despite his lack of interest in theology, Darwin still managed to pass his degree.

Darwin sets sail for South America

In 1831, Henslow introduced Darwin to Robert Fitzroy, the captain of HMS *Beagle*. The *Beagle* was due to set sail for South America to carry out a geographical survey of the coastline. Victorian conventions meant that Fitzroy could not socialise with the officers on his ship. He needed someone to act as the ship's naturalist, but he also needed that person to be his intellectual equal, someone with whom he could share his dinner table. Darwin was chosen and the *Beagle* left England on 27 December that year.

Darwin was not a good sailor and he was often unwell. He was over six foot tall and his cabin was so low he could not stand up straight in it. The cabin also served as the map room and part of one of the masts went through it. When he was not on his expeditions, it was in these very cramped conditions that Darwin had to examine, prepare and label the specimens he collected.

Darwin's experiences changed the way he imagined the world to be

As the *Beagle* progressed down the coast of South America, Darwin was dropped ashore for several days or weeks at a time while the ship carried out its survey of that part of the coastline. His collecting started in the jungle around Rio de Janeiro, where he was overwhelmed by the sights and sounds. He had never seen such a variety of plants and animals. As the journey continued, he found large fossilised bones that were bigger than any animal he knew. In the Andes, he found fossilised sea shells 12,000 feet up in the mountains. To explain these observations, Darwin speculated that the whole landscape had been changed by a huge force. He experienced an earthquake for the first time and he saw how the landscape could be changed. Through these experiences and through studying the work of the geologist Charles Lyell, Darwin's knowledge and understanding of geology grew considerably. His study of fossils was crucial in helping him to develop his theory of evolution.

Mary Anning was a famous fossil hunter who lived at the same time as Darwin. Her fossils helped scientists to develop their understanding of evolution. By studying fossils found in different layers of sedimentary rocks scientists have been able to tell when an organism first appeared and when it became extinct. They have produced a timeline of how organisms have changed and evolved over millions of years.

Portrait of the young Charles Darwin.
Source: Graphica Artis / Archive Photos / Getty Images

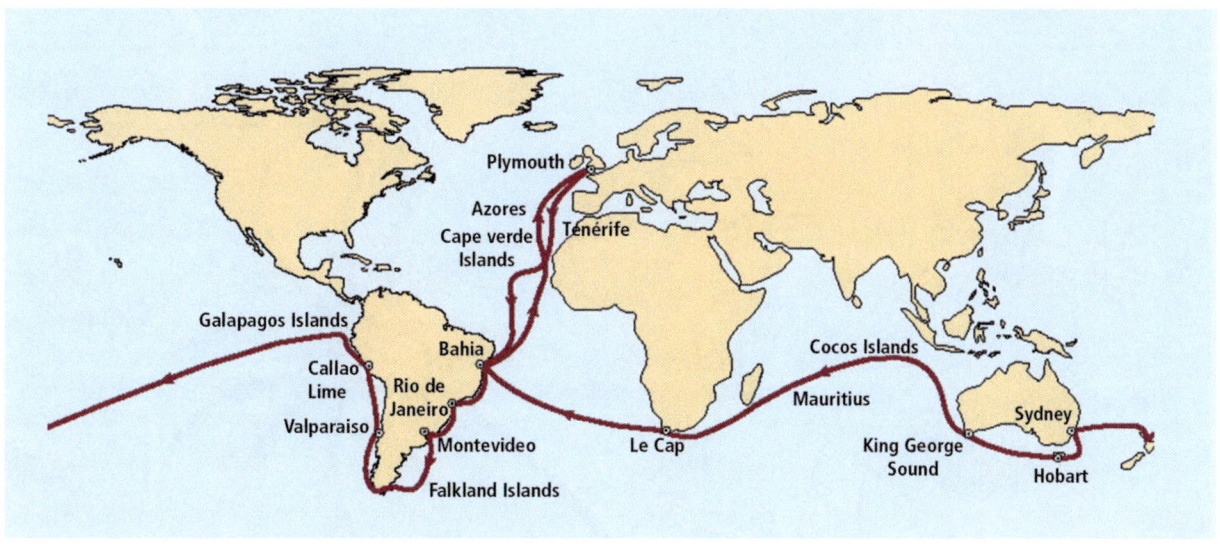

The voyage of the *Beagle* from 1831 to 1836.

How are fossils formed?

Sedimentary rock (see Chapter 11) can hide the fossilised remains of plants and animals. Fossils are the preserved remains or traces of dead organisms. When most organisms die they rot away but fossils may form if the conditions are right. The sea bed has all the conditions needed for fossils to form.

1. When a marine animal dies it sinks to the sea bed. The soft parts of its body decay leaving behind its skeleton. This skeleton is then covered by sediment such as sand and mud. This also happens to any land animals that are washed out to sea when they die.

2. As more layers or sediment build up, pressure increases on the lower layers. They become hard sedimentary rock and the skeleton becomes trapped in this rock.

3. The trapped skeleton dissolves and leaves behind a mould of its shape.

4. Water rich in minerals flows into the mould. Over time the minerals become crystals which fill the mould and take on the same shape as the skeleton.

5. Over millions of years, as a result of movements such as earthquakes, the rocks may rise to the Earth's surface. As the rock is eroded the fossil becomes exposed.

(Oxford University Museum of Natural History, 2012)

Triassic underwater scene illustration, featuring ammonites in their habitat.
Source: Science Photo Library / Getty Images

Fossil of an ammonite.
Source: iStock

Darwin was puzzled by the variety of animals on the Galapagos Islands

In September 1835, nearly four years after leaving England, the *Beagle* arrived in the Galapagos Islands, a small group of islands off the coast of Ecuador. Some of the plants and animals on the islands were similar to those he had seen on the mainland, but they were not the same species. He found that each of the small islands in the group had its own unique animals. He saw animals that he had never seen before, such as giant tortoises, and on each island the tortoises had their own distinct characteristics. Where the islands were grassy, the shells were close to the tortoises' necks, but on the islands where there was little grass and the tortoises had to eat shrubs, the shell was arched away from the neck to allow it to stretch up. He found a number of 'strange' animals, like marine iguanas, that were excellent swimmers and grazed on underwater plants but spent most of their life on the rocky shores.

Something to think about

Imagine how the tortoises developed different-shaped shells. What further developments may have advantaged the shrub-eating tortoise?

A Galapagos tortoise with a shell that arches away from the neck to allow the tortoise to reach up for shrubs.
Source: Tui De Roy / Minden Pictures / Getty Images

How did Darwin develop the theory of natural selection?

In December 1836, the *Beagle* arrived back in England. The voyage made Darwin famous and he was elected as a Fellow of the Royal Geographical Society. He returned to Cambridge and spent two years classifying and cataloguing his collection.

Among the specimens Darwin collected in the Galapagos was a collection of birds that he thought were finches, blackbirds and wrens. He sent these specimens to another scientist, John Gould, for examination. Gould recognised that they were in fact all finches and their distinguishing features were the size and shape of their beaks. Darwin hypothesised that all these birds had arisen from one species of finch that had arrived in the islands from the mainland of South America. He thought the size of the beaks was related to particular conditions on the islands, but his notes were incomplete and he had not labelled some of the birds properly. He did not know which birds came from which island and this meant he did not have good evidence to support his theory.

The variations in animals on the different islands made Darwin start to question the immutability of species. He set about collecting more systematic evidence. His studies over the next twenty years led him to develop three major theories:

1. Organisms produce more offspring than can survive. Large numbers die due to lack of food, disease and predation.

2. While all organisms in a species are similar, they are not identical; there are small variations in their characteristics. Those organisms whose characteristics are best suited to, or adapted to, a particular environment survive and pass on these characteristics to the next generation. Individuals less well adapted die out. Their characteristics are not passed on to the next generation. This is described as the 'survival of the fittest'.

3. Over very long periods of time, the impact in selecting characteristics gives rise to new species; the species evolves.

Darwin needed evidence to support his theory

Because Darwin did not think it was possible to see evolution happening in nature, he developed a scientific model to investigate the effect of selected characteristics being passed down from one generation to the next. He started to breed pigeons. Darwin gathered a great deal of scientific evidence and kept rigorous notes on his work. He found that eventually, through selective breeding, the offspring were so different from the original birds that they could be considered a new species. He extrapolated his results to suggest that this could happen of its own accord in nature. These findings challenged the biblical view that species were unchangeable and, knowing that this theory would cause controversy, he initially kept his ideas to himself.

Charles Darwin was not the first person to suggest that animals evolved, but, on the basis of the evidence he collected during his pigeon breeding, combined with his experiences in the Galapagos, he was the first person to offer a scientifically plausible mechanism for evolution. He called this the theory of **natural selection**.

Something to think about

For many years, people have bred different varieties of farm animals. Could an agricultural show be used to provide evidence for Darwin's theory?

Breeding pigeons helped Darwin to develop his theory of evolution.
Source: iStock

A letter persuaded Darwin it was time to publish his work

Alfred Russel Wallace was a naturalist and an admirer of Darwin. Wallace studied plants and animals in the Malay Archipelago, and in February 1858 he sent Darwin a paper based on his studies. He presented ideas on evolution that were very similar to Darwin's. Although Darwin did not want to cause controversy neither did he want to be upstaged by Wallace, so he decided to publish his ideas on natural selection. Their work was presented jointly to the Linnean Society of London in July 1858. In 1859, Darwin published his famous book *On the Origin of Species by Means of Natural Selection*. Darwin's authority in the subject was based on rigorous analysis of evidence, which he used to support his theory.

The book caused the expected furore because it challenged the biblical view that God was the creator and designer of the world. Darwin developed his ideas further and his book *The Descent of Man* was published in 1871. He made comparisons between man and ape. He did not suggest that man had developed from apes but that they had a common ancestor. Even so, this challenged the view that man was created in God's image.

Scientists continue to develop and clarify Darwin's ideas

Our understanding of genetics, adaptation and evolution has developed considerably since Darwin's time. Gregor Mendel (1822–1884) developed his Laws of **Inheritance** through the research he carried out on breeding peas. He suggested that inheritable characteristics were either *dominant* or *recessive,* and this affected how they were passed on to future generations of peas. He published his work in 1865 but, even though they lived at the same time, Darwin was unaware of it. If he had been, he would have been able to explain more fully his theory of the 'survival of the fittest'. During the twentieth century there was an explosion of research into genetics. Genes are sections of **DNA (deoxyribonucleic acid)**, a large molecule that carries genetic information. Rosalind Franklin (1920–1958) took X-ray images of DNA and this contributed significantly to Crick and Watson's discovery of its structure in 1953. They were awarded the Nobel Prize in recognition of the importance of this discovery. Subsequent work on genetics, including the Human Genome Project, which was completed in 2003, has given us a more detailed understanding of the laws of inheritance and provides us with a clear picture of how natural selection works.

Survival of the fittest and adaptation

What do scientists mean by survival of the fittest?

In any species there is variation. Some humans are tall and some are short. Some have brown eyes and some blue. We come from different ethnic backgrounds and this determines, among other things, our skin colour and facial features. There are clear differences, but we are all easily recognisable as humans; we come from the same species. Similarly, other animals and plants exhibit variation.

When considering Darwin's theory of 'survival of the fittest', it is a common misconception that fittest means healthiest. Fittest, in the context of **adaptation**, means best suited to or adapted to the particular environment in which the organism lives. An example is provided by Rosemary and Peter Grant, who started a long-term project on Darwin's finches in the Galapagos Islands in 1973. They found that each island had its own particular species of finch, and there was a direct relationship between the size and shape of the birds' beaks and their diet.

The ground finches have crushing beaks to eat the seeds that are available. The bigger and stronger the beak, the bigger the seeds they can eat. The tree finches have grasping beaks to capture the insects. The warbler, woodpecker and cactus finches have probing beaks. In any species there is natural variation and those birds whose beaks enabled them to compete for the food supply available on their islands survived. On islands where there was a supply of large hard seeds, the finches with naturally larger beaks survived and passed on this characteristic. Gradually, the finches with smaller beaks died out. The species evolved. In times of food shortages, a difference of 1 millimetre in the size of the beak can mean the difference between the birds being able to eat the available food and starving to death. All these different species of finches have evolved from a single species of finch that arrived in the islands from the mainland. Those birds which have been successful in competing for the available food on the islands survived and passed their favourable characteristics to their offspring.

1 Geospiza mag irostris
3. Geospiza parvula.
2. Geospiza fortis.
4 Certhidea olivasea.

Finch beaks show a range of adaptations to different habitats.
Source: Print Collector / Hulton Archive / Getty

Which characteristics can be inherited?

Jean-Baptiste Lamarck (1744–1829), a French scientist, proposed that, through repeatedly stretching their necks to reach the taller trees, giraffes could make their necks longer and that they could pass on these longer necks to their offspring. This is not correct. Adaptation refers only to inheritable characteristics that are determined by our genes. Giraffes whose genes determined they had long necks survived when food was in short supply because they could reach the branches that shorter giraffes could not reach. A long neck also gives a giraffe an advantage when fighting another giraffe. They survived to pass on their 'long neck' gene. Characteristics acquired during our lifetime are not determined by our genes and cannot be inherited. For example, a weightlifter will train to develop his or her muscles in order to lift heavy weights, but these big muscles are not an inheritable characteristic and they will not be passed on to future generations. Adaptation is a slow process that takes place over many generations.

Adaptation in flowering plants

Just as there is variation within animal species, there is variation within plant species. Flowering plants first appeared in the Cretaceous period, when dinosaurs still existed. To survive, plants need to be attractive to pollinators and there is competition for these pollinators. The plants that have survived are those which have been successful in this competition.

> ### Something to think about
>
> Think about a bee flying over a field of wild flowers. How does it decide which flowers to land on?

There has to be a reason for a pollinator to visit a plant. Some plants contain nectar, a good food source for animals. The flowers advertise nectar by being brightly coloured or perfumed. The shape of the flowers on a plant will in some ways determine the type of pollinator that is attracted to it.

Flowers that do not contain nectar have to attract pollinators in a different way. Some orchids produce pheromones to attract insects. The bee orchid looks like a bee, and bees land on them, thinking that they have found a mate. The corpse flower emits a smell of rotten flesh which can be detected up to 100 metres away, and it is pollinated by flesh-eating beetles which are attracted by the smell.

Plants cannot actively think about how best to attract pollinators, but the plants with flowers that are attractive to pollinators will be pollinated and produce offspring, which will inherit these attractive characteristics. Over generations, through the process of natural selection, the appearance of the flower changes. Plants and pollinators well adapted to one another and the local environmental conditions are best fitted to survive.

Bees prefer warm purple flowers

In order to warm up enough to be able to fly, bees 'shiver' the flight muscles at the base of their wings. It takes a great deal of energy for a bee to take off from a flower, so they need to make sure that they collect pollen and nectar in the most efficient way possible.

The bee orchid attracts bees, who think they have found a mate.
Print Collector/Hulton Archive/Getty Images

Dyer et al. (2006) carried out a study of the colour preference of a population of young bumble bees and found that they preferred purple flowers. When these flowers were examined, they were found to have a high nectar content, but the nectar content of a flower was not the only thing to attract bees. They found that bees preferred to visit warm flowers with a high nectar content. They have hypothesised that drinking this warmer nectar and being on or in a warmer flower enables the bees to warm their bodies. This is a great advantage to them because they save the energy they would otherwise have used to warm themselves. Flowers that track the sun, those which have heat-absorbing pigments and those with specialised cell structures that can warm the flower, are all at an advantage when it comes to attracting bees. From an evolutionary point of view, successful plants are those which maximise their opportunities for reproduction.

Adaptation in animals

Why can camels survive in the desert?

The conditions that animals have to contend with in a desert are extremes of temperature, blowing sand, very infrequent water and food supplies and sandy conditions underfoot.

The camel has slit-like nostrils and thick eyelashes that keep out the blowing sand.
Print Collector/ Hulton Archive/ Getty Images

We are familiar with pictures of caravans of camels walking across the desert. The camels are well adapted to the harsh conditions in a number of ways. The reserve of body fat stored in their hump means they can survive for a number of weeks without eating or drinking. Their fur keeps the Sun off their backs during the day and keeps them warm at night. Their feet are broad and this spreads their weight out and enables them to grip the moving sand. They are able to close their slit-like nostrils and they have very long thick eyelashes, both of which protect them against blowing sand. One of the ways in which camels adjust their body temperature is by diverting the blood supply to the nostrils, where it is cooled before passing up to the brain, and this means they lose very little water through sweating.

Something to think about

Imagine you need to cross a desert and you only have a horse to carry you and your baggage. What problems would you have? Do you think you and the horse would survive?

What other animals have adapted to life in the desert?

A wide range of animals is adapted to life in the desert. Every group of animals is represented. There are species of mammals, birds, reptiles, amphibians, spiders, insects and even fish where there are pools and streams. Reptiles such as lizards and snakes survive well in desert areas because they are 'cold blooded' and largely rely on the Sun to warm their bodies. Small mammals such as rats and bats also survive well. Most feed at night and shelter from the heat of the Sun during the day. Whatever the environmental conditions, some living things will adapt and survive.

The effects of changing habitats

What is a habitat?

'Habitat' is a term used to describe the natural home of a group of plants and animals; the organisms within a habitat depend on each other. It can also be used to describe the specific set of conditions to which the animals and plants that live there have successfully adapted. It is a place where organisms live and reproduce. Factors that influence which animals and plants will thrive in a habitat include climate, light, seasonal changes, food supply, vegetation, soil and predators. Soil is made up of particles of eroded rock mixed with organic matter, air and water. The nature of the soil and therefore the plants that will grow in it will depend on the type of the underlying rock. For example, soil in limestone areas is alkaline and plants such as camellia will not grow in it.

Habitats are not unchangeable. For example, saplings are not big enough to support birds' nests and they cannot provide shelter for other common animals such as squirrels. Their canopies are very small and there is still light on the ground underneath them, which means a wide range of plants can grow there. As the trees mature, their trunk and branches offer food and shelter for a range of animals of different sizes. In a woodland, as the canopy starts to block out the sunlight, only plants that can tolerate shade will grow underneath it. The environment has changed and specific habitats within the environment change too.

Light penetrating the developing canopy of a woodland.
Source: iStock

Some changes are not so visible

There is currently international concern about the amount of carbon dioxide humans are emitting into the atmosphere and the impact this will have on life on Earth. One of the probable effects of increasing levels of carbon dioxide in the atmosphere is excessive global warming. This is causing an increase in the temperature of the seas. This is observable in the polar regions, where the warmer waters are already causing glaciers and ice sheets to melt. Ice packs are becoming smaller and cannot support larger animals such as polar bears, which need to move onto the ice to catch seals. As the seas become warmer, some marine animals that thrive in the icy waters will not be able to tolerate increases in temperature as small as two degrees Celsius. They will die out. As the habitat changes, different species will move in to replace those organisms that are not able to adapt to the changing conditions.

Some of the animals and plants in a tropical coral reef will be similarly intolerant of small rises in sea temperature, but coral reefs are also vulnerable to another change that is taking place. As the amount of carbon dioxide in the atmosphere increases, the amount of carbon dioxide being absorbed by the oceans is increasing. If this happens, there is a danger that the oceans will become slightly acidic and rapid changes could mean that corals will not have enough time to adapt to the altered conditions. In more acidic waters, they will not be able to form their skeletons. If the corals are threatened, all the plants and animals that depend on them will also be threatened.

Phytoplankton, which are microscopic green plants, are also susceptible to acidity levels. Phytoplankton cover large areas of the oceans and, because they are plants, they photosynthesise and produce oxygen: about 50 per cent of the oxygen available on Earth. If they were to die out, the impact would be potentially catastrophic.

Coral and some of the fish that depend on it for food and shelter.
Source: iStock

Global dimensions: Human evolution

Mary Leakey was a famous palaeontologist – a fossil hunter – who lived in Africa from 1933 until her death 63 years later. Her discoveries have helped us to understand how, starting in Africa, the human race has adapted and evolved over the last four million years. In 1959, working with her husband, Richard Leakey, in the Olduvai Gorge in the country we now call Tanzania, Mary found skull fragments which were the fossilised remains of an early hominid species. This species is called Australopithecus boisei and is one of the ancestors of modern humans. Among other notable fossil finds, in the late 1970s, she and fellow palaeontologists discovered the Laetoli trail of 70 footprints made by hominids who lived in Africa 3.6 million years ago. These prints showed the evolution of the foot structure from an ape-like foot to one that was similar to the modern human foot. The stride length between the prints indicated these early humans had very short legs, which have adapted and evolved into the longer leg of modern humans.

www.nhm.ac.uk/discover/the-origin-of-our-species.html www.becominghuman.org/node/interactive-documentary www.bbc.co.uk/ahistoryoftheworld/objects/l3I8quLCR8exvdZeQPONrw

Summary

Charles Darwin's theory of evolution explains how organisms change over time. The term 'survival of the fittest' refers to how well adapted an organism is, not how healthy it is. Animals and plants that are well adapted to their environment survive and pass on their characteristics to the next generation. Characteristics acquired during an organism's lifetime are not inheritable. Through studying peas, Gregor Mendel was the first to explain how characteristics might be inherited. Studies into DNA have provided a clear picture of the mechanism by which this occurs.

When there are slow changes to the environment, organisms adapt slowly over many generations in order to survive in these new conditions. Owing to the behaviour of humans, environmental changes are happening rapidly and there are concerns that some organisms may not have the time they need to adapt. Large reductions in the numbers of plants on Earth will increase the rate of climate change as less carbon dioxide will be removed from the atmosphere and less oxygen will be released into the atmosphere through photosynthesis. The loss of habitat and the effects of rapid climate change are potentially devastating for the current balance of life on Earth.

Part 2: Ideas for practice

Topic: Teeth and beaks

Age group: 7–9 years

Introduction

This topic provides opportunities for children to identify and compare the functions of different types of human and animal teeth. They also explore how the teeth of animals are adapted to the environment in which they live and how they help them survive. The application stage focuses on birds and how they use their beaks.

Scientific view

In order for animals to survive, they need to be able to compete for the available resources, including food. The mouth parts of an animal determine the type of food it eats. Different teeth have different shapes and sizes and their function relates to their shape. The functions are cutting, tearing, crushing and grinding.

Working scientifically

In these activities children will:

● ask questions and use scientific enquiries to answer them;

- classify and present information to help answer questions;
- record findings using drawings;
- make simple comparisons and identify associations;
- use results to draw conclusions and raise further questions;
- use evidence from information sources to support their findings.

Exploration stage

Children's talk involves trying out their own ideas

Setting the scene

Show children video clips of different mammals and reptiles and discuss what they eat and how they are adapted to their habitats. Working *collaboratively*, children create food chains which include mammals or reptiles. The food chains should include a producer, predator and prey.

Scientific enquiry

Children *talk together* about the animals in their food chains and focus on the range of things they eat. They use information sources to explore and compare the structure of the teeth of herbivores with those of carnivores. Children create displays which illustrate the differences between the teeth of herbivores and carnivores using examples from mammals and reptiles. Can children work out what animals eat from the shape of their teeth? Use the question to probe children's understanding of the relationship between the structure and function of an animal's teeth.

   Children compare the shape of their own teeth with those of a carnivore mammal such as a lion or tiger. They can inspect their teeth using mirrors and record their observations using simple drawings which can be compared with a 3-D model. Remember to maintain hygiene, especially if using dental mirrors. Refer to *Be safe!* (2011). *Talk together* about similarities and differences between their teeth and those of carnivores.

Talking points: true, false or not sure?

- Lions eat grass when they can't catch their prey.
- Sheep have teeth which can only be used to eat grass.
- Without large canine teeth a lion would starve.
- We have the same teeth as lions.
- You can tell what a creature eats by studying its teeth.
- All teeth are basically the same.

Discuss children's responses to the talking points, and explore what they know about the functions of different types of teeth.

Puzzle

We eat meat just like lions and tigers, so why are our teeth not the same shape?

Storytelling

To help solve the puzzle, children compare how we obtain our food compared to carnivores, which live in the wild. Children focus their story on a reptile and a mammal of their choice. The story should be well researched using information sources so it accurately describes the animals' diets and compares them to our own. As part of the storytelling children can explore whether the shape of our teeth have changed since the time we were hunter-gatherers. Children use their stories to explain the differences between the shape of our teeth and those of carnivores such as crocodiles, lions and tigers.

Formative assessment

Provide opportunities for children to voice what they have learnt in the exploratory stage. Use evidence from their responses to the puzzle, talking points and other activities to assess differences between children's ideas and the scientific view. Plan how you will use the re-describing stage to help the children address their *learning needs*. You may need to modify the activities depending on the collective and individual needs of your children.

Information and teaching resources

BBC Bitesize:

- BBC (2017). Mammal Class Clips. *www.bbc.co.uk/education/topics/zn22pv4/resources/1*
- BBC (2017). Reptiles and Amphibians Class Clips. *www.bbc.co.uk/education/topics/zsmmn 39/resources/1*

Re-describing stage

Children's talk involves making sense of scientific ideas

Teacher-led discussion

Ask children to record what they ate yesterday. What did they use to help them? Did they use a knife to cut up their food? Animals such as lions and tigers eat raw meat just with their teeth. How sharp must a lion's teeth be? *Talk together* about the purpose of different-shaped teeth and how they are used by various animals. Discuss why carnivores like lions and tigers need sharp incisors and why they have fang-like canines. They also have molars, which have a flat surface for crushing and grinding. Carnivores sometimes use their claws to hold on to their prey and to help in tearing the flesh. Use video clips to illustrate the key ideas.

Scientific enquiry

Talk about why we don't need teeth like a tiger's and help the children to finally resolve the puzzle. If we don't have teeth like a carnivore, perhaps our teeth are similar to those of herbivores? Children collect pictures of the skulls of plant-eating animals to compare with human skulls. Do our teeth suggest we are more adapted to eating plants or meat? Children can research how humans obtained their food long ago when they lived a life as hunter-gathers. Did they eat mainly plants or did they eat a lot of meat. Are our teeth well adapted to eating both meat and plants?

Do any animals have teeth which are similar to ours? Children can use information sources to identify omnivore mammals and compare the shape of their teeth with ours. They draw diagrams and download pictures to show similarities and differences and add them to their display from the previous stage. *Talk together* about the children's displays and probe children's understanding of the link between the shape of an animal's teeth and its diet. Address outstanding *learning needs* before moving on to the application stage.

Information and teaching resources

BBC Bitesize:

- BBC (2011). Explanation – Wobbly Teeth. *www.bbc.co.uk/education/clips/zy84d2p*
- BBC (2017). Teeth – How They Help Animals Eat. *www.bbc.co.uk/education/clips/zwfj39q*
- BBC (2007). Teeth and Feeding. *www.bbc.co.uk/education/clips/z3k4d2p*

Application stage

Children's talk involves trying out scientific ideas

Animals without teeth

Using information sources children identify a range of common birds and classify them as either carnivores, herbivores or omnivores. They should compare the shapes of their beaks and record them through drawings.

Show the children pictures of different-shaped beaks and ask them to predict what each bird eats. Include pictures of distinctive beaks, such as those of woodpeckers, pelicans, parrots, ducks and eagles. *Talk together* about how the shape of the beak is important because it helps the bird eat particular types of food.

Children can build models of birds' beaks using a range of materials including card, plastic, lolly sticks and chop sticks. The beak could be designed to fit on the thumb and index finger so it is easy to open and close. Children plan tests to compare how well different shaped beaks work. Groups demonstrate how their beaks work and identify birds with similar shape beaks. Probe children's understanding of the link between the shape of its beak and what a bird eats.

Finish this activity by giving children the following puzzle to solve. Why do birds not have any teeth? Can they think of any reasons why birds survive better with beaks? What other vertebrates do not have any teeth?

Design and make a hand puppet

Based on the previous activity, children can design and make a hand-puppet of a bird with a moving beak. Refer to the ASE publication *Be safe!* for H&S advice on making things.

Children investigating the best 'beak' for eating the available food.
Source: Peter Loxley

Information and teaching resources

BBC Bitesize:

- BBC (2017). Birds Class Clips. *www.bbc.co.uk/education/topics/ztjj6sg/resources/1*

Topic: Body colours and patterns

Age group: 9–11 years

Introduction

This topic provides opportunities to explore how animals have adapted to suit their environment and that adaptation may lead to evolution. The activities focus on how colour and body patterns can help animals survive. In the application stage children plan enquiries to test whether bright colours or camouflage potentially provide the best protection for animals.

Scientific view

Successful animals are those whose characteristics enable them to survive and reproduce in their habitat. If, for example, the most brightly coloured animals survive, then this characteristic is passed on to subsequent generations. The same applies to animals which survive best by camouflage.

Working scientifically

In these activities children will:

- plan scientific enquiries to find answers to questions, including recognising and controlling variables;
- record data using bar graphs;
- report and present findings from enquiries and draw tentative conclusions;
- use established scientific knowledge to make sense of observations.

Exploration stage

Children's talk involves trying out their own ideas

The spots on a peacock butterfly make it look like an owl in order to scare off predators.
Source: iStock

Setting the scene

Read *How the Leopard Got His Spots* by Rudyard Kipling or a similar story involving an animal with spots. In Kipling's story some vocabulary would not now be considered acceptable. You might want to change some of the words before sharing the story with the children. Encourage them to discuss why the leopard was successful in the first part of the story and why he needed to change in the second part. *Talk together* about whether stripes or spots provide better camouflage in a forest. Why are they both better than being 'golden-yellow from head to heel'? Children can draw pictures to illustrate their arguments.

The story illustrates the need for animals to be camouflaged, but it suggests that animals can change their skin colourings instantly. Ask the children whether they think this is possible?

Puzzle

It is not only leopards that have spots. Other animals, such as fish, ladybirds, butterflies and peacocks, also have spots. But these spots are not for camouflage purposes: they are bright, colourful spots, which are easily seen by predators. Lots of animals are brightly coloured, including types of bees, wasps and frogs. Why? Is this a problem or an advantage?

Talking points: true, false or not sure?

- Ladybirds have spots to look good and attract a mate.
- Some butterflies have spots to frighten predators.
- Some frogs are brightly coloured to encourage predators to eat them.
- The bright dark and yellow stripes on some wasps and bees warn predators that they may get stung.
- Peacocks and birds of paradise use bright colours so they can be seen in the dark.

Children *work collaboratively* to answer the talking points. Discuss children's ideas and examine their reasoning.

Storytelling

Which animals have the brightest colours? Children use information sources to discover the most colourful animals in the world. The task involves telling an animal's survival story and how it is influenced by its colour. Events described in the story should include how it keeps safe, how it gets its food and how it reproduces. Children use PowerPoint presentations to tell their stories with links to relevant video clips. Use the opportunity to probe their thinking and to address the puzzle.

Formative assessment

Provide opportunities for children to voice what they have learnt in the exploratory stage. Use evidence from their responses to the puzzle, talking points and other activities to assess differences between children's ideas and the scientific view. Plan how you will use the re-describing stage to help the children address their *learning needs.* You may need to modify the activities depending on the shared and individual needs of your children.

Information and teaching resources

BBC Bitesize:

- BBC (2009). How Do Animals Protect Themselves from Predators? *www.bbc.co.uk/education/clips/zw3fb9q*
- BBC (2013). Birds of Paradise. *www.bbc.co.uk/education/clips/zxgd2hv*
- BBC (2007). Introduction to Butterfly Varieties. *www.bbc.co.uk/education/clips/zqjkjxs*
- BBC (2007). Minibeasts. *www.bbc.co.uk/education/clips/z884d2p*
- BBC (2007). How Animals Survive in the Desert. *www.bbc.co.uk/education/clips/zxcb4wx*

Re-describing stage

Children's talk involves making sense of scientific ideas

Teacher-led discussion

Start with what the children learnt in the exploratory stage. Discuss whether bright colours can provide an advantage for some animals. Of course, there are many other animal characteristics which help them survive. Show children the BBC Bitesize animation called *Why did the brown bear evolve into the polar bear?* The animation describes how brown bears adapted to life in the Arctic. The story is told to Sam, a young tortoise, by his Grandad Charlie. The story tells of a group of hungry brown bears who went looking for food to an icy region inhabited by seals. The bears' paws weren't good for walking on snow and ice, their fur wasn't thick enough for the cold conditions and the seals could easily see them coming with their brown fur. After a long, long time, some bears were born with bigger, thicker paws and with warmer, lighter-coloured fur. The bears which flourished evolved into polar bears.

Do children think it makes sense for brown bears to evolve into polar bears in this way? Did it happen quickly or gradually? Could it have been that the first white bears were born in the forest and finding it hard to survive migrated to colder regions in search of food? Encourage children to speculate about how evolution takes place. Is it a result of an unusual event, such a baby bear being born white instead of brown, or is it due to changes to the environment in which an animal lives?

Children work *collaboratively* to create a case for how animals evolve, citing particular examples. For example, how did the giraffe get such a long neck? Was it by accident or did it evolve in response to its environment? *Talk together* about children's ideas and use video clips to illustrate how animals adapt to their environment and discuss how changes to their environment could lead to evolution.

Scientific enquiry

The purpose of this enquiry is to explore whether camouflage works. Provide each group with a large sheet of coloured paper or card. The sheet of paper represents the background for the animals' *habitat*. Ask children to make at least four butterflies out of different coloured paper. One of the butterflies should be made out of the same colour paper as the habitat. They then stick the butterflies lightly to the *habitat* in a random pattern and hang it on the wall of the classroom. How easy is it to see the camouflaged butterfly compare to the others? Which is the easiest to see.

Children plan how to use their model habitat scientifically to test whether camouflage is effective. What data can they collect to support or refute the idea? How can they make sure their tests are fair? They will probably need the help of children who are unaware of the existence of the camouflaged butterfly. One way of doing it is to ask children from other classes to stand a few metres away from the habitat with their eyes closed. They are only allowed to open their eyes for one second, and then close them again. Which butterflies did they see? Can they describe where you placed the camouflaged butterfly? Collect data from a number of different children. Move the butterflies around for each test. Groups record their data and use it to conclude whether camouflage works. Children can extend their enquiry into pattern matching by designing animals with patterned camouflage to match a habitat made up of similar colours and patterns.

Teacher-led discussion

Talk together about how animals' characteristics help them survive and reproduce in their habitat. Reflect on how animals pass on these successful characteristics to their offspring and how this may lead to evolution. From this perspective, ask the children to create a more reliable, scientific story of *How the Leopard Got His Spots*. Listen to children's stories, probe their thinking and address outstanding *learning needs* before moving on to the application stage.

Information and teaching resources

BBC Bitesize:

- BBC (2009). Why Did the Brown Bear Evolve into the Polar Bear? *www.bbc.co.uk/education/clips/zpqw2hv*
- BBC (2009). Why Do Giraffes Have Long Necks? *www.bbc.co.uk/education/clips/zk3ygk7*
- BBC (2017). How Animals Have Adapted. *www.bbc.co.uk/education/clips/zccbp39*
- BBC (2015). How Animals Adapt to Become Successful Predators. *www.bbc.co.uk/education/clips/z8gg2p3*
- BBC (2017). How Does Camouflage Help an Animal to Hide or Attack? *www.bbc.co.uk/education/clips/zrntsbk*

Application stage

Children's talk involves trying out scientific ideas

Warning colours or camouflage?

Children can test whether bright warning colours or camouflage provide the best protection against predators. The idea is to decorate an egg using colours and markings, which will prevent it from being eaten by local animals. Children start by surveying an area in the school grounds where they intend to leave the eggs. They can then camouflage an egg so it is difficult to see and paint warning signals on another to scare off local animals. Unpainted eggs can be used as a control to help create a fair test. Photographs can be taken to record each stage and the outcomes of the enquiry. Results are unpredictable but will provide discussion opportunities. Remember, animals have ways of detecting food other than their sense of sight. Maintain good hygiene throughout this activity. For H&S advice refer to *Be safe!* (2011).

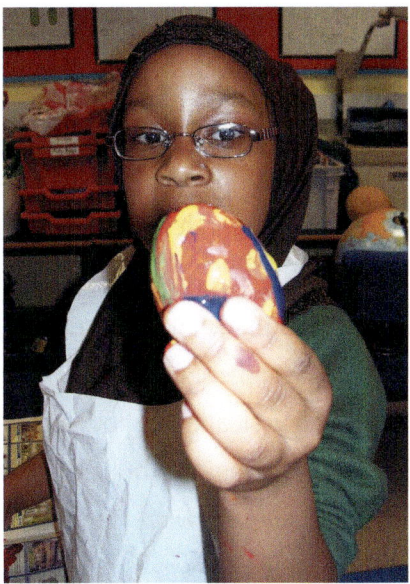

Warning signals painted on an egg.
Source: Peter Loxley

Colour-blind predators

National Geographic has a story on its website entitled *Shades of Prey: Can Colour-blind Predators See Warning Colours?* The story is fascinating and is supported with some amazing video footage. It is an opportunity for children to enjoy some real-life science. Children can explore and enjoy other stories especially in the kids' section.

Design an undiscovered animal

Groups of children research different habitats using information sources. They may include woodland, tropical rainforest, desert, river and arctic regions. Can they discover some of the animals that live there and suggest how they are adapted to their habitat? How do they keep safe? Children can then design an 'undiscovered' animal which would be suited to a particular habitat. Give it a name and describe its characteristics. What would it eat? What would be its predators? How would it keep safe? Children can create a 3-D model of the habitat and the imaginary animal. Groups present their models and explain why their animal is well suited or adapted to living there. Use the story to assess children's understanding of adaptation.

Information and teaching resources

Useful websites:

- National Geographic (2015). Shades of Prey: Can Colour-blind Predators See Warning Colours? *http://news.nationalgeographic.com/2015/11/151107-animals-science-insects-bugs-colors-vision/*
- National Geographic (2017). Weird and Wild. *http://news.nationalgeographic.com/weird-wild/*
- Science News (2016). Peacocks Twerk to Shake Their Tail Feathers. *www.sciencenews.org/article/peacocks-twerk-shake-their-tail-feathers?tgt=nr* – fascinating footage of peacock display.

Talk skills and science discussion: Elaborating

Ask groups to research a relevant topic such as:

- How fossils are formed
- How (e.g.) camels, polar bears, toadstools or sunflowers are adapted to their environment
- The life and work of Charles Darwin

Discuss in groups ideas arising from the topic. Ask children to ensure that they encourage one another to say as much as they can and to elaborate on ideas. Suggest using the talk tools: 'Can you say a bit more…?', 'What else do you know about it…?' and 'Could you explain what you mean by…?'
With the whole class, discuss issues such as:

- A comparison of how different species have adapted to their habitat over time, and why
- An evaluation of how fossils are formed and what the fossil record tells us
- An explanation of how a particular creature or plant fits (matches) the environment it lives in
- Charles Darwin – his journey and his thoughts on adaptation
- Charles Darwin – his life's work and his publication of evidence

Ask groups to say how well individuals elaborated on their ideas.

Ask children what they found difficult about elaboration and what they thought was useful.

Additional information and teaching resources

Companion book:

- Loxley, P. (2018). *Practical Ideas for Teaching Primary Science: Inspiring Learning and Enjoyment,* Abingdon: Routledge, Chapter 3: Flowering Plants, Chapter 4: Woodland Habitats, Chapter 5: Rocks and Fossils, Chapter 7: Decomposers, Chapter 14: Light and Chapter 15: Sound.

BBC Bitesize:

- BBC (2009). How Is a Camel Adapted to Live in the Desert? *www.bbc.co.uk/education/clips/z4ynvcw*
- BBC (2015). How Animal Skeletons Have Adapted. *www.bbc.co.uk/education/clips/zp6pk7h*
- BBC (2007). Interdependence and Adaptation. *www.bbc.co.uk/education/clips/z8cb4wx*
- BBC (2007). How Different Animals Adapted to Their Habitats. *www.bbc.co.uk/education/clips/z3hxpv4*
- BBC (2017). What Is Camouflage? *www.bbc.co.uk/education/clips/zcptsbk*

Websites:

- Widescreen Arkive. ARKive Education. *www.arkive.org/education*
- Wildscreen Arkive. *www.arkive.org*

- Oxford University Museum of Natural History: The Learning Zone (2006). *www.oum.ox.ac.uk/thezone/index.htm*

ASE journals:

- Primary Science 138 (May/June 2015). *Animals Don't Just Grow Feathers When They Want To…* by Terry Russell and Linda McGuigan.
- Primary Science Review 107 (March/April 2009). This issue focuses on the work of Darwin and related issues.

CHAPTER 16

HEALTH AND WELL-BEING

This chapter examines factors which influence the health and well-being of humans and other animals. We look at how our understanding of animal body systems and the ways in which they interconnect have developed slowly through history. Animals cannot manufacture their food in the way that plants do and so, for most animals, their way of life and continuing existence are limited by their ability to consume as widely as possible. Most humans, however, are able to make choices about what they eat and the ways in which they live, and the decisions they make will impact upon their health and development.

Topics discussed in the chapter

- Historical context
- Animal growth
- Animal nutrition – the digestive system
- The cardiovascular system
- Keeping healthy

Part 1: Subject knowledge

Historical context

Balancing the humours

Until the sixteenth century, our understanding of anatomical systems was dominated by the work of a Roman physician of Greek origin, Claudius Galen (c. 129–c. 216 CE). Because the dissection of human beings was considered unacceptable, Galen's work was based on clinical observation and the dissection of pigs and apes. Poor health was often attributed to imbalance between the four humours – blood, phlegm, yellow bile and black bile. Bloodletting was a common remedy for supposedly restoring the body's balance and remained so well into the eighteenth century.

Understanding of human disease was hampered by the persistence of Galen's four humours theory throughout Western medicine. The nature of infection and the transmission of contagious diseases were not fully understood, and doctors were unable to cope with the epidemics that swept Western Europe in the Middle Ages.

In Arab cultures, physiological investigation and medical trials were well known from the ninth century onwards. The philosopher and doctor Avicenna, also known as Ibn Sina (980–1037 CE), is thought, for example, to be responsible for the identification of a range of infectious diseases and a systematic approach to their treatment. Many of the hospitals established by religious orders in the medieval period owe their foundation to the medical practices witnessed by the soldiers and priests who returned from the crusades in the Middle East.

Human dissection led to major advances

In the early sixteenth century, Galen's ideas were increasingly questioned. Wider acceptance of human dissection enabled physicians to revise and review his ideas. In 1542, Andreas Vesalius (1514–1564) published a volume on human anatomy which raised the status of anatomy and surgery and led directly to William Harvey's classic explanation of the dual circulation of the blood in 1628. However, even Harvey (1578–1657) still believed in the mystical nature of the human body and the 'vital spark' that sustained life. It was René Descartes (1596–1650) in 1637 who initially described the heart as a mechanical pump and the body as a machine. Our knowledge of the process by which nutrition and breathing come together to provide the energy to sustain life was not developed until Antoine Lavoisier's (1743–1794) descriptions of the role of oxygen in combustion. This led to an understanding of the way in which energy is released through respiration in each cell to yield the energy needed for growth and to repair and drive the body's systems. There was a gradual realisation that animals are made up of interrelated and complex systems which govern their well-being.

Animal growth

How do we and other animals grow?

Growth in animals takes place through **cell division**. In the moments after fertilisation, the fertilised egg begins to divide into 2, 4, 8, 16 cells and so on. Cell division begins with the replication of the genetic material, the chromosomes, in the nucleus. Following this, the cell splits into two to produce two identical daughter cells, each containing the same genetic material as the parent cell.

Something to think about

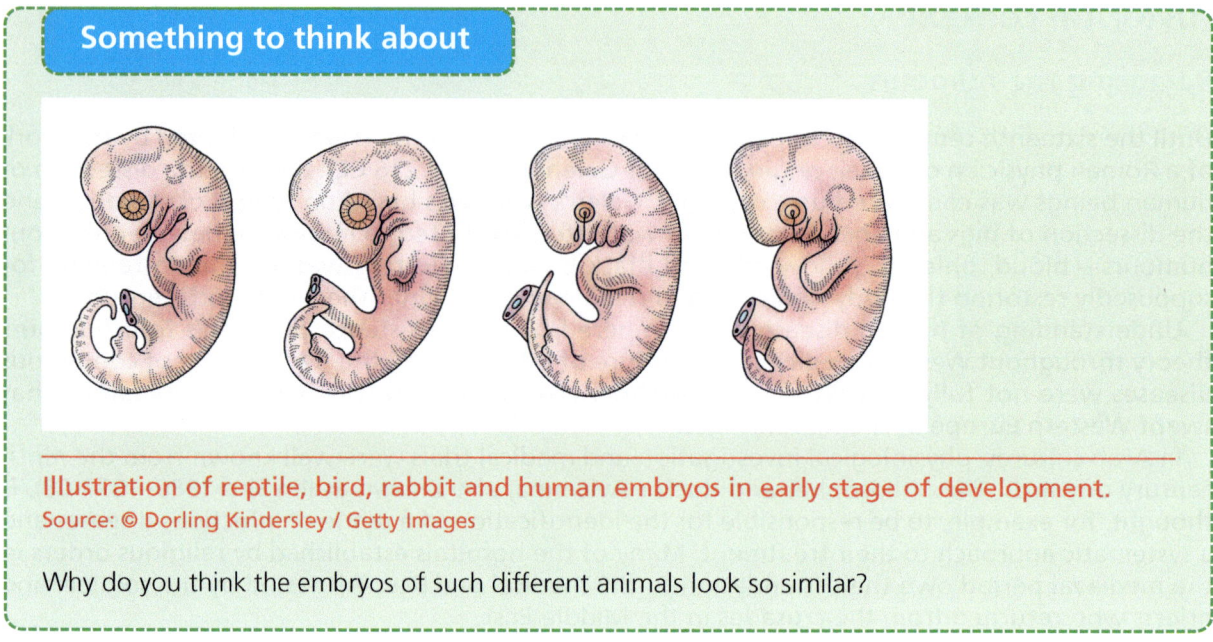

Illustration of reptile, bird, rabbit and human embryos in early stage of development.
Source: © Dorling Kindersley / Getty Images

Why do you think the embryos of such different animals look so similar?

How do we grow and why do we stop growing?

Different parts of an animal grow at different rates. A human baby's head grows quickly before birth to house and protect the developing brain, whilst the limbs grow more quickly after birth. As the cells that make up muscle tissue and organ systems divide, the skeleton itself needs to grow to accommodate the growing organism. Eventually, this process stops and the adult ceases growing. However, there will always be some cells that need to be replaced in the body. New blood cells, for example, are formed in the bone marrow throughout life. When the body is damaged, cells at the site begin dividing again, wounds heal and damaged tissue is replaced.

What are bones made from?

Human babies are born with over 300 bones but by the time a child becomes an adult these have reduced to 206. This reduction occurs because the infant bones are mostly cartilaginous and not made from the hard calcium-based bone material. **Cartilage** is a form of dense **connective tissue** and is flexible. Over time, this is converted to bone by a process known as **ossification**. This flexibility allows for movement and growth and for fusing of bone material – most notably in the skull, which is made up of separate plates in the uterus to enable slight compression and distortion of the head during birth. It is the cartilaginous nature of the infant bones that enables growth. The long bones of the body (such as the femur) grow from each end in areas called growth plates. This happens when the cartilage cells divide and increase in number. The new cartilage cells push the older cells towards the middle of the bone, where they die and the space they occupied is replaced by bone. When a bone has reached its full size, its growth plates are also converted into bone and growth stops.

What limits the size of different animals?

To grow large, an animal needs a strong internal skeleton to support it. The dinosaur skeletons displayed in many natural history museums are testament to this. The largest aquatic mammals, the whales, grow to such a size because their body weight is supported by the water. Even though they have strong skeletons, beached whales are in great danger, and unless they are quickly returned to the sea their internal organs will collapse under their own weight.

Invertebrates, such as earthworms, that have no skeletons are restricted in size and some live in water for support. On land, many invertebrates tend to be slow-moving and vulnerable. Those that have hard **exoskeletons,** such as crabs, can move with more speed but need to shed their skeletons in order to grow and at these times are vulnerable to predators. **Molluscs,** such as snails, grow as their shells grow. The size of insects is limited by their inefficient breathing mechanisms. In **vertebrates**, oxygen is efficiently transported to the cells by the circulatory system. However, insects rely on oxygen being delivered directly through a series of dead-end tracheal tubes, bottlenecks which limit the amount of oxygen that can be received at the insect's extremities. It is thought that the large insects that lived during the Palaeozoic era (543 to 248 million years ago) only did so because atmospheric oxygen levels were then at a record high.

Animal nutrition – the digestive system

Animals need food to live

In order to live, all animals need energy. The ultimate source of this energy is the food produced by plants through photosynthesis (see Chapter 13). Animals need a mechanism to release energy from the food they eat. Energy is used for growth, repair and to keep vital internal systems working. Animals can consume a wide range of foods. Those that have the greatest range, normally the omnivores, are the most likely to survive successfully. Those that consume higher up the food chain (see Chapter 13), the carnivores, need only spend a fraction of their time finding food as the meat they eat is high in energy. For example, lions may well only hunt every few days and the boa constrictor can survive for months without eating. This is in contrast to the **ruminants**, the herbivorous mammals such as cattle, that need to graze constantly in order to consume sufficient food to release enough energy to survive. Giant pandas (part of the bear family) consume a highly restricted diet mainly of bamboo. As a result, they need to spend most of their time feeding and cannot build up sufficient energy reserves to hibernate through the worst of the winter, as bears in temperate climates generally do. As a result, pandas struggle to survive in winter when the leaves that are available are often frozen and difficult to consume. From a survival point of view, an animal that has a highly specialised and restricted intake is vulnerable to alterations in the environment, either naturally or as a result of human actions.

Something to think about

Myth has it that we are never more than a few feet away from a rat. Why do rats survive so successfully? Is this anything to do with their diet?

What happens to the food that we eat?

Animals need to process their food so that it can be used effectively throughout the body to sustain life. The higher-order vertebrates – that is, birds, reptiles, fish, amphibians and mammals – have the most complex digestive systems, particularly those that are capable of eating a wide range of foodstuffs, including both vegetation and meat.

Human digestion – where does it begin?

Digestion begins in the mouth mechanically through biting, gnawing and chewing. Humans have three different types of teeth, incisors, canines and molars, each with a different function. Incisors cut, canines tear and molars grind the food which is then mixed with saliva so that it can be easily swallowed.

Swallowing is aided by a process of muscle contraction, known as **peristalsis**, that forces food down the oesophagus, or gullet, towards the stomach. The process of digestion begins with saliva (a mixture of mucus to lubricate and amylase to break down starch) in the mouth and continues as the food passes to the stomach, which secretes **gastric juices** (hydrochloric acid and pepsin to break down the proteins) that attack the ingested food. The acid in a human stomach is highly corrosive, with a pH of between 1 and 2. Depending on its nature, food will remain in the stomach for a variable amount of time. Water passes through quickly, whilst more complex foods – that is, those that contain proteins, carbohydrates and fats – will remain for two to three hours.

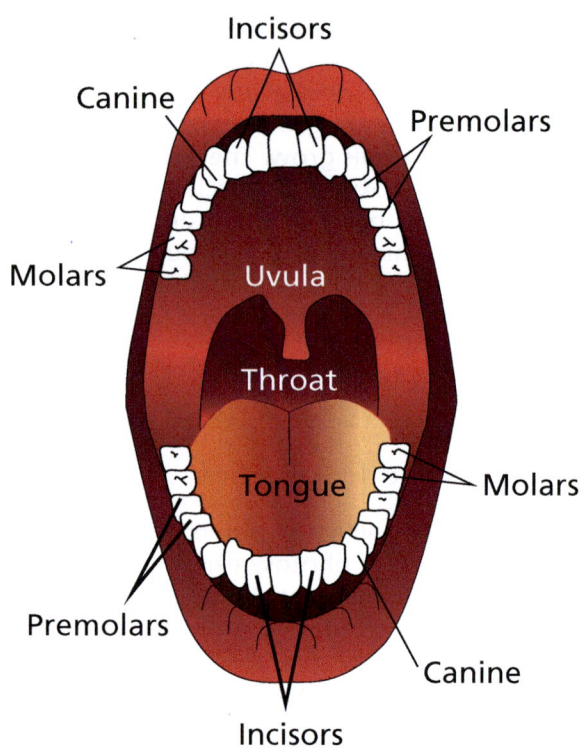

Different types of human teeth.

Beyond the stomach

As the food passes out of the stomach into the duodenum, **bile**, stored in the gall bladder, and other digestive juices produced in the pancreas and small intestines help to break down the complex foods into soluble forms that can pass through the intestinal lining and directly into the bloodstream. The small intestine is long and has a large absorbing surface, which is greatly increased by the thousands of tiny finger-like projections called 'villi'. Any undigested food and water passes into the colon, where the water is absorbed into the bloodstream. The semi-solid waste remaining (the faeces) is passed into the rectum by peristalsis and is expelled at intervals through the anus.

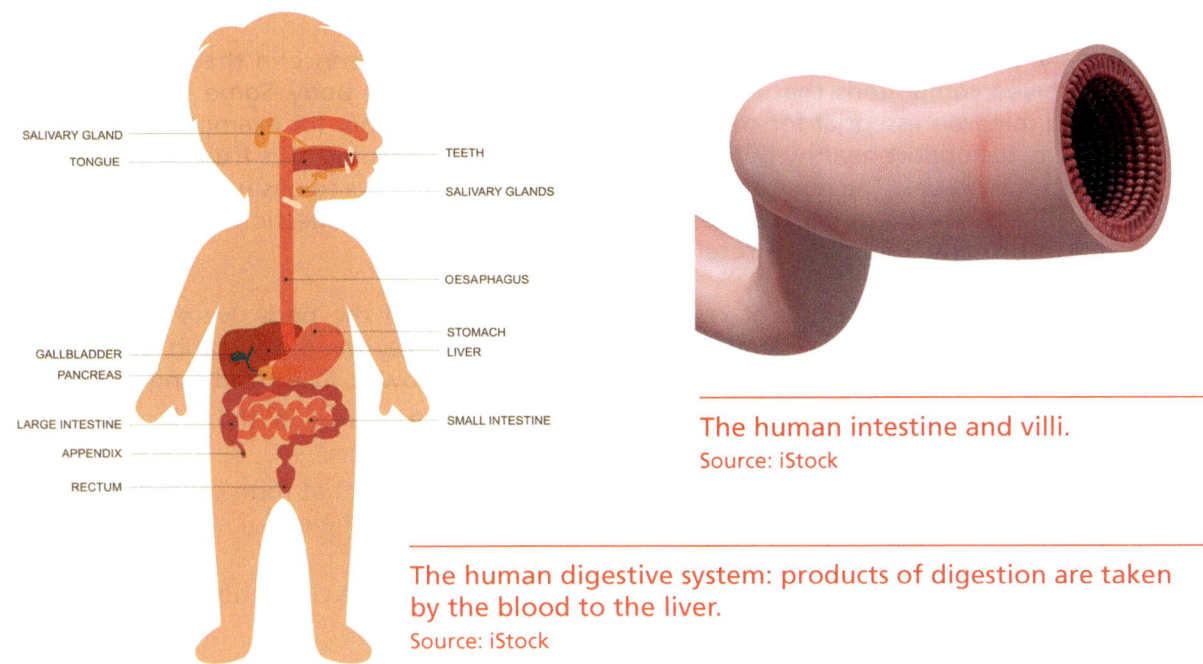

SALIVARY GLAND
TONGUE
TEETH
SALIVARY GLANDS
OESAPHAGUS
STOMACH
LIVER
GALLBLADDER
PANCREAS
LARGE INTESTINE
SMALL INTESTINE
APPENDIX
RECTUM

The human intestine and villi.
Source: iStock

The human digestive system: products of digestion are taken by the blood to the liver.
Source: iStock

Why can't humans eat grass?

At the end of the caecum, connecting the ileum with the colon, humans have a vestigial organ, the appendix. This structure is more prominent and important in herbivorous mammals, where it contains the bacteria essential for the digestion of cellulose. Without these bacteria, the outer cellulose shell of sweetcorn, for example, passes through the human digestive tract virtually untouched. It seems likely that the human appendix is an evolutionary relic from the times when human ancestors existed on mainly herbivorous diets.

Snail watch

It can be fascinating to observe digestion first-hand in snails. Giant African land snails have a nearly transparent gut. Feeding them on strawberries for a time will enable you to watch the passage of food through the snail's gut and even observe the muscular contractions that move the food forward towards the stomach.

Giant African land snail.
Source: iStock

257

Digestion releases nutrients into the bloodstream

Whatever the actual process of digestion, the outcome is the presence in the bloodstream of various dissolved **compounds** that can be transported around the body. Some of these will be vitamins and minerals essential for continued health and well-being: for example, calcium from dairy products to support healthy bones and teeth or vitamin C from citrus fruit to produce and repair connective tissues. The main purpose of digestion, however, is to ensure a constant supply of fuel to all cells for the process of respiration. The products of digestion are glucose (from carbohydrates), amino acids (from proteins) and fats:

- Glucose is used in the process of respiration in every cell of the body. Here it is oxidised, releasing energy to drive the chemical processes in the cells. Carbon dioxide and water are by-products of this reaction. Respiration provides energy for growth, living and renewal.
- Fats are incorporated into cell membranes and other structures in the cells or used in respiration, releasing twice as much energy as glucose.
- Amino acids are absorbed by cells and used to build the proteins that form cell membranes or form enzymes which control and coordinate chemical activity in the cells.

Respiration also requires oxygen, which is brought to the cells via the circulation of the blood.

The cardiovascular system

How is oxygen transported around the body?

The heart (as a pump), the lungs (for the supply of oxygen) and the blood vessels (arteries, veins and capillaries) make up the cardiovascular system. Blood is able to transport dissolved oxygen, food and the waste products of respiration around the body. Deoxygenated blood flows from every tissue of the body to the right side of the heart, where it is pumped to the lungs. Here the carbon dioxide produced as a by-product of respiration **diffuses** out of the blood plasma into the lungs and oxygen diffuses from the lungs into the blood, where it combines with **haemoglobin** in the red corpuscles. Oxygenated blood returns to the left side of the heart and is pumped around the body. The two circulations run simultaneously, giving the characteristic double heartbeat with which we are all familiar. Flow of the blood in the heart is controlled by non-return valves. Contractions of the left side of the heart (systolic) are stronger than those of the right (diastolic) because oxygenated blood has to be pumped around the whole body. This contraction can be felt as a 'pulse' in various locations (neck, wrist, behind the knee) where blood vessels carrying this blood run just below the surface of the skin. The normal adult human heart contracts about 70 times a minute, increasing to 100 times a minute during activity. In smaller animals, such as mice, the heartbeat can be as high as 600 times a minute, whilst an elephant's heart beats only about 30 times a minute.

> ### Something to think about
>
> Mice live on average 3 years and elephants 60. Do you think there is a connection between the rate at which an animal's heart beats and its longevity? What implications does this have for humans?

HUMAN CIRCULATORY SYSTEM

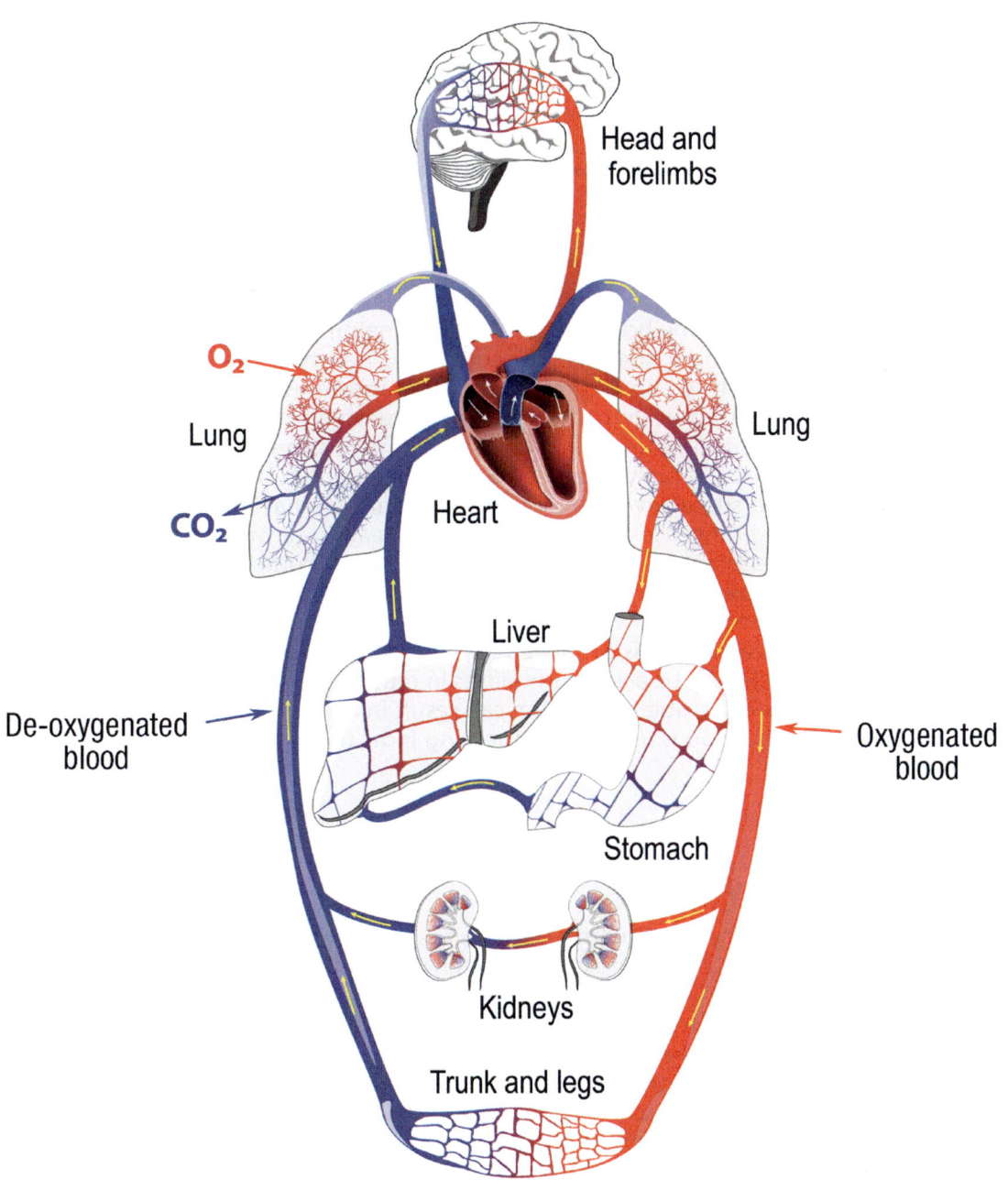

Head and forelimbs

O_2

Lung

CO_2

Lung

Heart

Liver

De-oxygenated blood

Oxygenated blood

Stomach

Kidneys

Trunk and legs

Double circulation with the heart as a pump.
Source: iStock

Respiration

Respiration takes place in every living cell of every organism – animals and plants. It is the process by which glucose is oxidised to form carbon dioxide, and water and energy is released to maintain the organism's vital functions. This process happens most efficiently in the presence of oxygen (aerobic respiration). The oxygen is supplied via the lungs and the bloodstream through the process of breathing. The fuel, glucose, is from digested food in animals and from photosynthesis in plants. Aerobic respiration can be described as:

glucose + oxygen $\longrightarrow$ carbon dioxide + water + energy transfer

$$C_6H_{12}O_6 + 6O_2 \longrightarrow 6CO_2 + 6H_2O$$

About 60 per cent of the energy gained from aerobic respiration is in the form of heat. In 'warm-blooded' animals this maintains the body temperature. Remaining energy is used for growth and repair or for muscular movement such as in locomotion, heartbeat or breathing. As activity increases, the need for oxygen to support respiration also increases. As a result, the heart beats faster to deliver oxygen more quickly to the cells and breathing rate increases to supply this. Certain **hormones** will also increase the heart rate: for example, adrenaline is known as the 'fight or flight' hormone because it is rapidly produced under the stimulus of fear. Adrenaline increases both heart rate and blood sugar levels, allowing an animal to react rapidly to a threatening situation – usually by defending itself or running away. Heart rate may also increase in colder conditions so that a greater amount of heat can be produced to compensate. If the demand for oxygen through vigorous exercise becomes greater than the rate at which the body is able to supply it, then anaerobic respiration will take place. The process is less efficient than aerobic respiration and as a result lactic acid is produced as a waste product. In humans this can happen during strenuous exercise. The lactic acid accumulates in muscle tissue and can cause stiffness and aching ('cramps'). In plants anaerobic respiration can result in the production of ethanol (alcohol) and carbon dioxide. This reaction is used in the brewing industry.

Keeping healthy

Limeys, sauerkraut and gum rot

On sea voyages prior to the mid-eighteenth century, many more sailors died due to poor health than any other reason. In the 1740s, for example, when Admiral Anson's expedition to the Pacific Ocean eventually returned, well over half the sailors aboard had perished. The majority of these deaths were due to the sailor's scourge, the dreaded illness, scurvy. In desperation, the Admiralty in London invited scientists to suggest manageable ways of staving off the onset of this debilitating condition during the increasingly long voyages that were being undertaken.

It was considered at the time that scurvy was the result of poor sanitation, diet, living conditions aboard ship or even feebleness of mind in the sailors themselves. Although it was known that foods such as sauerkraut could combat the development of scurvy, there was no understanding that it was a deficiency condition resulting from lack of a vital vitamin. Sailors lacked vitamin C, which maintains the health of connective tissues in the body. Without it, wounds do not heal, gums rot, lethargy and depression set in and eventually sailors die. Many weird and wonderful solutions were proposed, such as burying the sailor up to the neck in sand or drinking sulphuric acid, but it was James Lind, a naval surgeon, who in 1747 conducted a carefully structured investigation to prove conclusively that lack of a vital element in the diet caused scurvy. In doing so, Lind provided the first recorded example of a clinical trial using control subjects. He introduced a much-needed rigour into medical research. As a result of his work, the provision of green vegetables and citrus fruits became commonplace on British naval vessels, earning the sailors the nickname 'limeys' and in the process saving untold numbers of lives.

Factors which influence health and well-being

The health and well-being of animals depends on a number of factors. For most animals, these are the ability to find and consume appropriate amounts of food, freedom from disease or debilitating injury, shelter from adverse weather conditions and safety from predators. Today, we have a clear understanding of the nature of infection and communicable bacteriological diseases and the role **micro-organisms** play in human health. In the eighteenth and nineteenth centuries, the Industrial Revolution saw rural populations move to the cities to live in crowded and insanitary conditions. Public health became a matter of real concern when, in 1848, an epidemic of cholera led to the death of 14,000 people in London. The writings of Charles Dickens and others exposed the problems associated with poor diet and sanitation, and helped to bring about the development of great engineering works such as the building of the London sewerage system by Joseph Bazalgette. This effectively lifted the scourge of waterborne diseases from the city. In the early twentieth century, the mass mobilisation of men to fight in two world wars exposed the impact of poor nutrition on the population and brought a clearer understanding of the importance of diet in promoting health and general well-being.

Humans are able to make choices about the food they consume and the ways in which they live and these can have a direct impact on health and well-being. Some choices are personal ones for which we can take direct responsibility – whether we eat a balanced diet or give up smoking. Some choices we may feel are beyond our direct control – industrial pollution, exposure to epidemics or the predicted outcomes of increased global warming.

There is an increased emphasis within education on the ways in which individuals can take responsibility for the impact of lifestyle on health and well-being. With growing levels of childhood obesity and falling levels of exercise, children need to be aware of the ways in which they can determine their future well-being. However, these are sensitive issues and need careful and measured treatment in the primary context.

What is a balanced diet?

We know that a variety of different foods is essential to support our body systems and maintain our health. The human body uses carbohydrates as a source of energy for growth, movement and repair. We eat carbohydrates in the form of sugars or starch (found in grains such as rice and wheat). These are broken down through the process of digestion and changed into glucose, which is the main energy source for respiration. Our bodies cannot store excess carbohydrate, so if more sugar and starch is eaten than the body can use, it is stored as fat. Similarly, the fats that we eat are broken down and used by the body to fuel respiration. Proteins, either from meat or pulses, yield a range of chemicals that are used to replace and repair damaged tissue. They also provide some of the enzymes that control our metabolic rate. Within a balanced diet, we also need to consume foods rich in vitamins to help control reactions within the body and minerals, such as calcium, to support the building of bones and maintain nerve function. Living tissue is made up mostly of water, so we need to replace water lost through urination, sweating and exhalation. Finally, although we can no longer digest cellulose (fibre found in vegetables, fruits and whole grains), it still forms an essential part of our daily diet as our bodies need it to speed up the passage of food through the gut. This fibre is also known as roughage.

Poor diet is a global issue. In areas of poverty and deprivation, people are often malnourished and underweight, whereas in developed countries, the abundance and relative cheapness of foodstuffs have led to a growing concern about rising levels of obesity. Many foods are highly processed and contain high levels of sugars, fats and salt. Maintaining a healthy lifestyle requires good nutrition and exercise, and children need to be encouraged to recognise the link between the two.

A balanced diet: can you identify the five food groups?
Source: iStock

Global dimensions: Clean water and public health

Inadequate water supplies and poor sanitation have long been responsible for some of the most devastating public health epidemics. In 1854, a severe outbreak of cholera killed over 600 people in London. Popular belief at the time held that cholera was caused by breathing 'bad air', but local doctor John Snow mapped the incidence of the disease and was able to show that cases clustered around one public water pump. He established that cholera was a water-borne disease and persuaded the local council to disable the pump. London's rapid growth in the nineteenth century had meant that its woefully inadequate sewer system was unable to cope with the huge amount of sewage produced each day. Open sewers ran through densely populated areas and contributed to the contamination of public water sources. An extensive system of sewers was eventually developed as a result of Snow's work and most of this Victorian system is still in use.

Cholera remains a problem today, especially in emergency situations such as devastating floods or areas where war, civil unrest or famine result in sudden movements of population to makeshift refugee camps. It can be prevented by access to safe drinking water, sanitation and good hygiene. The charity Water Aid estimates that one in eight people globally do not have safe water, and diseases such as cholera, typhoid and dysentery are common across the developing world and result in the deaths of 4,000 children a day. The charity concentrates on the use of low-cost, appropriate and sustainable technologies that are within the capacity of local communities to operate and maintain. SODIS (solar water disinfection) is a simple procedure to disinfect drinking water by putting contaminated water into PET (polyethylene terephthalate) bottles and exposing them to sunlight for 6 hours where UV-A rays from the sun kill the viruses, bacteria and parasites that cause diarrhoea.

http://wellcomecollection.org/mike-jay-john-snow-and-soho-cholera-outbreak-1854

www.wateraid.org/uk/

www.sodis.ch/index_EN

Summary

Developments in understanding of the way in which our bodies function, combined with understanding of the nature of disease, have led to improvements in health and well-being. Food contains stored energy which was originally captured from the Sun by plants, and the digestive system enables animals to break down these foods into soluble forms. The blood carries dissolved food, along with oxygen, through the circulatory system to all animal cells. Respiration is the process by which this energy is released and made available for animals to carry out all of the life processes. Respiration takes place in all cells.

Animals produce offspring that are similar to themselves. Growth occurs through the process of cell division and each new cell contains the same genetic material as the parent cell. The skeleton supports and protects an animal's body and determines its size. Continuing health and well-being depend on the choices we make about what we consume and how we live our lives.

Part 2: Ideas for practice

Topic: Healthy eating

Age group: 7–9 years

Introduction

In this topic children explore why animals and humans need the right types and amount of nutrition to stay healthy. In the application stage, children plan and prepare a suitably balanced meal.

Scientific view

We obtain the nutrients we need to grow and develop healthily from the foods we eat. To keep healthy, we must choose a balanced diet from the different food groups.

Working scientifically

In these activities children will:

- gather, record and classify data to help in answering questions;
- use results to draw conclusions and raise questions;
- use evidence to answer questions and develop their ideas.

Exploratory stage

Children's talk involves trying out their own ideas

Setting the scene

Read the story of *The Very Hungry Caterpillar* by Eric Carle. *Talk together* about what it ate each day. Were the children surprised that the caterpillar had stomach-ache on Saturday? Which of the foods are best for a growing caterpillar? Which foods will keep it healthy? Is it best to eat lots of fruit or lots of things like chocolate cake, ice cream and sausages? If the children could choose, which foods would they eat? Can they explain why?

Storytelling

In words and pictures children create their own stories entitled *The Very Hungry Gorilla.* The plot should be similar to the *Hungry Caterpillar* in that the Gorilla eats all the wrong foods with something happening to it as a consequence. Discuss and display children's stories and talk about their reasons for the types of food which they have chosen for the Gorilla to eat. What do gorillas normally eat? Why are the foods in the story not healthy for the Gorilla? Use the stories to assess children's ideas about healthy eating.

Scientific enquiry

Ask the children what they would eat if they could choose their own meals for a week. How would they make their decisions? Would it be based only on what they like best or would they choose 'healthy foods'? Children can *work collaboratively* to plan their meals for a week. They should come to an agreement for the whole group. Younger children can plan for a shorter time and use drawings to record their choices. The groups should compare and justify their choice of meals.

Puzzle

How do we know which are the best foods to choose? Which foods keep us healthy?

Discuss children's responses to the puzzle and probe their thinking about the nature of a balanced diet.

Formative assessment

Provide opportunities for children to voice what they have learnt in the exploratory stage. Use evidence from their responses to the puzzle, story and enquiry to assess differences between children's ideas and the scientific view. Plan how you will use the re-describing stage to help the children address their *learning needs.* You may want to modify the activities depending on the shared and individual needs of the children.

Re-describing stage

Children's talk involves making sense of scientific ideas

Teacher-led discussion

The purpose of this part is to introduce children to the different food groups so that they can make informed choices about what they should eat. Start by showing the children the video clip entitled, *'Why animals need a healthy diet'*. This includes footage about the diet of a gorilla. Children may be surprised that gorillas are vegetarians. Use the clip to illustrate the value of fruit and vegetables in a diet. Use other video clips to talk about the different food groups and how they help us keep healthy.

Food from the major food groups.
Source: iStock

Scientific enquiry

Provide the children with pictures of foods from all the major food groups:

a)   Fruit and vegetables;
b)   Meat, fish and alternatives;
c)   Foods containing fat and sugars;
d)   Milk and dairy foods;
e)   Bread, other cereals and potatoes.

Which of these were included in the children's choice of meals in the exploration stage? How many children chose to eat lots of fruit and vegetables? How many chose lots of foods containing fats and sugars, such as crisps, chips and cakes? Which was the most popular choice? Help the children match their foods to each of the groups. Use pictograms to record how frequently they chose a particular type of food.

Make children aware that their bodies perform best when they eat a balance of these foods. Use a food pyramid diagram to talk about the balance. They can use this information to decide whether their choices of food provided a healthy diet or whether they would likely end up with stomach-ache like the caterpillar! What changes do they need to make to their original choices? Discuss their reasons for making changes and address the puzzle.

Teacher-led discussion

Start by making the point that too much sugar is not good for our health. Discuss how it rots our teeth, causes us to put on weight and can make us ill. Children aged between 7 to 10 years should have no more than 24 grammes (6 teaspoons) a day, younger children should have less. The problem is we don't know most of the time how much sugar we are eating. For example, there are 35 grammes (9 teaspoons) of sugar in a 333 millilitres can of Coca Cola. So, just one can a day can damage children's health.

Scientific enquiry

Children bring into school the packaging from all their favorite foods including drinks. Add your own packaging to the collection. Make sure all the items are clean and safe to handle. Gloves are recommended when handling packaging. For this activity, children will need a big jar of sugar and electronic scales to weigh it in grammes.

Working in groups, children choose the types of foods which they typically eat in a day from the collection. From the labels, groups record the amount of sugar in each product. Then, for each product, they weigh out that amount of sugar contained in the food. The idea is to end up with a container of sugar which represents the amount of sugar the children eat in a day. If they are eating a healthy diet the sugar should not weigh more than 24 grammes per child. Children may be surprised how much sugar they consume in a day. Discuss the outcomes of the enquiry and the potential implications for the health of the children. Address outstanding *learning needs* before moving on to the application stage.

Information and teaching resources

BBC Bitesize:

- BBC (2007). Why Animals Need a Healthy Diet. *www.bbc.co.uk/education/clips/zv6mhyc*
- BBC (2007). Why Do We Need to Eat Fruit and Vegetables? *www.bbc.co.uk/education/clips/zbnhfg8*
- BBC (2007). Eating a Varied Diet. *www.bbc.co.uk/education/clips/zv84d2p*
- BBC (2007). Five Types of Food. *www.bbc.co.uk/education/clips/z4x76sg*
- BBC (2009). Food Needed by the Human Body. *www.bbc.co.uk/education/clips/ztr3cdm*

Application stage

Children's talk involves trying out scientific ideas

Preparing a balanced meal

An enjoyable way of developing children's understanding further would be to involve them in planning, shopping for and preparing a balanced meal for a picnic or other occasion. *Working collaboratively*, children can decide what they would like to eat on the picnic and then justify their choices with regard to a healthy balance. Listen to conversations and assess children's understanding of a healthy diet.

Once a decision has been made, children can be taken to the local supermarket to choose and buy their food. Added sugar in any packaged food should be monitored to ensure a healthy picnic. Back in the classroom, they can then prepare their picnic. Issues of hygiene, safe use of equipment and special diets can be brought into the discussion. Refer to ASE publication *Be safe!* for health and safety guidance. Calculation of costs of the meals could be included in the project. While on their picnic, they could go on a caterpillar hunt and photograph what the caterpillars are eating!

Topic: Keeping Healthy

Age group 9–11 years

Introduction

In this topic, children will explore the impact of exercise on the way our bodies function and discover how our digestive and circulatory systems work to provide the energy our bodies need. In the application stage children explore diets for athletes, carry out sport science activities and find out about the work done by sports scientists.

Scientific view

The circulatory system is the means by which blood is pumped by the heart around our bodies. The blood carries food and oxygen to provide the energy the body needs to support its natural functions. As we make greater demands on our bodies through exercise, the heart pumps more quickly to supply additional energy.

Working scientifically

In these activities children will:

- plan scientific enquiries to answer questions, controlling variables where necessary;
- take measurements using scientific equipment, taking repeat readings when necessary;
- use observations, measurements and other data to draw conclusions;
- use scientific knowledge to explain observations and measurements.

Exploration stage

Children's talk involves trying out their own ideas

Setting the scene

Start with video footage of athletes competing in a recent event, a world championship, a marathon or the Olympics, for example. Ask the children to watch them closely and discuss how they might be feeling when they finish their race. Do they notice if the athlete is sweating or breathing heavily or even falls on the ground as they finish?

Scientific enquiry

Talk together about how the children feel when they have been exercising – during PE in school, for example. Do they experience similar effects to the Olympic athletes?

In a PE session, ask the children to undertake a series of simple exercises. This may need to be adapted to meet the needs of particular children in the class. This could be a simple circuit-training exercise, for example, with set numbers of star jumps, running on the spot, step-ups, etc., for 2 minutes altogether. When the children have finished, ask them to sit immediately and discuss in pairs how they feel. Encourage the children to be precise about how they describe this. They can discuss whether they feel hot, whether they are sweating or if their heart is beating faster. Also, focus their attention to their breathing and whether their legs feel stiff or ache.

Discuss children's responses and focus on how their heartbeat changes during exercise. Time spent practicing finding and recording a pulse before the investigation will be well spent. Children work in pairs to alternately exercise and measure pulses for each other. Avoid the investigation turning into a competition. They need to be reminded that the idea is not to tire themselves completely; moderate exercise is enough.

The children should record in some detail the changes that occur during exercise. To do this they will need to measure and record their at-rest results for heart rate and breathing. They could also describe their appearance and use a forehead thermometer to take their temperature. Once they have the base data, the pairs can take it in turns to exercise and record physiological readings. At this point, it would also be useful to ask the children to take the same readings five minutes after exercising has finished to see if anything has changed.

Taking a pulse at the wrist.
Source: iStock

Puzzle

Prompt the children to suggest reasons for why the changes occur, relating this back to existing knowledge about the body's need for energy. Why does our pulse rate rise and why do we breathe more heavily when exercising? Why do we get hot?

Talking points: true, false or not sure?

- My heart beats faster when I run because I need more blood.
- My heart stops beating when I am sleeping because my body doesn't need any energy.
- When I run, my heart beats faster because I get excited.
- I breathe more deeply when I run because I need more oxygen.
- I breathe more deeply when I run because I need more energy.

Talk together about children's responses to the puzzle and talking points. Encourage them to share their ideas and to provide reasons for their points of view.

Formative assessment

Provide opportunities for children to voice what they have learnt in the exploratory stage. Use evidence from their responses to the puzzle, talking points and other activities to assess differences between children's ideas and the scientific view. Plan how you will use the re-describing stage to help the children address their *learning needs.* You may want to modify the activities depending on the shared and individual needs of the children.

Information and teaching resources

- Olympic (2017). Athletics. *www.olympic.org/videos/athletics* - official website of the Olympics movement.
- BP Educational Service (2017). Animals, Including Humans Topic Starter. *http://bpes.bp.com/ primary-resources/science/ages-9-to-11/animals-including-humans/animals-including-humans-topic-starter/* - heart rate activities.

Re-describing stage

Children's talk involves making sense of scientific ideas

Teacher-led discussion

The purpose of this stage is to help children understand that we get energy from our food, which is used to make our limbs move and also to warm our bodies. The faster or longer we run, the more energy our bodies require. Start with the video clip entitled, *'Five types of food'* in which an athlete talks about the types of food she eats to keep fit. A point made in the video is that food for our bodies is like petrol for a car. Put the wrong petrol in a car and it does not work properly; similarly, if we eat the wrong food our bodies will not perform so well. The food we eat and the performance of our bodies are closely linked. Discuss what children know about the value of a balanced diet.

Talking points: true, false or not sure?

- Eating lots of sugar provides all the energy I need.
- Pasta is an energy food.
- Foods with too much fat in them should be avoided.
- A balanced diet has meat in it.
- Fruit provides more than just energy.

Talk together about children's responses to the talking points and probe the reasons for their ideas. Assess their understanding of a balanced diet and, if necessary, use activities from the previous topic to address their *learning needs.* Use video clips to help children review their understanding of nutrition.

Scientific enquiry

Turn the conversation back to the puzzle. Why does our pulse rate rise and why do we breathe more heavily when exercising? Why do we get hot? To answer the puzzle, children need to know what happens to food when we eat it. Where does it go and what happens to it inside our bodies? Children work *collaboratively* to answer the enquiry questions. They start by drawing around the body of one member of the group on a large piece of paper and draw in what they think are the key organs. They can then use information sources to check and improve the accuracy of their diagrams. Children *talk together* about how food is digested and transported around the body. Focus on the role played by the heart. Encourage each group to arrive at a shared view. Each group can present and compare their ideas in whole-class discussion.

Modelling

Starting from the children's ideas, introduce the concept of respiration. In simple terms, respiration is the process by which our bodies gain energy from the food we eat. Use diagrams, 3-D models and video clips of the digestive and circulatory systems to explain how food combines with oxygen in our muscles (cells) to release energy for movement and heat. Children can modify their drawings to make them consistent with the scientific model and use their understanding of respiration to solve the puzzle. Probe their thinking and address any outstanding *learning needs*. What else would they like to find out? Children can raise their own questions for further learning.

Storytelling

Review the different stages as food passes through our bodies. Children use musical instruments to compose a piece of music based on the journey of the food as it passes stage by stage through the body. The children can choose a musical theme, maybe based on heartbeat or breathing, which continues throughout their piece and on which other sounds representing the different stages are imposed. (This activity is based on *Explore Music Through Science* by David Wheway and Shelagh Thomson, 1993).

Information and teaching resources

BBC Bitesize:

- BBC (2007). Five Types of Food. *www.bbc.co.uk/education/clips/z4x76sg*
- BBC (2017). How Our Circulatory System Keeps Us Alive. *www.bbc.co.uk/education/clips/zg2chv4*
- BBC (2077). Respiration – How Is Oxygen Transported Round the Body? *www.bbc.co.uk/education/clips/ztctk7h*
- BBC (2017). Digestion – How Does Breakfast Affect Your Day? *www.bbc.co.uk/education/clips/zs2bxsg*

Application stage

Children's talk involves trying out scientific ideas

Diets for athletes

Children investigate the diets and training routines of athletes through information sources. What effects are the routines designed to have on their bodies and performances? Does exercise increase breathing rate or an athlete's ability to take in more oxygen at each breath: in other words, does lung capacity increase? Does the diet help to build muscle or provide the energy to perform better? As part of the project, children can design and make high-energy meals which are designed for sprinting or endurance running. They can compare these with the diets of top athletes.

Sports science

Explore activities from websites devoted to sports science for children. There are many interesting ideas such as games, enquiries, projects, quizzes and videos. They can learn about forces in action, healthy eating and how science relates to various types of sports.

Careers in sports science

Invite a STEM ambassador into school to talk about the work done by sports scientists. Courses about sports science are offered by a wide range of universities and colleges round the country. Children can explore the range of courses available on the web and find out about the jobs which sports scientists do.

Information and teaching resources

- Science Kids (2016). Sports Science for Kids. *www.sciencekids.co.nz/sports.html*
- Science Kids (2016). Sports Science Videos. *www.sciencekids.co.nz/videos/sports.html*
- Education.com (2017). Sports Science Fair Projects. *www.education.com/science-fair/sports/*

Talk skills and science discussion: Challenge

Ask groups to research a topic of interest to them which relates life style choices to health – for instance, swimming, cycling, running, healthy eating, vegetarian diet, drinking water, clean air, etc.

Ask groups to discuss their points of view about exercise, diet and health. Clarify the need for a respectful challenge in the discussion. Ask groups to use the talk tools '*I agree because*' and '*I disagree because*'.

As a whole class, carry out role-plays to dramatise ideas raised. Discuss a range of points of view and suggest how compromise and tolerance are useful. Establish the idea that in science, we work towards finding evidence which will answer questions and help us make decisions. Ask groups to consider the importance of challenging ideas, in science, and more generally. Emphasise the difference between challenging an idea and challenging the person who offers the idea.

Additional information and teaching resources

Companion book:

- Loxley, P. (2018). *Practical Ideas for Teaching Primary Science: Inspiring Learning and Enjoyment,* Abingdon: Routledge, Chapter 6: Living Things, Chapter 7: Decomposers and Chapter 8: Nutrition.

BBC Bitesize:

- BBC (2009). The Importance of Fitness. *www.bbc.co.uk/education/clips/zgqw2hv*
- BBC (2017). What Do Humans Need to Stay Healthy? *www.bbc.co.uk/education/clips/zw3jxsg*
- BBC (2017). An Introduction to the Major Organs of the Body. *www.bbc.co.uk/education/clips/zyqfg82*
- BBC (2009). The Heart and How It Works. *www.bbc.co.uk/education/clips/zncg9j6*

Websites:

- BBC Good Food (2016). How Much Sugar Should Children Have? *www.bbcgoodfood.com/howto/guide/children-and-sugar-how-bad-it*
- NHS Choices (2015). How Does Sugar in Our Diet Affect Our Health? *www.nhs.uk/Livewell/Goodfood/Pages/sugars.aspx*
- Food a Fact of Life (2017). *www.foodafactoflife.org.uk* – lots of activities.
- The Children's University of Manchester (2012). The Body and Medicines. *www.childrensuniversity.manchester.ac.uk/interactives/science/bodyandmedicine/* - interactive website designed for primary education.
- BBC. Science: Human Body and Mind. *www.bbc.co.uk/science/humanbody/*

ASE journals:

- Primary Science 136 (Jan/Feb 2015). *Playground Science* by Alan Cross and Jon Board.
- Primary Science 133 (May/June 2014). *'Vegecating' Children* by Katherine Bagshaw, Hannah Barham, Rebecca Betts, Amie Felton and Joshua Knatt.
- Primary Science 128 (May/June 2013). *A Child-Centered Approach to Learning About Healthy Eating* by Francesca Telford.
- Primary Science 127 (March/April 2013). *Taking a 'Giant Tour' to Explore the Human Body* by Dan Davies.
- Primary Science 123 (May/June 2012). *Using Models to Promote Children's Scientific Understanding* by Jane Maloney and Sheila Curtis.
- Primary Science Review 102 (March/April 2008). *The Benefits of Being Physically Active* by Sue Chedzoy and Craig Williams.

CHAPTER 17

THE PARTICLE NATURE OF MATERIALS

In everyday contexts, we heat water to make tea or melt chocolate to cover a cake. Puddles on the pavement dry up in the sunshine and water turns into ice cubes in the freezer. The words that we use to describe what we observe, such as solidifying, melting, boiling and condensing, label these events in scientific terms but give no explanation of the processes taking place. In order to help to explain why materials such as water change their properties when they change from a solid to a liquid and to a gas, we need to offer a story or a model which will help in visualising the processes involved. This chapter explores the particle nature of matter and how this can be used to make sense of phenomena such as ice cubes melting and sugar dissolving in water.

Topics discussed in the chapter

- Historical context
- Properties of materials
- The particle model of matter
- Reversible and physical changes

Part 1: Subject knowledge

Historical context

What the ancient Greeks believed

The idea that matter is not continuous but can be understood as being made up of tiny particles originally came to us from Greek thinking. The philosopher Democritus (460–370 BCE) proposed a thought experiment to ask what would happen if we try to divide matter (a piece of gold, say) into smaller and smaller pieces by continually cutting it in half. He suggested there would be a limit to the number of times this could be done and that eventually the smallest possible piece would result and that this would be indivisible. This he named an atom, meaning 'cannot be cut'. He proposed that these atoms were very small, hard particles that were different in size and shape for each different material but were capable of moving about and joining together.

However, Democritus' ideas were ignored in favour of the 'four elements' theory, supported by more eminent Greek philosophers such as Aristotle and Plato. This idea – that matter is made up of differing proportions of the elements earth, fire, air and water and that matter could be transmuted from one form to another – formed the basis of alchemy. The pursuit of alchemy and the search for the magical 'philosopher's stone' that would transform base metals into gold were ultimately a dead end in our developing understanding of the nature of matter, although many eminent scientists, including Newton, became fascinated with its study.

New ideas emerge in the nineteenth century

In the early nineteenth century, the atomic ideas of Democritus were resurrected by the work of John Dalton, who calculated the relative sizes and characteristics of atoms and laid the foundations for modern chemistry. Our understanding of the form that these atoms actually take was later refined by the research of J. J. Thomson and Ernest Rutherford and culminated in Niels Bohr presenting his 'solar system' model of the atom in 1913 (see Chapter 18). Nowadays, we see the atom as no longer indivisible but comprised of **protons**, **neutrons** and **electrons** and other particles which determine the nature of matter itself.

Properties of materials

Common experiences

The common materials with which we come into contact in everyday life exist in one of three familiar forms: as a solid (e.g. wood), a liquid (e.g. water) or as a gas (e.g. oxygen). There are obvious physical features that distinguish a solid from a liquid. Solids tend to have a shape of their own which they maintain without support. Even a malleable solid such as play dough will retain its new shape once manipulated. A liquid, however, flows and takes on the shape of its container or, if allowed to run freely, will spread out into a thin film on a level surface. The extent to which a liquid spreads is dependent on its viscosity: water and syrup offer two contrasting examples of this. Defining the properties of gases in a similar way is more problematic. Experience of blowing up balloons tells us that a gas, like liquid, has no shape of its own but, unlike liquid, will fill a container completely rather than collecting at the bottom.

> ### Something to think about
>
> Consider the gas that fills the rooms we live in. Wherever we are in the room, we can breathe easily, whether we're up a ladder changing a light bulb or lying on the floor watching TV. How does air get everywhere?

Solid or liquid or gas?

Some solids, like sand and flour, can mimic the behaviour of liquids. We can pour flour and see the flow of sand. Does this mean that sand and flour should be classified as liquids?

If we investigate the structure of sand and flour more closely by looking through a magnifying glass or digital microscope, we can see the individual bits of solid material or grains from which they are made. An analogy is to compare a sack of sand or a bag of flour with a bag of marbles. Each is a mixture made up of solid pieces of material and air. Each grain of sand or flour is classified as a solid. A bag of sand or flour is a **mixture** of a solid and a gas, and the ability to flow is a property of the mixture. An observable property that distinguishes a gas from a liquid or a solid is that it can be squashed or compressed. Generally, solids and liquids are difficult to compress, whilst gases are springy and compress easily.

> ### Something to think about
>
> A sponge holds its own shape but is obviously squashy. Does this mean that some solids are easily squashed or is there another way of looking at it?

The need for a model

The previous discussion draws on features of solids, liquids and gases, which we can observe but offers no explanation about why these differences occur. How can we offer an explanation when we cannot see what is causing materials to behave as they do? To do this we need to think creatively and imagine what the structure of the materials may look like. To help us do this we need a model which behaves in the same way as the materials. The particle model of matter offers a fairly simple and understandable way of explaining the behaviour of materials.

> ### Something to think about
>
> Imagine you have been given a block of chocolate and asked to divide it into as many pieces as possible. Imagine using finer and finer instruments until you are working at a microscopic level, rather like a surgeon performing intricate keyhole surgery using a microscope to focus on the operation site. As you continue cutting, what do you imagine the chocolate would look like? When you look through the microscope, what would you see? Could you imagine going on like this forever?

The particle model of matter

What you would end up with would be individual 'particles' of chocolate that are the smallest pieces possible and can no longer be divided – but are still chocolate. Every substance has unique particles that are different from the particles of any other substance. These particles are not static; they have energy, are in constant motion and are attracted to each other by very strong electrical forces. Energy in the form of heat will affect the speed of the particles. The higher the temperature, the more energy the particles have and so the more quickly they move. In a small square of chocolate there will be many millions of particles. When the chocolate is in a solid block we can imagine particles arranged in a tightly packed uniform structure, rather like a lattice, with the particles held firmly in place by the mutual attraction between them. They can vibrate but cannot move freely. This structure is rigid and not easily pressed out of shape. A solid is **dense** because the particles are packed tightly together. It has a fixed volume and its shape is fixed unless subjected to a force (think of Plasticine being moulded). Solids are difficult to compress as there is no empty space between the particles.

Something to think about

Imagine what happens if you now decide to make a chocolate cake and so heat a block of chocolate in a microwave oven. What will happen to it as it gains more energy?

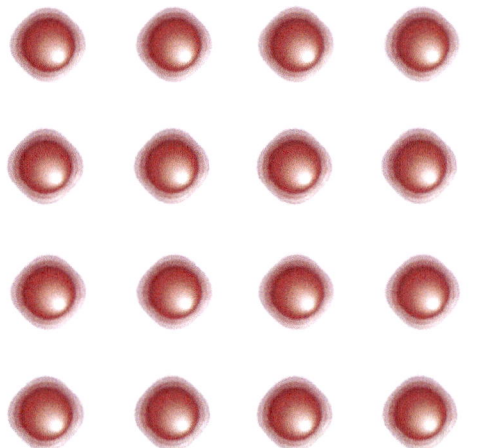

Source: iStock

Model of a solid.

More to think about

In the model above, imagine the supermarket shelf is shaken from side to side (given more energy). The regular arrangement of the stacked apples will break down and the apples will roll across the floor. Compare the behaviour of the apples to the behaviour of chocolate when it is heated. Do you think this is a useful model?

How do solids change into liquids?

As we heat materials, we give more energy to the particles. They are able to move apart from each other and are less constrained by the forces that attract them. They are freer to move randomly over and around each other. The chocolate can be poured out of the basin and will spread across a plate. A liquid will flow as the particles, although still close together, clump randomly and show no particular order. A liquid has a surface and fixed volume, although its shape is defined by its container. A liquid is not easily compressed as there is no empty space between the particles. An analogy is a children's ball pool. The balls take up the shape of the pool but there is little space between them and so they cannot be compressed. As the children play in the pool, the balls roll over each other and become thoroughly mixed.

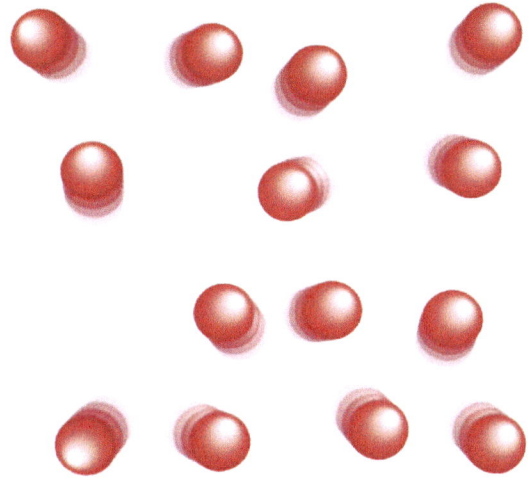

Source: iStock

Model of a liquid.

Why are gases easily compressed?

In a gas such as air, the particles move with more energy and greater speed than in a liquid and are able to break the bonds that hold them together. A gas has no surface and no fixed shape or volume and will spread out to fill any container. Gases are much less dense than solids or liquids. The particles move rapidly, bouncing off one another and off the sides of their container. There are wide gaps between the particles, and the volume of gas becomes smaller as the size of the container decreases. A model for this might be the National Lottery balls in the drum of the machine.

Something to think about

Imagine your chocolate cake is baking in the oven. How does the smell of the cake baking spread throughout the house?

Model of a gas.

How can the particle model explain melting and evaporation?

As a solid warms, the particles begin to vibrate more vigorously until they are able to overcome the forces of attraction between them and move more freely. The solid has melted or liquefied to become a liquid: we call this a change of state. As warming continues, the particles continue to gain energy until they move so vigorously that they break away from each other and escape as free-moving gas particles. The liquid evaporates and changes state. The amount of heat (and so energy) needed to achieve this change will be different for different substances. Evaporation does not always require high temperatures. For example, a saucer of water left on a windowsill will eventually 'dry up'. The water takes in heat from the surrounding air and so the water particles begin to move more quickly. Faster-moving particles close to the surface have enough energy to resist the pull of the surrounding water particles and so escape the liquid. Evaporation happens more quickly if the surrounding air temperature is warmer and also if there is a greater surface area of water exposed to the air.

When materials are cooled, the reverse happens. Cooling removes energy from the particles and so they slow down and are unable to overcome the attraction between them. Gases become liquids again by condensing and liquids return to solids by solidifying.

Something to think about

You pour yourself a large glass of water, add ice and leave it on the table on a hot day. When you return to the glass after some minutes, you notice the outside of the glass is wet. Can you explain why this happens?

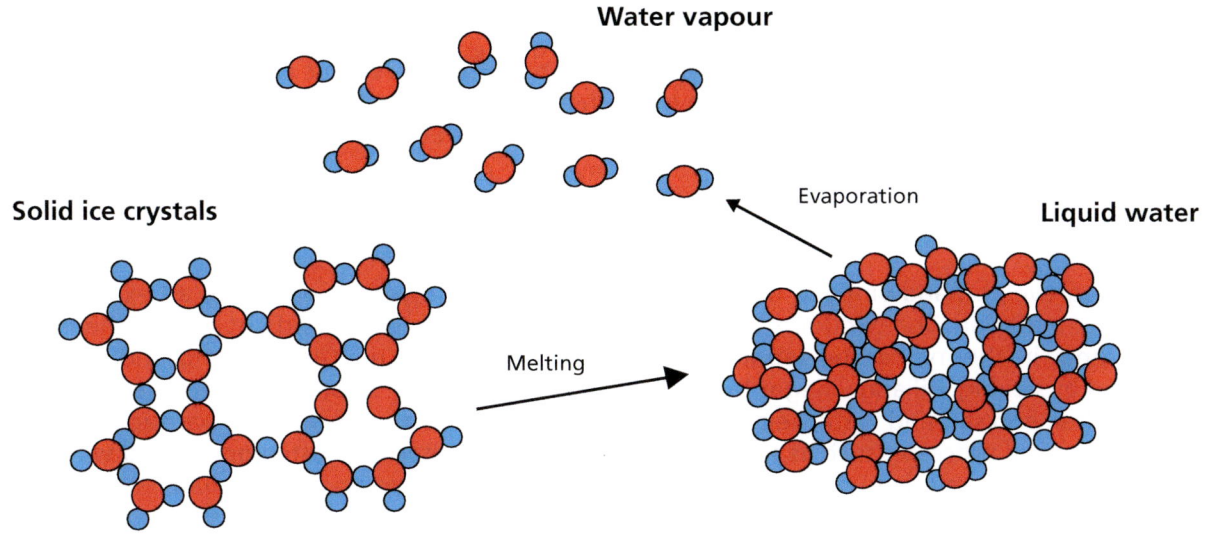

The changing structure of water.

The water cycle

The water in lakes, seas, oceans and rivers is involved in a constant cycle of evaporation, condensation and precipitation. Pollution in the atmosphere can affect the quality of falling rain. When factory chimneys emit sulphur dioxide gases this dissolves in the rain and falls as acid rain damaging the environment.

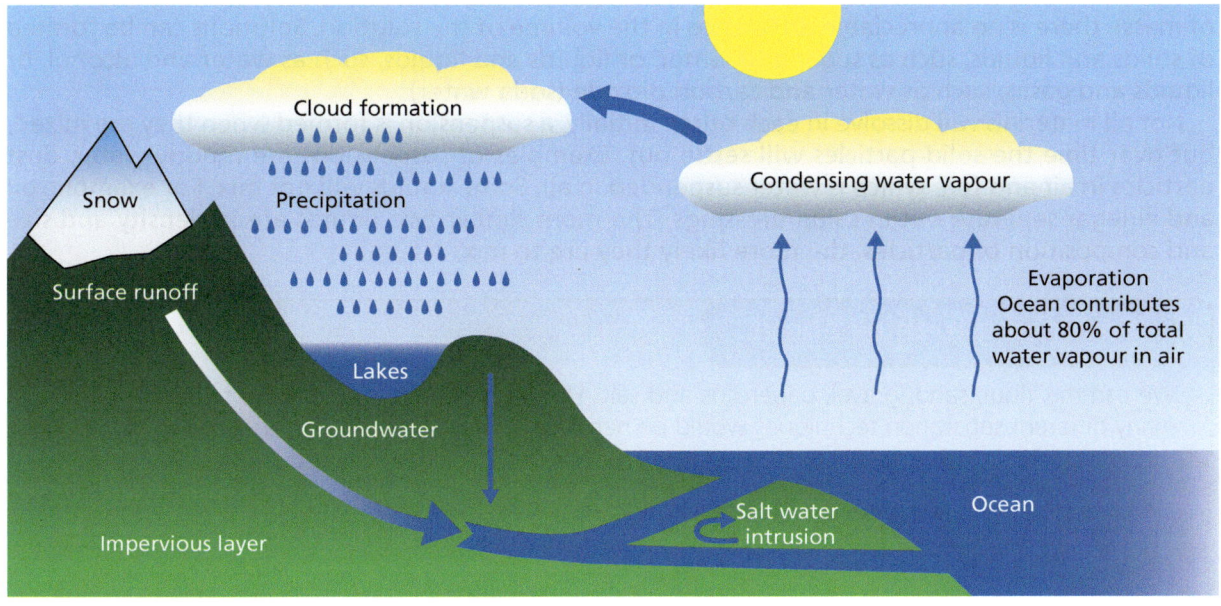

The water cycle.

Reversible and physical changes

The change of state of a material from solid to liquid to gas is a *reversible change* and an example of a *physical change* to that material. Physical changes may alter the appearance and physical properties of a material but the nature of the particles involved stays essentially the same.

What other changes are reversible?

Sand and gravel, oil and vinegar, dust in the air and salt dissolved in water are all examples of mixtures of materials. The two (or more) substances are physically combined but remain chemically distinct and, in theory, can be separated by physical means. A mixture of sand and gravel is separated by sieving, oil and vinegar by settling and then pouring. Dust can be removed from the air by a filter, and salt and water separated by evaporation. Most methods of separation are one-step, mechanical processes such as sieving (sand and gravel), filtering (coffee grinds and water) or pouring off (fat from gravy). However, other mixtures may require an intermediate step, such as the addition of water. For example, to separate a mixture of sand and salt it is first mixed with water. The mixture can then be filtered to remove the insoluble solid (sand) and evaporated to separate out the soluble solid (salt).

Solutions and suspensions

When materials such as sugar or salt dissolve, a solution is formed. A solution is a clear liquid, which is often, but not always, colourless. Instant coffee, for example, gives a clear, brown solution. The liquid which forms a solution is called a **solvent** and the substance that dissolves is called the solute. Water is a common solvent. Weighing reveals that although the **weight** of a solution is the same as the combined weight of the solvent and solute (a phenomenon known as conservation of mass), there is no appreciable difference in the volume of the solution. Solutions can be formed of solids and liquids, such as sugar and water, or liquids and liquids, such as water and alcohol, or liquids and gases, such as water and carbon dioxide (soda water).

Not all materials will dissolve in each other. Initially, a suspension is formed when they are mixed, but over time the solid particles will settle out. Examples of suspensions are muddy water, dust particles in air and fog, which is water suspended in air. Some liquids will not mix. For example, oil and vinegar separate out in salad dressings. The more similar two liquids are in density and size and composition of particles, the more likely they are to mix.

> ## Something to think about
>
> We can mix flour, sand, gravel, paperclips and salt. How can we retrieve all the constituents? How many different separation techniques would be needed to achieve this?

An example of dissolving – where did the sugar go?

Water and sugar are made up of tiny particles. The particles in the solid sugar are held in tight arrays, whilst those of the liquid water are freer to move around each other. The water particles have more energy than the sugar particles as they have been able to break the strong bonds of attraction between them. The individual sugar particles are grouped together into granules, their size depending on the type of sugar: granulated, caster, icing, etc. When the sugar is added to the water, we can imagine the more energetic water particles knocking and bumping against the particles on the surface of the solid sugar. Gradually, these particles will be dislodged from the sugar granule and then slip into the spaces between the water particles. Gradually, more particles are dislodged, slip into the spaces and eventually a solution is created. This explains why the mass of the resultant solution increases but its volume does not.

What difference does heat make?

When we make instant coffee, we use hot water and stir. How can we explain this in terms of the particle nature of materials? If the water is hotter then the water particles will have more energy and so move faster and bump into the coffee granules with more energy, breaking them down more quickly. Similarly, stirring will impart more energy to the water and speed up the mechanical breaking down of the coffee granules. The smaller the granules, the more quickly they will dissolve, as smaller granules have proportionally greater surface area for their volume. The particle model also helps to explain why there is a limit to the amount of sugar we can dissolve in our tea. When there is no more space between the water particles, the solution is described as 'saturated' and the sugar particles drop to the bottom of the cup.

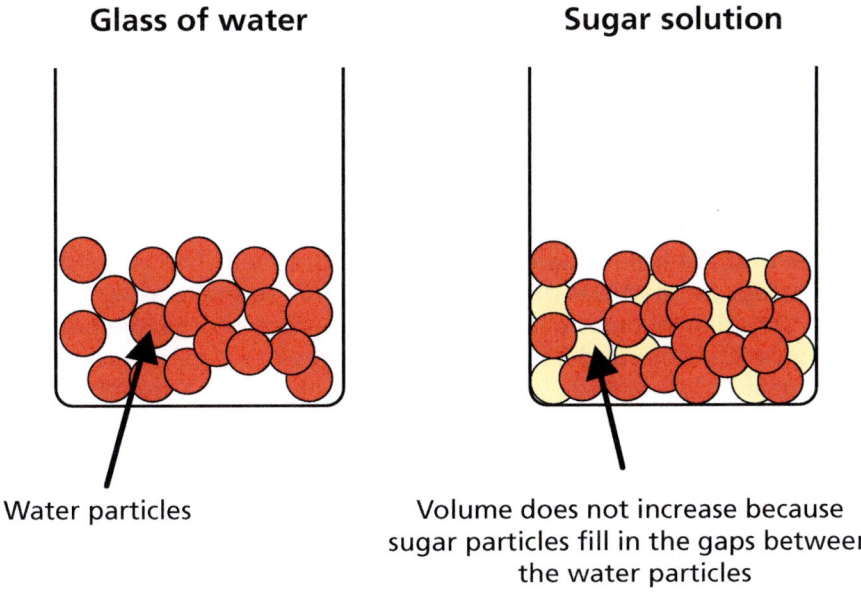

Glass of water   **Sugar solution**

Water particles   Volume does not increase because sugar particles fill in the gaps between the water particles

Simplified model of a sugar solution.

Global dimensions: Climate change and melting ice caps

It is at the Earth's poles that the impact of global warming is most noticeable. A rise of half a degree in the Earth's temperature over the past 100 years has resulted in the retreat of many glaciers and a noticeable shrinking of the sea ice at both poles. When ice which is formed over water melts, there is little effect on sea level as the floating ice displaces a volume of water equal to its own weight. However, it would be a different matter if ice formed over land began to melt in significant quantities. The main ice-covered land mass is Antarctica at the South Pole where about 90 per cent of the world's ice is found, along with 70 per cent of the world's fresh water. Ice here is on average 2000 metres thick and, with very low temperatures, it is unlikely that significant melting will occur in the near future.

At the North Pole, however, the ice is much less thick and floats on the Arctic Ocean. Recent satellite images show that there has been a significant decrease in the amount of ice at the North Pole during winter, so much so that it may well soon be possible to sail the North West passage from the Atlantic Ocean to the Pacific Ocean throughout the year. Images from NASA also show how the ice fields of Greenland are being affected. As more land becomes ice-free, the traditional ways of the peoples of Greenland will become increasingly threatened. Their traditional ways of hunting will be endangered as investors clamour to mine the wealth of minerals known to exist beneath the surface.

http://science.howstuffworks.com/environmental/earth/geophysics/question473.htm

www.nasa.gov/topics/earth/features/thick-melt.html

www.guardian.co.uk/environment/2011/jul/04/ice-caps-arctic-white-gold-rush

Summary

All matter exists either as a solid, a liquid or a gas: these are known as states of matter. Many substances are capable of changing from one form to another when they are either heated or cooled. The amount of heating or cooling needed to produce a change of state differs for each material. Changes of state are reversible changes or physical changes.

These processes can be explained by imagining materials made up ultimately of tiny indivisible particles that are held together by mutual attraction. This is the particle model. When a solid is heated, the particles gain energy and start to move away from each other and as they do so the solid becomes a liquid. As a liquid gains energy, the particles are able to break away from each other and become a gas. The reverse happens when the material is cooled. As they gain or lose energy (through heating or cooling), the physical properties of the material itself change.

When solutions are formed, the particles of the solute slip into the spaces between the particles of solvent. The volume of a solution is the same as the initial volume of the solvent. The mass of a solution is the same as the combined masses of the solvent and solute. This phenomenon is known as the conservation of mass.

Part 2: Ideas for practice

Topic: Ice and water

Age group: 7–9 years

Introduction

This topic provides opportunities to explore the nature of ice and how it behaves in different environmental conditions. Children take and record accurate measurements to determine the freezing or melting point of water and the effect on the melting point of adding different chemicals. Activities in the application stage focus on the water-cycle and weather.

Scientific view

The temperature of water determines its state. Liquid water turns into solid water (ice) when it is cooled below 0°C. Ice becomes a liquid when it is heated above 0°C. Water does not normally exist as liquid above 100°C.

Working scientifically

In these activities children will:

- ask and try to find answers to questions;
- perform tests;
- observe closely, using suitable equipment;
- record and communicate what happened using drawings;
- use their observations and ideas to suggest answers to questions.

Exploration stage

Children's talk involves trying out their own ideas

Setting the scene

Ice balloons have their own built-in 'wow' factor and never fail to prompt an excited response from children, especially if they are presented as 'ice animals'. Make ice balloons in various shapes and sizes, one for each group.

Scientific enquiry

Children can spend time initially observing, drawing, photographing or describing their ice balloon. What does it look like? What does it feel like? Does it make any sounds? Discourage children from handling the ice for too long. Children can listen to the balloons as they crinkle and crack in the warm classroom atmosphere. Make a list of all the key words which children use to describe the properties.

Ice balloons.
Source: Peter Loxley

Talking points: true, false or not sure?

- The ice balloon is made from water.
- If left for a long time, the ice will melt.
- The ice is too cold to melt.
- The ice will only melt when its temperature rises above 0°C.
- We can stop it melting by wrapping it up in a woolly coat.

Use the talking points to encourage the children to share their understanding of the properties of ice. Discuss children's reasons for their answers.

Scientific enquiry

Ask the children to predict the temperature of the ice balloon. Do they think the temperature in the middle and the outside will be the same? Help children drill a hole into the ice so they can measure the internal temperature. Children work out how to fix a thermometer to the outer part of the ice. Avoid using mercury-filled thermometers. Children compare temperatures. What reasons can they think of for the differences? Use data recorders to measure the change in internal and external temperatures over time as the ice melts. Children record the results and draw conclusions regarding the temperature at which ice melts.

Puzzle

Discuss results of the enquiry and establish that ice changes state at 0°C. The puzzle is whether ice always melts at the same temperature? Listen to children's ideas and encourage them to explain to each other what they know about melting.

Storytelling

Show children pictures from the web of icy roads in winter. Talk about the problems caused by icy conditions and how roads are salted in winter to prevent them becoming covered in ice. Also talk about how we use de-icer spray on car windscreens when they become iced up. Listen to children's stories on the topic and ask them to think of a reason why salt melts the ice. Does the salt warm up the ice, or is there another reason? Do they think any other substance could be used?

Scientific enquiry

Provide groups with a tray of ice cubes and a range of materials including salt, sugar, sand, vinegar, liquid soap and washing-up liquid. Children plan tests to find out which substance makes the most effective de-icer. Tests need to be fair and melting temperatures recorded. Children record the temperature of the water as long as it is in contact with the ice. Does the ice always melt at 0°C or does the melting temperature depend on the added substance? Children explain the effects of adding salt to ice. In the light of the enquiry, explore children's responses to the puzzle.

Formative assessment

Provide opportunities for children to voice what they have learnt in the exploratory stage. Use evidence from their responses to the puzzle, talking points and other activities to assess differences between children's ideas and the scientific view. Plan how you will use the re-describing stage to help the children address their *learning needs*. You may want to modify the activities depending on the shared and individual needs of the children.

Re-describing stage

Children's talk involves making sense of scientific ideas

Teacher-led discussion

Compare the properties of ice with liquid water. Why are they so different, considering they are made from the same material? Use models and suitable video clips to illustrate the difference between solids and liquids.

Modelling

Ask children to imagine they are a particle of water and to mime how they might move in solid ice. While they are miming being a solid particle, tell them the 'ice is melting' and they should mime accordingly. Then, when all the 'ice has melted' the water heats up until it all evaporates and turns into a gas.

Storytelling

Children come together to put words to their mime and discuss how their actions portrayed water in its various states. Ask children to describe what it felt like being a water particle trapped inside a solid as it changed into a liquid. How did the change of temperature affect their behavior? How did they react when the temperature reached boiling point? Pick up on children's ideas and, if you feel it is appropriate, help them build a picture in their minds of the particle structure of water. Address any outstanding *learning needs* identified in the exploratory stage.

Scientific enquiry

Ask children whether they think chocolate melts at the same temperature as ice. Provide children with milk chocolate buttons and challenge them to plan an enquiry to discover the melting temperature. Extend the enquiry to find out whether different types of chocolate have different melting points. For H&S advice on suitable sources of heat refer to *Be safe!* (2011). Also remind children that the chocolate is not for consumption during or after the test.

   Children can use information sources to compare the melting/freezing points of other common materials with ice and chocolate.

Information and teaching resources

BBC Bitesize:

- BBC (2007). The Behavior of Particles in Solids, Liquids and Gases. *www.bbc.co.uk/education/clips/zpbvr82*
- BBC (2007). Solids, Liquids and Gases. *www.bbc.co.uk/education/clips/zmx76sg*
- BBC (2007). The Temperature of Ice. *www.bbc.co.uk/education/clips/z23ygk7*
- BBC (2007). Turning Glass from a Liquid to a Solid. *www.bbc.co.uk/education/clips/zvqw2hv*
- BBC (2007). Building Sculptures Out of Snow and Ice. *www.bbc.co.uk/education/clips/zqmqxnb*

Application stage

Children's talk involves trying out scientific ideas

Design and make their own gauges

In preparation for the following weather activities, children design and make their own wind and rain gauges. There are lots of ideas on the web.

Predicting the weather

Take children out into the playground at the same time every day for a week. Each time observe and describe the weather. Take photographs of the sky and clouds, take temperature readings, measure relative wind speed and direction and record rainfall over the last 24 hours. Back in the classroom, children record their weather data on charts and use the information to predict the weather for the following day. They can present their forecast in the style of a TV presenter using a chart. Children compare their forecast each day with the forecast from the met office. Next day, they can use their data to assess which was most accurate. At the end of the week, discuss how successful they have been at predicting the weather. Is there a link between one day's weather and the next? What causes changes in the weather?

Where does the rain come from?

Children use information sources, including video clips, to research the water-cycle and present their findings using PowerPoint presentations. They can make simple evaporation or condensation models to help explain the key ideas. They can find suitable ideas for the models on the web.

Storytelling

Children imagine they are a rain drop who meets another rain drop in a cloud. As the cloud gets colder and darker as it fills up with rain, the two rain drops get to talking about where they come from and how they ended up in this cloud, wondering what will happen to them next. Children can tell a story based on a conversation between the rain drops as they anticipate their fate.

Modelling

Explore pictures of snowflakes in all their beautiful diversity. Ask the children to imagine they are individual snowflakes and to model how they combine to make snow. Groups of children could then look at developing a snowflake dance, thinking about appropriate music to convey the different stages of the snowflake's life. They can interpret through dance how the snowflakes form when the weather is cold and how they 'melt' as the temperature rises. Children can make models of snowflakes or create their own paintings. Use information sources to explore the different patterns. They can also write their own stories or poems inspired by their experiences of snow and the ephemeral beauty of snowflakes.

Snowflakes.
Source: iStock

Information and teaching resources

- Met Office (2017). *wow.metoffice.gov.uk* – weather observation website.
- Met Office (2015). Make Your Own Weather Station. *www.metoffice.gov.uk/learning/weather-for-kids/weather-station*

Topic: Melting ice in the polar regions

Age group: 9–11 years

Introduction

This topic provides opportunities for children to explore what is happening to the ice in the polar regions and predict consequences for rising sea levels. In the application stage children find out about the work of polar scientists and design clothing and accommodation to keep them warm and safe.

Scientific view

When water is in a solid state (ice), its particles of hydrogen and oxygen are joined together in a crystalline structure. When ice melts, the crystal structure collapses and, as a result, the particles move closer together. Consequently, the volume of a given amount of ice decreases when it changes into liquid water. This helps to explain why melting icebergs do not raise sea levels. Only ice which is formed on land has the potential to raise sea levels when it melts.

Working scientifically

In these activities children will:

- plan scientific enquiries to find answers to questions;
- make systematic observations and measurements;
- use observations and measurements to draw conclusions;
- use scientific knowledge and understanding to explain observations.

Exploration stage

Children's talk involves trying out their own ideas

Setting the scene

'ARCTIC ICE MELTING AT "AMAZING" SPEEDS, SCIENTISTS FIND', was the headline of an article published by BBC News in 2012. The article was based on research carried out by the Norwegian Polar Institute which is at the forefront of arctic research. Show children video footage documenting the melting ice in the Arctic and find out what children know about the polar ice caps and what they think is happening to them.

Talking points: true, false or not sure?

- Polar ice caps are sheets of ice and snow.
- Due to climate change the polar ice caps are shrinking.
- Melting ice caps are causing sea levels to rise.
- Melting ice caps can cause flooding.
- Melting ice caps are causing global warming.

Children *work collaboratively* to reach agreement on talking points. Groups come together to share their ideas. Encourage groups to respectfully challenge each other's ideas and to share their reasoning.

Puzzle

Do melting icebergs contribute to rising sea levels? What type of ice in the Arctic and Antarctic regions is most likely to cause flooding? Ask children with knowledge of the subject to explain what they know to the rest of the class.

Scientific enquiry

There are two types of ice in the Arctic and Antarctic regions. There is sea ice which floats on water, and land ice that is formed on land. There is no land at the North Pole and therefore it is covered by sea ice. Icebergs float on water, although they were originally formed on land before falling into the sea. Focus on how melting ice in the Arctic and Antarctic regions may be contributing to rising sea levels. *Talk together* about whether the melting of sea ice or land ice will cause the sea levels to rise. Children make their own predictions and plan enquiries to find out if they are right.

Have ready frozen water-filled balloons to make big icebergs. Strip off the rubber skin. They can be floated in tanks of warm water. Children mark the level of the water before the icebergs start to melt. At intervals in time they record any changes in the water level. The same experiment could be done on a smaller scale with ice cubes and plastic beakers. Ask groups to explain their results and conclude whether melting land ice or sea ice presents the greatest danger to coastal communities. The class can use information sources to identify communities around the world which are in most danger from rising sea levels and display the results on a giant map in the classroom.

Ice balloons floating in water.
Source: Peter Loxley

Formative assessment

Provide opportunities for children to voice what they have learnt in the exploratory stage. Use evidence from their responses to the puzzle, talking points and other activities to assess differences between children's ideas and the scientific view. Plan how you will use the re-describing stage to help the children address their *learning needs.* You may want to modify the activities depending on the shared and individual needs of the children.

Information and teaching resources

- Shukman, D. (2012). Artic Ice Melting at 'Amazing' Speed, Scientists Find. *www.bbc.co.uk/news/world-europe-19508906*
- Science Kids (2016). Arctic Sea Ice. *www.sciencekids.co.nz/videos/earth/arcticmelting.html*
- European Space Agency (2016). The Threat of Melting Ice. *www.esa.int/esaKIDSen/SEMFEO7CS5G_Earth_0.html*

Re-describing stage

Children's talk involves making sense of scientific ideas

Teacher-led discussion

To understand why sea ice does not contribute to rising sea levels children need to know the difference between the structure of ice and water. Use models and video clips to discuss the particle nature of materials. Talk about how most materials expand when they change from a solid to a liquid. When it comes to water, however, the opposite is true; water expands when it changes from a liquid to a solid.

Modelling

Illustrate how particles are arranged to form a solid with simple analogies such as stacking apples. Talk about what would happen if the stack of apples were pushed over. The apples would roll along the table in a similar way to a liquid. Use this analogy to talk about the different particle structure for ice (solid) and water (liquid).

Children can take on the role of the particles. Groups model the structure and behaviour of ice and water. They model how heating solids makes the particles vibrate vigorously, resulting in a collapse of the solid structure into that of a liquid. Children can explore through modelling how it is possible for the water to have a smaller volume than ice. They can then create their own theories about why melting sea ice does not increase sea levels. Groups use diagrams to explain and compare their ideas.

Due to expansion on freezing, some of the ice floats above the surrounding water. If the iceberg melts back into the water, it will contract to its original volume and hence will not cause the sea level to rise.
Source: iStock

Teacher-led discussion

Discuss how an iceberg floats in water. Much of it floats beneath the surface. Use an ice balloon to demonstrate. Establish that when ice melts into water its volume reduces so that it only has the volume previously taken up by that part of the iceberg beneath the water. This is why the volume of the water does not rise when ice melts. *Talk together* about why melting sea-ice cannot be responsible for increases in sea levels. Address any outstanding *learning needs* identified in the exploratory stage. Children can raise their own questions for further learning.

Storytelling

What has changed since the BBC News article warned us in 2012 that the ice in the Arctic was shrinking? Has the situation improved since then or got worse? Children use information sources to find out what we know today about the threat of melting ice in the Artic. They can start by exploring the Norwegian Polar Institute website. Children are encouraged to email scientists at the Institute with questions about the Arctic and their work. Groups present the results of their research in the form of an e-newspaper article with links to engaging and informative video clips.

Information and teaching resources

BBC Bitesize:

- BBC (2007). The Behavior of Particles in Solids, Liquids and Gases. *www.bbc.co.uk/education/clips/zpbvr82*

Other websites:

- Norwegian Polar Institute. Climate and Climate Change. *www.npolar.no/en/themes/climate/*

Application stage

Children's talk involves trying out scientific ideas

Blogging about science

Children can use information sources to discover the type of work done by scientists in both the Arctic and Antarctic Regions. Field scientists often blog about things they see and discover. Choosing an area of research, children can find out some of things scientists have discovered and communicate the ideas in the style of a blog entry.

Keeping safe and warm

Weather conditions in the polar regions can be extreme, including very low temperatures, high winds, snowstorms and icy blizzards. Children use information sources to investigate the environmental conditions polar scientists have to endure and design clothing and accommodation to keep them warm and safe. The accommodation should be designed to be easily portable, yet large enough and strong enough for scientists to live in for months at a time. Designs should include a rationale for the use of materials, drawings to show how materials are used and a 3-D model of the accommodation.

Information and teaching resources

- British Antarctic Survey (2015). *www.bas.ac.uk*
- International Arctic Science Committee. *http://iasc.info/*
- Ocean Portal (2016). Arctic Scientists at Work. *http://ocean.si.edu/ocean-videos/arctic-scientists-work*
- Norwegian Polar Institute. Climate and Climate Change. *www.npolar.no/en/themes/climate/*
- Exploratorium (2015). Ice Stories: Dispatches from Polar Scientists. *http://icestories.explor atorium.edu/dispatches/*
- Literacynet.org. What Is Polar Science? *http://literacynet.org/polar/what.html*

Talk skills and science discussion: Explaining

Ask each group to find out all they can about a different topic and prepare to explain their scientific ideas to the class. They can choose among evaporation, condensation, melting, boiling, freezing, solids, liquids or gases.

Emphasise the need to explain ideas in order to generate and consolidate understanding. Ask groups to ensure that they can explain their ideas to one another before they are expected to explain to the whole class. Every child in a group should be able to explain ideas not just a spokesperson. Children in a group can choose to support one another by each explaining separate sections of understanding. So each member of the group should actively contribute to the oral explanation.

The group can prepare a poster, PowerPoint or Prezi presentation or web page if needed, but they must explain their ideas aloud to the class. Suggest that groups use the talk tools 'We found that...', 'It's interesting to know that...', 'We are going to tell you about...', 'The next thing we thought of was...' and 'Do you have any questions?'

Ask the class to comment positively on the presentation, saying what they have learned. Ask groups to talk about explanation – when is it easy or difficult and why is it so important to scientists?

Additional information and teaching resources

Companion book:

- Loxley, P. (2018). *Practical Ideas for Teaching Primary Science: Inspiring Learning and Enjoyment,* Abingdon: Routledge, Chapter 9: The Material World and Chapter 10: Changing Materials.

BBC Bitesize:

- BBC (2017). How Polar Bears Adapt to Melting Ice Caps. *www.bbc.co.uk/education/clips/zg94d2p*
- BBC (2013). Polar Bears in Their Habitat. *www.bbc.co.uk/education/clips/z8h34wx*
- BBC (2017). Why Antarctica Is So Important in Measuring Climate Change. *www.bbc.co.uk/education/clips/zykrp39*

Websites:

- Polar Bears International (2017). Research. *www.polarbearsinternational.org/our-work/scientific-research*
- SchoolScience (2017). *www.schoolscience.co.uk*
- ABPI (2016). Interactive Resources for Schools. *www.abpischools.org.uk/page/modules/solids-liquids-gases/.cfm*
- Royal Society of Chemistry (2017). Learn Chemistry: Enhancing Learning and Teaching. *www.rsc.org/learn-chemistry*

ASE journals:

- Primary Science 138 (May/June 2015). *Adventures on the Thames* by Sarah Parker.
- Primary Science 132 (March/April 2014). *Learning About the Weather Through an Integrated STEM Approach* by Gokhan Serin.
- Primary Science 129 (Sept/Oct 2013). *Now Here's the Weather Forecast* by Mathew Richardson.
- Primary Science 125 (Nov/Dec 2012). *Polar Science is Cool!* By Sophie Weeks.

CHAPTER 18
CHANGING MATERIALS

It has always been the alchemist's desire to turn base metals, such as lead, into gold and silver. The legendary tool supposedly capable of achieving this was the philosopher's stone. Although the alchemists never succeeded, their work led to the development of what we now call chemistry. This chapter looks at how substances can be chemically combined to form new materials and uses the particle model to explain the nature of the changes involved.

Topics discussed in the chapter

- Historical context
- Elements, compounds and mixtures
- The periodic table
- The formation of materials
- Spectacular chemical reactions

Part 1: Subject knowledge

Historical context

The plum pudding model

John Dalton (1766–1844) suggested that all known substances could be formed from different combinations of tiny particles (see Chapter 17). He was convinced by the evidence available that the atom was truly indivisible. However, this was later found not to be true and we now know that atoms can be split up into even smaller particles.

The mystery of the atom and its true nature began to unfold in the late nineteenth century, when the physicist J. J. Thompson (1856–1940) discovered within matter a negatively charged particle, which was named the electron. This led to a new way of visualising an atom. Instead of imagining it to be a solid sphere, Thompson visualised it as a mass of positive matter with negative electrons scattered throughout, like plums in a suet pudding.

From plum pudding to solar system model

In 1909, the New Zealand physicist Ernest Rutherford (1871–1937) and his colleagues tested Thompson's 'plum pudding' model. Their investigation showed the plum pudding model was inadequate in explaining their results. As a result, Rutherford suggested a 'solar system' model with a cloud of negatively charged electrons orbiting a tiny, densely packed, positively charged nucleus. Rutherford's subsequent work led in 1918 to the discovery of protons, the positively charged particles within the nucleus that neutralise the negatively charged electrons surrounding it. However, measurement of the mass of atoms indicated that a further, neutral particle must exist within the nucleus. This constituent of the atom, the neutron, proved harder to find and it wasn't until 1932 that James Chadwick identified what was seen as the last piece in the atomic puzzle.

However, it is now known that both the neutron and the proton are in fact made of even smaller particles, known as quarks. Today, scientists continue to seek the most fundamental particles from which materials are constructed. The Large Hadron Collider at CERN (The European Organisation for Nuclear Research) in Geneva has been designed to answer questions about the nature of quarks and to explore in greater depth their composition and formation.

Positive matter

Electron

The plum pudding model of the atom.
Source: iStock

Elements, compounds and mixtures

What is our world made of?

The materials which make up the Earth are **elements**, mixtures or compounds.

An element is a pure substance consisting of one type of atom. There are 118 known elements, such as hydrogen, oxygen, gold and lead. These elements are combined in different ways to form all the materials which make up the Earth. In a mixture like air, the elements such as oxygen and nitrogen are not chemically bonded together and can be separated. On the other hand, water is a compound in which hydrogen and oxygen are chemically bonded together and cannot be easily separated. The creation of a compound from two or more elements is described as a chemical or permanent change, as opposed to the non-chemical or reversible changes which we associate with mixtures.

Something to think about

Common salt, which we have used for centuries to add flavour to food, is a combination of the highly volatile metal sodium and the noxious gas chlorine. Why isn't salt more of a danger to our health?

How do elements combine to make new materials?

An answer to the salt puzzle can be found when we consider the way elements combine to form new materials which are very different from their original constituents. Rutherford's model of the atom allows us to tell convincing stories of the ways in which elements combine to form new substances.

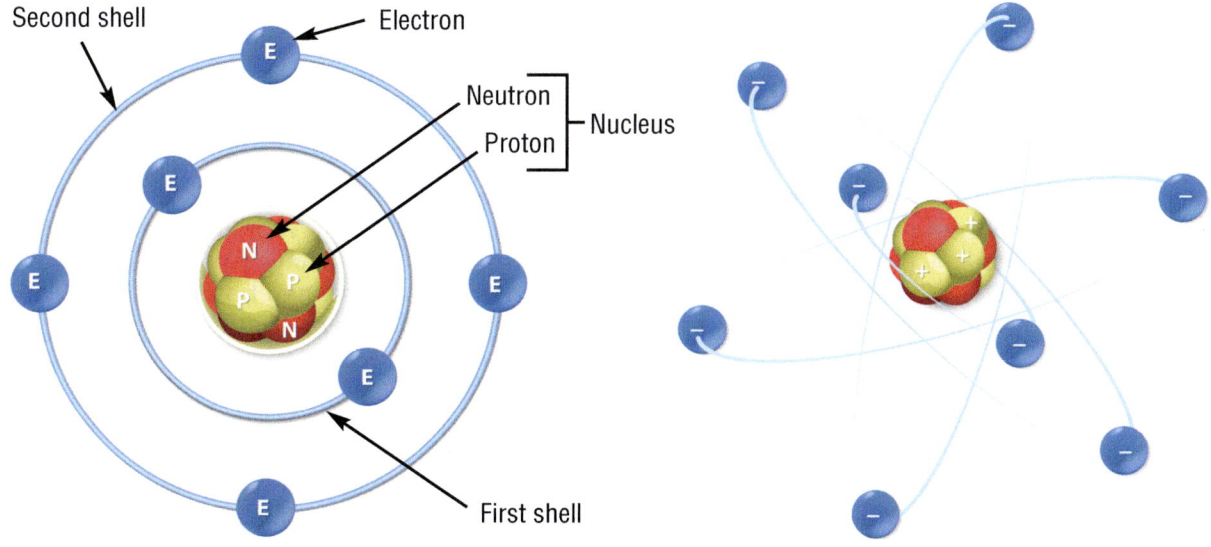

The solar system model of the atom – a single atom of carbon.
Source: iStock

Imagine the atom as a central nucleus surrounded by a cloud of negatively charged electrons. The resultant charge is always neutral so the number of protons in the nucleus must equal the number of electrons. Each of the known elements has a unique number of protons and corresponding electrons. Hydrogen, the simplest atom of all, has a nucleus containing just one proton and so has one orbiting electron. The much heavier silver atom has 47 neutrons and 61 protons in its nucleus and so 61 orbiting electrons.

Why are some elements, like sodium, very reactive?

It is the arrangement of the orbiting electrons that determines the reactivity of an element. Electrons are confined to orbit in particular arrangements. The first orbital shell (see diagram on p. 299) cannot contain more than 2 electrons, the second cannot contain more than 8 and the maximum number is also 8 for the third shell. If the outer shell of an atom is not complete, it will combine easily with other elements until it is 'filled up'. The ease with which this takes place is largely due to the number of spaces on the outer shells. For example, sodium has an outer shell with 1 single electron where 8 are possible and therefore is highly reactive. Chlorine is reactive because it has only 7 electrons in its outer shell and needs an additional 1 to make it stable. Atoms that have full shells do not tend to react easily with other chemicals. For example, the noble gases helium (2 electrons), neon (10 electrons) and argon (18 electrons) all have full outer shells and are all odourless, colourless and unreactive.

Sodium and chlorine combine to make common salt.

What happens when sodium and chlorine combine?

When sodium and chlorine combine to form sodium chloride (common salt), the electrons in the outer shells are rearranged. The single electron in the outer shell of the sodium atoms transfers to fill the outer shell of chlorine atoms. This means that both atoms now have full outer shells and are therefore much less reactive. The atoms of chlorine and sodium are then bonded together by electrical forces to form sodium chloride molecules, which have their own unique properties.

What does an atom really look like?

Scientists do not know what an atom actually looks like. The solar system model provides us with a useful way of visualising it but scientists do not actually think that it looks this way in reality. There are, however, some things that scientists are certain about. Firstly, they believe that the majority of the mass of an atom is contained in its nucleus – the electrons can be considered to have negligible mass. Although the nucleus is so massive, its volume is believed to be small compared to the size of the atom. The majority of the volume occupied by the atom is empty space as the orbits of the electrons extend far beyond the nucleus. The atom overall is believed to be about 100,000 times bigger than the nucleus.

Something to think about

Imagine you needed to make a scale model of an atom. If you used a ping-pong ball to represent the nucleus, how far away would you place the orbiting electrons?

The periodic table

In 1869, the Russian chemist Dmitri Mendeleev succeeded in representing the known elements in a graphical format, the periodic table. The elements were grouped in the table according to their atomic structure and other properties. The first table had gaps, which Mendeleev believed belonged to elements which had not yet been discovered. Some of the first missing elements to be discovered were gallium (1875) and scandium (1879). These discoveries demonstrated to scientists the immense value of the periodic table in helping to develop their understanding of the structure of matter.

The periodic table has become one of the icons of science. Using atomic mass to order the elements means that reactive elements are grouped on the left-hand side of the table and the stable elements on the right. Within the table all the metals are grouped together. Metals are distinguished by their ability to conduct electrical charge. This charge is carried on electrons and in metals the electrons in the outer shell are only loosely attracted to the nucleus. This allows the electrons to exist in what is often termed a 'sea of electrons', free to move in response to an externally applied voltage. For example, when a length of copper wire is attached to the opposite ends of a battery, negatively charged electrons are free to move round the circuit.

		Chemical symbol		Number of protons		He 2
						Helium
						Balloons
B 5	C 6	N 7	O 8	F 9	Ne 10	
Boron	Carbon	Nitrogen	Oxygen	Fluorine	Neon	
Solar cells	Basis of living things	Protein	Air	Toothpaste	Advertising signs	
Al 13	Si 14	P 15	S 16	Cl 17	Ar 18	
Aluminium	Silicon	Phosphorous	Sulphur	Chlorine	Argon	
Drink cans	Computer chips	Matches	Volcanoes	Swimming pools	Light bulbs	

Part of periodic table (simplified) including possible uses of elements

The formation of materials

Atoms rarely exist on their own

Individual atoms of elements tend not to exist singly: they clump together into arrangements that are called molecules. Oxygen, for example, is always written as O_2 because it occurs naturally as two oxygen atoms joined together into a stable molecule. When hydrogen joins with oxygen to form water, the resulting molecule is made up of two hydrogen atoms and one oxygen atom. Oxygen has 8 electrons in total – so there are two empty spaces in its outer electron shells. The two hydrogen atoms slot neatly into place, their single electrons filling the gaps. The resulting water molecule is written as H_2O.

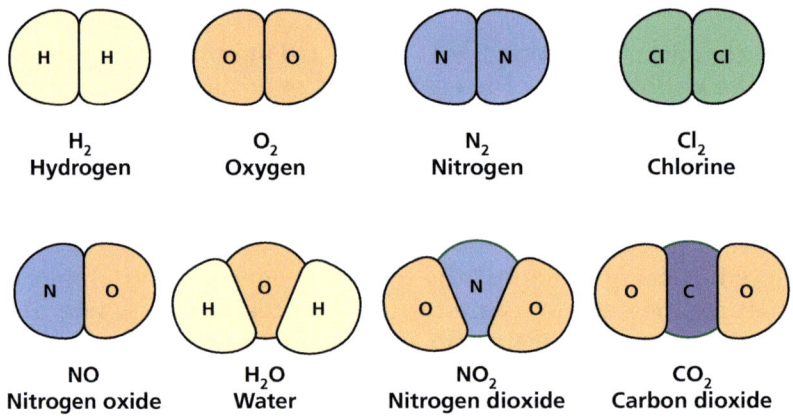

Some common molecules.

Can the same atoms be used to produce different materials?

When atoms combine together they form continuous structures that give us the materials with which we are familiar. The ways in which these structures form will often define the properties of the material itself. For example, diamond, which is made from densely packed carbon atoms, has a very rigid internal structure which gives it hardness and durability. In contrast, graphite, which is softer and much less durable than diamond, is made from carbon atoms joined together in layers. The bonds between the layers are relatively weak, which means that the layers can slide across each other. Graphite is a useful material for drawing with because it is soft, slippery and the layers of carbon are easily rubbed off onto the paper.

> ### Something to think about
>
> Clay used for making pottery is a layered compound of silicon, oxygen, aluminium and hydrogen. When it is wet, water molecules can get between the layers and the clay is slippery and malleable. When the clay is dried, the water evaporates, but the structure of the clay remains the same so it is crumbly. If it is wetted, it will once again be workable. However, if the clay is fired in a kiln, a chemical reaction takes place and a new, stronger material is produced. Can you imagine what the firing does to the atomic structure of the clay to change its properties so radically?

Does energy always play a part in the formation of new materials?

Whether a change in materials is physical or chemical, energy will always play its part. For example, rolling and shaping play dough takes energy, as does squeezing water out of a sponge. When dissolving sugar in water, the movement energy of the water molecules helps to break down the solid lumps of sugar. These changes are relatively easily reversed. However, the changes that occur when two or more substances join together chemically are not easily reversed and usually take place as a result of an exchange of energy. Everyday examples of chemical change include baking a cake, frying an egg and firing clay.

Energy is released when new materials are formed by burning

Heating involves raising the temperature of a material: for example, to melt gold so that it can be cast into different solid shapes. This can be reversed. Burning involves a chemical change that results in the formation of new substances: for example, when a common fuel, such as wood, burns. Carbon and hydrogen from the wood combine with oxygen in the air to produce carbon dioxide and water; a residue, ash, results. Burning is an irreversible chemical reaction that requires fuel, oxygen and a high enough temperature. This is described as the 'fire triangle' and all three have to be present for burning to occur. The reaction is capable of emitting huge amounts of energy and has proved useful to humans over a long time.

What happens to the original materials when things burn?

Things appear to diminish as they burn. A candle decreases in size and wood disintegrates to ash. We see burning as a destructive process. However, in chemical terms, it is in fact a constructive process since it results in the formation of new materials. It is difficult to demonstrate that mass is conserved when things burn, but this is so.

Something to think about

Candle wax is a hydrocarbon – a carbon-based material. If mass is conserved when materials burn, can you think what happens to the wax when the candle is lit?

Other chemical changes involving oxygen

Chemical changes involving the combination of oxygen with other materials are described as oxidising reactions. Respiration is an important example of **oxidation**. This is the process by which energy is released to the body when carbohydrate molecules combine with oxygen in our cells (see Chapter 16). This is an example of oxidation which does not involve burning. Another example is rusting. Most metals will react with oxygen: for example, the oxidisation of copper creates a green discolouration, which is easily removed. 'Rusting' happens when iron and steel oxidise. Rusting iron can weaken built structures and cause

A candle burning.

irreversible damage. For oxidation of iron to occur, water needs to be present. Water is always present in the atmosphere, but rusting is more rapid in damp climates or when salt is present to speed up the reaction. There are a number of ways to prevent rusting: for example, painting the iron or mixing it with a metal that is resistant to oxidation, such as chrome, to form stainless steel.

Spectacular chemical reactions

Mixing bicarbonate of soda and vinegar is a popular way of creating a spectacular volcano effect.

A vivid description of the fate of Pompeii during a topic on the Romans encouraged a class of 8-year-olds to try to recreate the eruption of Vesuvius. They built a model from papier mâché and then wondered how to model the eruption itself. A mixture of bicarbonate of soda and vinegar, with red powder paint for authenticity, gave a satisfying result, with the lava bubbling out of the crater and pouring down the mountainside.

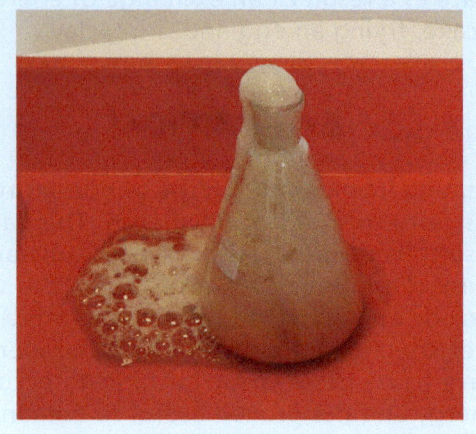

The volcano effect.
Source: Peter Loxley

What causes the volcano effect?

Bicarbonate of soda is an alkaline substance; its constituents are hydrogen, carbon and oxygen and the reactive metal sodium. Vinegar is an acid. Highly alkaline and highly acidic substances are dangerous but we use milder forms of them in many household contexts. Toothpaste is alkaline to combat the acidity of saliva. Acidic lemon imparts a tart flavour to foods, whilst vinegar kills bacteria and so is useful in preserving food. Generally, an acid will react with an alkaline to produce a new substance and, typically, a gas – carbon dioxide – will be produced. It is the release of the gas which causes the mixture of vinegar and bicarbonate of soda to bubble up and create the volcano effect. Another example of this can be seen when an effervescent vitamin C tablet is placed in water. The tablet contains a dry mixture of vitamin C, an alkaline material such as sodium bicarbonate and citric acid. When placed in water, the tablet dissolves and the citric acid and sodium bicarbonate combine chemically. New substances are produced, including carbon dioxide, which provides the fizz.

Could we use the volcano effect to prove that mass is conserved?

Mix sodium bicarbonate and citric acid in a small plastic bag and weigh it. Weigh some water, add this to the bag and seal it. The mixture will bubble and the bag will expand. Weighing again should demonstrate that, although the constituents have combined and changed and new substances have been produced (carbon dioxide, for example), the overall mass has remained the same. The conservation of mass is one of science's big ideas because it applies to all types of chemical and physical changes, regardless of the materials involved.

Mass is conserved in a chemical reaction.
Source: Peter Loxley

Something to think about

If you held the plastic bag while the reaction was taking place you would have noticed a change in temperature of the mixture. What may have caused it?

Global dimensions: Mining metals and high-tech industries

Since early times, humans made use of metals found near the Earth's surface to manufacture tools and weapons. However, as technologies advanced, chemical means of extraction of metals was increasingly used to obtain rarer metals or extract large quantities of metals from naturally occurring ores. Modern-day hard rock mining on an industrial scale involves the blasting, excavating and crushing of thousands of acres of land and the use of huge quantities of chemicals such as cyanide and sulphuric acid, resulting in the pollution of groundwater with toxic by-products. The scarred cliffs that once marked the highly profitable Cornish copper and tin mining industry of the late eighteenth and early nineteenth centuries are long gone, but similar effects are still seen around the world today in the intensive mining of gold, silver, copper and uranium. Whilst exploitation of workers and damage to local populations has been highlighted in some of the poorer areas of the world, intensive mining impacts across the globe. The US Environmental Protection Agency, for example, estimates that 40 per cent of drainage basins in the Western USA are contaminated by pollution from hard rock mines. Metals themselves are relatively easily recyclable (with a few exceptions, such as uranium) and less energy is often used during recycling than in initially mining the metals.

The development of high-tech industries, however, has had an impact on the demand for traditional metals. For instance, copper, once the mainstay of Zambia's mining industry, is no longer in such high demand for electrical cables as its function has now been overtaken by fibre optics. Many Zambian copper workers have lost their jobs or are now on lower wages. This has had enormous impacts on the health and education of their families as well as on the Zambian economy. In addition, many newer technologies, such as smart phones, flat screens, electric cars and wind turbines, make use of the rare earth metals. Despite their name, these are not rare but dispersed and seldom found in sufficient quantities to make mining economical. New demand has produced a growing concern that the world may soon face a shortage unless major new sources are exploited. At present, 90 per cent of the world's supply of these metals is mined in China.

www.renewableworld.org.uk/

http://topics.nytimes.com/top/reference/timestopics/subjects/r/rare_earths/index.html

Summary

As research into the nature of materials continues, our understanding of the complexity of the structure of atoms continues to develop. Materials can exist as elements, compounds and mixtures. The periodic table is a classification of elements based on their atomic mass, and the position of an element in the table will indicate its properties. The fundamental structure of atoms of different elements determines their properties and how they combine together to form more complex materials. The resulting compounds often have very different properties from their constituent elements. Energy is a part of the process of forming new compounds as electrons are either exchanged or shared by the atoms. When new compounds are formed, the mass of the resulting materials is the same as the combined mass of the reacting materials – mass is conserved. Mixtures consist of elements or compounds which do not react chemically together and they can be relatively easily separated.

Part 2: Ideas for practice

Topic: Materials at the seaside

Age group: 5–7 years

Introduction

This topic is about materials children could experience on a visit to the seaside. In the exploration stage children use enquiry skills to explore the properties of sand and the best sand/water mixture for making sandcastles. Activities in the re-describing stage enable children to compare the properties of materials, which they may use at the seaside. Children further develop their understanding of materials and their properties in the application stage by making bread for a seaside picnic.

Scientific view

Objects are made from materials. Materials have properties which determine how they behave when they are used. For example, dry sand is runny and collapses when made into a shape. Properties of materials can be described using words such as hard, soft, stretchy, stiff, shiny, dull, rough, smooth, bendy and brittle.

Working scientifically

In these activities children will:

- ask questions and use first-hand experience to answer them;
- perform simple tests and make comparisons;
- identify and classify different objects and materials;
- use their observations and ideas to suggest answers to questions.

Exploration stage

Children's talk involves trying out their own ideas

Setting the scene

Ask children to bring in pictures of themselves at the seaside. Listen to their holiday stories and talk about making sandcastles. Show the class photographs of different types of sandcastles from the web.

Puzzle

Demonstrate how to make a sandcastle using a tray of dry safe sand and a small container. When it collapses, ask children why it will not keep its shape? Do they know how to make a sturdy castle?

Scientific enquiry

Discuss children's ideas regarding how to make sandcastles. Focus on the idea that the sand needs to be wet. Working in groups, children explore making sandcastles using different amounts of water to discover the best mixture. They need to work systematically and record their results so that they can identify the amount of sand and water they need for the best sandcastle. Use only 'silver sand' not 'builder's sand'. Explain how sand can get in their eyes and they must handle it carefully. They should wash their hands after the activity. Refer to *Be safe!* (2011) for H&S guidance.

Building sandcastles at the seaside.
Source: iStock

Modelling

Through mime, children act out running through sand. At first they run on top of the sand, then they imagine wading through it up to their knees. Finally, they mime running through a wall of sand. Watch their mimes and ask them to explain their movements. Which words would they use to describe what the sand feels like?

Scientific enquiry

Provide children with magnifiers and let them look closely at the structure of sand. Ask them to draw a picture of what they think it is made from and describe how it behaves when they handle it.

Talking points: true, false or not sure?

- Sand feels soft like cotton wool.
- Sand feels hard like wood.

- Sand feels runny like water.
- Sand feels stretchy like rubber.
- Sand is crumbly like a biscuit.
- Sand is shiny like metal.

Discuss the talking points and help children choose words, which best describe the properties of sand. Let children test and describe the properties of the alternative materials listed in the talking points.

Formative assessment

Provide opportunities for children to voice what they have learnt in the exploratory stage. Use evidence from their responses to the puzzle, talking points and other activities to assess differences between children's ideas and the scientific view. Plan how you will use the re-describing stage to help the children address their *learning needs.* You may want to modify the activities depending on the shared and individual needs of the children.

Information and teaching resources

ASE journals:

- Primary Science (123, May/June 2012) *Dramatic Science at Key Stage 1* by Deb McGregor and Wendy Precious.

Useful website:

- Making Sandcastles: Materials. *www.practicalprimaryscience.org*

Re-describing stage

Children's talk involves making sense of scientific ideas

Teacher-led discussion

Recap on what children learnt from the exploration stage and list words, which can be used to describe the properties of sand. Provide a display of objects which children and their families may take with them to the beach. For example, a beach ball, a football, beach cricket set, a Frisbee, towels, sunhat, sun glasses, plastic bottles of suntan cream, bucket and spade, fold-up chair, beach umbrella, different types of games, bags to carry things in, a picnic set and what else you can think of. Choose one of the objects, and together with the children, model suitable words to describe the properties of the material(s) from which it is made. If appropriate for your children introduce the words 'properties' and 'materials' when talking about the objects.

Scientific enquiry

Each group takes two objects from the display and *working collaboratively* identify their uses and think of words which describe the properties of the materials from which they are made. Children draw the objects and annotate their properties.

Teacher-led discussion

Groups can describe their objects to the class and add them to a display in which objects made from the same materials are grouped together. Address outstanding *learning needs.* Use video clips to talk about the properties of materials and their uses.

Teaching and information resources

BBC Bitesize:

- BBC (2007). Materials and Their Properties. *www.bbc.co.uk/education/clips/z7qd7ty*
- BBC (2007). What Are Bridges Made From? *www.bbc.co.uk/education/clips/zwys34j*

Application stage

Children's talk involves trying out scientific ideas

Food for the seaside

It would be ideal if you could organize a trip to the seaside. Otherwise, tell children they are going on an imaginary trip to the seaside and it is up to them to design and make their own sandwiches. Tell them the sandwiches will be very special because they will make their own bread. Provide them with a list of things to choose from, which they can put on their sandwiches.

Children start by examining the properties of flour. Does it have the right properties to shape in a roll of bread? What needs to be added? Children can then be shown how to make small bread rolls. This provides opportunities to develop their measuring skills. Discuss how the properties of the materials change in each stage when making the dough and after the bread has been baked. Children can compare the properties of their baked rolls with the flour from which they were made. Some dough can be left uncooked to compare with the cooked bread. Throughout the activity help children use suitable scientific language when describing the properties.

Next, children decide what they want to put on their rolls and with the help of an adult can make their sandwiches. Take a trip to the 'beach' (school hall) and use sounds and images of the seaside to help children imagine they are sat on the beach. Children close their eyes, listen to sounds, eat their sandwiches and tell stories about things they like to do by the seaside.

When planning any activity involving food preparation pay close attention to good hygiene, and follow the guidelines set out in the ASE publication *Be safe!*

Information and teaching resources

ASE journals:

- Primary Science Review 88 (May/June 2005) *Crunchier on the Outside – Investigating Bread* by Sarah Marks and Emma Ranger.
- Primary Science Review 90 (Nov/Dec 2005) *Snow in the Nursery* by Collyer and Ross.

Topic: Burning and global warming

Age group: 9–11 years

Introduction

In this topic, children explore the effects of burning and how it can contribute to global warming. The activities help children to understand that chemical changes caused by burning can result in the formation of new materials which pollute the air. The application stage provides opportunities for children to discover some of the causes and effects of global warming, and explore what is being done to address the problems.

Scientific view

Burning is a process in which an existing material chemically combines with oxygen to produce a new material. Heat energy is released as part of the process. Carbon-based materials such as oil, wood, coal and paper readily burn in oxygen to produce gases, which can be harmful and pollute the atmosphere. The chemical changes produced by burning produce new materials and are not reversible.

Working scientifically

In these activities children will:

- plan scientific enquiries to answer questions and control variables where necessary;
- use simple equipment and materials appropriately and take action to control risks;
- make comparisons and identify simple patterns in their observations;
- use results to draw conclusions and raise further questions;
- report on findings orally and through formal presentations;
- use established scientific knowledge to answer questions and support their findings.

Exploration stage

Children's talk involves trying out their own ideas

Setting the scene

Start this topic by show showing children the video clip entitled *Global warming: the effect it has on the planet*. Discuss what children know about global warming.

Talking points: true, false or not sure?

- Exhaust fumes from traffic are the main cause of global warming.
- Global warming is mainly caused by rising sea levels.
- Cattle and sheep contribute to global warming.
- Burning fossil fuels is the major cause of global warming.
- Pollution from factories does not contribute to global warming.
- Chopping down trees makes global warming worse.
- Airplanes do not contribute to global warming because they fly high above the Earth.

Children *work collaboratively* to find answers to the talking points. Groups come together to share ideas. Explore the reasons for their views.

Puzzle

How does the burning of fossil fuels contribute to global warming? Present the puzzle to the children and ask groups to prepare an explanation. Encourage each member of the group to contribute and to rehearse their explanations before presenting them to the class. Use their explanations to assess what they know about the subject.

Storytelling

One of the earliest scientific attempts to explain burning (combustion) was made by Johannes Baptista van Helmont (1580–1644), a Flemish physician and alchemist. Van Helmont carefully observed how different materials burnt and concluded it involved the escape of a 'wild spirit' (*spiritus silvestre*). He was the first person to understand that air is not a single substance but is a mixture of substances which he called gases. He discovered the gas carbon dioxide and showed that it is produced both in the burning of coal and in the fermentation process of winemaking. Children use information sources to explore the work of Johannes Baptista van Helmont. They can focus on his work on gases and burning. Children can tell his story in the form of a cartoon, entitled *Wild Spirit*, using captions to explain the science.

Scientific enquiry

Children plan an enquiry to find out whether a 'wild spirit' is released into the air when organic materials are burnt. In a well-ventilated room, children burn various things, such as small pieces of paper, wood and nuts. (Check for any allergies to nuts beforehand.) If they weigh the objects before and after burning, they can collect data to find out whether some residue must have escaped into the air. (Use sand trays, safety glasses, safety candles and fire-proof tongs. Refer to the ASE publication *Be safe!* for health and safety guidance when planning this investigation.) Discuss children's results and establish that burning the materials creates a substance, which is released into the air. Explore children's ideas about what the substance is, where it came from and how it could contribute to global warming.

Formative assessment

Provide opportunities for children to voice what they have learnt in the exploratory stage. Use evidence from their responses to the puzzle, talking points and other activities to assess differences between children's ideas and the scientific view. Plan how you will use the re-describing stage to help the children address their *learning needs.* You may want to modify the activities depending on the shared and individual needs of the children.

Information and teaching resources

BBC Bitesize:

- BBC (2017). Global Warming: The Effect It Has on the Planet. www.bbc.co.uk/education/clips/zt9wcwx

Re-describing stage

Children's talk involves making sense of scientific ideas

Teacher-led discussion

Start by discussing what children learnt about burning in the exploration stage. Establish that the 'wild spirit' is in fact carbon dioxide. Point out that the process is not reversible. In other words, it is not possible to burn a material such as paper and then reverse the process to produce paper again. Compare burning to melting. When a solid melts, the material is not chemically changed, it just changes state. For example, solid chocolate when it melts only changes state. The liquid is still made from the same particles as the solid and the process is easily reversed.

Scientific enquiry

Is burning the only irreversible process? Children can mix different materials together to see whether the process is reversible or irreversible. Some suggestions for materials to combine are:

1. Sand and water
2. Flour and water
3. Sugar and water
4. Microwaveable porridge oats and water

5.   Bicarbonate of soda with vinegar

6.   Whole milk and vinegar

To discover which combinations are irreversible groups, first mix the materials together at room temperature and then test whether they can be separated by sieving, filtering and evaporation. Use the scientific terms mixtures and solutions when talking about the reversible processes. Next, children can investigate the effect heat has on how the materials react. Use warm water to test the effect it has on the sugar solution. Will more sugar dissolve in warmer water? Will flour dissolve in warmer water? Microwave the oats according to instructions on the packet. Is the process reversible? Choose suitable sources of heat and supervise the activities to ensure children's safety. For H&S guidance refer to the ASE publication *Be safe!* (2011).

With the help of an adult warm some milk in a saucepan and stir in the vinegar. Do not boil. Use a ratio of 3 parts milk to 1 part vinegar. When lumps appear turn off the heat, continue to stir for a minute and then leave to cool. Wearing protective gloves, sieve out the lumps, wash them and leave on a towel to dry. Children can compare the 'lumps' with the original materials milk and vinegar and talk about how they have created a new material, which is a form of plastic. They can measure the amount of plastic they produced in grammes and work out how much milk they would need to make enough plastic to manufacture a lunch box. Extend this investigation by exploring plastics made from different types of milk and kitchen acids. For example, try goat's milk and lemon juice. Use these activities to reinforce children's understanding of irreversible changes. Supervise these activities to ensure children's safety. Refer to *Be safe!* (2011) for guidance.

Application stage

Children's talk involves trying out scientific ideas

Burning changes the gases in the atmosphere

Start this part by demonstrating that potential burning has to change the gases in the atmosphere. Use a sand tray, candles and different-sized glass jars to demonstrate that something in the air is used for burning. Choose suitable glassware which can resist changes in temperature. Invert a jar full of air over a burning candle. The candle goes out: this is evidence that a constituent of the air has been used up. With bigger jars, which contain more air, we would expect the candle to burn for longer. It is important not to allow any more air to get into the jar after it is placed over the candle. If a burning candle stands in a tray full of water and a jar is put over it, what do the children notice happens to the water as the candle burns and goes out? They can use information

What part of the air has been used up when the flame goes out?
Source: iStock

sources to find out more about burning and how it can release carbon dioxide and other substances into the air.

Children can take on the role of carbon and oxygen particles to model the process of burning. They can represent the carbon in a solid (candle wax) by bunching together and holding on to each other. Now what happens? How does the wax burn? Is there something else involved which we cannot see? *Talk together* about the possibility of some invisible substance being involved. What happens when a scented candle is burnt? How is the scent transferred around the room? Which substances do the children know exist but cannot be seen? Explore children's ideas and help them model the burning process in which carbon dioxide is formed. Address any outstanding *learning needs* identified in the exploratory stage.

The greenhouse effect

Return to the puzzle and talk about how carbon dioxide created when burning fossil fuels pollutes the atmosphere and contributes to global warming. Identify fossil fuels such as coal, oil including petrol and diesel, and natural gas. Talk about fossil fuels as carbon-based materials, which produce huge amounts of carbon dioxide when they are burnt. Use video clips to show how fossil fuels are formed and how carbon dioxide released in the air after they are burnt contributes to the greenhouse effect.

Problems caused by cars

This activity will help the children to apply their understanding of burning and make them aware of the problems associated with burning fossil fuels. Bring in a 2-litre water bottle. Tell the children that if it were filled with petrol it would weigh approximately the same. Ask the children to guess its mass in kilogrammes. They can try to lift the bottle and review their estimate and then measure its mass accurately using electronic scales. Children research how many litre bottles it would take to fill a typical family car. Establish there must be a lot of material in a tank full of petrol which ends up polluting the air. How long would it take to use a tank full of petrol? How far could the car go? Discuss what will happen to all the carbon in the petrol after it has been burnt in the engine of the car. Talk about the car journeys we take each week and work out an estimate of how many kilogrammes of petrol are used by the average family in one week. Estimates for the whole school could be calculated. Now try to imagine the scale of the pollution created by cars in a city like London, in a country like Britain and throughout the world. The figures are staggering.

Design a pollution-free car

Children research recent developments towards designing 'pollution-free' cars. They could use their findings and imaginations to design the pollution-free car of tomorrow. They produce posters to advertise the design features and the benefits their cars will have for society.

Climate change conference

Organize your own climate change conference by inviting a STEM Ambassador to give the key note speech. In preparation for the conference, children form research groups to find out about climate change in different parts of the world and report on their findings at the conference. The title of the conference could be *'What is being done about climate change'*. The purpose of the conference is to report on the problems in different parts of the world, identify what is being done at present and to make proposals for future initiatives. Use children's reports to assess their progress.

Information and teaching resources

- Fossil Fuels. *https://www.youtube.com/watch?v=jakJ-Tf79ac*
- Fossil Fuels 101. *https://www.youtube.com/watch?v=zaXBVYr9Ij0*
- BBC (2007). Carbon Dioxide Experiment. *www.bbc.co.uk/education/clips/zb4g9j6*
- BBC (2007). Does Gas Weigh Anything? *www.bbc.co.uk/education/clips/zt3fb9q*
- BBC (2016). April Breaks Global Temperature Record. *www.bbc.co.uk/news/science-environment-36303046*
- BBC (2014). Climate Change: The Possible Effects. *www.bbc.co.uk/news/science-environment-26817593*

Talk skills and science discussion: Thinking of a summary

Ask groups to research and discuss a relevant topic. They can choose among heating materials, reversible change, irreversible change, cooking or oxidation. Ask groups to talk about what they have found out, and then to summarise their discussion into three sentences to share with the class.

Discuss the summaries with the class. Help groups to explain how they identified key points and what was difficult about thinking of a summary. Talk about the value of specific vocabulary, precisely used.

Additional information and teaching resources

Companion book:

- Loxley, P. (2018). *Practical Ideas for Teaching Primary Science: Inspiring Learning and Enjoyment,* Abingdon: Routledge, Chapter 10: Changing Materials.

Websites:

- Royal Society of Chemistry (2017). Learn Chemistry: Enhancing Learning and Teaching. *www.rsc.org/learn-chemistry/*
- The Science Museum London. Teachers' Resources: Kitchen Science. *www.sciencemuseum.org.uk/educators/classroom-resources*

ASE journals:

- Primary Science Review 88 (May/June 2005). *Crunchier on the Outside – Investigating Bread* by Sarah Marks and Emma Ranger.
- Primary Science Review 90 (Nov/Dec 2005). *Snow in the Nursery* by Collyer and Ross.

CHAPTER 19

ELECTRICITY AND MAGNETISM

Analogies are used to help visualise concepts such as electrical current, voltage and resistance. Analogies are an important meaning-making tool in science because they enable learners to use familiar images and experiences to make sense of unfamiliar scientific concepts. However, it is important to remember that the analogies presented do not provide exact representations of electricity and therefore have limited explanatory power. When teaching electricity, we need to be aware of the limitations of the analogies and discuss them with the children.

Topics discussed in the chapter

- Historical context
- Static electricity
- Electrical circuits
- The mysteries of voltage explained
- Electrical resistance
- Links between magnetism and electricity

Part 1: Subject knowledge

Historical context

Around 2,600 years ago, the ancient Greeks discovered that rubbing amber on lamb's wool produced **static electricity**. Once rubbed, the amber attracted materials such as feathers and straw. If it was rubbed hard enough, small sparks could be generated.

Although static electricity was demonstrated in the times of the ancient Greeks, little progress was made until the eighteenth century, when Benjamin Franklin (1706–1790) demonstrated that electricity could travel between objects. He demonstrated that electricity acted like a fluid (current) travelling from what he called a positive object to a negative one.

In 1800, Alessandro Volta (1745–1827) discovered how to produce electricity using zinc and copper discs. This discovery was the forerunner of the dry-cell battery and was a dependable and safe source of **electrical current**. Hans Christian Oersted (1777–1851) demonstrated the relationship between electricity and magnetism. He realised that when electricity flows in a wire it creates a magnetic field around the wire, which can be detected by a simple magnetic compass. André-Marie Ampère (1775–1836) used this discovery as a way of measuring electric current, which led to the development of instruments such as the ammeter and voltmeter.

Static electricity

Why does rubbing create static electricity?

Rubbing a balloon against your sweatshirt will make you and the balloon stick together. How does this work?

The force of attraction between a sweatshirt and the balloon is caused by static electricity. Rubbing the surface of the balloon with fabric creates a build-up of negative charge on the balloon and a build-up of positive charge on the fabric. Since negative and positive charges attract each other, the balloon sticks to the sweatshirt.

Where do the positive and negative charges come from?

All atoms are made up of positive and negative charges. The nucleus of an atom has a positive charge and the electrons, which surround it are negatively charged. Atoms are usually neutral because the combined negative charge of the electrons balances the positive charge of the nucleus. When a balloon is rubbed with a cloth, a great number of the electrons from the atoms in the cloth are transferred to the balloon. This increases the amount of negative charge on the surface of the balloon. At the same time, the amount of negative charge on the surface of the cloth is reduced and the cloth becomes

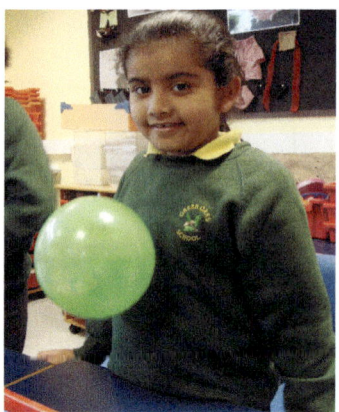

Static electricity in action.
Source: Peter Loxley

positively charged. In this way, both the balloon and cloth have become electrified. Static electricity is so called because it is only the *surface* of the cloth and balloon which is electrified. The charge does not flow in the materials.

Something to think about

You may have experienced the effects of static electricity when you brushed your hair on a dry day. Imagine what happens to your hair to create static electricity. Where does the static charge go eventually?

The build-up of static electricity can create lightning

Throughout history, different cultures have developed mythological stories to explain lightning. For example, the ancient Greeks thought it was a weapon used by Zeus, the king of all gods. We associate lightning with thunderstorms, but it has also been seen during volcanic eruptions, the testing of nuclear weapons, heavy snowstorms, extremely intense forest fires and large hurricanes.

Lightning is a gigantic discharge of static electricity. It is similar to the electric shock you sometimes get when you touch a doorknob but on a massively larger scale. Lightning is caused by a build-up of negative charge in the atmosphere which discharges down to the ground through the air. In doing so, it creates a large amount of heat and light.

Static electricity causes lightning.
Source: iStock

Electrical circuits

Electrical current refers to the movement or flow of electricity. Batteries enable **circuits** to be created in which a steady flow of electrical current can be maintained. The electrical current in a circuit is created by the flow of negative charge (electrons) in the connecting wires. Connecting wires are usually made from copper, which contains electrons which are free to move inside the metal. These mobile electrons are drawn to the positive terminal of the battery, creating a flow of negative charge. At the same time, the negative terminal of the battery feeds new electrons into the circuit, so maintaining the flow.

How do children visualise electric current?

Children imagine electric current in different ways. Some see it as little bright sparks that run through wires. Others imagine it to be like flashes of lightning, while some children imagine it to be like a fluid flowing from the battery to the bulb.

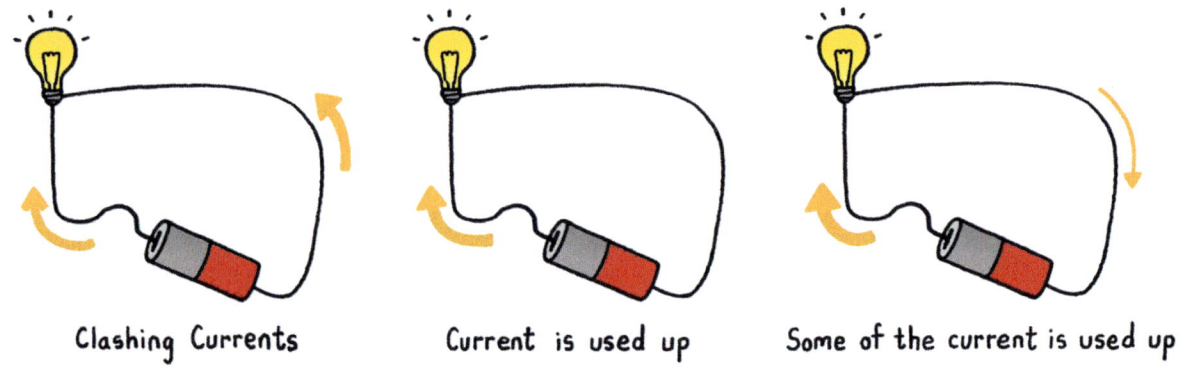

Clashing Currents   Current is used up   Some of the current is used up

Children's ideas about electrical circuits.
Source: Osborne and Freyberg, 1985

Generally, children's ideas derive from the belief that electricity is stored in the battery and flows down the wires to the bulb. The 'clashing current' idea is based on the belief that electricity flows out from both ends of the battery and collides in the bulb causing it to light up. Another common misconception is that electricity flows along one wire only and is then used up in the bulb. The 'some current used' model is a sort of compromise when children realise that an electric circuit will not work without a return path from the bulb to the battery. They imagine that any spare electricity would be returned to the battery via the second wire.

How do children's views differ from the scientific model?

Although the children's explanatory models are not scientifically correct, they are nevertheless quite powerful and can provide quite convincing explanations. The problem with these models is that they are not consistent with more detailed observations and do not stand up to rigorous testing. If instruments that measure the flow of electricity are used, we find that the flow (electrical current) is the same in all parts of the circuit. In other words, the same amount of electricity that flows out of the battery flows back into its other end, that is, the flow of electricity is conserved in all parts of the circuit.

What causes the bulb to light?

To understand how an electrical circuit lights up the bulb, we can use the analogy of an energy transport system. We can compare the battery to an energy storage depot and the electrical current to the flow of transporters or trucks which carry the energy from the depot (battery) to the bulb. Each of the transporters picks up energy at the depot and transfers it to the bulb. It then returns to the depot to collect more energy. The bulb shines brightly as long as the transporters provide it with enough energy.

Something to think about

Imagine if there was a problem, which slowed down the flow of transporters. What would happen to the brightness of the bulb? Can you think of other events that would influence how brightly the bulb would shine?

Electrical current is the same in all parts of the circuit.

What happens inside the wires?

Inside a wire the mobile electrons which are part of the metal act as transporters. Large numbers of mobile electrons exist inside the conducting wires. Imagine tiny energy transporters travelling in the wires that connect the bulb to the battery.

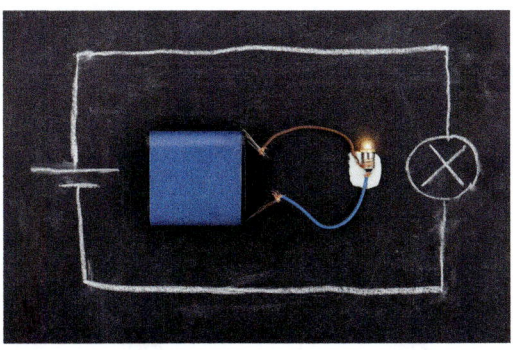
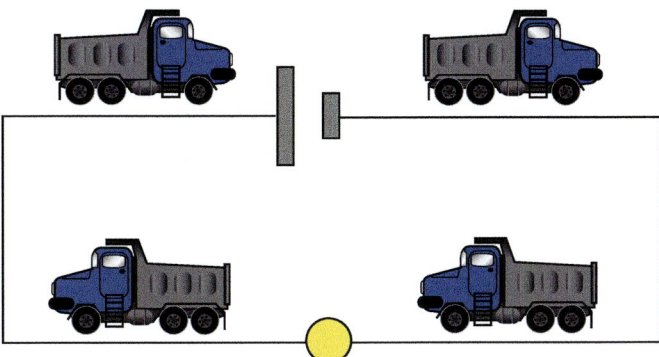

Energy transport model – the circuit (left); energy transport model (right).
Source: iStock

When the bulb and battery are connected in a circuit the mobile electrons move energy from where it is stored in the battery to the bulb. The flow of electrons around the circuit is called an electrical current, measured in ampere or amp (A). Because the numbers of electrons are so large, we measure electric current by the number of coulombs of charge, which flow in the circuit. One coulomb (C) of charge consists of approximately six million, million, million electrons. A current of 1 amp indicates that 1 coulomb of electrons flows through the bulb every second. If the current increases to 2 amps, the rate of flow of electrons is twice as much and so on. The coulomb is named after the scientist Charles-Augustin de Coulomb (1736–1806) and the amp is named after André-Marie Ampère (1775–1836). Both made major contributions to our understanding of the behaviour of electricity.

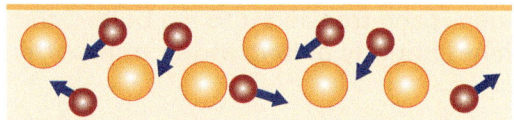   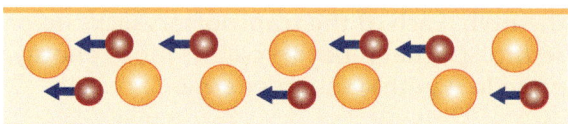

Random movement of electrons when the wire is not connected in a circuit   Flow of electrons when the wire is connected in a circuit

Mobile electrons are part of the structure of wires.

With regard to the transport analogy, each transporter represents one coulomb of charge. When the current is increased, each coulomb of charge flows more quickly around the circuit, delivering more energy to the bulb each second.

Connecting bulbs in series and parallel circuits

Bulbs can be connected together to form either a series or parallel circuit. In a series circuit, current flows through each bulb in turn (see diagram below). Adding bulbs in series reduces their brightness. The more bulbs we connect in series, the less brightly they shine. This is because the transporters have to share their energy between the bulbs. Two bulbs in series shine less brightly than a single bulb.

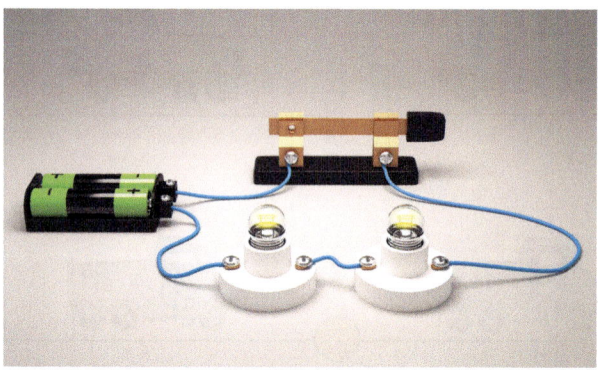   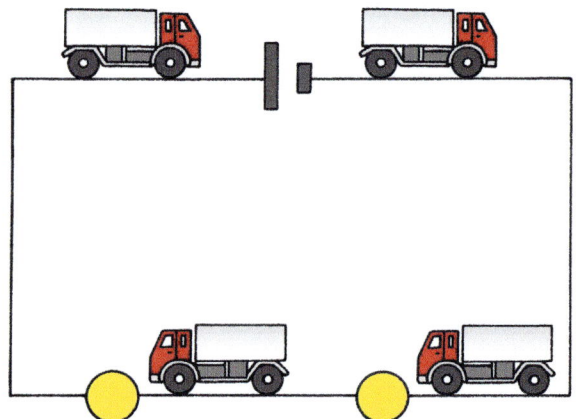

Series circuit.
Source: iStock

In a parallel circuit, current has a choice of routes and flows through either one or other of the bulbs (see diagram below). When bulbs are connected in parallel, the brightness of the bulbs is not affected. Two bulbs connected in parallel shine just as brightly as a single bulb. This is because different pathways can be taken by the transporters. Each of the transporters only passes through one bulb before returning to collect more energy from the battery (depot). Each bulb gets the same amount of energy as if it were the only bulb in the circuit.

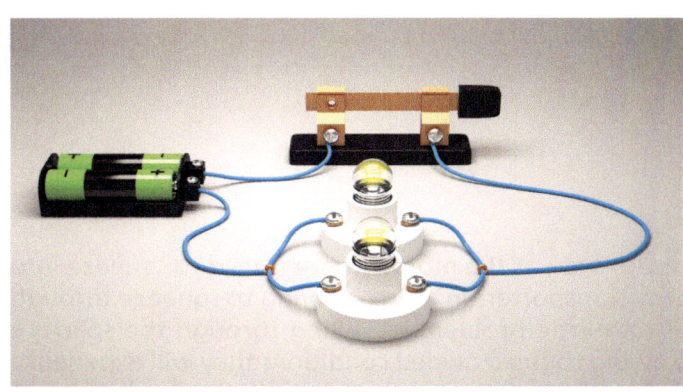

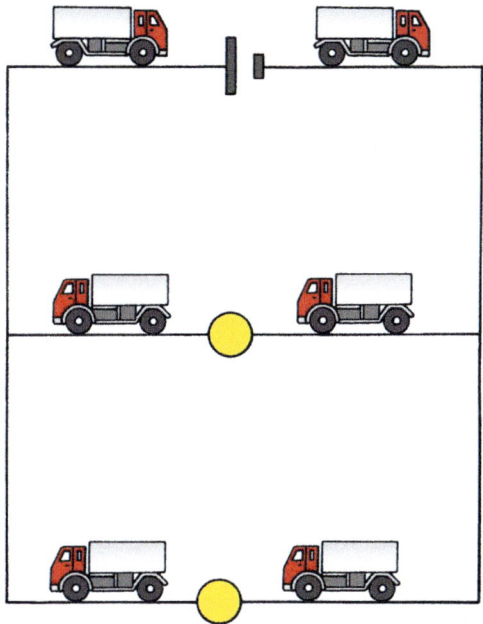

Parallel circuit.
Source: iStock

The mysteries of voltage explained

Matching bulbs to batteries

Batteries are made up of cells. In common dry-cell batteries, each cell has an **electrical voltage** of 1.5. Two cells combine to make 3 volts, four cells to make 6 volts and six cells to make 9 volts. As we increase the voltage in a circuit by adding more cells, the brightness of the bulb increases. However, if we increase the voltage too much, there is a danger that the filament of the bulb will overheat and 'blow'. Bulbs are labelled to indicate their recommended voltage. When connected to its recommended voltage, a bulb will shine brightly and is less likely to be damaged.

> ### Something to think about
>
> Imagine that you have a 9-volt battery and three 3-volt bulbs. How would you connect them together so that the bulbs would shine as brightly as possible without blowing?

What is voltage?

To help us imagine the nature of voltage, we can again use the energy transport analogy. Think of the voltage of the battery as an indication of how much energy each of the transporters will carry from the battery to the bulb. For example, a 1.5-volt battery provides each transporter with 1.5 units of energy to carry to the bulb. When the transporters return to the battery, they are each given another 1.5 units of energy and so on. A unit of energy is called a joule. A 3-volt battery, therefore, provides each transporter with 3 joules of energy, a 6-volt battery supplies 6 joules and so on. The larger the voltage, the more energy is carried by each of the transporters to the bulb.

Something to think about

All analogies have their limitations. What can't the transport analogy explain about the behaviour of an electrical circuit? Can you think of another analogy which could be used?

Electrical resistance

What happens inside a light bulb?

Chaos is caused by roadworks on a crowded motorway, as the motorists are forced to squeeze into one narrow lane. So we can imagine the energy transporters in a circuit trying to squeeze through the bulb's very thin filament wire. They will find little problem travelling through the spacious connecting wires, but hold-ups are inevitable owing to the crowded conditions they will experience inside the filament. The speed at which they travel through the filament will dictate the rate of flow of the transporters (electrical current) all around the circuit.

As the transporters enter the filament wire, they are packed together and inevitably crash into its atomic structure. It is through these collisions that they pass on their energy to the filament, which becomes very hot and gives out heat and light. Collisions with the atomic structure create **resistance** to the flow of electrical current. Thinner wires create more resistance because there are more collisions between the transporters and the atomic structure of the wire.

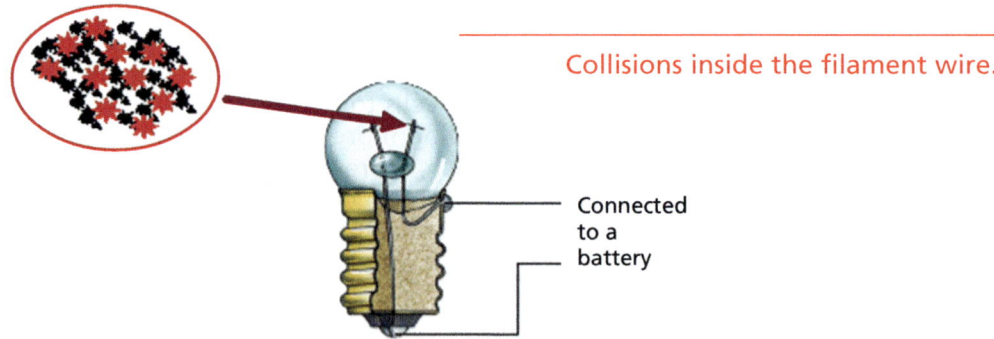

Collisions inside the filament wire.

Connected to a battery

The difference between conductors and insulators

Conductors allow the passage of electrical current. Good conductors have a structure, which provides a supply of mobile electrons (energy transporters). Metals are good conductors because they contain an abundance of mobile electrons. Generally, nonmetals, such as plastic, wood, wool, rubber and glass, are insulators. These materials have structures which prevent the flow of electrons and therefore cannot provide an adequate supply of energy transporters. The exception is graphite, a non-metal, which has a structure through which electricity can flow.

Solutions, which contain sugar, salt or lemon juice, are fairly good conductors. This is because when these materials dissolve, they produce a large supply of positive and negative energy transporters, which can travel relatively easily through the liquid.

Links between magnetism and electricity

What is a magnet?

A **magnet** is an object made of a material which creates a magnetic field. The magnetic field is strongest at the north and south poles of the magnet. An object can be described as a magnet if it repels a known magnet. Similar magnetic poles repel each other, while opposite poles attract. If a magnet is cut in half you have two magnets, each with a north and a south pole. The north pole of a magnet is sometimes called the north seeking pole because it will point to the Earth's North Pole when the magnet is freely suspended.

Which materials are magnetic?

A **magnetic** material is attracted to a magnet. A magnet can exert a force on a magnetic object without coming into direct contact with it. The force can act at a distance. Magnets are surrounded by an invisible force field. Not all materials are attracted to magnets; only objects made of iron, cobalt or nickel are magnetic.

Something to think about

What are the differences between magnetic and gravitational force fields? Do you think it curious that magnets can attract and repel each other, while gravity can only act in one way? Is it possible that there could be a gravitational force which repels objects?

The Earth is a giant magnet

The Earth behaves like a giant magnet. Its magnetic field is similar to that of a bar magnet which is tilted 11 degrees from Earth's axis.

Scientists think that the rotation of the Earth plays a part in creating its magnetic field. The rotation of the Earth generates electrical currents in its iron core, which are thought to be the cause of the magnetic field. How the currents and magnetic field are created is not clear, but it is known that Venus does not have such a strong magnetic field, although it has an iron core similar to the Earth's. It seems that Venus, which takes 243 Earth days to rotate, does not spin fast enough to create a strong magnetic field.

Something to think about

Some magnets are stronger than others. What makes them stronger? Is it related to the size of the magnet? How could you find out?

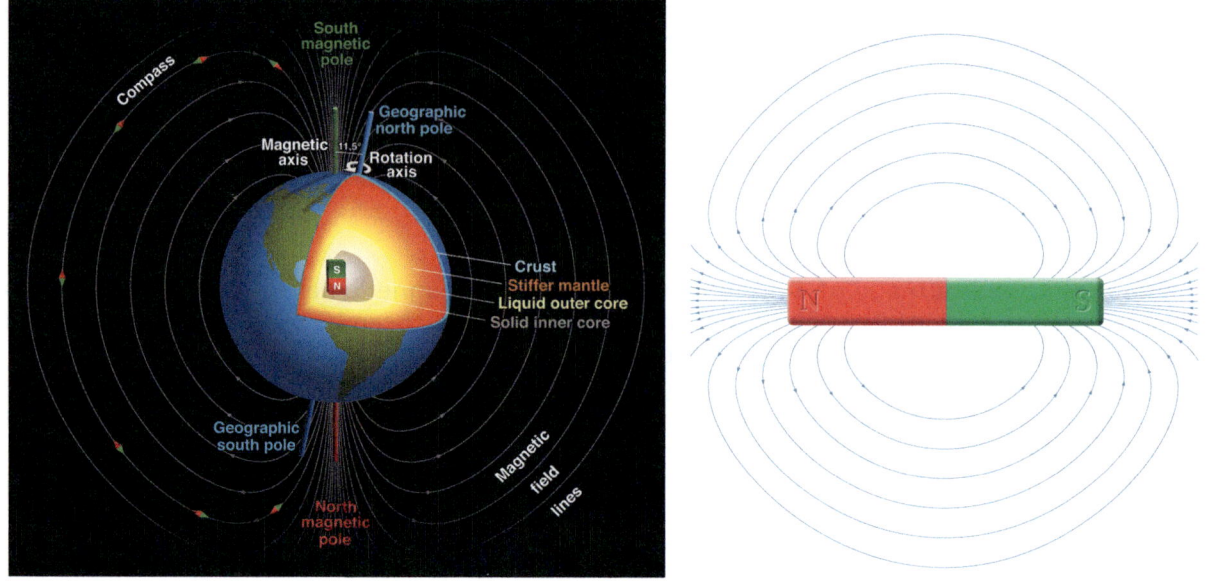

Earth's magnetic field (left); magnetic field of bar magnet (right).

Is there a connection between electricity and magnetism?

Hans Christian Oersted (1820) accidently discovered that when an electrical current flows it creates a magnetic field. He was demonstrating to friends the heating effect of electrical currents when he noticed that a nearby compass needle moved every time he turned on the circuit. This has become known as the electromagnetic effect. When a current flows through a wire, it creates a magnetic field in the space around the wire. This discovery led to the development of electro-magnets, which are made from coils of wire around an iron core. Increasing the number of coils increases the strength of the magnetic field.

Can we use magnetism to create electricity?

If electricity can be used to make magnetism, can magnetism be used to make electricity? In 1831, Michael Faraday demonstrated that by moving a magnet in and out of a coil of wire an electric current could be produced. Faraday's discovery led to the development of the electrical generator, which has had profound effects on the way that we live and work. Today's power stations use giant turbines to move magnets inside huge coils of wire (generators) to produce the electricity we need. Many of these power stations use fossil fuels such as coal, gas and oil to power the turbines. Alternative technologies include the use of wave power, wind power, tidal power, nuclear power and biofuels.

Global dimensions: Solar electricity

In the developed world, householders worry about the size of their electricity bills and the sustainability of electricity generated by the burning of fossil fuels. But in many less developed areas of the world, the raw material for generating green electricity is something they have in abundance – sunlight. In some countries, areas of open land have been fitted with huge arrays of solar panels to produce large amounts of electricity. These projects have expensive start-up costs and tend to provide power for cities. It is only recently that effective and affordable technologies can turn solar energy into clean electricity for small communities. In southern India, for example, a simple solar panel is sufficient to power two light bulbs and a socket. Now a rural family can enjoy cheap, safe lighting at night, rather than relying on expensive and polluting kerosene lights – and they can also recharge a mobile phone or run a radio.

However, solar panels using photovoltaic (pv) cells will work even in less sunny climates. The Centre for Alternative Technology (CAT) in Wales gives advice to those planning to install solar technology in this country, and pv roof tiles are becoming more common on new houses across Europe. Small-scale solar electricity usage is also growing, with pv cells used to power weather stations, parking meters and even street lighting, and to recharge laptops and mobile phones.

www.energysavingtrust.org.uk/Generating-energy/Choosing-a-renewable-technology/Solar-panels-PV

http://info.cat.org.uk/pv

www.guardian.co.uk/environment/2012/jul/03/solarpower-renewableenergy

Summary

Electricity is a phenomenon made possible by the structure of materials. All materials are made up of atoms, which contain positive charges called protons and negative charges called electrons. Usually the two types of charge cancel each out and no electric effect can be detected. However, with various materials it is possible to remove some of the negative charges by rubbing the surface. Removing the negative charges leaves the surface of the material positively charged and creates static electricity.

In many metals, the negative charges (electrons) are not firmly fixed to atoms and are free to move around inside the material. When a battery is connected to the metal filament in a bulb, the mobile negative charges travel away from the negative end of the battery towards the positive terminal. This creates an electric current. Electric currents carry energy from the battery to appliances such as light bulbs, motors and buzzers.

Materials that contain iron have magnetic properties. The Earth behaves like a giant magnet because of its iron core. There is a close connection between electricity and magnetism. When an electric current flows in a wire, it creates a magnetic field. The reverse is also true. Moving a magnet inside a coil of wire can generate a voltage and cause an electric current to flow. The movement of a magnet inside a coil is the method by which electric power is produced in power stations.

Part 2: Ideas for practice

Topic: Electric circuits

Age group: 7–9 years

Introduction

This topic provides opportunities for children to construct simple series electrical circuits and to become familiar with basic components. Activities in the re-describing stage help children understand how switches can be used to turn a bulb on or off. Opportunities to make artefacts involving electrical circuits are provided in the application stage.

Working scientifically

In these activities children will:

- ask questions and use scientific enquiry to answer them;
- set up practical enquiries and comparative tests;
- record findings using scientific language, drawings and labelled diagrams;
- use results to draw conclusions, make predictions, suggest changes and raise further questions;
- think creatively to explain how the circuit works and to establish links between cause and effects;
- explain observations by drawing on established scientific knowledge.

Scientific view

A simple circuit is a one-way track around which electricity flows. The flow of electricity through the bulb causes it to light up. If the circuit is not a complete loop, the electricity is prevented from flowing and the bulb will not light up.

Exploration stage

Children's talk involves trying out their own ideas

Setting the scene

There are lots of stories about lighthouses, real and imaginary. Start this chapter by reading a story to the children. Show the children some pictures of real

Model lighthouse.
Source: Peter Loxley

Making a simple circuit.
Source: Peter Loxley

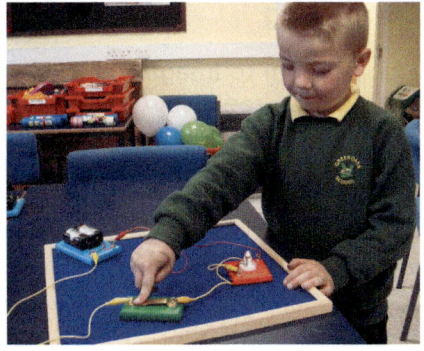

lighthouses and talk about their structure and purpose. Ask the children to talk about how a lighthouse works. Are lighthouses today manned by keepers or are they automatic? Children use information sources to identify where light-houses can be found around the coastline and find out how many have a lighthouse keeper.

Show the children a model lighthouse, which you can make from a cardboard tube. Use a simple electric circuit consisting of a bulb, battery and wires. Make sure the battery and wires are hidden inside the tube and the children can only see the bulb fixed to the top. Children can guess what must be inside the model lighthouse to light the bulb. Children talk about and draw a picture of what they think is inside the model which causes the bulb to light. Discuss children's pictures and compare to a torch. Establish that there must be a battery inside the model.

Scientific enquiry

Talk with the children about the purpose of the battery and how it can be connected to the bulb. Provide the children with a simple 1.5-volt battery and point out that it has a positive and negative end. Challenge the children to use the battery to light a 1.5-volt bulb. Encourage them to place the bulb in turn against each end of the battery. Ask them to suggest why the bulb does not light. What else do they need? Children can try to use one wire to light the bulb. When successful, they can draw the circuit. Use magnifiers so the children can see the filament clearly and draw the part of the bulb which lights up. They can consider why the bulb has to be connected in a loop to the battery to make it work. Once the children are familiar with the concept of an electrical circuit, they can use bulb holders and battery holders to make a circuit. Explain that the holders make the job easier. Guidance on batteries and circuits is provided by the ASE in their *Be safe!* booklet.

Puzzle

Talk together about why a bulb will not light until it is connected in a circuit to both ends of the battery. Why do we need a complete circuit?

Talking points: true, false or not sure?

- A complete circuit stops electricity leaking out of the battery into the air.
- A complete circuit enables electricity to flow from both ends of a battery to light the bulb.
- A battery is filled with light which travels through the wires to light up the bulb.
- A battery goes flat when it runs out of light.
- If a wire is missing the bulb only receives half of the electricity from the battery.

A complete circuit provides a pathway for electricity to flow through the bulb.

Discuss children's responses to the puzzle and the talking points and probe children's under-standing of how electric circuits work.

Modelling

Ask children to imagine they were small enough to fit inside the wires in an electric circuit. What would they see? Now ask them to mime moving through different parts of the circuit. Imagine they were travelling through the battery, then inside the wires and finally through the thin filament of the bulb. Freeze-frame the action inside each of the components and ask children to explain their mime. Discuss what they imagined when they performed their mimes. Probe their ideas about the nature of electricity.

Formative assessment

Provide opportunities for children to voice what they have learnt in the exploratory stage. Use evidence from their responses to the puzzle, talking points and other activities to assess differences between children's ideas and the scientific view. Plan how you will use the re-describing stage to help the children address their *learning needs.* You may need to modify the activities depending on the collective and individual needs of your children.

Teaching and information resources

- We Like Viral (2015). Creepiest Lighthouses in the World: Their Stories Will Give You CHILLS! *www.welikeviral.com/creepiest-lighthouses-world-stories-will-give-chills.html*

Re-describing stage

Children's talk involves making sense of scientific ideas

Teacher-led discussion

The purpose of this stage is to provide an analogy which children can use to make sense of why a battery and bulb need to be connected in a complete circuit. Start by using a simulated model of an electric circuit to explain how electricity travels around a loop. The BBC Bitesize clip, '*How an electric circuit works'*, contains a useful simulation.

Modelling

A useful analogy for a circuit is a toy train carrying goods from the depot (battery) along the track (wires) to a station (bulb) and then returning to collect more goods. If the track is not a complete loop, the train will get stuck and will not be able to complete its journey. A toy track can be set up in the classroom and compared with the circuit. Children can also act out this analogy if a track is marked out in the playground. Listen to the children's conversations when they are modelling and ask them to explain the answer to the puzzle.

Scientific enquiries

1. Adding components

Children explore the effects of changing the components in a circuit. Construct a circuit with a 1.5 V battery and 1.5 V bulb. Then add another bulb and observe the effects. What difference does adding another battery make? Children investigate the effects of adding bulbs and batteries and try to identify patterns. To avoid blowing the bulbs, always add bulbs to a circuit before adding extra batteries. Short circuits are inevitable, so choose batteries which tolerate short circuits safely (See *Be safe!* 2011). Children record their results by drawing annotated circuit diagrams using their own symbols. They can use the analogy to explain how each of their circuits works. Children can raise further enquiry questions involving other components such as buzzers and LED's.

2. Controlling circuits

Children can make switches and use them to control a simple circuit. They use materials such as paper clips, paper fasteners, foil, card and wire to make simple switches to try their own designs. Encourage the children to draw their circuits and talk about how the switch turns the bulb on and off using the train analogy. Address any outstanding *learning needs.*

Information and teaching resources

BBC Bitesize:

● BBC (2007). How an Electric Circuit Works. *www.bbc.co.uk/education/clips/zq3fb9q*

Application stage

Children's talk involves trying out scientific ideas

Design and make a model lighthouse

Children can design and make a model lighthouse, torch or a standing lamp which is turned on and off by a simple switch.

Games and activities

The BBC Bitesize clip entitled *'Using circuits to make games and activities'* provides some ideas for designing and making activities. Having watched the video, children can design their own games, cards or models which involve the use of a simple electric circuit.

Information and teaching resources

BBC Bitesize:

● BBC (2007). Using Circuits to Make Games and Activities. *www.bbc.co.uk/education/clips/zxrb4wx*

Topic: Series and parallel circuits

Age group: 9–11 years

Introduction

Activities in this topic focus on designing circuits, which control the brightness of lamps connected in series and parallel. Children explore how the brightness of the lamps in a circuit change depending on how they are arranged and on the voltage of the cell. Children compare and give reasons for variations. In the application stage, children research recent developments in motor car design, and design and make a model car with working headlights.

Scientific view

An electrical circuit can be thought of as a transport system, which uses electrical current to transfer energy from the battery to the bulbs. A series circuit is a one-way track along which electricity flows to deliver energy to each of the bulbs. When bulbs are connected in parallel, the electrical current splits up in order to flow through each branch of the circuit. Bulbs shine brighter when connected in parallel because the arrangement allows more electrical current to flow and hence more energy per second is delivered to each bulb.

Working scientifically

In these activities children will:

- try to find answers to questions through scientific enquiry;
- think creatively to explain how the circuits work and to establish links between cause and effects;
- make comparisons based on their observations and use test results to make predictions and set up further comparative tests;
- report findings from enquiries in written and oral form;
- use established scientific knowledge to help explain observations.

Exploration stage

Children's talk involves trying out their own ideas

Setting the scene

Introduce the lesson by exploring video clips, pictures and models of different types of cars. Talk about the children's favourites. What do they like best about them? Discuss the main parts of a car and their purposes. Focus the discussion on the design criteria for the headlights. What should they be able to do? Talk about the source of energy, which powers the lights. Establish there is a battery in the car which provides energy to light up the bulbs in the headlights.

Puzzle

Tell the children that later on they are going to design and make a model car with working headlights. The puzzle is how are they going to connect the headlights together in an electric circuit?

Scientific enquiry

In small groups, children can systematically test different circuits to discover the best circuit arrangement for headlights. They start off with a circuit containing a 1.5-volt lamp and a 1.5-volt battery. Children observe the brightness of the bulb. They then test two 1.5-volt lamps and a 1.5-volt dry-cell battery connected in series. Why are the bulbs so dim and how could they make them brighter? Children *work collaboratively* to construct an explanation on which they can agree. Provide them with an additional 1.5-volt cell so they can construct a circuit with two cells and two lamps. Ask children to explain the effects. When planning these activities refer to ASE guidelines in *Be safe!* (2011) for using electrical equipment.

Introduce the standard symbols for components in an electric circuit. Children then draw circuit diagrams to record the different ways they connected the bulbs and annotate them to explain the results. Now, challenge the children to find ways of connecting two 1.5-volts lamps together so that they shine brightly using only one 1.5-volt cell. Ask each group to draw a diagram of their successful circuit and compare to the diagram of the series circuit.

Talk about the similarities and differences in the circuits and introduce the term 'parallel circuit'. Ask each group to list the differences between a parallel and a series circuit. What advantages do parallel circuits have over series circuits? Are there any disadvantages? What would happen if they used 6-volt bulbs and a 6-volt battery? Children can design and test different circuits using a range of components.

Return to the puzzle. Ask the children to decide, on the basis of their investigations, which circuit arrangement is best for their model car. Probe children's reasons and discuss what they have learnt from their enquiries.

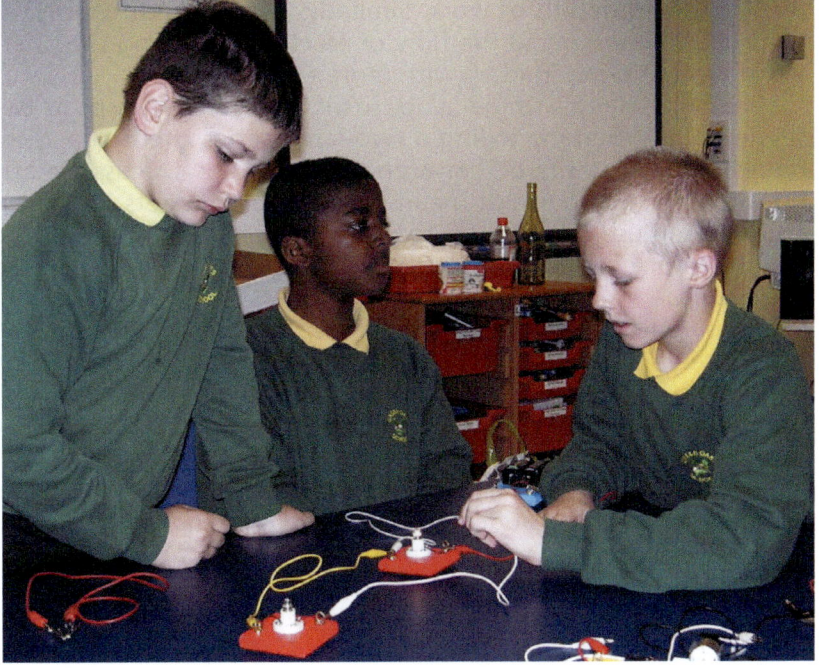

Children testing different circuits.
Source: Peter Loxley

Formative assessment

Provide opportunities for children to voice what they have learnt in the exploratory stage. Use evidence from their responses to the puzzle and other activities to assess differences between children's ideas and the scientific view. Plan how you will use the re-describing stage to help the children address their *learning needs.* You may need to modify the activities depending on the collective and individual needs of your children.

Re-describing stage

Children's talk involves making sense of scientific ideas

Teacher-led discussion

Choose an analogy which you think will be most meaningful for your children. The transport analogy described in the subject knowledge section of this chapter is a useful one. Use suitable drawings to represent the tiny 'energy transporters' inside the wires, which carry energy from the battery to the bulb. Compare this model with the BBC Bitesize waterwheel model entitled *'The power of batteries in a circuit'*.

Modelling

Children can model the transport analogy, using sweets or dried fruit as the energy, which is stored in the battery. Discuss the concept of energy with the children. Energy is needed to make things happen. They can talk about what they are able to do when they have lots of energy. They can run about and do lots of work. Similarly, a bulb needs energy, which it gets from the battery, to light up. Children mime the flow of electricity carrying the energy from the battery to the bulb before returning to load up with more energy.

When modelling a single-lamp circuit, each child transports two sweets from the battery to the single bulb. When modelling a two-lamp series circuit, each child carries two sweets from the battery, which are shared between the two bulbs. Discuss the effect of sharing the energy on the brightness of the bulbs. It means each bulb only gets half the energy supplied by the battery. Children can use this analogy to predict what will happen if three bulbs are connected in series. Use the term 'electric current' to describe the flow of electricity, modelled by the children, around the circuit.

In a parallel arrangement, each transporter only passes through one bulb before returning to the battery. This means each bulb is supplied with a full load (two sweets) of energy, the same amount it would receive if it were the only bulb in the circuit. Children can hypothesise about the brightness of the bulbs if a third bulb were to be connected in parallel. Compare the energy drain on a battery when it is connected in parallel and series circuits.

Challenge children to create their own analogies which explain the way electric circuits behave. Probe their ideas and address outstanding *learning needs.*

Information and teaching resources

BBC Bitesize:

- BBC (2007). The Power of Batteries in a Circuit. *www.bbc.co.uk/education/clips/z7ys34j*

ASE journals:

- Primary Science 135 (Nov/Dec 2014). *The Red and Blacks Developing 10–11 Year Old's Understanding of Electricity.*
- Primary Science 135 (Nov/Dec 2014). *Teaching the Big Ideas of Electricity at Primary Level* by Steven Chapman.
- Primary Science 135 (Nov/Dec 2014). *Tricky Circuitry* by Tony Davies.

Application stage

Children's talk involves trying out scientific ideas

Model car with working headlights

Children design and make a model car with working headlights. For a further challenge, they could design one which is also powered by an electrical motor. Ideas for designing and making a model car can be found on the STEM Centre website. The Nuffield project entitled *'How fast should your buggy be?'* is a useful resource which describes the materials required and how to use them to make a battery-powered vehicle.

Children start designing their model car by researching recent developments in the design of headlights and find out how LED's are used. They can incorporate LED's in the design of their model cars instead of filament bulbs. Designing a model electric-powered car could be part of a project into sustainable development, taking in recent electric-powered vehicle design.

Information and teaching resources

STEM Centre resource:

- STEM Learning. How Fast Should Your Buggy Be? *https://www.stem.org.uk/elibrary/resource/ 25794/how-fast-should-your-buggy-be*

BP educational services:

- BP Educational Service (2017). Electricity Topic Starter. *http://bpes.bp.com/primary-resources/ science/ages-9-to-11/electricity/electricity-topic-starter/*

Talk skills and science discussion: Making comparisons

Ask groups to discuss changes made to simple electrical circuits by adding components or changing the set-up of the circuit. Ask groups to explain to one another what they think is happening using comparative words, such as *more* or *less*, and particular words, such as 'brighter'.

With the whole class, discuss the effects of modifying simple circuits and bring out the scientific point of view. Use comparisons as evidence. Establish the importance of evidence. Emphasise the idea of replicating an enquiry as a basis for ongoing scientific discussion.

Additional teaching and learning resources

Companion book:

- Loxley, P. (2018). *Practical Ideas for Teaching Primary Science: Inspiring Learning and Enjoyment,* Abingdon: Routledge, Chapter 12: Electricity and Chapter 13: Forces and Magnetism.

BBC Bitesize:

- BBC. BBC Science Clips (animations). *www.bbc.co.uk/schools/scienceclips/*
- BBC (2017). Electromagnetism and Magnetism. *www.bbc.co.uk/education/guides/z3g8d2p/revision*

ASE journals:

- Primary Science 136 (Jan/Feb 2015). *Playground Science* by Alan Cross and Jon Board.
- Primary Science 123 (May/June 2012). *Using Models to Promote Children's Scientific Understanding* by Jane Maloney and Sheila Curtis.
- Primary Science Review 98 (May/June 2007). *Understanding Simple Circuits* by Jenny Mant and Helen Wilson.

CHAPTER 20

FORCES AND MOTION

Although we rarely think about forces, they are part of everything that we do. On Earth, it is not possible to imagine a situation in which forces are not involved. Gravity causes objects to fall to the ground; friction causes our shoes to wear out and, when cycling or driving in our cars, air resistance slows us down. This chapter looks at a range of situations in which forces are involved.

Topics discussed in the chapter

- Historical context
- Relationship between force and motion
- Gravity and weight
- Air resistance
- Floating and sinking
- Friction
- Simple machines

Part 1: Subject knowledge

Historical context

Our understanding of how **forces** control motion can be traced back to the time of the ancient Greeks and in particular to the work of Aristotle (384–322 BCE). Aristotle's ideas about why things moved were intuitive and based on common sense. For example, he thought objects could not move without a force to push them. This understanding was based on his everyday experience. If he rolled a rock along the ground, it would stop after travelling a certain distance. The distance depended on how hard he pushed it. He concluded from this that the rock stopped because it ran out of force. Bigger forces lasted longer and hence the rock travelled further.

A more reliable view of force and motion

Aristotle's explanation of how forces control motion is a powerful view because it is built on observation and experience. However, it is not reliable because it does not predict the motion of objects accurately in a wide range of contexts. It was Sir Isaac Newton (1643–1727) who eventually provided us with a more dependable understanding of forces and motion. Newton recognised that objects continue to move naturally without the help of forces. He realised that forces change motion. In other words, forces make objects go faster, or slower or change direction. If there are no forces acting on an object, it will continue to move at a constant speed or remain at rest.

Relationship between force and motion

Imagine you are travelling on a spaceship towards Mars. The journey will take you nearly a year, even though you are travelling very fast. The rockets which fired you into space have detached from the main capsule. What is keeping the spaceship moving so fast? Would we expect the spaceship to slow down as it gradually 'runs out' of force?

From a scientific perspective, we should ask ourselves not what is keeping the spaceship going but if there is anything out there that could slow it down. On Earth, objects that move are slowed down by air resistance and friction. If you travel fast on a bicycle, you can feel the force of the air pushing against you. When you stop pedalling, the force of the air will slow you down. In space, there are no air particles to smash into and hence no force of air resistance to slow the spaceship down. Once travelling at a particular speed, a spaceship will continue travelling at that speed. Some spaceships have small engines, which can be used to create forces to alter their direction or speed. The same law of motion applies to the Earth; an object will continue moving at a constant speed until a force acts on it.

Spacewalk

Now imagine that a fault develops on a radio aerial on the outside of the spaceship. You open the door and take a step outside while the ship is still travelling very fast. What would happen next?

1.   Would you fall away from the spacecraft?

2. Would the spacecraft speed on past you, leaving you behind?

3. Would you continue moving alongside the spacecraft?

Remember that you were travelling at the same speed as the spaceship when you were inside it. As you step outside, would that situation change? In space there is no air and hence nothing to bump into which will slow you down. If there are no forces to speed you up, slow you down or change the direction of your motion, then you will continue moving at the same speed as the spacecraft. Indeed, if you could only see the spacecraft, you would not sense that you were moving.

Spacewalk.

Gravity holds the universe together

Have you ever thought why the Moon doesn't fly off into space? Why does it keep moving around the Earth? Isaac Newton worked out the answer to this question when he realised that the force of gravity pulls the Moon around the Earth. To explain how it works, Newton imagined a cannon ball being fired from the top of a very high mountain. When the ball is fired, gravity would pull it down towards the ground. Where it lands would depend on how fast it was fired. If the speed of the cannon ball is too slow, it will crash into the Earth. If the speed is too fast, the cannon ball will fly off into space. But, if the speed is just right, then the cannon ball will continually fall towards the Earth but never reach it – it will orbit the Earth. Because the Earth is curved, the cannon ball would fall all the way around. His thought experiment ignores the effects of air resistance, which would influence the motion of the cannon ball. However, it explains the movement of the Moon because there is no air in space to affect its movement.

The force of gravity can act over very large distances and keeps all the planets orbiting around the Sun. Without the force of gravity, the Solar System would never have been formed (Chapter 11).

Newton's thought experiment: A–E show different speeds of the cannon ball.

Gravity and weight

What is the weight of a 2kg bag of sugar?

The concepts of weight and mass are often confused in everyday life. From a scientific point of view, the mass of the sugar is 2kg but its weight is different because it is a measure of the force of gravity acting on it. For every kilogram of mass, gravity exerts a force of 10 newtons (N). If an object has a mass of 2kg then its weight will be 20N. This means that you need to pull with a force of 20N to lift the bag of sugar off the supermarket shelf.

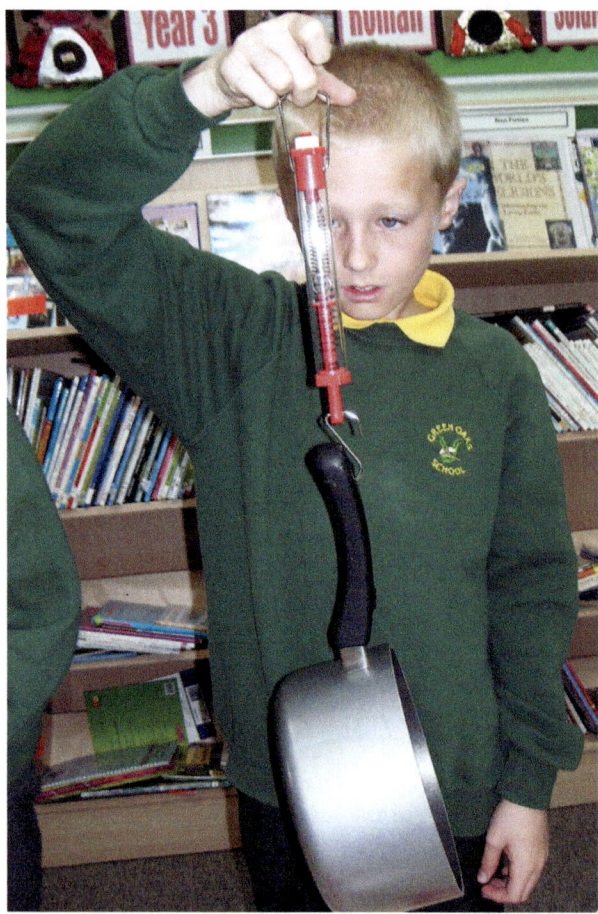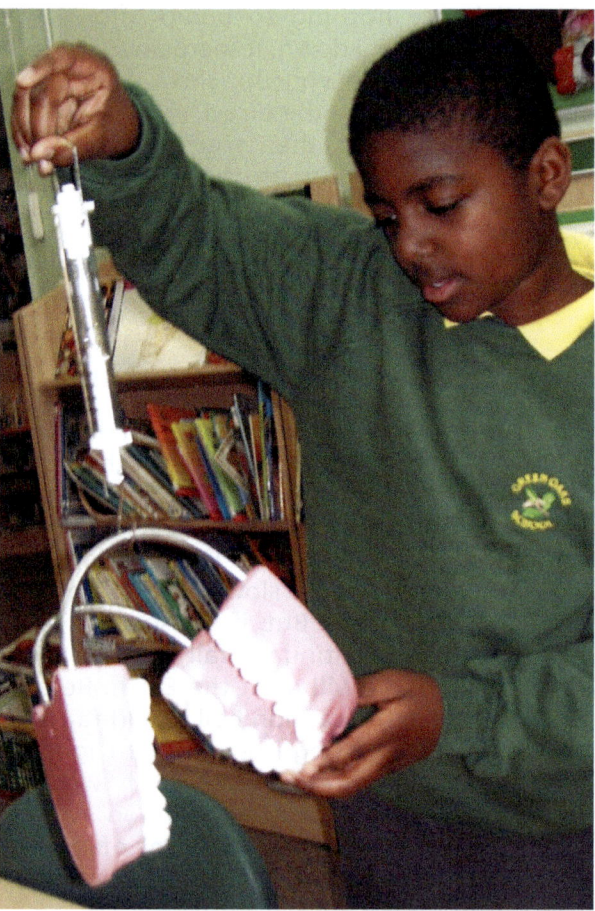

Using force meters.
Source: Peter Loxley

Something to think about

Use force meters to compare the weights of different objects. What does a mobile phone weigh in newtons? Estimate before measuring with the force meter. Do this for a range of objects until you become skilled at estimating weights.

Gravity is a natural force

Scientists are not sure about what causes gravity. Gravity is a natural force that pulls objects together. All solid objects exert a gravitational force. The strength of the pull of gravity depends on the mass of the objects and the distance between them. All objects have gravitational attraction, but we may only notice the force of its pull when massive objects like the Earth are involved. If we took a bag of sugar into space, we would not be able to detect its weight. It would become weightless because the force of gravity from Earth would be so weak. The sugar would be weightless but we would still have a mass of 2kg to sweeten our tea. Mass is a measure of how much sugar there is in the bag, measured in kilograms, while weight is a measure of the force of gravity pulling it down towards the Earth, measured in newtons. In our everyday lives, we often use the word 'weight' because mass on Earth is always under the influence of the Earth's gravity.

Something to think about

Imagine what it would be like living on a planet with an atmosphere similar to that on Earth but with one-tenth of the gravity. How would this affect the evolution of the animals and plants? What would a tree look like?

Air resistance

Why is it difficult to run with an open umbrella?

On Earth, the motion of objects is controlled by a number of interacting forces. One of the most common forces is air resistance. When running with an open umbrella, we feel the resistance that air creates to anything that moves through it. In effect, we live at the bottom of a sea of air, and in order to move we need to push the air in front of us out of the way. An open umbrella makes this task even more difficult because more air has to be pushed out of the way. The bigger the umbrella, the harder it is to push the air out of the way and hence the greater the air resistance.

Something to think about

Imagine that you are an animal that lives on the seabed. Would you notice all the water around you? Would resistance from the water affect your movement? Is living on the seabed comparable to living at the bottom of a sea of air?

Choosing the best words

Air resistance is a force created by collisions between the air and objects which push their way through it. Bigger objects create more air resistance because they have to push more air out of the way. Faster objects create more air resistance because they smash through the air more violently. Imagine what words you could use to explain the effect air has on the motion of objects. Explain the motion of a falling feather without using the words 'air resistance'. Which words do you think are appropriate?

Balanced and unbalanced forces

We can use arrows to depict the direction and magnitude of the forces, which control the motion of an object. Consider a hippopotamus called Hypo who has just jumped out of a plane with a parachute on her back. Two forces control her motion. There is a downward force caused by the pull of gravity (Hypo's weight), which tends to speed it up, and an upward force caused by air resistance, which tends to slow it down. In this case, the opposing forces are unbalanced. That is, the pull of gravity is larger than the air resistance and consequently Hypo's speed will increase. If the air resistance which opposes her motion were greater than the force of gravity, Hypo would slow down (decelerate).

Air resistance

Weight of Hypo (force of gravity pulling her down)

Forces in action.

If Hypo's weight and the air resistance were of equal magnitude then she would fall at a constant speed because the effect of one force would be balanced by the other. Balanced forces do not change motion – they have the same effect as if there were no forces involved.

> ### Something to think about
>
> Imagine if gravity was turned off halfway through Hypo's fall. Describe what would happen.

Unbalanced forces change the motion of objects. Objects speed up when the forces are unbalanced in the same direction as their movement and slow down when the unbalanced forces act in the opposite direction. When the forces are balanced, the motion of an object is unaffected; it will either continue moving at a constant speed or remain at rest. These are big ideas because they apply to all situations. The concept of balanced and unbalanced forces can be used to explain and predict the motion of all objects in every situation, including our next topic – floating and sinking.

Floating and sinking

Why is it hard to sink a beach ball?

Pushing a beach ball under the water in a pool or at the seaside is not easy. The bigger the ball, the harder it is to push under the water. This is because water exerts an upward force on the beach ball. The bigger the ball, the greater is the upward force, or **upthrust**, created by the water.

The forces that control the motion of an object in water are its weight and the upthrust exerted by the water. If the weight of the object exceeds the upthrust then the object will sink. If the forces are balanced, the object will float.

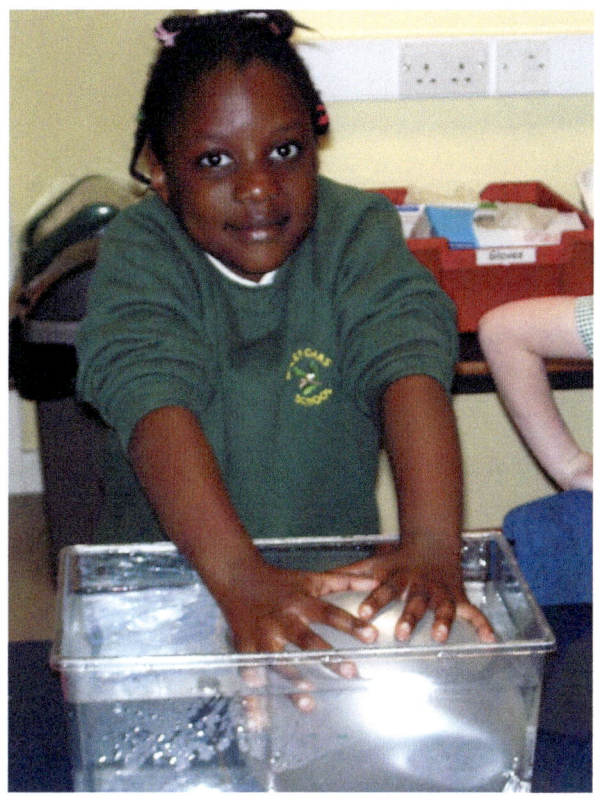 

Having fun trying to sink a balloon.
Source: Peter Loxley

343

Factors which influence upthrust

The upthrust exerted on an object is dependent on the amount of water that the object pushes out of the way (displaces). The upthrust is dependent on the amount of space the object takes up in the water. Big objects create more upthrust because they take up more water space. Try submerging a big balloon and a small balloon. The upthrust created by the big balloon will be greater than the smaller one because it displaces more water.

The shapes of boats are designed to optimise the amount of space they take up in the water. Cargo boats are designed to float more deeply in the water when they are fully laden. This means they take up more space and hence create more upthrust to support the weight of the boat and its cargo.

> ### Something to think about
>
> Imagine how a submarine is made to sink and then rise to the surface again by taking in and letting out water. How can the concept of balanced and unbalanced forces explain the way the motion of a submarine is controlled?

Friction

> ### Something to think about
>
> Why do things wear out? A simple explanation is that things, such as shoes, wear out because of friction. However, this explanation is only meaningful if you understand how friction works. Can you explain why shoes wear out, without using the term 'friction'? Are words such as rubbing, rasping, grating, scratching, ripping, sliding, colliding and bumping appropriate?

Friction is caused by tiny 'potholes'

If you have driven a car on a very bumpy road with lots of potholes, you will know what it feels like when your wheels smash into the bumps and potholes.

Pothole analogy.

Exploring the effects of friction.
Source: Peter Loxley

Equivalent collisions happen when an object, such as a brick, is dragged over a rough surface. The roughness of both the base of the brick and the surface over which it is dragged are the cause of friction between the surfaces. No surfaces are perfectly smooth; if you look at most surfaces under a powerful microscope, you will see they have bumps and 'potholes' in them.

To drag an object over a surface you need to apply a force to overcome friction. The amount of friction created will depend on the smoothness of the object and the surface. Very smooth surfaces, such as that on an ice rink, create little friction.

To help us move objects over rough surfaces we use wheels. Wheels make use of friction. It is the force of friction between the surface of the wheel and the surface of the road, that is, the 'grip' of tyres, that enables a vehicle to move forwards.

Something to think about

Imagine what life would be like without friction. Start by thinking about how friction helps you to run or walk up a hill.

Simple machines

Levers, pulleys and gears are simple machines. We use them every day to make it easier to complete simple tasks such as levering off the top of the syrup tin with a spoon or more strenuous actions such as lifting heavy weights. Levers and pulley systems can increase the effect of a force. Even simple pulleys can make it easier to lift loads. By passing a rope over a pulley, workers are able to pull down on the rope and use their body weight to help them lift the load. Lifting a bucket out of a well is much easier when the rope passes over a pulley. Levers are used when we open a bottle with a bottle opener, pull out a nail with a hammer or use scissors. A gear is a wheel with teeth (sometimes called a cog), which interlocks with another gear to increase the force or change the speed or direction of movement. A smaller cog connected to a larger cog will rotate faster, for example, in a clock, gears control the difference in speed of movement of the minute and hour hands.

A bottle opener is a simple lever.
Source: iStock

A simple pulley system.
Source: iStock

Single gear system on a bicycle.
Source: iStock

Something to think about

Think about the gears on your bike, there are two sets joined by a chain. How do they work to move you forward and enable you to go faster than you could on foot?

Global dimensions: Wind-up technology

The inventor Trevor Baylis produced the original clockwork radio in 1994. His radio was capable of receiving news and information in areas where mains electricity supplies were intermittent or nonexistent and where people couldn't afford batteries for portable radios. His original idea was taken up by a company that quickly realised the potential for self-sufficient electronics in developing countries. With the help of government grants and charitable donations, the wind-up radio was born.

Since then wind-up technology has produced wind-up lights, torches, water purification plants, mobile phone chargers and even foot-driven generators to power laptops. These are proving useful and popular – not just in areas where mains electricity supplies are erratic but also among energy-conscious consumers across the world. Wind-up radios are widely used in Africa, where community radio programmes are a useful tool for education as well as entertainment and news. There is now even a wind-up MP3 player which can play music and video, show photos, charge phones and act as a voice recorder.

http://electronics.howstuffworks.com/gadgets/travel/wind-up-cell-phone-chargers.htm

http://windupradio.com/trevor.htm

Summary

The relationship between force and motion can be surprising. Our everyday experiences lead us to think that objects require a force to keep them moving. After all, when we stop pushing something on a flat surface, we normally expect it to slow and stop. Science shows us that this is not the case. Things change their motion not because a force is used up or removed but because of the action of forces. For example, shopping trolleys slow down when we stop pushing them because frictional forces act on their wheels to stop them turning freely. If there were no forces acting on the trolley after we stop pushing, it would keep moving at a constant speed until it collided with something.

Forces owing to friction and air resistance can rarely be avoided on Earth and so objects appear to slow down naturally when they are not being pushed or pulled along. Out in space, the conditions are different. Objects can travel great distances at constant speeds without being pushed or pulled along. In the Solar System, the motion of objects, both natural and man-made, is mainly controlled by gravity. Planets, moons and manufactured satellites are kept in their orbits by the pull of gravity.

Part 2: Ideas for practice

Topic: Friction

Age group: 7–9 years

Introduction

This topic provides opportunities for children to explore the nature of friction and the effect it has on movement. Activities enable children to picture how frictional forces are created and how their actions cause surfaces to wear down. In the application stage children apply their knowledge to design a pair of non-slip slippers.

Scientific view

Most things we do involve forces. For example, pushing forces help us jump and run. Rubbing or sliding forces help us slow down and stop. Forces even help warm our hands when we rub them together. Rubbing forces are also responsible for wearing out our clothes. When we walk and run, our shoes rub against the ground and bits are torn off. Friction is another name for rubbing forces. Frictional forces can slow objects down and can scratch and damage surfaces. Friction can also help us to move by providing 'grip' between surfaces.

Working scientifically

In these activities children will:

- raise and try to find answers to questions;
- put forward their own ideas and make simple predictions;
- make simple comparisons and identify simple patterns;
- compare what happened with what they expected would happen;
- plan a fair test with help from their teacher;
- provide explanations for their observations.

Exploration stage

Children's talk involves trying out their own ideas

Setting the scene

Arrange for the children to bring their favourite shoes to school. *Talk together* about what the children like about their shoes. Why are they their favourites? When do they wear them? Why do they need to wear shoes? Why do we wear different types of shoes?

Scientific enquiry

Working in groups children compare the soles of their favourite shoes. First, sort the shoes according to their uses and then according to the types of soles. Children predict which shoes provide the best grip and plan an investigation to find out if they are right. Ask the children to explain their results and describe the forces involved. Explore their thinking and use of scientific language.

Puzzle

Show the children a shoe with a hole in it. *Talk together* about what could have caused the hole. What causes our shoes to wear out?

Use the concept cartoon to generate discussion. The cartoon is available on the book's website.

Encourage the children to hypothesise about why the soles of their shoes wear out. Explore types of activities, such as running, sliding, jumping and dancing, which are likely to wear shoes out more quickly.

Storytelling

Working in groups, children develop a scientific theory for how shoes wear out. Ask them to describe the process and explain where all the bits of shoe, which are missing, can theoretically be found. Each group presents their theory to the class. Use children's ideas to assess what they know about friction.

Scientific enquiry

Ask children to describe the types of surfaces that are likely to wear shoes out most quickly. They can set up their own practical enquiries to test and compare different surfaces and from their results draw conclusions regarding which are likely to cause the most damage to a pair of shoes. Surfaces could include floor tiles, different types of carpet, wood, concrete, gravel, sand and tarmac. Some of the tests will need to be made outdoors or in different parts of the school building. Children can collect data by pulling a flat shoe with a weight inside across the surfaces using a newton meter to measure the rubbing (frictional) force.

Question the children to make sure their tests are fair. Children record their findings using charts. Groups present their results and explain their findings. They should use drawings to explain why particular types of surfaces, which they tested, are likely to wear out shoes quicker than others.

Formative assessment

Provide opportunities for children to voice what they have learnt in the exploratory stage. Use evidence from their responses to the puzzle and other activities to assess differences between children's ideas and the scientific view. Plan how you will use the re-describing stage to help the children address their *learning needs.* You may want to modify the activities depending on the shared and individual needs of the children.

Re-describing stage

Children's talk involves making sense of scientific ideas

Teacher-led discussion

Discuss what children learnt from the exploration stage. Which surface created the greatest rubbing force? Use video clips to introduce the idea of friction as a force that acts between two surfaces. Help children to imagine how friction works when two surfaces are rubbed together.

Scientific enquiry

Children can make simple models of shoes with polystyrene soles. They explore how the soles of shoes wear out by rubbing their model shoes against textured surfaces including various grades of sandpaper. Manual rubbing by small numbers of children for a short time is unlikely to produce dangerous levels of dust if the room is well ventilated. Refer to *Be safe!* (2011) for guidance.

Children *work collaboratively* to discover which surfaces are more likely to wear shoes out. Discuss their reasons. Encourage the children to use a range of words to describe the actions, which wear out their shoes. Words such as rubbing, scratching, ripping, gripping, grating, scraping, cutting and scuffing are all appropriate. Children can draw pictures to show how friction causes things to wear out. They can explain their pictures to each other.

Help the children re-describe the outcomes of their enquiry in the exploratory stage in terms of friction. They can classify the surfaces on a friction scale from high to low. Return to the puzzle and reinforce the idea that frictional forces are what cause our shoes to wear out. Bearing the puzzle in mind, children explain what causes their trousers, jumpers and tyres on their bikes and carpets at home to wear out? Discuss their ideas and address any outstanding *learning needs.* Children can raise their own questions for further learning.

How friction wears things out.
Source: Peter Loxley

Information and teaching resources

BBC Bitesize:

- BBC (2007). Friction Between a Tyre and the Road. *www.bbc.co.uk/education/clips/z462tfr*
- BBC (2008). Friction on Ski Slopes. *www.bbc.co.uk/education/clips/zkhxpv4*
- BBC (2008). How Does Friction Work as a Force? *www.bbc.co.uk/education/clips/zjr3cdm*
- BBC (2007). How Is Friction Created? *www.bbc.co.uk/education/clips/z79rkqt*
- BBC (2012). Investigating Friction. *www.bbc.co.uk/education/clips/z67w2hv*
- BBC (2008). Testing Friction on the Road. *www.bbc.co.uk/education/clips/zk2qxnb*

Application stage

Children's talk involves trying out scientific ideas

Design and make 'non-slip' slippers

Children apply their understanding of friction to choose the best material from which to make a pair of 'non-slip' slippers. Discuss the properties of suitable materials. How can they make the soles of the slippers both hard wearing, comfortable and not slippery? Children explore through information sources and products how commercial soles are often made from layers of different materials. There is information on the web about how to make slippers.

Children test the properties of a range of materials and use the results to inform the design of their slippers. Encourage them to explain their choice of materials. Once they are sure of their design they can use the tested materials to make their slippers. Follow ASE guidance in *Be safe!* (2011) on 'making things'.

Children test their slippers on different indoor surfaces to make sure they are non-slip. Costing, sizing, measuring and marketing the slippers involve the use of mathematics and communication skills, which make the project more STEM inclusive.

Information and teaching resources

- DIY Bedroom Slippers. *https://www.youtube.com/watch?v=0k_2Tg0_JTU*
- Making Slippers. *https://www.youtube.com/watch?v=Yn0fqvply6U*

Topic: Air resistance

Age group: 9–11 years

Introduction

In this topic children explore the nature of air resistance and use their scientific knowledge to inform their decision-making in a range of practical activities. In the application stage children have opportunities to find out how knowledge of aerodynamics is used in real-life situations.

Scientific view

We live in a sea of air. To move through air, we need to push it out of the way. The force with which objects push their way through air is called 'air resistance'. Air resistance is a force which impedes movement and is a type of friction.

Working scientifically

In these activities children will:

- plan scientific enquiries to answer questions, including recognizing and controlling variables;
- take accurate measurements and repeat readings when appropriate;
- record data using tables and graphs;
- report and present findings orally and in various other ways;
- use established scientific knowledge to make sense of their findings and to inform their decision making.

Exploration stage

Children's talk involves trying out their own ideas

Setting the scene

Leonardo da Vinci was much more than just a painter: he was also a scientist, engineer, inventor, town planner and sculptor. Children can use information sources to explore some of his inventions, which included designs for flying machines and a parachute.

Leonardo da Vinci's parachute.

Scientific enquiry

Children *work collaboratively* to make and test a model of Leonardo's parachute design. There is a lot of helpful information on the web. *Talk together* about how it works and how the design could be improved. Compare his design with modern day parachutes.

Puzzle

How do parachutes work? Can children explain how parachutes work without using the term air resistance?

We often use the term 'air resistance' as if it provides an explanation without being able to picture in our minds what it means. Before trying to explain how a parachute works, ask the children to explain what air resistance means to them. What does it look like? Ask them to draw a picture of it.

Talking points: true, false or not sure?

- Air resistance and wind are the same thing.
- Stationary objects experience most air resistance.
- We only feel air resistance when we move fast.
- Umbrellas can create a lot of air resistance.
- Air resistance is a force which slows us down.
- Air resistance is similar to water resistance.
- Air resistance can make us go faster, as well as slowing us down.
- Birds could not fly without air resistance.

Discuss children's reasons for their responses to the talking points. Ask each group how they arrived at their answers. Did they share ideas, did they challenge each other's ideas and was there any negotiation? Encourage groups to describe challenges and negotiations where different points of view were discussed.

Scientific enquiry

Children plan enquiries to demonstrate the effect of air resistance on objects of different sizes and shapes. Use sloping runways as test tracks and fix various shaped and sized fronts to the same 'test vehicle' to ensure the tests are fair. Children record and compare results and use them to identify the least and most aerodynamic shapes. Children can explain their results by drawing pictures showing how the shape of an object affects air resistance. Discuss their drawings and assess their understanding of air resistance.

Formative assessment

Provide opportunities for children to voice what they have learnt in the exploratory stage. Use evidence from their responses to the puzzle, talking points and other activities to assess differences between children's ideas and the scientific view. Plan how you will use the re-describing stage to help the children address their *learning needs.* You may want to modify the activities depending on the shared and individual needs of the children.

Information and teaching resources

BBC Bitesize:

- BBC (2012). Investigation Air and Water Resistance. *www.bbc.co.uk/education/clips/zxqd7ty*
- BBC (2012). The Effects of Air Resistance and Air Density. *www.bbc.co.uk/education/clips/zpg3cdm*

Other websites:

- Da Vinci Parachute and Testing Reliability of Leonardo's Inventions. *www.youtube.com/watch?v=tAoXi_uDDgw*
- Da Vinci's Parachute. *www.youtube.com/watch?v=uvsV5aqrN9k*

Re-describing stage

Children's talk involves making sense of scientific ideas

Teacher-led discussion

The purpose of this part is to introduce the children to models which will help them visualise the nature of air resistance. Start by discussing the video clip 'What is air resistance?' and review what children know about friction. Frictional forces are created when two objects rub against each other. Describe air resistance as the frictional force created when a moving object rubs against the air.

Scientific enquiry

To understand air resistance children need to experience its force. Explore the effect an open umbrella has on how fast children can run. Start by measuring how fast they can move without an umbrella and then compare with how fast they can go holding various sized umbrellas. Record and graph the results. Ask the children to describe how the running speed and size of umbrella influence the force exerted by the air. Share results of the enquiry and explore reasons why running through air with an open umbrella creates such a powerful force. *Talk together* about why air resistance doesn't remain the same but depends on the speed and size of the object moving through the air.

Modelling

It helps if the children have something tangible with which to compare air resistance. Encourage the children to compare moving through air to moving through water. Talk about living at the bottom of a sea of air and compare it with moving through water. To move around we have to push the air out of the way, just like moving through water.

Air resistance can be modelled using the children to represent air molecules. Children who represent the air stand relatively close together with little room for anyone to squeeze through. A child can then be chosen to gently push his/her way through the crowd. Encourage the children to visualise air resistance as a series of collisions between the moving object and the air. The collisions with the air create forces, which oppose or resist the movement of the object. The faster the object moves, the greater the number of collisions and hence the greater the air resistance. Can the model be used to explain why bigger objects create more air resistance? *Talk together* about whether the children think this is a good model. Could they use it to explain how a parachute works? Could they think of another model?

Experiencing the effects of air resistance.
Source: Peter Loxley

Storytelling

Give each group a feather to observe falling through the air. Ask them to describe its motion and to explain it with regard to the collisions it makes with the air particles. Children should draw pictures to illustrate their stories. In talking about the pictures, encourage the children to use their own words to describe the forces involved. Use children's stories to assess their progress and address outstanding *learning needs*. Children can raise their own questions for further learning.

Information and teaching resources

BBC Bitesize:

- BBC (2007). Could You Use an Umbrella to Parachute? *www.bbc.co.uk/education/clips/zpvs34j*
- BBC (2008). What Is Air Resistance? *www.bbc.co.uk/education/clips/zsjd7ty*

Application stage

Children's talk involves trying out scientific ideas

Parachute design

Children can apply their understanding of forces to the design of a parachute. Ask them to predict how the shape and size of a parachute influences its rate of fall. Children should justify their predictions based on their understanding of air resistance. They can make simple parachutes using polythene bags and string to test their predictions. When testing from a height, follow ASE guidance in *Be safe!* (2011). Encourage them to draw diagrams, which clearly show the forces which control the motion of the parachute.

Comparing different sizes of parachute is quite easy. It is more difficult to fairly compare different shapes because the sizes need to be kept the same. This activity provides opportunities for children to apply their mathematical knowledge of shape and their understanding of how forces control the motion of the parachute.

Children can explore the design of commercial parachutes using a range of information sources and perhaps compare them to Leonardo's original design. They finally use the outcomes of their enquiry to help design and test their own working model of a modern day

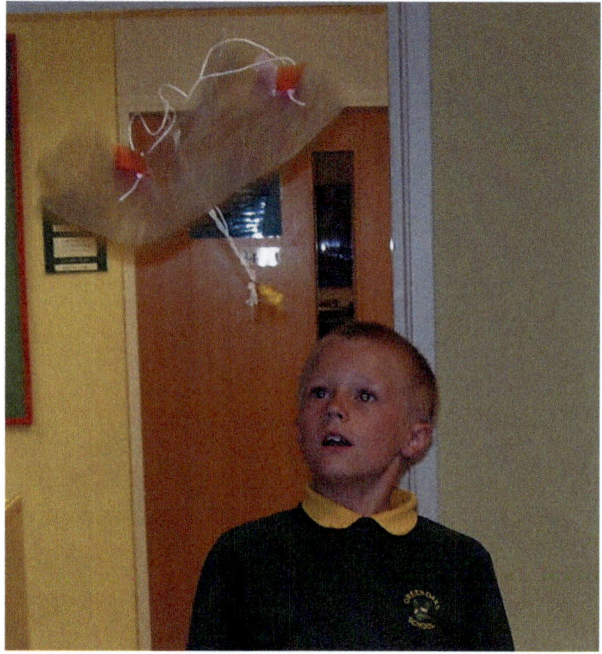

Testing out a parachute.
Source: Peter Loxley

parachute. Children report their findings in the form of an advertising poster, which promotes the efficiency of their design on the basis of performance statistics, similar to the way new car designs are promoted.

Aerodynamics: the Bloodhound Project

Aerodynamics is the study of the movement of air and the way objects, such as airplanes and cars, move through the air. Children use information sources to learn about the science of aerodynamics and discover what engineers and scientists do who work in the field.

The Bloodhound Project is an attempt to build a car which can travel at 1000mph. Children can explore their website and find out about the design of the car and the progress the engineering team have made. The website also contains a range of teaching resources associated with the project. There are also opportunities to post questions for the project team and to arrange a STEM ambassador to visit your school.

Use the Bloodhound Project as the starting point for children to design their own world record breaking super car based on their understanding of aerodynamics. Working in groups, children can design an aerodynamic car and make a model which is powered by an elastic band. Groups can test their models to see which can create a school land speed record.

Information and teaching resources

BBC Bitesize:

- BBC (2007). Streamlining in Nature and Industry. *www.bbc.co.uk/education/clips/zxspyrd*
- BBC (2012). How Air Resistance Slows Down Vehicles. *www.bbc.co.uk/education/clips/zwynvcw*

Other websites:

- The Bloodhound Project. *www.bloodhoundssc.com/project*
- Real World Physics Problems (2017). Aerodynamics – For Kids. *www.real-world-physics-problems. com/aerodynamics-for-kids.html*

Talk skills and science discussion: Negotiation

Ask groups to research and discuss their ideas about a relevant topic, preparing an oral presentation for the class. They can choose from: gravity, friction, air resistance, submarines, parachutes, floating and sinking, movement, change of direction, and balance.

Ask each group to make note of a point at which *negotiation* was needed in their discussion; that is, where there were different points of view, where turn-taking was complicated or where a summary had to include more than one idea.

Clarify the difference between negotiating *ideas* and negotiating the organisation and running of the group discussion. Ask groups to provide examples of how negotiation can proceed and what happens when it breaks down. Ask groups to provide examples of negotiating ideas, where different points of view were aired and discussed.

Additional information and teaching resources

Companion book:

- Loxley, P. (2018). *Practical Ideas for Teaching Primary Science: Inspiring Learning and Enjoyment,* Abingdon: Routledge, Chapter 13: Forces and Magnetism.

Websites:

- Experiment Da Vinci parachute. *https://www.youtube.com/watch?v=h6M3hftiHow*
- Da Vinci's Parachute WHS. *https://www.youtube.com/watch?v=PPGJiJY9MfQ*
- Da Vinci's Parachute Tutorial. *https://www.youtube.com/watch?v=ZPfsFAQe10w*
- Science Kids (2016). Flight Aerodynamics. *www.sciencekids.co.nz/videos/engineering/flightaero-dynamics.html*
- The Indianapolis Public Library (2013). Aerodynamics – Paper Airplanes. *www.indypl.org/kids/blog/?p=7360*
- Watch Know Learn (2017). Drag and Biomimetics. *www.watchknowlearn.org/Video.aspx?VideoID=13218&CategoryID=468*
- National Aeronautics and Space Administration (2015). What Is Aerodynamics? *www.nasa.gov/audience/forstudents/k-4/stories/nasa-knows/what-is-aerodynamics-k4.html*

ASE journals:

- Primary Science Review 103 (June 2008). *Leonardo Flies Again – Integrating Science and Art* by Ivor Hickey, Deirdre Robson, Mary Flanagan and Paula Campbell.

CHAPTER 21

LIGHT

Light is a fascinating physical phenomenon. Light travels at astonishing speed; it bounces off some objects and is absorbed by others. Because we can sense light, we see images, shadows and colour. Most living things rely on light for their survival. Plants need light to grow, and animals rely on plants for their food. Without light, there would be no hope of survival for the majority of the living things that inhabit the Earth. In this chapter, our main focus is on the behaviour of light as a form of radiant energy and how it helps living things to survive. We also look briefly at the language of light and how it has been used by writers to powerful effect.

Topics discussed in the chapter

- Historical context
- The nature of light
- How living things sense light
- The language of light

Part 1: Subject knowledge

Historical context

What the ancient Greeks believed

The ancient Greeks knew that light travelled but thought that vision worked by *intromission*, that is, that eyes send out beams which we see when they return to us. This idea is disproved by the way that we can see distant objects. Aristotle (384–322 BCE) puzzled over the nature of light and decided that light can be thought of as waves of energy similar to ocean waves. Other Greek scientists thought that light moved as particles. This dichotomy of ideas still exists; sometimes light appears to behave as a wave and sometimes as a particle. What these theories have in common are the key ideas that light travels; it needs no medium to travel through and it is a form of energy.

Newton and Huygens hold conflicting views

New ideas started to emerge during the seventeenth century. Dutch mathematician Christiaan Huygens (1629–1695) thought that light travelled in waves. He believed light crossed space through the mysterious medium of ether – a weightless, invisible substance existing in space and the Earth's atmosphere. Huygens' contemporary Sir Isaac Newton (1642–1727) conducted a series of investigations into the nature of light and colour, which indicated that light travelled as particles. Newton was not wholly convinced that this was the complete picture but he was so influential that his 'corpuscular' theory took precedence. In his 1704 book *Opticks* Newton says: 'Light is never known to follow crooked passages nor to bend into the shadow'. Light as particles must always travel in straight lines.

Thomas Young provides a different picture

Newton's particle theory dominated optics until the nineteenth century, when it was augmented by the wave theory of light. British physicist Thomas Young (1773–1829) showed that different wavelengths of light corresponded to different colours. This paved the way for new ways of explaining the nature of light, which eventually led to the development of the electromagnetic theory based on the work of James Clerk Maxwell (1831–1879). We now use both the wave and particle models of light to explain how it behaves in a range of contexts.

The nature of light

What do we know about light?

Light is radiant energy which we can sense with our eyes. Because we can see light, we literally have a vision of our surroundings. We interpret this vision, focusing on different aspects of what we see, and learn to make meaning of constantly changing images.

Imagine what the physical world would be like without light or colour.

Light can be pictured as a type of **wave**. It has two key properties – intensity and wavelength. The light that we see is a part of a spectrum of **electromagnetic energy**; other wavelengths include radio and television waves, microwaves and infrared waves. Light travels through a vacuum at 300 million metres per second (700 million miles per hour) or seven times round the Earth in one second.

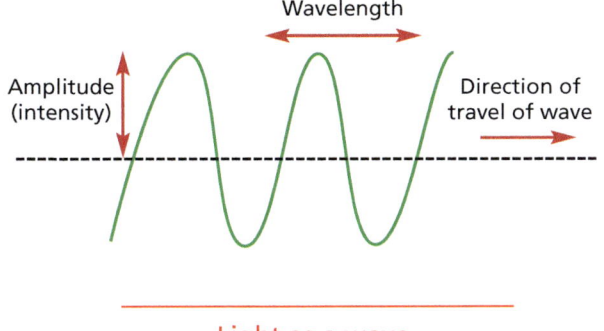

Light as a wave.

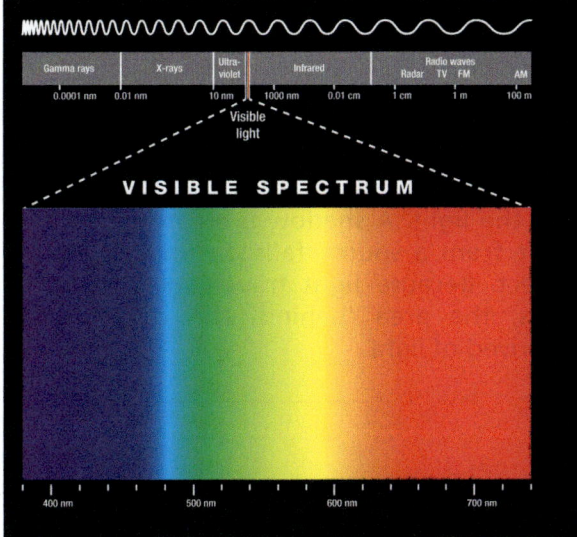

The visible part of the electromagnetic spectrum.
Source: iStock

What is a light year?

A **light year** is a measure of distance, not time. A light year is the distance that light would travel in one Earth year, roughly 10 million, million kilometres or about 6 million, million miles. The extremely high speed at which light travels means that here on Earth we see light from nearby sources at practically the instant it is produced. This is not true of very distant, interplanetary objects; light takes eight minutes to reach us from the Sun. We see the Sun as it was eight minutes ago. Light from distant stars can take many thousands of years to arrive on Earth. When we look at distant stars, we see them as they were many, many years ago.

Amazingly, light can travel through a vacuum

Light needs no material (solid, liquid or gas) to travel through. Space is empty; there is no air or anything else between us and the Sun or the planets, but we see them because light waves move through a vacuum. In contrast, if the Sun or planets are making any sound, we cannot hear it because sound cannot travel across space like light. Sound needs something to move through.

Light can also travel through some materials

Light travels through clear air largely unaffected by the particles of its gases. Similarly, light is transmitted through clean water. Particles and pollutants may scatter or absorb light, making air or water appear murky. Solid materials are interestingly varied in the way they do, or do not, let light through. Transparent solids such as glass, some plastics, some crystals and cellophane transmit light. Coloured glass or cellophane can be just as transparent as clear glass. Transparency is not to do with lack of colour but with the ease of transmission of light. Some materials allow us to see light through them, but we cannot see clear images. These materials are translucent. Some plastics, tracing paper, obscure glass, ceramics and unpolished crystals are translucent. Other materials halt light entirely by absorbing or reflecting all of it. These materials are opaque. Metals, wood, cork, cardboard, clay and some fabrics are opaque.

What causes a shadow?

The importance of opaque materials is that they create distinct shadows by blocking out the light. A shadow is created when light from a source falls on an opaque object. Because light travels in straight lines, the area 'behind' the object is deprived of light.

Shadow theatre displaying children's silhouettes.
Source: Karen Blumberg / Getty Images

Something to think about

Where does your shadow go when you turn off the light? Can you make a red shadow? Can you make darker or lighter shadows?

Reflection enables us to see objects

Light falling on an object is transmitted through it, absorbed by it or **reflected** from it. When light is absorbed by materials, its energy is used to heat the object. Some materials appear black because they absorb all the visible wavelengths, reflecting little into our eyes. White materials reflect the entire spectrum. Other materials reflect some colours and absorb others; a red book reflects red and absorbs the other colours or wavelengths.

Things which are not luminous are visible because they reflect light. Some surfaces, such as that of a mirror or still water, are almost perfect reflectors, bouncing back much of the light that lands on them. The mirrors we use in our homes reflect light extremely well, giving us a clear image of what is before them. They are usually 'plane' (flat) so that the images we see look like things as they are. Curved mirrors can invert, magnify or distort images and can be used for a range of purposes, such as viewing mirrors on cars or as part of a telescope.

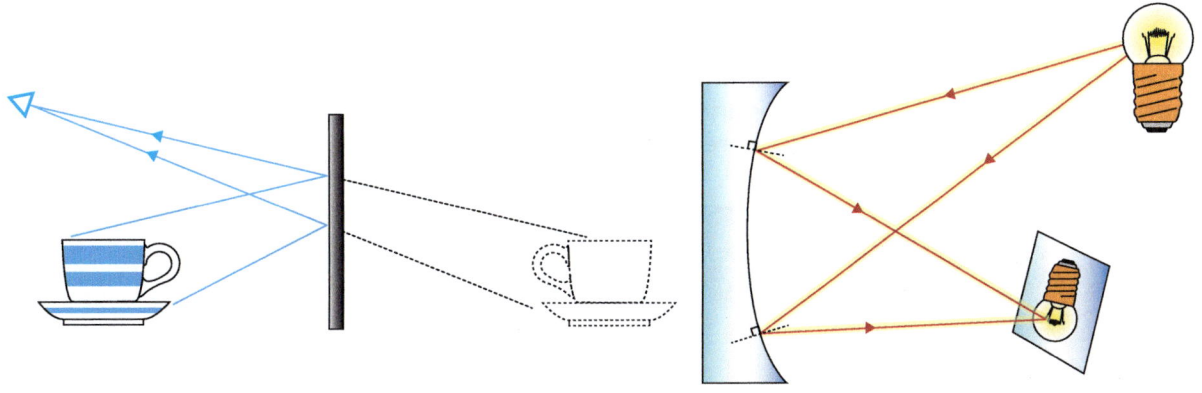

An image as seen in a mirror.

Light reflected from a concave surface such as a spoon.

Absorption can transform light energy into different forms

Solar cells (often used to power classroom calculators) absorb **radiant** light **energy,** which is then transferred into electrical energy. They need good levels of sunlight to work effectively. Solar water heaters work by absorbing heat energy from sunlight to directly heat water and will work even on dull days. Solar absorption panels of different types increasingly provide a form of sustainable energy.

Green plants absorb light (blue and red light, reflecting green) and, fortunately for life on Earth, have found a way of storing its energy. Inside the leaf, a light-fuelled set of reactions goes on. This is photosynthesis – literally, *light used for making* (see Chapter 13). The resources required are the simple particles of water and carbon dioxide; using these, in the presence of light and chlorophyll, plants produce simple sugars. These are used to make the more complex organic (carbon-based) proteins, carbohydrates, fats, oils and other materials that plants need to live and grow. Plants offer animals two life-sustaining things: a source of energy contained in compounds like sugars and a source of oxygen.

How living things sense light

Worm's eye view

Some living things have the ability to sense light even though they don't have eyes. For example, scientists have discovered that worms have light-sensitive cells on the front and end of their bodies. It is thought that worms that live in soil use their light-sensitive cells to detect when they are close to the surface. Worms can detect not only the radiation wavelengths of visible light but also ultraviolet light.

Bees and birds can detect ultraviolet light

Humans have very complex eyes and we can be forgiven for thinking that our vision is among the best of all the animals. We classify the wavelengths of light that we can see as 'visible' light, which suggests that all other light is 'invisible'. This is not the case. Some animals, including birds and certain insects, can detect ultraviolet light and are able to sense more colours than we can. Birds and some invertebrates, such as bees and spiders, can sense different parts of the electromagnetic spectrum. What they 'see' is very different from what we see.

A primrose as seen by the human eye and a bee.
Source: Bjorn Rorslett / Science Photo Library Ltd.

Something to think about

What would our world look like to an alien whose eyes were only sensitive to ultraviolet light? Imagine trying to explain why you had to stop at traffic lights. What would be the advantages to an alien of eyes which were highly sensitive to infrared light? Think about how we use infrared cameras.

Can any animals see in the dark?

Cats are said to be able to 'see in the dark'. Does this mean cats do not need light to see? Confusion can stem from how we use the term 'dark'. Often we use 'dark' to mean dim light, not its total absence. Cats can vary the size of their pupils much more than humans; they can let in more light or contract the pupil to a very small size to protect the eyes in bright sunlight. Cats also have special cells behind the retina which act as mirrors, reflecting light back through the retina; this gives their sensitive cells a second chance to absorb the light and gather information. Light reflecting from the back of cats' eyes seems to make them glow in the dark.

Cat's eyes glowing in the dark.
Source: iStock

Cats can see about six times better than humans in dim light. Most sharks, which live in dim and murky water, can see even better. Sharks have extremely light-sensitive retinas and also reflect light back into their eyes. Since sharks can see about ten times better than us in murky water, it means that a shark will inevitably see you before you see it.

How our eyes work

We can only see things because light travels; it has to move to get to us. Light entering the eye through the pupil is focused by a lens, and its energy is captured by sensitive cells at the back of the eye. These cells, the rods and cones of the retina, respond to different wavelengths of light and different light intensities. The brain interprets the patterns made by light on the retina and so we see images, colours, shades and movement.

Because we have two eyes, we see the world in three dimensions; we are able to judge distances and understand textures, deciding whether things are solid or liquid. We have colour vision, which allows us to note the warning colours of dangerous creatures that give other creatures the chance to camouflage themselves and hide. Ingenious uses of technology, such as television and cinema, enable us to see other lives and other scenes from around the world. Microscopes and telescopes magnify things so that we can see the very small or the very far away. Technology can enhance what we are able to see so that our view of the world, and our place in it, is enriched.

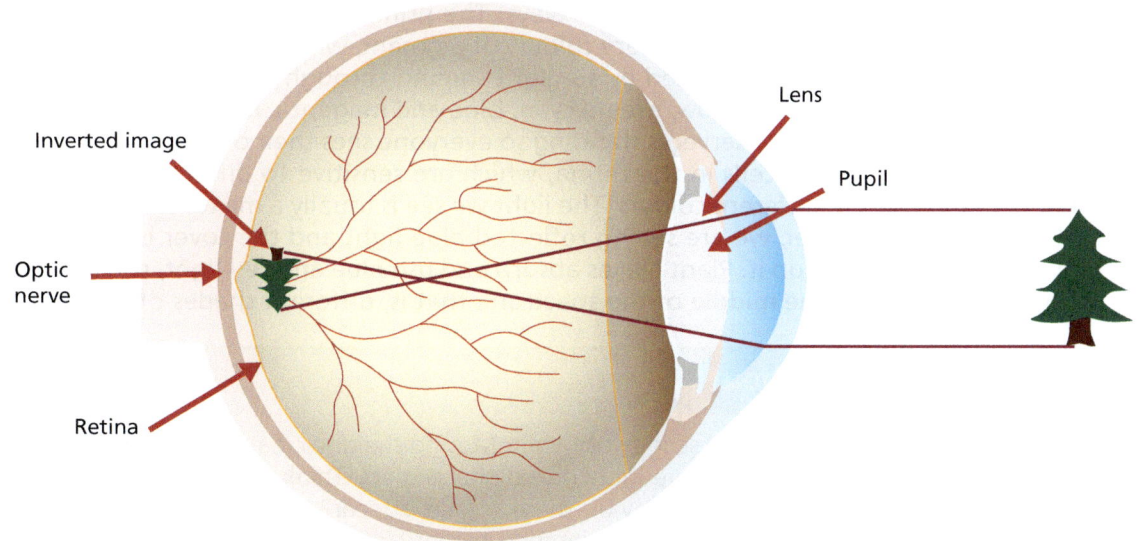

Diagram of the human eye.

Our eyes control the amount of light which enters them

Some light sources have lots of energy and are intensely bright. Others have little energy and appear dim. Brightness and dimness are simple visual descriptions. The intensity of light is measured in units called **lux**. At 5 lux, things appear dim; at 500 lux, they are bright. Humans can see in an extremely wide range of light intensities, from starlight to spotlights, but our eyes are damaged by bright lights, which leave an after-image on the retina. The iris controls the amount of light which enters our eyes. In dim conditions, the pupil dilates to let in more light. In bright light, the pupil contracts to stop too much light entering the eye.

Mixing light.
Source: iStock

What are colours?

White light, such as sunlight, is a mix of different wavelengths. Newton separated and recombined white light and went on to describe seven colours of the visible light spectrum as red, orange, yellow, green, blue, indigo and violet. Newton liked the number 7 but actually the colours merge into one another and can be described in other ways. The primary colours of light are red, blue and green. They are different from the primary colours of pigment, which are red, blue and yellow. If you look at a rainbow spectrum created by sunlight shining through rain, you can see that its colours could be described as red, yellow, green, cyan, blue and magenta. Rainbows are an optical illusion dependent on where an observer is standing so everyone sees their own separate rainbow. We see colour because of cone cells in the retina, which are sensitive to different wavelengths, which our brains interpret as different colours. The light we see is usually a mixture of wavelengths. If we look at a blue book cover, we are seeing reflected blue light and the cover is absorbing all other wavelengths, which fall on it. Plant leaves absorb and use blue and red light, reflecting back to us mixtures of light from the middle of the spectrum, that is, different shades of green.

Something to think about

Look at the shiny side of a CD-ROM disc in bright light. Moving the disc creates different shapes of rainbow or spectra; it is possible to capture this with a digital camera. Think about the CD rainbows. What colours are there? In what order? Why do these colours appear? What other objects can be used to create a spectrum? How would you describe the order of the colours? Compare with Newton's observations.

A rainbow.
Source: iStock

Coloured objects reflect some colours and absorb others.

The language of light

Light influences how we think and talk about the world

Although light is a physical phenomenon, a radiant wave, our emotional response to light is dependent on what it tells us about our surroundings. We enjoy our sense of sight. We like colours, patterns, pictures, scenery, sunsets, certain arrangements of human features – that is, what we interpret as physical beauty. The idea of light is used as a metaphor for some things, which are profoundly important to people; the Roman poet Catullus uses the phrase *brevis lux* – brief light – to describe life itself. The world's great religions relate light and life. 'Then spake Jesus again unto them, saying, "I am the light of the world: he that followeth me shall not walk in darkness, but shall have the light of life"' (John 8:12). The Hindu festival of Holi (colour) and the Indian and Nepalese festival of light, or Diwali, are examples of how people interpret and celebrate the ways that light changes as the world moves around the Sun. Children may have encountered the idea that light is a metaphor for life and have heard stories in which the concept of light is used when considering notions of spirituality.

Darkness represents a step into the unknown

Conversely, we use the idea of darkness as a metaphor for things that are fearful or even evil. Children may think of darkness as having a substance of its own. People are rightly afraid of the dark. Darkness – absence of light – robs us of our ability to see where we are and what is happening, and this loss of perception means we have much less control or chance to make informed choices. It is not dark we fear but what happens 'under cover of darkness'. Put scientifically, we would not imply that darkness is a cover or cloak or that dark has agency and collaborates to offer concealment to villains; we would say that we fear what happens in the absence of light.

Colours also perform important functions in figurative vocabulary. We see 'red', we feel 'blue' and we go through 'purple patches'. Light and dark, day and night, colour and reflection, all figure largely in stories and poems and offer ways into thinking about the physics of light. Helping children to understand the physical nature of light is an opportunity to help them distinguish real from imaginary fears and to learn to cherish their sense of sight.

How the concepts of light and dark are used in stories

'Darkness fell …' 'Her face lit up …' Such phrases in stories may influence children's perception of light and dark. We commonly use the concepts of light and dark metaphorically: 'light streamed in', 'colour drained from her face', 'his eyes shone', 'the wizard was in a dark mood' and 'the gold coins glowed'. A further source of confusion might be that *light* is also the opposite of *heavy*. Traditional stories make great use of light and dark, mirrors, crystals, rainbows and colour, and the changes that happen throughout a day or because of the seasons. The Sun, Moon and stars figure largely in traditional tales, as do magic potions that make things invisible and spells that cast darkness. Rainbows have a long tradition in stories, from the sign of hope seen by Noah to the pots of gold buried by leprechauns. Phases of the Moon, eclipses and the way the positions of the planets change all contribute excitement to stories. This is to our advantage as science teachers. Children's everyday ideas are valuable starting points for discussion and can lead on to activities, which help to establish a more scientific point of view. We can tap into the power of stories and poems. We can also ensure that we encourage children to create hypothetical and testable concepts of how the world works, without dimming their capacity to enjoy fantasy. Imagination is a resource for science.

Global dimensions: Light bulbs without electricity

The Litre of Light Project in the Philippines brings light into the cramped shanty dwellings of many of Manila's poorest inhabitants. Families living on less than $2 a day either cannot afford electricity or live in areas where there are no mains supply. As a result, their corrugated roofed houses and the passageways between them are dark all the time and fires started by candles are common amongst the overcrowded dwellings. One innovative solution uses plastic bottles. These are filled with a solution of bleach and water and slotted into holes in the corrugated iron roofs. In the daytime, sunlight is refracted through the solution into the room below. The bottle lights are quick to make and use easily available materials to provide a light equivalent to a 55W bulb. This simple scheme uses a sustainable, appropriate and green technology that is easily transferrable to other situations.

http://phys.org/news/2011-09-bottle-brighten-millions-poor-homes.html http://physicsbuzz.physics-central.com/2011/09/solar-bottle-superhero.html

Summary

Light is a form of energy which travels as an electromagnetic wave or as high-energy photon particles. It needs no medium to travel through. Our sense of vision is profoundly important. What we perceive as dark is absence of light. Green plants use trapped light energy to synthesise sugars, providing themselves and animals with a source of chemicals for respiration, growth and repair. The oxygen we breathe is a by-product of photosynthesis. Materials may be transparent, translucent or opaque, and opaque objects block light, creating shadows. White light comprises a spectrum of colours with each colour of light having a slightly different wavelength. Blue light has more energy than red light. Different colours of light are absorbed by some surfaces and reflected by others. This creates the colourful world in which we live.

The concepts of light and dark lend texture to our use of language. A mix of stories and children's own ideas about light and dark can provide an interesting basis for considering a more scientific perspective.

Part 2: Ideas for practice

Topic: Shadows

Age group: 7–9 years

Introduction

This topic provides opportunities for children to explore how shadows are formed and to find patterns in the way the size of shadows change. Children also learn that dark is caused by the absence of light and that this is the reason that shadows are formed. In the application stage children design and make their own shadow puppets and make use of their knowledge of shadows to put on a show.

Scientific View

Light enables us to see and recognise different objects and to make sense of the world in which we live. Without light, the world would be dark. Shadows are formed when objects block out light to create areas of darkness.

Working scientifically

In these activities children will:

- ask questions and use scientific enquiries to answer them;
- set up practical enquiries;
- make careful observations and identify simple patterns;
- use results to draw conclusions and raise further questions;
- use straight forward scientific evidence to answer questions.

Exploration stage

Children's talk involves trying out their own ideas

Setting the scene

Read the extract from *Peter Pan*. Mrs. Darling has just spotted Peter. Nana is a big dog who looks after the children Wendy, John and Michael.

Peter Pan

Mrs. Darling screamed, and, as if in answer to a bell, the door opened, and Nana entered, returned from her evening out. She growled and sprang at the boy, who leapt lightly through the window. Again Mrs. Darling screamed, this time in distress for him, for she thought he was killed, and she ran down into the street to look for his little body, but it was not there; and she looked up, and in the black night she could see nothing but what she thought was a shooting star.

She returned to the nursery, and found Nana with something in her mouth, which proved to be the boy's shadow. As he leapt at the window Nana had closed it quickly, too late to catch him, but his shadow had not had time to get out; slam went the window and snapped it off.

You may be sure Mrs. Darling examined the shadow carefully, but it was quite the ordinary kind. Nana had no doubt of what was the best thing to do with this shadow. She hung it out at the window, meaning 'He is sure to come back for it; let us put it where he can get it easily without disturbing the children.'

But unfortunately Mrs. Darling could not leave it hanging out at the window. It looked so like the washing and lowered the whole tone of the house. She thought of showing it to Mr. Darling, but he was totting up winter great-coats for John and Michael, with a wet towel around his head to keep his brain clear, and it seemed a shame to trouble him; besides, she knew exactly what he would say: 'It all comes of having a dog for a nurse.'

She decided to roll the shadow up and put it away carefully in a drawer, until a fitting opportunity came for telling her husband.

Barrie (2007)

Puzzle

Ask the children whether they have ever lost their shadows like Peter Pan. If so, do they think a drawer would be a good place to keep it? Is it possible to lose a shadow? What is a shadow?

Scientific enquiry

Go out into the schoolyard on a sunny day and see if the children can manage to lose their shadows. Remind them never to look directly at the Sun. Let them try to pick their shadows up or try to run away from them. *Talk together* about the children's experiences and reasons why they could not lose their shadows.

In the classroom, children explore how shadows are formed using torches and screens. They can compare the shadows formed by opaque and transparent objects. They can also investigate how to change the size of a shadow and whether different-coloured objects make different-coloured shadows.

Talking points: true, false or not sure?

- Shadows are caused when an object blocks the light.
- Shadows are caused when light passes through an object.
- Green objects create green shadows.
- Little objects can create big shadows.
- Bigger light sources create bigger shadows.
- The shape of a shadow never changes.
- Shadows are made from black light.

Children *work collaboratively* when exploring the talking points and produce drawings showing how shadows are created in support of their answers. Encourage groups to share their ideas and explain their reasoning.

Formative assessment

Provide opportunities for children to voice what they have learnt in the exploratory stage. Use evidence from their responses to the puzzle, talking points and other activities to assess differences between children's ideas and the scientific view. Plan how you will use the re-describing stage to help the children address their *learning needs*. You may want to modify the activities depending on the shared and individual needs of the children.

Re-describing stage

Children's talk involves making sense of scientific ideas

Teacher-led discussion

The purpose of this stage is to help the children to visualise a shadow as an area of darkness where an object is blocking light. *Talk together* about the nature of darkness. What does darkness mean to the children? Give them time to discuss in groups and then present their ideas. Offer the scientific view that darkness is the absence of light.

Modelling

Create a dark cave from opaque material and tables in the classroom. Put different coloured objects in the corners of the cave. Make it big enough for at least two children. Allow volunteers to go into the cave two at a time. When they come out, ask them what they could see. Did they notice the objects in the corner? Did they recognise them? Can they describe their colours? By the end of the activity most children will have experienced the sense of dark and been able to talk about it. Let children go back into the cave with a torch and describe what they can see. Discuss how light from the torch enables them to see the objects.

Storytelling

In the story, Mrs. Darling ran down into the street to search for Peter Pan. The night was so 'black' that 'she could see nothing but what she thought was a shooting star'. Ask children whether they have been out in the 'black night'? What did it feel like? What could they see? Children can write about what it feels like to be in the dark. They can describe the darkest place they have ever experienced and what they imagine it would be like to stand inside a very dark shadow. Use their stories to assess their understanding of the nature of shadows.

Teacher-led discussion

Talk again about the Peter Pan story and whether it is possible for people to lose their shadows. Where do shadows go at night? Using a strong light source, create silhouettes of different objects. Ask children to explain them and suggest how to make them sharper and change their size. Children can draw their own silhouettes and use them to create a display. Remind children not to look directly at bright lights.

Use evidence of children's ideas from their storytelling and other activities to assess their progress and identify any outstanding *learning needs*. Use video clips to illustrate how shadows are formed and talk about how a shadow is caused by the absence of light.

What else do children want to find out? They can raise their own questions for further investigations.

Information and teaching resources

BBC Bitesize:

- BBC (2008). How Do Different Materials Affect Shadows? *www.bbc.co.uk/education/clips/zsqd7ty*

- BBC (2015). Understanding Darkness and Light. *www.bbc.co.uk/education/clips/zpp86fr*
- BBC (2015). What Are Shadows? *www.bbc.co.uk/education/clips/zwh86fr*

Application stage

Children's talk involves trying out scientific ideas

Design and make a shadow theatre

Make a small shadow theatre using a box or a large one using a sheet suspended from the ceiling. Children can design and make shadow puppets to act a scene from *Peter Pan* or they can create their own stories. Use a range of opaque and translucent materials. Encourage each group to *work collaboratively* to design their own shadow scenery, props and characters. During rehearsals, encourage the children to use their knowledge of shadows imaginatively. For example, sizes can

Children rehearsing their shadow puppet show – the audience are on the other side of the giant screen.
Source: Peter Loxley

be changed dramatically by moving the puppet closer to the light source. Giant monsters and carnivorous plants can be produced this way. Talk to the children about the effects they want to achieve and help them put their ideas into action. Finally, children need to spend time preparing their script and rehearsing their performance.

Ask classmates to evaluate performances, commenting positively on use of puppets, story, sound effects and so on. Children should be taught not to make negative comments but instead make suggestions, which might support the group's work. Discuss light, dark and shadows and find out what the children think they need to know next.

Information and teaching resources

BBC Bitesize:

● BBC (2007). Shadow Puppets. *www.bbc.co.uk/education/clips/z87jmp3*

Other websites:

● TES (2015). Teachers TV: Making Shadows. *www.tes.com/teaching-resource/teachers-tv-making-shadows-6085139*

Topic: How we see the world

Age group: 9–11 years

Introduction

This topic provides opportunities for children to experience and talk about how light travels in straight lines and to explain that objects are seen because light travels from the objects into our eyes. In the application stage, children look at the world through coloured spectacles and begin to understand the problems colour blindness can cause. A local optician or STEM ambassador can be invited to answer children's questions.

Scientific View

We use our eyes to make sense of a world full of objects. We see objects because the light they reflect travels from the objects in straight lines into our eyes. Reflected light also enables us to see images of the objects in shiny surfaces such as mirrors. Dark is the absence of light. Shadows are formed when objects block light creating areas of darkness.

Working scientifically

In these activities children will:

● plan enquiries to find answers to questions;

- use first-hand experience and information sources to help answer the question;
- use scientific drawings and diagrams to record and explain observations;
- use established scientific knowledge to explain observations.

Exploration stage

Children's talk involves trying out their own ideas

Setting the scene

Start this topic with role-play activities. You will need a large space, such as the school hall.

Activity 1: Dancing with my shadow

Working in pairs, one child takes on the role of a dancer and the other one becomes the shadow. Start off with music with a slow beat. As the dancer moves around the floor, the other child must shadow his/her movements. Change the beat of the music, while the children swap roles.

Activity 2: Dancing with my reflection

Again working in pairs, children role-play dancing in front of a large mirror. One child takes on the role of a dancer and the other one becomes the reflection mirroring his/her movements. Again, change the beat of the music and swap roles.

Puzzle

At the end of the activities children form into larger groups and discuss the differences between their shadows and reflections. The puzzle is, if light causes shadows and reflections, why are they so different?

Talking points: true, false or not sure?

- Shadows are dark reflections.
- Shadows are dark because they are created by dark light.
- Reflections we see in a mirror are coloured shadows.
- Objects block out light to create shadows.
- Light bounces off mirrors to create reflections.
- Most objects reflect light, which is why we can see them.
- Reflections are the wrong way round in a mirror.

Children *work collaboratively* on the talking points and try to reach agreement on what they think is the difference between a shadow and a reflection. Groups produce drawings to show how they believe shadows and reflections are formed. Groups then come together to present their ideas and compare different points of view.

Scientific enquiry

Children use torches, screens and plain mirrors to create shadows and reflections of objects to explore differences and similarities. Remind them not to shine torch light directly into their eyes. Groups record and discuss the main differences and try to explain the causes. Compare their results with their previous drawings. Listen to, and probe, children's reasoning for why shadows and reflections behave the way they do.

Formative assessment

Provide opportunities for children to voice what they have learnt in the exploratory stage. Use evidence from their responses to the puzzle, talking points and other activities to assess differences between children's ideas and the scientific view. Plan how you will use the re-describing stage to help the children address their *learning needs.* You may want to modify the activities depending on the shared and individual needs of the children.

Re-describing stage

Children's talk involves making sense of scientific ideas

Teacher-led discussion

Show children a picture of the Sun streaming through clouds and talk about how light travels in straight lines. Explain that it is because light travels in straight lines that shadows and reflections are created. Help children resolve the puzzle using video clips showing how shadows, and reflected images in mirrors, are created because light travels in straight lines. Use the following activities to enable children to explore and talk about how reflected light also enables us to see objects.

Modelling

Children can use flexible tubes to show that light must travel in straight lines. The only way they can see objects through the tube is when it is held straight. They can also cut holes in cards, which need to be lined up before they can look through them to see an object at the other end. In a darkened room they can shine a torchlight through the holes onto a target at the end. Use string to show that the holes need to be set in a straight line for the light to pass through.

Scientific enquiries

1. How we see objects

    For this activity you will need shoe boxes with circular peepholes in one end and a window in the top. Cover the window with a flap to control the light. Objects placed in the 'dark box' beneath the flap are first viewed through the peephole with the flap closed and then viewed again with it open. Torch light can be shone through the flap onto the object. Children compare what they see with and without the flap in place and use drawings to explain how the light enables them to see the object. Encourage them to explain their drawings.

2. Viewing objects in different coloured lights

   Use 'dark boxes' to view the objects in different coloured light. Children will need a torch and various colour filters to place over the window. They can start by looking at a range of objects in torchlight and then view them in a selection of coloured lights. Children record and compare their results. What effect does shining coloured lights have on how they see the objects? Ask children to explain their observations in terms of how light is reflected off objects.

3. High visibility clothing

   Children may use high visibility jackets and arm-bands when they ride their bicycles and go on school trips. Children can design their own tests to compare high visibility material with normal fabrics of various colours to evaluate how well it works. They can use information sources to find out about retroreflective materials and their uses.

Storytelling

Ask children to imagine what the world would look like if the Sun were blue. They can use their dark boxes with a blue filter to help imagine how different objects in the world would appear. Children can create picture stories entitled 'Blue World'. Encourage children to explain the reasons for their ideas and address any outstanding *learning needs*.

Information and teaching resources

BBC Bitesize:

- BBC (2007). Light Travels in Straight Lines. *www.bbc.co.uk/education/clips/zyntsbk*
- BBC (2015). What Are Shadows? *www.bbc.co.uk/education/clips/zwh86fr*
- BBC (2007). How Light Can Be Reflected and Distorted. *www.bbc.co.uk/education/clips/zbfjxnb*
- BBC (2007). Seeing in the Dark – Reflective Materials. *www.bbc.co.uk/education/clips/zs3ygk7*
- BBC (2007). The Use of Reflective Materials for Safety. *www.bbc.co.uk/education/clips/ztcg9j6*

Application stage

Children's talk involves trying out scientific ideas

Viewing the world through coloured spectacles

Design and make simple spectacles out of card and different-coloured transparent materials. Ask the children to note how the world seems to change when they look through the different-coloured 'glasses'. What problems do they have in distinguishing between various colours? Ask groups of children to choose one pair of coloured glasses and *talk together* about the problems they would have if the world always appeared as it does when they look through the glasses.

Make children aware that the world does not look the same to all people. Children can use information sources to research the nature and causes of vision problems, including colour blindness. Discussion could focus on social problems experienced by children who wear glasses, with an examination of the motivation behind this. Provide positive role models and encourage the class to accept that sight problems create difficulties with which many children live every day. Invite a local optician or STEM ambassador to talk to the children about her/his work and to answer questions about the causes of common eye problems. Plan the visit with the professional and provide a list of children's questions in advance so that resources can be prepared.

Talk skills and science discussion: Presenting ideas

Ask groups to research and discuss a 'Light' topic, such as how rainbows are formed, how shadows are formed, mixing colours of light, correcting vision, how the eye works and what lenses and mirrors do.

Alternatively, ask groups to set up and run a focused investigation involving light, colour or shadow.

Ask groups to suggest ways that a group of scientists might present their ideas to others.

Organise a conference on 'Light' and ask each group to present their findings. The presentations must involve an oral component and plenary discussions in which the group of children orchestrate the discussion. Suggest ways to ensure that presentations are clear, articulate and well organised.

Ask groups what problems arise in preparing and giving a presentation. Ask for positive feedback on presentations and highlight good practice. Discuss why scientists present their work at conferences and in peer-reviewed journals. Collect the presentations and reviews into a journal and ask children what they think they need to work on next.

Additional information and teaching resources

Companion book:

- Loxley, P. (2018). *Practical Ideas for Teaching Primary Science: Inspiring Learning and Enjoyment,* Abingdon: Routledge, Chapter 14: Light.

BBC Bitesize:

- BBC (2007). A Torch as Light Source. *www.bbc.co.uk/education/clips/zb3s34j*
- BBC (2017). Light. *www.bbc.co.uk/education/clips/zg6r82p*
- BBC (2007). Where Does Light and Shade Come From? *www.bbc.co.uk/education/clips/z8vfb9q*

Websites:

- Science Experiment: Light Travels in Straight Lines. *www.youtube.com/watch?v=4xq6TTsyyOI*
- BP Educational Service (2017). Light Topic Starter. *http://bpes.bp.com/primary-resources/science/ages-9-to-11/light/light-topic-starter/*
- Annenberg Learner (2016). The Science of Light. *www.learner.org/teacherslab/science/light/*

ASE journals:

- Primary Science 125 (Nov/Dec 2012). *The Owl Who Was Afraid of the Dark* by Kevin Smith.
- Primary Science Review 93 (May/June 2006). This issue focuses on Light and Sound.

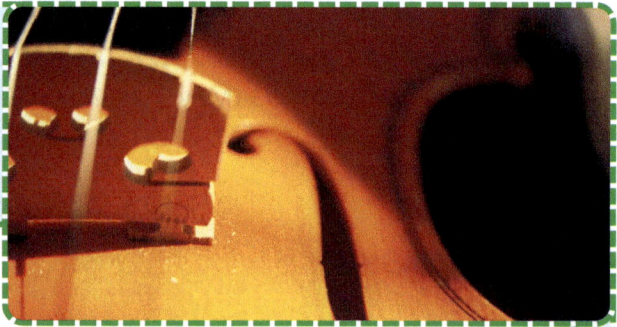

CHAPTER 22
SOUND

Sound figures largely in our world. Every day we experience noise, music and voices. We use sound to communicate and entertain. Some sounds we find satisfying and enjoyable, others can be unpleasant and even threatening. At times, we use sounds aggressively as warning signals, at other times, to portray affection and trust. Music is one of our great cultural achievements and exemplifies how sound can be used to enrich our lives. In this chapter, we look at the physical nature of sound and how different sounds are produced. We also explore the similarities and differences between the way we and other animals detect sound.

Topics discussed in the chapter

- Historical context
- The nature of sound
- Acoustics
- Hearing sounds

Part 1: Subject knowledge

Historical context

In the sixteenth century, Leonardo da Vinci (1452–1519) studied hearing; he compared the sound of a bell to a stone creating ripples when dropped into water. This analogy enabled him to picture how sound could travel in waves. A hundred years later, Italian astronomer and physicist Galileo Galilei (1564–1642) noticed that vibration creates sound and that objects can resonate. As part of his study of sound, he explained everyday effects, such as how a wet finger can make a wine glass ring. He also demonstrated that the frequency of sound waves determined their pitch.

Enquires into the speed of sound

In the 1600s, French scientist and monk Marin Mersenne, interested in musical composition, considered the speed of sound and studied acoustics and vibrating strings. Robert Boyle (1627–1691), the Irish theologian, soldier and physicist whose work on air pressure is well known, first measured the speed of sound in air in 1660. Isaac Newton (1642–1727) looked at the way sound travels, describing the relationship between the speed of sound and the density and compressibility of the medium in which it is travelling. So, for example, he knew that sound travels more readily in water than in air. Newton realised that sound can be interpreted as 'pressure' or thought of as pulses, which are transmitted through adjacent particles of matter.

Mathematics, music and acoustics

The eighteenth-century Dutch mathematician Daniel Bernoulli (1700–1782) studied the flow of air. He considered the relationship of music and mathematics. He found that, for example, a violin string could vibrate at more than one frequency. Such vibration consists of a series of natural frequencies, the higher frequencies superimposed on the lower. Bernoulli's understanding of the mathematical and physical nature of sound enabled him to see that complex musical sound, such as the sound made by a musical instrument, consists of a series or mix of simple sounds, such as those produced by a tuning fork.

Acoustics is the science of sound, including its production, transmission and effects. Acoustic research has led to the development of the electronic communication and entertainment systems which enrich our lives today.

The nature of sound

How vibrations create sounds

To exist, sounds need a vibrating source and a medium to travel through. To hear sounds, creatures need sensitive cells arranged to detect vibrations. Sound waves must move through a solid, a liquid or a gas. They cannot move through the vacuum of space. Sound around us is produced when the air is disturbed by vibrations in some way and these vibrations are detected as sound in our ears. The source of sound vibrations can be the speaker cone of a sound system, the air in a flute, people talking by vibration of vocal cords in the larynx, the mechanical disturbance of traffic noise or the vibration created as a jet engine or thunder moves enormous amounts of air. A cymbal creates sound. In its ordinary position, it is silent. Once it is struck, it moves rapidly to and fro. Air immediately next to it is compressed, causing a slight increase in air pressure; it then moves back *past* its rest position, causing a reduction in the air pressure. As this continues, a wave of alternating high and low pressure radiates away from the cymbal in all directions. These patterns of high and low pressure are interpreted as sounds in our ears and brain.

So it is that sounds are generated by rapid movement or vibration. Objects vibrate in different ways to make their own unique sounds. When a gong is struck, the entire object is made to vibrate. Sounds made by a violin are created by the vibrations of its strings. The vibrating strings set up vibrations in the body of the violin, which amplify the sounds.

A model to explain how sound travels

Materials are made from moving particles, which can pass their energy on to others. This is how sound moves. The closer the particles are to one other, the more easily they pass on sound vibrations. This means sounds travels better in liquids, where particles are close together, than in air, where they are further apart. The particles of a solid such as steel are tightly packed and pass on vibrations to their neighbours very readily. Sound moves more rapidly in a solid than a liquid or gas. Sound vibrations (waves) travel away from their source, radiating out in all directions. As the sound wave travels further from the source, the more its energy is dissipated and the fainter the sound becomes.

The body of the stringed instrument amplifies the sound made by vibrating the strings.
Source: Peter Loxley

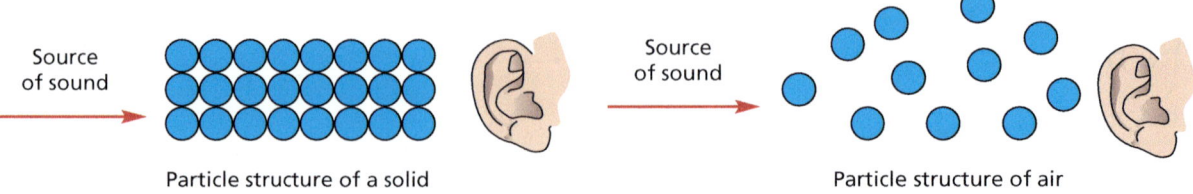

Particle structure of a solid

Source of sound

Particle structure of air

Source of sound

Sound travels faster in a solid than in air because the particles, which transfer the sound, are closer together.

Leonardo da Vinci imagined sound waves to be like ripples spreading out on the surface of water. Do you think this is a useful analogy? Could it help explain about the behaviour of sound?

Problems with the water model

The water analogy is not a perfectly accurate picture, but it does enable us to understand how the sound from a source such as a bell can be heard in all parts of a room simultaneously. The analogy breaks down when we consider the movement of the particles of water. In water waves the particles move up and down at right angles to the direction of travel of the wave. This is called a **transverse wave** and is consistent with the way light travels. Sound is a **longitudinal wave**, which means that its energy travels in the same direction in which the source vibrates.

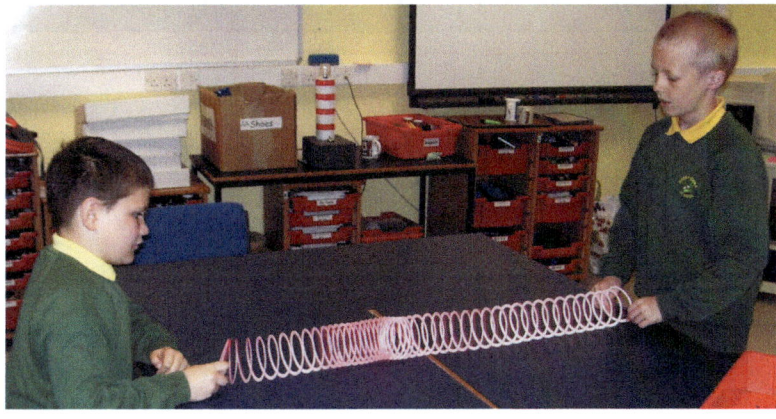

Using a slinky to model how sound travels in longitudinal waves.
Source: Peter Loxley

Ripples on water.
Source: iStock

Can sound be reflected like light?

Sound is reflected from surfaces. When sound is reflected from hard surfaces, echoes can be created. Bats have very sensitive ears and use echoes to locate their prey. In effect, they locate their prey by 'shouting', but their voices are at such a high pitch that we humans cannot hear them. Their ultrasound calls bounce off the hard exoskeleton of their prey, such as a moth, and are returned so that they hear an echo a fraction of a second later. Bats calculate the decreasing distance between themselves and insects by listening. Some water creatures can also locate things or one another in this way. Bottlenose dolphins produce clicking sounds, which they use to navigate around their habitat. There is even a Madagascan shrew that explores its terrain by echolocation. We have developed technology which imitates animals' use of sound to locate underwater objects. Ships use sonar (Sound Navigation and Ranging) equipment to detect and locate submerged objects or to measure distances underwater.

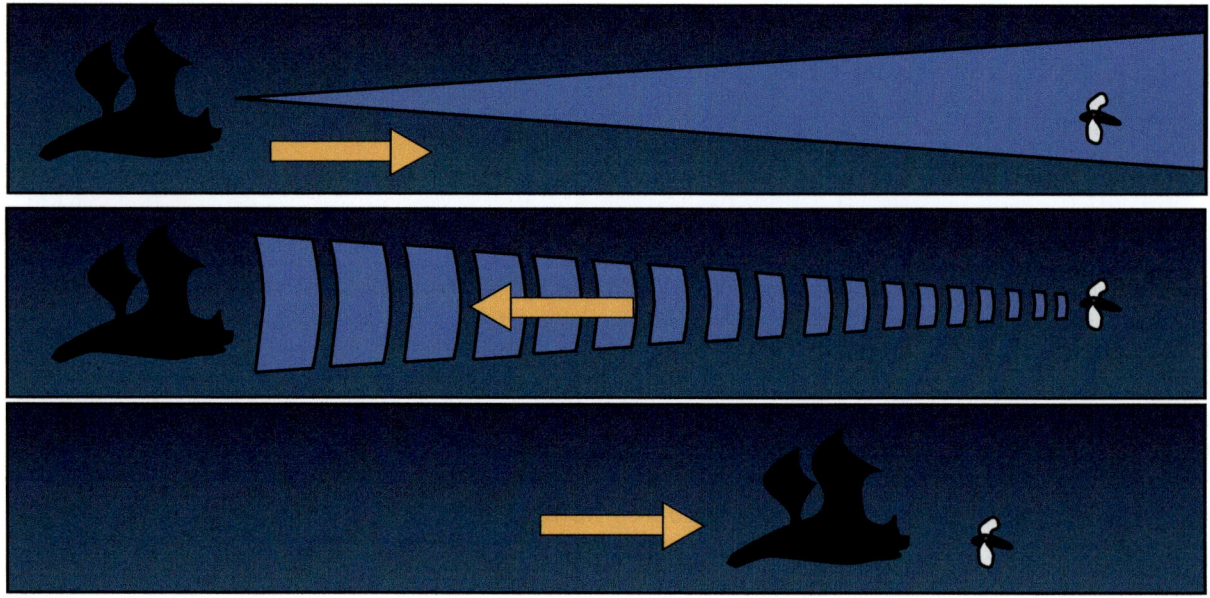

Bats use echoes to locate their prey.

Something to think about

If sound travels better in solids than it does in air, then why do we shut doors and windows to block out unwanted sounds? It could be argued that closing doors should enable the sound to travel more easily into the room.

Which materials absorb sound?

Some surfaces absorb rather than reflect sound. Curtains and carpets make an appreciable difference to the acoustics of a room. Good absorbers of sound are often a mixture of a gas (air) and a solid. For example, woollen curtains and carpets are good absorbers; so are some manufactured materials, such as polystyrene and foam, which are commonly used as insulators of sound. Sound vibrations dissipate when they are continuously transferred from one medium to another.

Acoustics

Pitch and frequency

Sound waves have the same measurable characteristics as light waves, that is, wavelength, frequency and amplitude.

The number of vibrations produced by a source during one second is the *frequency* of the sound. We use the term **pitch** to describe how we interpret different frequencies. As the frequency of vibration increases, the sound we hear gets higher and higher. High-frequency sounds have a high pitch. If vibrations have a low frequency, the resulting sound has a low pitch. We start a column of air vibrating as we blow into a recorder; we can change the frequency of the vibrations by changing the length of the air column that is vibrating. Small piccolos have higher-pitched sounds than large bassoons because they make it possible to vibrate an air column at a higher frequency. Interestingly, vibration in air columns is unaffected by the shape of the column – so we can bend and twist tubes which would otherwise be long and unwieldy to make such things as trumpets, cornets, trombones and horns with the same range of notes as they would have if straight.

How can we measure the loudness of a sound?

The loudness, or volume, of a sound is dependent on the amplitude, or size, of the vibrations. For human ears, the loudness of a sound cannot be measured with complete accuracy. Everyone perceives sound slightly differently and perception of loudness by individuals is affected by the duration of a sound. However, machines can measure sound volume by measuring the amount of energy the sound wave contains. The more energy the wave contains, the greater the intensity of the sound. Sound is measured in **decibels (dB)**.

The measure zero decibels (0dB) of sound is about the lower limit of human perception. The dB scale is logarithmic, that is, an increase of one on the scale represents a doubling of sound intensity. People talk at about 40dB, car engines run at about 60dB, a rock concert is 120dB, a blue whale humming at 1 metre, 183 dB, and above 130 dB, sound becomes painful to our ears. The explosion of the volcano Krakatoa in 1883 is estimated to have been 180dB from a distance of 100 miles in air.

Sound wave made by a percussion instrument, showing variation in amplitude (loudness).

Hearing sounds

Are all animals' ears the same?

The ears of mammals are specialised to detect sound and convey detailed information about direction, pitch, loudness and quality to the brain. The external shape of the ear may differ. Some animals can move their ears to track sounds. Others, like elephants, use the shape of their outer ears to help cool their bodies.

The ear is a delicate and complex mechanism which converts sound vibrations to electrical impulses. Vibrations in the air entering the ear canal vibrate the eardrum. This in turn vibrates the three small bones of the middle ear: the hammer, anvil and stirrup. This vibration is transmitted to the oval window and then to the cochlea in the inner ear. The cochlea is a coiled tube containing liquid. Hair-like structures in the cochlea resonate to different frequencies of sound; their movement generates a chemical neuro-transmitter. In this way, sound in air is moved through solid and then liquid to create nerve impulses. The auditory nerve transmits the impulses to the brain.

Humans have well-developed brains and can use highly complex patterns of sound to communicate ideas through language. Other highly intelligent animals, which produce complex

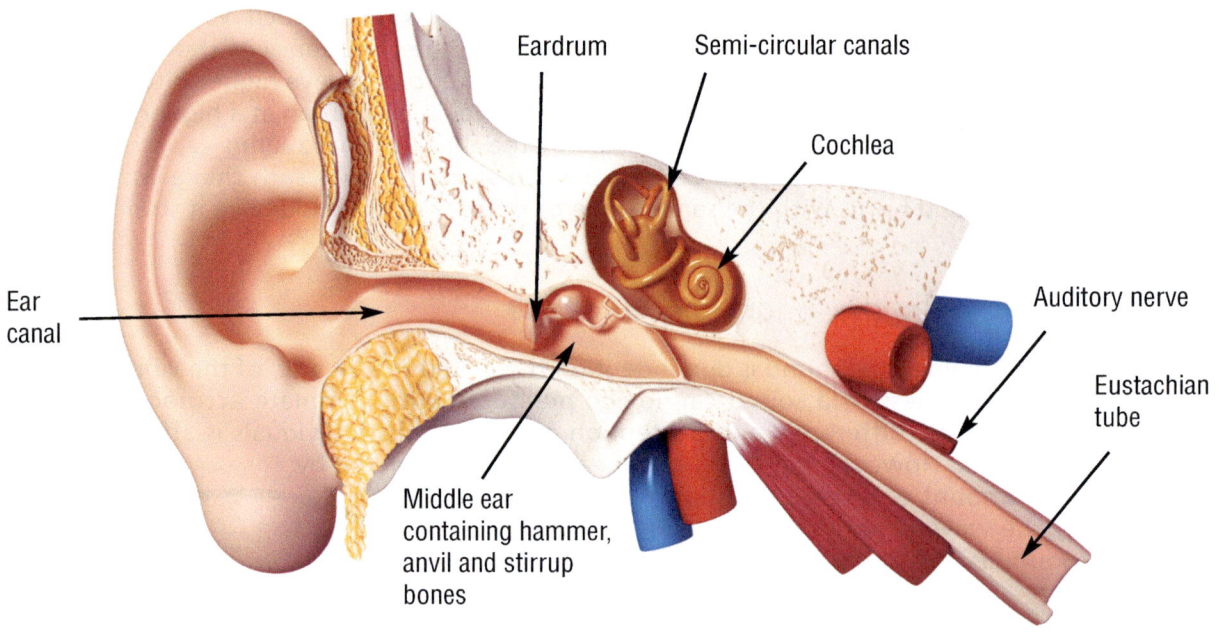

Structure of the human ear.
Source: Jacopin / Science Photo Library Ltd.

patterns of sound for communication, are whales and dolphins. Many other animals use systems of sounds to communicate.

Although generally only mammals have large outer ears, fish, birds, reptiles and amphibians have eardrums and inner ears. For example, frogs have eardrums behind their head on both sides of their body. Sound vibrations picked up by the eardrums are sent to the brain in a similar way to a mammal's. However, frogs also use another organ to detect sound: they use their lungs. Scientists have found that frogs have an unbroken air link from the lungs to the eardrums. It seems that this link helps the frog to locate sounds and also possibly to protect the ears from its own loud calls. Frogs can call extremely loudly (up to about 95 decibels) – the sound equivalent of a train whistle. It is thought that the lungs help to protect the ears by equalising the pressure on the inside and outside of the eardrum. Since fish were the original vertebrates, and therefore have a common ancestor with frogs, it is perhaps not surprising to find that many types of fish also use a lung-like air bladder as an eardrum.

Do owls really have big ears?

Some owls seem to have tufty ears on top of their heads. Actually, these feathers are not associated with hearing. Like other birds, owls have ear openings or apertures on the sides of the head. To be successful night hunters, owls need to have a highly developed sense of hearing. Some owls have the parts of their faces around the ear aperture shaped like radar dishes to funnel in the sound. When a noise is detected, an owl is able to tell its direction because of the minute time difference between hearing the sound in the left and right ears.

The tufts of feathers on an owl's head look like ears.
Source: iStock

Why don't birds have bigger ears?

Why don't owls have big ears like rabbits and foxes? Think about having a conversation on a windy day. When wind races past the ears, it creates a loud roaring noise, which limits the ability to distinguish separate sounds. Lack of external ears significantly cuts down wind noise, enabling birds to hear other sounds when they fly.

Some butterflies have ears on their wings

A fascinating recent discovery is that some butterflies active at night have ears located in their wings. Previously it had been assumed that, although butterflies could detect air vibrations through their wings, they did not have specialised organs for detecting sound. As far as we understand, it is only butterflies that are active at night which have ears. Moths, which are mainly active at night, have a well-developed sense of hearing to enable them to detect the **ultrasonic sound** used by bats to locate their prey. It is thought that night-flying butterflies have evolved sound sensors to help avoid being eaten by bats.

Something to think about

The first chapter in the book explores the pleasure of finding out that the natural world may not be how we first imagine it to be. Frogs hear sound through their lungs, and butterflies hear sound through their wings to avoid being eaten by bats. What other wonderful things can children find out?

Global dimensions: Music around the world

Each culture has its own musical traditions and the world enjoys an astonishing range of music derived from different cultures. Even though the same techniques of striking, plucking and blowing are used to produce the sounds, the nature of the material used to make the instrument will affect the quality of the sound it makes. Western orchestras have instruments made from wood, brass and other metals. Traditional instruments are made from locally available materials – for example, in West Africa the gourd plant is used to make a stringed instrument called a kora and in China bamboo is used to make flutes. It is interesting to consider in what ways instruments from around the world are the same and in what ways they are different.

The scales used in musical compositions vary from culture to culture and this can affect the emotional impact the music has on us.

Gamelan orchestra: www.youtube.com/watch?v=Fsn0RKc5N3Q

Indian instruments: www.youtube.com/watch?v=EOxD77LDUQY

Chinese orchestra: www.youtube.com/watch?v=Lykgg5phVJE

Australian traditional music: www.youtube.com/watch?v=dFGvNxBqYFI

www.bbc.co.uk/schools/gcsebitesize/music/world_music/

Summary

Someone speaks; the vibrations set up in their larynx move particles of air. The sound wave is transmitted; the complexity of the vibration carries all sorts of information about the voice. Hearing involves the ear in capturing the vibration and converting it to neural information to be sent to the brain for processing. Sound, like light, is a physical phenomenon, a form of energy profoundly and extensively important for human life. With sound we can have language, music and story, we can be alerted to danger or ask for help and we can identify one another and learn.

Animals use sound for various purposes. They use it to locate their prey, to avoid their predators and warn others of approaching danger. Animals make sounds to attract a mate, defend a territory and challenge a competitor. In social groups, animals use sound to identify others, to coordinate group activities and to generally pass on information.

Part 2: Ideas for practice

Topic: Detecting sound

Age group: 5–9 years

Introduction

This topic introduces children to the idea that sounds travel out from their sources and are detected by our ears. Throughout the stages children explore the value of having two ears and apply their knowledge in the application stage to gain insights into why some animals have such big ears.

Scientific view

Sound travels from its source in all directions. We hear sound when it enters our ears. Having two ears enables us to distinguish between different sounds and also helps us decide where the sounds are coming from.

Working scientifically

In these activities children will:

- ask questions and answer them in different ways;
- observe closely and make comparisons;
- perform simple tests;
- use their observations and ideas to suggest answers to questions.

Exploratory stage

Children's talk involves trying out their own ideas

Setting the scene

Read a story involving sound, for example 'The King's Keys', and use this as a basis for games involving sound.

Storytelling

The King had locked away all his gold in a room with a thick door and a very strong lock. There was only one special key which could unlock the room. Every afternoon, the King had a nap on his favourite throne. He ordered the whole palace to go to sleep too so that it was very, very quiet. To keep the special key safe while he was asleep, he always put it in a gold box underneath the throne.

One day, a thief who wanted to steal the gold tiptoed into the King's room. He saw the King asleep. Without even breathing, the thief crept silently up to the throne. He knew where the key was kept. Gently, his fingers closed round it … he lifted it up … and as he did so, a loud 'Ding dong! Ding dong! Ding dong!' rang through the room. The thief froze in horror. He hadn't realised that attached to the key was a small but very loud silver bell!

With his eyes closed, the King smiled to himself. As he had expected, it was his own son Prince Echo trying to steal the key. Of course Prince Echo wasn't a real thief. This was a game they played together. The King had promised that, on the day his son was clever enough to steal the key, he would make him King! Sometimes he used gold bells, sometimes silver and sometimes bronze; the little bells always warned him before the thief could escape.

Scientific enquiry

Play the King's keys game with the children – if possible, in a large space, such as the school hall. Place the 'throne' in the middle of the space and choose a child who doesn't mind being blindfolded to be the King. The King sits on the throne and places the keys to the treasure on the floor underneath. The rest of the children form a large circle surrounding the throne. One at a time, the children try to sneak up and steal the keys without the King knowing. The thief is caught if the King is able to point in the direction of the approaching child. Any child who is able to steal the keys becomes the King. The game can be played in smaller groups so that more children can have the opportunity to be the King.

Puzzle

After playing the game, *talk together* about how the children could tell when a thief was trying to steal the keys. How did they know the thief was getting closer? How did they know which direction the thief was coming from? How did they know when the thief was behind them? Listen to children's responses and assess what they know about how we use our ears to detect sounds.

Talking points: true, false or not sure?

- We need two ears to listen to a sound.
- We only use one ear at a time to listen to a sound.

- We can listen to two sounds because we have two ears.
- It is hard to listen carefully.
- Some sounds are easier to listen to than others.
- We hear better with two ears.

Discuss children's responses to the talking points and ask them to describe how they use their ears to listen to sounds. Ask them whether they really need two ears?

Scientific enquiry

Provide children with ear muffs which they can use to cover their ears. Working in groups, with the help of an adult, children carry out the following tests. If possible, use a recording of a sound to make sure the volume remains the same in each case.

1. Listen to a quiet sound with and without the muffs.
2. Listen to a quiet sound close up and then after it has been moved further away from them.
3. Listen to a quiet sound with and without one ear covered by the muff.
4. Listen to a quiet sound in front of them and then the same distance behind them.

For each activity ask children to talk about how the sounds differed and to draw annotated pictures to explain why. Ask them to draw pictures to show how they think sound travelled from the source to their ears. Talk about the purpose of having two ears.

Formative assessment

Provide opportunities for children to voice what they have learnt in the exploratory stage. Use evidence from their responses to the puzzle, talking points, drawings and other activities to assess differences between children's ideas and the scientific view. Plan how you will use the re-describing stage to help the children address their *learning needs.* You may want to modify the activities depending on the shared and individual needs of the children.

Re-describing stage

Children's talk involves making sense of scientific ideas

Teacher-led discussion

Focus on the idea that sounds travel from their sources and having two ears helps us to locate the sounds. Start by asking what the children learnt from the enquiry. Do they think they are better off with two ears? Explore their reasons. Use video clips to discuss how we use our ears to detect and locate sounds which travel out from their sources.

Modelling

To explore the advantages of having two ears, play a different version of the King's keys game. Again, the King sits blindfolded on his throne with the other children surrounding him in a big circle. This time, each child has an instrument with which to make a sound. Children are chosen randomly to make a sound with their instruments and the King has to point to where he thinks the sound is coming from and to describe the instrument. The game continues until all the children have had the opportunity to contribute a sound.

Observe and talk about how the King identifies the direction of the sound. How does he move his head? Record the number of correct responses made by the King. The King now puts a disposable foam earplug in one of his ears and the game is repeated. Try the experiment with different Kings or Queens. Compare the accuracy of the responses for two ears to one ear. *Talk together* about the advantages of having two ears compared with only one.

Develop the game with two children in different parts of the circle making sounds with their instruments at the same time. Are two ears better than one when it comes to distinguishing between the two sounds?

Children draw new pictures to show how they use their ears to locate sounds. Encourage them to explain their drawings. Return to the puzzle to assess children's progress. Address any outstanding *learning needs* identified in the exploratory stage. What else would they like to find out about sound, ears and hearing in humans and animals? Children can raise and investigate their own questions.

Information and teaching resources

BBC Bitesize:

- BBC (2017). Sound. *www.bbc.co.uk/education/clips/zt9tfrd*

Application stage

Children's talk involves trying out scientific ideas

Animal ears

Collect pictures of animal ears for display. Include some unusual ones like those of the long-eared bat. Children compare the shape and size of a range of different animals' ears. Discuss reasons for why the ears of animals are not all the same.

Children use information sources to discover animals with the biggest ears. They find out why they have such big ears and tell their stories in words and pictures. Probe children's understanding of how their animals use their ears to detect sound.

Making model ears

Ask the children whether having huge ears could improve their hearing. Would they hear better if they had ears like the animals in their stories? With the help of adults, they can make simple ear models to test out their ideas. Models can be designed so they fit over the children's ears for testing.

Wearing their 'big ears', children can role-model acting like the animals in their stories. Children move and make sounds like their animals and use their ears to locate prey or escape from predators. At intervals, freeze-frame the acting and ask children to explain how their animal would be using its ears. What would it be listening out for?

Long-eared bat.
Source: iStock

Design and make an imaginary animal

Children can design and make simple models of an imaginary animal, which can hear and locate very quiet sounds, such as the movement of an ant or worm.

Topic: How vibrations create sound

Age group: 7–9 years

Introduction

This topic provides opportunities for children to explore how different sounds can be created and how they travel through the air. The exploratory stage focuses on factors which affect pitch and volume. In the application stage children design and make their own instruments and use their understanding of sound to control pitch and volume.

Scientific view

Sound is caused by objects when they vibrate. When objects vibrate, they cause the air around them to vibrate. These vibrations travel through the air and, if they enter our ears, we hear them as sound. The sound we hear depends on the nature of the vibrations. For example, more rapid or faster vibrations create a higher pitch and bigger vibrations create louder sounds.

Working scientifically

In these activities children will:

- ask questions and use scientific enquiries to answer them;
- set up practical enquiries and comparative and fair tests;
- make systematic observations including the use of ICT for data-logging;
- use charts and drawings to record and communicate data;
- use results to make comparisons and draw conclusions;
- use appropriate scientific language to discuss their ideas and communicate their findings.

Exploratory stage

Children's talk involves trying out their own ideas

Setting the scene

Have available a range of musical instruments. Ask for volunteers to form a band. Give each member a different instrument (a range of wind, stringed and percussion) and ask them to play along with a recorded tune together. Now ask the children in the audience to close their eyes while each member of the group plays their instrument independently. The game is to identify the instrument just by listening to it. *Talk together* about how the sounds made by each of the instruments could be changed. How can sounds be made lower or higher in pitch, quieter or louder, more or less tuneful? Is it possible to make a guitar sound like a drum? Encourage children to provide reasons for their views.

Scientific enquiry

Focus on how each of the instruments makes its sound. Use a drum with rice placed on the skin to demonstrate how it vibrates. Suspend a table tennis ball from a length of cotton. Strike a tuning fork and bring it close enough to tap the ball so that children can see vibration as movement.

In groups, children can explore a range of instruments and record their ideas as set out below:

Instrument	How do you make the sound?	What vibrates?	How can you change the volume of the sound?	How do you alter the pitch?

Encourage the children to interpret and make sense of the scientific terms for themselves. They can *talk together* about the meanings of the terms vibrations, volume and pitch. Check the children's understanding and encourage them to compare the sounds made by the instruments to help make sense of scientific vocabulary. For example, which instruments have the highest pitch and which produce the most volume?

Children's drawings

Ask children to choose one instrument and draw an annotated picture of how it makes its sound and how they are able to hear it. Children can *talk together* about how instruments are able to change the pitch and loudness of the sounds they produce. Encourage them to use comparative terms, such as *high* and *low* pitch and *loud* and *quiet* sounds. Display the drawings and encourage children to annotate each other's work positively with additional information.

Puzzle

What does sound look like as it travels through the air? Is it possible to see sound? Discuss children's responses to the puzzle and introduce the idea of an analogy. *Talk together* about the purpose of an analogy. Can children think of an analogy for sound?

Modelling

Children use information sources to explore answers to the puzzle. They present their ideas through drawings and models. Children come together to share their ideas. Encourage them to compare and evaluate different analogies and ideas. Discuss what makes a good analogy or model.

Formative assessment

Provide opportunities for children to voice what they have learnt in the exploratory stage. Use evidence from their responses to the puzzle and other activities to assess differences between children's ideas and the scientific view. Plan how you will use the re-describing stage to help the children address their *learning needs.* You may want to modify the activities depending on the shared and individual needs of the children.

Re-describing stage

Children's talk involves making sense of scientific ideas

Teacher-led discussion

The purpose of this stage is to provide a model that children can use to help them develop a mental picture of how sound travels through the air. Start by discussing children's responses to the puzzle. Use appropriate video clips to build on their understanding and address their *learning needs*.

Modelling

Compare children's ideas with the following models. Ask them which they think make most sense and whether they could be improved.

1. Children standing in a line can model the air. Have a pile of cards with the word 'sound' written on each. Children stand close enough so that they can touch hands. A child at the start of the line who represents the instrument, gives out the sound cards one at a time. The 'sounds' are then passed from child to child down the line until they reach the listener at the other end.

2. Use a slinky coil to show how a vibrating source can cause pulse patterns to be passed along the coil. Talk about the springiness of air and how it behaves like a slinky.

3. Ask children to stand behind each other with their arms outstretched and their hands on the shoulders of the person in front. The child, acting as the instrument, at the back end of the line gives the child in front a gentle push which is then passed on down the line from child to child. The model can be developed with gentle vibrations being passed down the line. If the vibrations are made continuous then the observing children will be able to see the patterns of vibrations repeated along the line.

4. Use a line of dominoes to represent the air. When the first is knocked over, each domino knocks over the next and so on, causing a pulse of sound to travel down the line.

Make it clear to the children that these models are analogies, which behave in similar ways to sound. *Talk together* about the strengths and limitations of each model. Explore how the models can be used to demonstrate changes in loudness and pitch.

To assess progress, ask the children to look again at their own pictures created earlier. How could they be revised in light of what they have learnt? Address any outstanding *learning needs* identified in the exploratory stage. What else would they like to find out? Children can raise and investigate their own questions.

Information and teaching resources

BBC Bitesize:

- BBC (2015). How Are Sounds Produced? *www.bbc.co.uk/education/clips/zcy7sg8*
- BBC (2007). How Distance from a Sound Source Will Affect How Loud It Will Seem. *www.bbc.co.uk/education/clips/z47w2hv*
- BBC (2007). How Does Sound Travel Through Air. *www.bbc.co.uk/education/clips/ztwkjxs*
- BBC (2017). Making Sounds with Different Pitches. *www.bbc.co.uk/education/clips/ztptsbk*
- BBC (2014). What Is Sound? *www.bbc.co.uk/education/clips/zc3qp39*

Application stage

Children's talk involves trying out scientific ideas

Design and make musical instruments

Tell the children they are going to be songwriters and performers. They have to design and make their own instruments. Allow children to choose and name their own bands. Each band needs to design and make three types of instrument: stringed, wind and percussion. There are lots of ideas on the web. Encourage children to bring resources from home. To help plan this activity refer to ASE guidance (*Be safe!* 2011) regarding safe use of tools, materials and glues when making things.

Children playing their own musical instruments.
Source: Peter Loxley

Design criteria should focus on the range of volume and pitch the instruments can make. They can use electronic data-loggers to measure the volume. Ask the children to provide annotated drawings of their instruments, explaining how they create sound and how the pitch and volume of the sound can be changed. Bands perform a favourite song or they can write their own to a popular tune. They can then evaluate each other's instruments using the design criteria. What are the strengths of each instrument? How can designs be improved?

Ask each band to create a presentation for the class in which they demonstrate how their instruments work, compare the sounds they make and say what they would like to try next to improve the pitch and volume.

Information and teaching resources

BBC Bitesize:

- BBC (2014). How Drums and Percussion Make Sounds. *www.bbc.co.uk/education/clips/zcrkxsg*
- BBC (2014). How String Instruments Make Sound. *www.bbc.co.uk/education/clips/zx4whv4*

Talk skills and science discussion: Exploratory talk and interthinking

Ask groups to research three musical instruments to find out the physics of the sounds they produce (pitch, tone and volume): piano or drum (percussion); recorder, trumpet or flute (wind); violin or guitar (stringed).

Ask groups to discuss and design a new musical instrument, or an adaptation of an existing instrument, for use by younger children. The focus of the discussion is to ask for and give ideas and information and to encourage everyone to contribute.

Children in groups should be asked to conduct an exploratory discussion. The idea of 'interthinking' is useful; inclusive, exploratory discussion enables people to think aloud together – to interthink. It is interthinking that has enabled scientists to work with one another to build up knowledge of how the world works. Using historical and contemporary thinking, scientists are able to replicate and build on one another's work to establish a robust understanding of phenomena.

Design drawings should be displayed and the class encouraged to annotate each other's drawings with positive comments and suggestions for modifications.

Ask the class to discuss the value of group talk and whole-class discussion for thinking and learning. What are the advantages of interthinking? Bring out the importance of dialogue for a community of scientists working in similar fields.

Additional information and teaching resources

Companion book:

- Loxley, P. (2018). *Practical Ideas for Teaching Primary Science: Inspiring Learning and Enjoyment,* Abingdon: Routledge, Chapter 15: Sound.

ASE journals:

- Primary Science Review 103 (June 2008). *The Sound of Music* (Wobbly Corner).
- Primary Science Review 93 (May/June 2006). This issue focuses on light and sound.

APPENDIX A Information and teaching resources

Books

The following books cover a wide range of concepts and can be used to help address gaps in subject knowledge:

- Cross, A. and Bowden, A. (2014) *Essential Primary Science (2nd ed)*, Maidenhead: OUP.
- Farrow, S. (2006) *The Really Useful Science Book*, Abingdon: Falmer Press.
- Peacock, G., Sharp, J., Johnsey, R. and Wright, D. (2014) *Primary Science Knowledge and Understanding (7th ed),* London: Sage.
- Roden, J., Ward, H. and Ritchie, H. (2007) *Extending Knowledge and Practice Primary Science*, Exeter: Learning Matters.
- Wenham, M. and Ovens, P. (2010) *Understanding Primary Science (3rd ed)*, London: Sage.

The following books address specific areas of knowledge:

- Allen, M. (2014) *Misconceptions in Primary Science (2nd ed)*, Maidenhead: OUP.
- Asoko, H. and de Boo, M. (2001) *Analogies and Illustrations: Representing Ideas in Primary Science*, Hatfield: ASE Publications.
- Pierce, P. (2014) *Jurassic Mary: Mary Anning and the Primeval Monsters*, Stroud: The History Press.
- Rutledge, N. (2010) *Primary Science Teaching the Tricky Bits*, Maidenhead: Open University Press.
- Thomson, K. (2005) *A Very Short Introduction to Fossils*, Oxford: Open University Press.

Websites

The following websites provide a wide range of resources for teaching primary science:

- Hamilton Trust. *www.hamilton-trust.org.uk*
- Primary Resources. *www.primaryresources.co.uk/science/science.htm*
- Primary Science Teaching Trust. *https://pstt.org.uk/*
- Science Museum London, Teachers' Resources. *www.sciencemuseum.org.uk/educators/classroom-resources*

- Science resources from New Zealand. *http://sciencelearn.org.nz/*

These websites provide ideas for teaching science in real-life contexts.

- ASE SchoolScience. *www.schoolscience.co.uk*
- Practical Action. *http://practicalaction.org/schools*
- STEM Centre. *www.stem.org.uk/resources*
- STEM clubs. *www.stemclubs.net*
- The Royal Society of Chemistry. *www.rsc.org/learn-chemistry*

These websites provide resources regarding the natural world:

- Arkive Education. *www.arkive.org/education*
- Oxford University Museum of Natural History: The Learning Zone. *www.oum.ox.ac.uk/thezone/index.htm*
- Royal Horticultural Society. *https://schoolgardening.rhs.org.uk/home*
- Science and Plants for Schools. *www.saps.org.uk/primary*
- Weather for kids. *www.metoffice.gov.uk/learning/weather-for-kids*
- Weather observations website. *http://wow.metoffice.gov.uk/#*
- Wildscreen Arkive. *www.arkive.org/*
- Woodland Trust. *www.woodlandtrust.org.uk*

These websites provide video clips which support all areas of science learning:

- BBC Bitesize. *www.bbc.co.uk/education*
- Planet SCICAST. *www.scicast.org.uk/films*

The following websites provide ideas and interactive games for teaching science:

- ABPI resources for schools. *www.abpischools.org.uk/page/*
- BP Educational Service. *http://bpes.bp.com/primary-resources/*
- Children's University of Manchester. *www.childrensuniversity.manchester.ac.uk*
- Duck Builder Game. *www.cgpbooks.co.uk/online_rev/duck/duck.htm*

These websites provide access to up-to-date stories about real-world science:

- BBC Earth. *www.bbc.com/earth/uk*
- BBSRC. *www.bbsrc.ac.uk*
- National Geographic. *http://news.nationalgeographic.com/*
- Science News. *www.sciencenews.org*
- The Naked Scientists. *www.thenakedscientists.com*

These websites provide resources regarding Earth and Space:

- ESERO-UK. *https://www.stem.org.uk/esero*
- Great Space Explanations.
  www.bbc.co.uk/science/space/universe/collections/great_space_explanations
- Hubble telescope site. *http://hubblesite.org/gallery/*
- Mars for Kids. *http://mars.nasa.gov/participate/funzone/*
- NASA Space Place. *http://spaceplace.nasa.gov/*

APPENDIX B Links to the companion book

Contents of companion book, Loxley, P. (2018) *Practical Ideas for Teaching Primary Science: Inspiring Learning and Enjoyment,* Abingdon: Routledge. **Links to core book** refer to relevant subject knowledge chapters.

Companion book	Ideas for practice	Key ideas	Links to core book
Ch.2: Growing Plants	Yrs 5–7: Growing plants from seeds Yrs 7–9: Growing healthy plants Yrs 9–11: Bulbs and cuttings	Germination of seeds Conditions for healthy plant growth Different ways of propagating plants	Ch.13: Interdependence Ch.14: Diversity
Ch.3: Flowering Plants	Yrs 5–7: Flowering plants Yrs 7–9: Pollination Yrs 9–11: Adaptation	Plant structure and variety Structure of flowers Pollination Life cycles Adaptation	Ch.14: Diversity Ch.15: Adaptation and Evolution
Ch.4: Woodland Habitats	Yrs 5–7: Autumn in the woodland Yrs 7–9: Spring in the woodland Yrs 9–11: Habitats and food chains	Seasons Habitats Food chains Interdependence Adaptation	Ch.13: Interdependence Ch.15: Adaptation and Evolution
Ch.5: Rocks, Habitats and Fossils	Yrs 5–7: Micro-habitats Yrs 7–9: Rocks and fossils Yrs 9–11: Fossil hunters	Habitats Structure of rocks Fossils Evolution	Ch.11: The Earth and Beyond Ch.15: Adaptation and Evolution
Ch.6: Living Things	Yrs 5–7: Living or non-living? Yrs 7–9: Body parts Yrs 9–11: Life cycles	Characteristics of living things Digestive system Skeleton and muscles Life cycles Changes as humans develop	Ch.14: Diversity Ch.16: Health and Well-being

Companion book	Ideas for practice	Key ideas	Links to core book
Ch.7: Decomposers	Yrs 5–7: What have woodlice ever done for us? Yrs 7–9: What have mushrooms ever done for us? Yrs 9–11: What has mould ever done for us?	Habitats Detritivores Nature's recyclers Decomposers: mushrooms and mould Microbes and science's fight against disease	Ch.13: Interdependence Ch.15: Adaptation and Evolution Ch.16: Health and Well-being
Ch.8: Nutrition	Yrs 5–7: Five a day Yrs 7-9: Eating the right kinds of foods Yrs 9–11: The circulatory system	Balanced diet Benefits of exercise Sugar and obesity Circulatory system History of medicine Links between diet and performance	Ch.16: Health and Well-being
Ch.9: The Material World	Yrs 5–7: Everyday materials Yrs 7–9: Fabrics Yrs 9–11: Plastic waste	Properties of materials and their uses Natural materials – properties and uses Man-made materials – properties and uses	Ch.17: The Particle Nature of Materials
Ch.10: Changing Materials	Yrs 5–7: In the kitchen Yrs 7–9: The water cycle Yrs 9–11: Solutions and suspensions	Temporary change Melting and freezing Evaporation and condensation Mixtures Permanent change	Ch.17: The Particle Nature of Materials Ch.18: Changing Materials
Ch.11: Earth and Space	Yrs 5–7: Journey to the Moon Yrs 7–9: Mission to Mars Yrs 9–11: In search of Goldilocks Planets	Conditions on the Moon Conditions on Mars NASA missions Solar System Beyond the Solar System	Ch.11: The Earth and Beyond
Ch.12: Electricity	Yrs 5–7: Introducing electric circuits Yrs 7–9: Electric circuit challenge Yrs 9–11: Saving energy	Electrical components Simple series circuits Conductors and insulators Electrical current Designing, making and using circuits	Ch.19: Electricity and Magnetism

Companion book	Ideas for practice	Key ideas	Links to core book
Ch.13: Forces and Magnetism	Yrs 5–7: Forces in action Yrs 7–9: Gravity and magnetism Yrs 9–11: What has gravity ever done for us?	Actions of forces – pushes, pulls and twists Links between force and motion Gravity and magnetism Weight Universal effects of gravity	Ch.19: Electricity and Magnetism Ch.20: Forces and Motion
Ch.14: Light	Yrs 5–7: Night animals Yrs 7–9: Reflections and shadows Yrs 9–11: Chasing shadows	Light and dark Light and vision Reflecting light Blocking light Light travels in straight lines	Ch.15: Adaptation and Evolution Ch. 21: Light
Ch.15: Sound	Yrs 5–7: How noisy is our world? Yrs 7–9: Elephants: the ultimate sound machine Yrs 9–11: How marine animals use sound	Noise Creating sounds Vibrations, frequency, pitch and volume Detecting sound Sound in solids and liquids	Ch.15: Adaptation and Evolution Ch.22: Sound

REFERENCES

Alexander, R.J. (2001) *Culture and Pedagogy: International Comparisons in Primary Education*, Oxford: Blackwell.

Alexander, R.J. (2006) *Towards Dialogic Teaching*, York: Dialogos.

Allen, M. (2010) *Misconceptions in Primary Science*, Milton Keynes: Open University Press.

Allen, M. (2014) *Misconceptions in Primary Science (2nd ed)*, Maidenhead: Open University Press.

Asoko, H. (2000) *Learning to Teach Science in the Primary School*, in R. Millar, J. Leach and J. Osborne (eds), *Improving Science Education: The Contribution of Research*, Buckingham: Open University Press.

Asoko, H. (2002) Developing Conceptual Understanding in Primary Science. *Cambridge Journal of Education*, 32(2): 153–164.

Asoko, H. and de Boo, M. (2001) *Analogies and Illustrations: Presenting Ideas in Primary Science*, Hatfield: ASE Publications.

Association for Science Education (2011) *Be Safe! Health and Safety in School Science and Technology for Teachers of 3- to 12-year-olds (4th ed)*, Hatfield: Association for Science Education.

Avraamidou, L. and Osborne, J. (2009) The Role of Narrative in Communicating Science. *International Journal of Science Education*, 31(12): 1683–1707.

Banks, F. and Barlex, D. (2014) *Teaching STEM in the Secondary School*, London: Routledge.

Barnes, D. (1976) *From Communication to Curriculum*, Harmondsworth: Penguin Books.

Barnes, D. (2008) *Exploratory Talk for Learning*, in N. Mercer and S. Hodgkinson (eds), *Exploring Talk in School*, London: Sage.

Barnett, J. and Feasey, R. (2016) *Jumpstart Science Outdoors*, London: Routledge.

Barrie, J.M. (2007) *Peter Pan*, London: Penguin.

Barzun, J. (1991) *Begin Here: The Forgotten Conditions of Teaching and Learning*, Chicago: University of Chicago Press.

Bell, B. and Cowie, B. (2001) The Characteristics of Formative Assessment in Science Education. *Journal of Science Education*, 85: 536–553.

Bianchi, L. and Feasey, R. (2011) *Science Beyond the Classroom Boundaries for 3–7 Year Olds*, Maidenhead: Open University Press.

Black, P. and Harrison, C. (2000) Formative Assessment, in M. Monk and J. Osborne (eds), *Good Practice in Science Teaching: What Research Has to Say*, Buckingham: Open University Press.

Black, P., Harrison, C., Clare, L., Marshall, B. and Wiliam, D. (2002) *Working Inside the Black Box: Assessment for Learning in the Classroom*, London: King's College.

Borges, A.T. and Gilbert, J.K. (1999) Mental Models of Electricity. *International Journal of Science Education*, 21(1): 95–117.

Brady, J. (1982) Halley's Comet: AD 1986 to 2647 BC. *Journal of the British Astronomical Association*, 92(5): 209–215.

Braund, M. (2009) Talk in Primary Science: A Method to Promote Productive and Contextualized Group Discourse, *Education 3–13*, 37(4): 387–397.

Braund, M. and Reiss, M. (2004) *Learning Science Outside the Classroom*, Abingdon: RouledgeFalmer.

Braund, M. and Reiss, M. (2006) Validity and Worth in the Science Curriculum: Learning School Science Outside the Laboratory. *The Curriculum Journal*, 17(3): 213–228.

Brown, H. (1994) *The Wisdom of Science: Its Relevance to Culture and Religion*, Cambridge: Cambridge University Press.

Bruner, J.S. (1986) *Actual Minds, Possible Worlds*, London: Harvard University Press.

Campaign for Science and Engineering (2014) *CaSE Report – Improving Diversity in STEM*, www.sciencecampaign.org.uk/resource/ImprovingDiversityinSTEM2014.html

Carle, E. (1981) *The Honeybee and the Robber*, J. MacRae Books.

Carle, E. (1994) *The Very Hungry Caterpillar*, London: Hamish Hamilton Ltd.

Carver, R. (2005) Principles of a Story. *Prospect*, 114: 32–34.

Casterton, J. (2005) *Creative Writing: A Practical Guide*, London: Palgrave Macmillan.

Centre for Alternative Technology. www.cat.org.uk/information/info_content.tmpl

Cerini, B., Murray, I., and Reiss, M. (2003) *Student Review of Science Curriculum: Major Findings*, London: Institute of Education, University of London.

Clarke, S. (2008) *Unlocking Formative Assessment*, London: Hodder & Stoughton.

Confederation of British Industries (2015) *Tomorrow's World: Inspiring Primary Scientists*, www.cbi.org.uk/tomorrows-world/assets/download.pdf

Cox, B and Cohen, A. (2011) *Wonders of the Solar System*, London: Harper Collins.

Cox, B. and Cohen, A. (2013) *Wonders of Life,* London: Harper Collins.

Cross, A. and Bowden, A. (2014) *Essential Primary Science (2nd ed)*, Maidenhead: OUP.

Crowley, K. and Jacobs, M. (2002) *Islands of Expertise and the Development of Family Scientific Literacy*, in G. Leinhardt, K. Crawley and K. Knutson (eds), *Learning Conversations in Museums*, Mahwah: Erlbaum.

Crump, T. (2002) *Science: As Seen Through the Development of Scientific Instruments*, London: Constable and Robinson Ltd.

Cutting, R. and Kelly, O. (2015) *Creative Teaching in Primary Science,* London: Sage.

Darwin, C. (1974) *The Descent of Man and Selection in Relation to Sex*, Detroit: Gale Research (reprint of 1874 edition).

Darwin, C. (1998) *The Origin of Species*, Hertfordshire: Wordsworth.

Davies, D. (2011) *Teaching Science Creatively*, London: Routledge.

Davies, D. and Howe, A. (2003) *Teaching Science and Design and Technology in the Early Years*, London: David Fulton.

Davies, D., Collier, C., Earle, S., Howe, A. and McMahon, K. (2014) *Approaches to Science Assessment in English Primary Schools*, Bristol: Primary Science Teaching Trust.

Dawes, L. (2004) Talk and Learning in Classroom Science. *International Journal of Science Education*, 26(6): 677–695.

Dawes, L. (2008a) 'Encouraging Students' Contributions to Dialogue During Science. *School Science Review*, 90(331): 1–7.

Dawes, L. (2008b) *The Essential Speaking and Listening: Talk for Learning at Key Stage 2*, London: Routledge.

Dawes, L. (2012) *Talking Points: Discussion Activities in the Primary Classroom*, London: Routledge.

Dawkins, R. (1986) *The Blind Watchmaker: Why the Evidence of Evolution Reveals a Universe Without Design*, London: Penguin Books.

Dawkins, R. (1998) *Unweaving the Rainbow*, London: Penguin Books.

de Boo, M. (2006) *Science in the Early Years*, in W. Harlen (ed.), *ASE Guide to Primary Science Education*, Hatfield: ASE.

DeCoito, I. (2016) STEM Education in Canada: A Knowledge Synthesis. *Canadian Journal of Science, Mathematics and Technology Education,* 16(2): 114–128.

Department for Business Innovation and Skills (2014) *Project STEM: Book of Insights*, https://www.gov.uk/government/uploads/system/uploads/attachment_data/file/351433/BIS-14-899-STEM-book-of-insights.pdf

Driver, R. (1983) *The Pupil as Scientist*? Milton Keynes: Open University Press.

Driver, R. and Easley, J. (1978) Pupils and Paradigms: A Review of Literature Related to Concept Development in Adolescent Science Students. *Studies in Science Education*, 5(1): 61–84.

Dunlop, L., Crompton, K., Clarke, L. and McKelvey-Martin, V. (2015) Child-led Enquiry in Primary Science, *Education 3–13*: 43(5).

Dunne, M. and Peacock, A. (eds) (2015) *Primary Science: A Guide to Teaching Practice,* London: Sage.

Dyer, A.G., Whitney, H.M., Arnold, S.E.J., Glover, B.J. and Chittka, L. (2006) Bees Associate Warmth with Floral Colour. *Nature*, 442: 525.

Earle, S. (2014) Formative and Summative Assessment of Science in English Primary Schools: Evidence from the Primary Science Quality Mark, *Research in Science & Technology Education*, 32(2): 216–228.

Einstein, A. and Infeld, L. (1961) *The Evolution of Physics*, Cambridge: Cambridge University Press.

Ellwood-Friery, K. (1996) *The Moon*, in M. Rosen (ed), *Poems for the Very Young*, London: Kingfisher.

Falk, J. and Dierking, L. (2000) *Learning from Museums*, Walnut Creek: Altamira Press.

Fara, P. (2010) *Science: A Four Thousand Year History*, Oxford: Oxford University Press.

Farley, F. and Rainey, R. (2006) *Anaconda, the Bulge Wave Sea Energy Converter* at www.bulgewave.com/.

Farrow, S. (2006) *The Really Useful Science Book*, Abingdon: Falmer Press.

Feynman, R.P. (1964) *The Feynman Lectures on Physics*, Reading: Addison-Wesley.

Feynman, R.P. (1999) *The Pleasure of Finding Things Out*, London: Penguin Books.

Fortey, J. (2007) *Eyewitness Great Scientists*, London: Dorling Kindersley Ltd.

Francis, G. (2015) *Adventures in Human Being*, London: Profile Books.

Gillies, R.M., Nichols, K., and Khan, Asaduzzaman. (2015) The Effects of Scientific Representations on Primary Students' Development of Scientific Discourse and Conceptual Understanding During Cooperative Contemporary Inquiry-science. *Cambridge Journal of Education*, 45 (4): 427–449.

Goldsworthy, A., Watson, R. and Wood-Robinson, V. (2000) *Developing Understanding in Scientific Enquiry*, Hatfield: ASE Publications.

Greca, I.M. and Moreira, M.A. (2000) Mental Models, Conceptual Models and Modelling. *International Journal of Science Education*, 22(1): 1–11.

Gregory, A. (2003) *Eureka: The Birth of Science*, Cambridge: Icon Books.

Harlen, W. (ed) (2011) *ASE Guide to Primary Science Education*. Hatfield: ASE.

Harlen, W. (2012) *The Fibonacci Booklet*, http://fibonacci.uni-bayreuth.de/resources/fibonacci-booklet.html

Harlen, W. (2014) *Assessment, Standards and Quality of Learning in Primary Education*, York: Cambridge Primary Review Trust.

Harlen, W. and Qualter, A. (2014) *The Teaching of Science in Primary Schools*, London: Routledge.

Heiney, P. (2014) *Can Crocodiles Cry?* Stroud: The History Press.

Hodson, D. (1999) Building a Case for a Sociocultural and Inquiry-oriented View of Science Education. *Journal of Science Education and Technology*, 8(3): 241–249.

Howard, S. and Scott, L. (2014) *Success with STEM: Ideas for the Classroom and Beyond*, London: Routledge.

Johnson, C., Peters-Burton, E. and Moore T. (2016) *STEM Road Map*, New York: Routledge.

Johnson-Laird, P. (1983) *Mental Models*, Cambridge: Harvard University Press.

Kosso, P. (2002) The Omniscienter: Beauty and Scientific Understanding, *International Studies in the Philosophy of Science*, 16(1): 39–48.

Kubli, F. (2001) Can the Theory of Narratives Help Science Teachers Be Better Storytellers? *Science & Education*, 10(6): 595–599.

Layton, D. (1993) *Technology's Challenge to Science Education*, Buckingham: Open University Press.

Leach, J. and Scott, P. (2002) Designing and Evaluating Science Teaching Sequences: An Approach Drawing Upon the Concept of Learning Demand and a Social Constructivist Perspective on Learning. *Studies in Science Education*, 28(1): 115–142.

Levinson, R. (2008) Promoting the Role of the Personal Narrative in Teaching Controversial Socio-scientific Issues. *Science & Education*, 17(8–9): 855–871.

Lijnse, P. (2000) Didactics of Science: The Forgotten Dimension in Science Education Research?, in R. Millar, J. Leach and J. Osborne (eds), *Improving Science Education: The Contribution of Research*, Buckingham: Open University Press.

Lijnse, P. (2004) Didactical Structures as an Outcome of Research on Teaching – Learning Sequences? *International Journal of Science Education*, 26(5): 537–554.

Livesey Museum for Children. *Myths and Legends*. www.liveseymuseum.org.uk/pdf/TheDreamtime.pdf

Loughland, T. and Kilpatrick, L. (2015) Formative Assessment in Primary Science, *Education 3–13*, 43(2): 128–141.

Loxley, P.M. (2009) Evaluation of Three Primary Teachers' Approaches to Teaching Scientific Concepts in Persuasive Ways. *International Journal of Science Education*, 31(12): 1607–1629.

Loxley, P.M. (2018) *Practical Ideas for Teaching Primary Science: Inspiring Learning and Enjoyment,* Abingdon: Routledge.

McGough, R. (1983) *Snowman*, in *Sky in the Pie*, London: Puffin/Penguin.

McGregor, D. and Precious, W. (2012) Dramatic Science: At Key Stage 1. *Primary Science,* 123: 10–13.

McGregor, D. and Precious, W. (2014) Just Imagine: Using Drama to Support Science Learning with Older Primary Children. *Primary Science,* 132: 35–37.

McMahon, K. (2012) Case Studies of Interactive Whole-class Teaching in Primary Science: Communicative Approach and Pedagogic Purposes. *International Journal of Science Education,* 34(11): 1687–1708.

Mercer, N. (1995) *The Guided Construction of Knowledge*, Clevedon: Multilingual Matters.

Mercer, N. (2000) *Words and Minds: How We Use Language to Think Together*, London: Routledge.

Mercer, N., Dawes, L. and Staarman, J.K. (2009) Dialogic Teaching in the Primary Science Classroom, *Language and Education*, 23(4): 353–369.

Mercer, N., Dawes, L., Wegerif, R., and Sams, C. (2004) Reasoning as a Scientist: Ways of Helping Children to Use Language to Learn Science. *British Educational Research Journal*, 30(3): 359–377.

Moggach, T. (2012) *The Urban Kitchen Gardener*, London: Kyle Books.

Mosley, M. and Lynch, J. (1996) *The Story of Science*, London: Mitchell Beasley.

Murphy, C. and Beggs, J. (2003) Children's Perceptions of School Science. *School Science Review*, 84(308): 109–116.

National Foundation for Educational Research (2013) *Improving Young People's Engagement with Science, Technology, Engineering and Mathematics (STEM)*, https://www.nfer.ac.uk/publications/99927/99927.pdf

Naylor, S. and Keogh, B. (2000) *Concept Cartoons in Science Education*, Sandbach: Millgate House Publishers (concept cartoons are also available on CD ROM).

Naylor, S., Keogh, B. and Goldworthy, A. (2004) *Active Assessment*, London: David Fulton.

Newman, M. (2012) An Inferential Model of Scientific Understanding. *International Studies in the Philosophy of Science*, 26(1): 1–26.

Newton, I. (2003) *Optics: Or a Treatise of the Reflections, Inflections, and Colours of Light (reprint edition)*, New York: Prometheus Books.

Norris, S.P., Guildbert, S.M., Smith, M.L., Hakimelahi, S. and Philips L.M. (2005) A Theoretical Framework for Narrative Explanation in Science. *Science Education*, 89(4): 535–563.

Nuffield Foundation (2012) *Developing Policy, Principles and Practice in Primary School Science.* www.nuffieldfoundation.org/primary-science-assessment

Ogborn, J., Kress, G., Martins, I. and McGillicuddy, K. (1996) *Explaining Science in the Classroom*, Buckingham: Open University Press.

Osborne, J., Simon, S. and Collins, S. (2003) Attitudes Towards Science: A Review of the Literature and Its Implications. *International Journal of Science Education*, 25(9): 1049–1079.

Osborne, R. and Freyberg, P. (1985) *Learning in Science: The Implications of Children's Science*, Auckland: Heinemann.

Passy, R. (2014) School Gardens: Teaching and Learning Outside the Front Door. *Education 3–13*, 42(1): 23–38.

Peacock, G., Sharp, J., Johnsey, R. and Wright, D. (2014) *Primary Science Knowledge and Understanding (7th ed),* London: Sage.

Pierce, P. (2014) *Jurassic Mary: Mary Anning and the Primeval Monsters*, Stroud: The History Press.

Pine, K., Messer D. and St. John K (2001) Children's Misconceptions in Primary Science: A Survey of Teachers' Views, Research. *Science & Technological Education*, 19(1): 79–96.

Poole, M. (1990) The Galileo Affair. *School Science Review*, 72(258): 39–48.

Poskitt, K. (1991) *The Moon*, in J. Foster (ed), *Twinkle Twinkle Chocolate Bar: Rhymes for the Very Young*, Oxford: Oxford University Press.

Posner, G.J., Strike, K.A., Hewson, P.W. and Gertzog, W.A. (1982) Accommodation of Scientific Conception: Toward a Theory of Conceptual Change. *Science Education*, 66(2): 211–227.

Primary Science Teachers Trust (2015) The Teacher Assessment in Primary Science (TAPS). https://pstt.org.uk/resources/curriculum-materials/assessment

Project STEM (2014) *https://www.gov.uk/government/uploads/system/uploads/attachment_data/file/351433/BIS-14-899-STEM-book-of-insights.pdf*

Ramirez, R. (2013) *Save Our Science: How to Inspire a New Generation of Scientists*, Kindle Single, TED Books.

Reed, A.W. (1993) *Aboriginal Myths, Legends and Fables* [compiled by A.W. Reed], Chatswood: N.S.W.

Roberts, A. (2015) *The Incredible Unlikeliness of Being: Evolution and the Making of Us*. London: Heron Books.

Roden, J. (2005) *Reflective Reader: Primary Science*, Exeter: Learning Matters.

Roden, J., Ward, H. and Ritchie, H. (2007) *Extending Knowledge and Practice Primary Science*, Exeter: Learning Matters.

Rogers, E.M. and Wenham, E.J. (eds) (1980) *Nuffield Physics*, London: Longman.

Rogoff, B. (1990) *Apprenticeship in Thinking: Cognitive Development in Social Context*, New York: Oxford University Press.

Rosen, M. (2000) *Centrally Heated Knickers*, London: Puffin.

Rowell, P.M. and Ebbers, M. (2004) Constructing Explanations of Flight: A Study of Instructional Discourse in Primary Science, *Language and Education*, 18(3): 264–280.

RSPB (2006) *Out-of-Classroom Learning: Practical Information and Guidance for Schools and Teachers*, Sandy: RSPB.

Rutledge, N. (2010) *Primary Science Teaching the Tricky Bits*, Maidenhead: Open University Press.

Sagan, C. (1997) *The Demon-Haunted World: Science as a Candle in the Dark*, London: Headline Book Publishing.

Science and Engineering Education Advisory Group (2012). *Supporting Scotland's STEM Education and Culture*, www.gov.scot/resource/0038/00388616.pdf

Scott, P. (1998) Teacher Talk and Meaning Making in Science Classrooms: A Vygotskian Analysis and Review. *Studies in Science Education*, 32(1): 45–80.

Seimears, C.M., Graves, E., Schroyer, M.G., and Staver, J. (2012) How Constructivist-Based Teaching Influences Students Learning Science. *The Educational Forum,* 76(2): 265–271.

Silver, A. and Rushton, B.S. (2008) Primary-school Children's Attitudes Towards Science, Engineering and Technology and Their Images of Scientists and Engineers. *Education 3–13,* 36(1): 51–67.

Simon, S. (2000) *Students' Attitudes Towards Science,* in M. Monk and J. Osborne (eds), *Good Practice in Science Teaching: What Research Has to Say,* Buckingham: Open University Press.

Sobel, D. (1999) *Galileo's Daughter: A Drama of Science, Faith and Love,* London: Fourth Estate.

Solomon, J. (1994) The Rise and Fall of Constructivism. *Studies in Science Education,* 23(1): 1–19.

Sustainable Development Commission (2007) *Every Child's Future Matters.* www.sd-commission.org.uk/publications/downloads/ECFM_report.pdf

Sutherland, R., Armstrong, V., Barnes, S., Brawn, R., Breeze, N., Gall, M., Mathewson, S., Olivero, F., Taylor, A., Triggs, P., Wishart, J. and John, P. (2004) Transforming Teaching and Learning: Embedding ICT into Everyday Classroom Practices. *Journal of Computer Assisted Learning,* 20(6): 413–425.

Sutton, C. (1992) *Words, Science and Learning,* Buckingham: Open University Press.

Sutton, C. (1996) *The Scientific Model as a Form of Speech,* in G. Welford, J. Osborne and P. Scott (eds), *Research in Science Education in Europe,* London: Falmer Press.

Tharp, R. and Gallimore, R. (1988) *A Theory of Teaching as Assisted Performance,* in R. Tharp and R. Gallimore (eds), *Rousing Minds to Life: Teaching, Learning and Schooling in Social Context,* New York: Cambridge University Press.

Thompson, M. (2016) *A Space Traveller's Guide to the Solar System,* London: Transworld Publishers.

Thomson, K. (2005) *A Very Short Introduction to Fossils,* Oxford: Open University Press.

Traianou, A. (2006) Understanding Teacher Expertise in Primary Science: A Sociocultural Approach. *Research Papers in Education,* 21(1): 63–78.

Treagust, D.F., Duit, R., Joslin, P. and Lindauer, I. (1992) Science Teachers' Use of Analogies: Observations from Classroom Practice. *International Journal of Science Education,* 14(4): 413–422.

Turner, J. Keogh, B., Naylor, S. and Lawrence, L. (2011) *It Fair – or Is It Not?,* Sandbach: Millgate House.

University of St. Andrews (2013) *Quotations by Galileo Galilei.* www-history.mcs.st-andrews.ac.uk/Quotations/Galileo.html

Warwick, P. and Sparks Linfield, R. (2000) *The Past, the Present and Possible Futures,* London: Routledge Farmer.

Weinberg, S. (2015) *To Explain the World: The Discovery of Modern Science,* London: Penguin Books.

Wenham, M. and Ovens, P. (2010) *Understanding Primary Science (3rd ed),* London: Sage.

Wertsch, J.V. (1991) *Voices of the Mind: A Sociocultural Approach to Mediated Action,* London: Harvester Wheatsheaf.

Wheway, D. and Thomson, S. (1993) *Explore Music Through Science,* Oxford: Oxford University Press.

Woods-Townsend, K., Christodoulou, A., Rietdijk, W., Byrne, J.B., Griffiths, M.M. and Grace, J.B. (2016) Meet the Scientist: The Value of Short Interactions Between Scientists and Students. *International Journal of Science Education,* Part B, 6(1):89–119.

Wootton, D. (2015). *The Invention of Science: A New History of the Scientific Revolution*, New York: Harper Collins.

Zhai, J., Jocz, J.A. and Tan A. (2014) 'Am I Like a Scientist?': Primary Children's Images of Doing Science in School. *International Journal of Science Education*, 36(4): 553–576.

Zollman, A. (2012) Learning for STEM literacy: STEM Literacy for Learning. *School Science and Mathematics,* 112(1): 12–19.

GLOSSARY

acid rain – Rainfall that can cause environmental damage. It occurs when the waste gases (sulphur and nitrogen oxide) produced by burning coal and other fossil fuels combine with atmospheric water to form an acid.

adaptation – The process by which creatures adapt to their habitat. Those with the most suitable characteristics survive to breed, creating creatures fitted to their habitats.

asteroid – Rocky or metallic material left over from the formation of the Solar System. Most asteroids orbit the sun between the orbits of Mars and Jupiter. Some cross the Earth's path and have collided with the Earth.

atom – The basic unit of matter. The smallest particle of an element that still displays the properties of that element.

autotroph (primary producer) – An organism that produces organic compounds from simple molecules, using energy from light or chemical reactions (e.g. green plants and some bacteria); also known as a primary producer.

bacteria – Single-celled micro-organisms. Bacteria exist everywhere on Earth including inside living organisms. In soil, they recycle nutrients. In the human body, some are a vital part of digestion but others cause disease, e.g. cholera.

Big Bang – Model of the events at the beginning of the universe. The Big Bang considers that the universe began from an extremely hot and dense singularity 13.7 billion years ago and that the universe continues to expand.

bile – Yellowish substance secreted by the liver and stored in the gall bladder. Bile aids the digestion of fats.

biodiversity – The variety of life forms within any given ecosystem often used as a measure of the health of biological systems.

biofuel – Fuel for cooking, powering vehicles and heating that comes from often specifically grown crops (e.g. wood, palm oil, corn and sugar cane).

biomass – Living or recently dead biological matter that can be used for fuel.

carbohydrate – Chemical used for food, consisting of carbon, hydrogen and oxygen atoms combined (e.g. glucose). Sugars or starch (potatoes, rice or bread, for example) contain carbohydrates. Glucose is used as a fuel in respiration to release energy to the body.

carnivore – Animal with a diet consisting mainly of meat obtained by predation or scavenging.

cartilage – Connective tissue providing structure and support (as in the nose or the ears) or cushioning joints (as between the discs of the spinal column).

cell division – Mechanism by which the contents of the cell, including the nucleus and DNA, divide equally. Organisms grow or repair tissue by cell division.

cellulose – The material in the cell wall of green plants which gives them structure. Some ruminants have micro-organisms in the gut to digest cellulose. It is not digestible by humans but useful as dietary fibre to move food through the gut.

chlorophyll – Green pigment found in plants and algae and contained in the chloroplasts. It absorbs light energy during process of photosynthesis.

classification – Biologists group, or classify, different species of organisms by means of shared physical characteristics.

cog – A wheel with teeth around its edge that engage with another cog to transfer motion.

colloid – Chemical mixture where the particles of a substance are suspended evenly within another but not dissolved (e.g. fog, clouds, smoke, whipped cream, milk and blood).

combustion – Combustion happens when a fuel (e.g. wood or oil) combines with oxygen through burning to give off heat. When organic substances, such as wood, burn they release carbon dioxide.

comet – Ball of ice and dust that orbits the Sun. As it approaches the Sun, the ice vaporises and streams away from the comet, carrying dust with it, to form a tail that may be visible from Earth (e.g. Hale-Bopp in 1997).

compound – Chemical substance consisting of two or more chemical elements that cannot be separated by simple means. A compound often has very different properties from its constituents. For example, common salt is made from a poisonous gas (chlorine) and a highly reactive metal (sodium).

connective tissue – Collagen-based substance that holds organs in place and forms ligaments and tendons.

constellation – A collection of astronomical bodies, usually stars, that appear to form a pattern in the sky.

decibel (dB) – Unit used to express the intensity of sound (e.g. 0 dB = threshold of human hearing, 60–70 dB = spoken conversation and 110–115 dB = a rock concert).

decomposers – Micro-organisms that consume dead or decaying organisms from which they get energy and nutrients for growth. Primary decomposers are bacteria and fungi.

density – A physical property of matter; the relationship between the mass of an object (in kilogrammes) and its volume (in cubic metres). Dense metals such as lead and gold are heavy for their size whilst polystyrene has low density and is light for size.

detritivore – Organisms that derive nutrients from decomposing organic matter (e.g. worms and woodlice). They form an important part of food webs in ecosystems.

diffusion – Process by which particles mingle as a result of their constant motion and resulting collisions (e.g. perfume diffuses throughout the air in a room).

DNA – Deoxyribonucleic acid, DNA, is the hereditary material in humans and most other organisms. Contained in every cell of the body, DNA stores the genetic code that defines an individual.

eclipse – An eclipse occurs when one astronomical object moves in front of another. For example, when the Moon moves in front of the Sun, the shadow of the Moon crosses the Earth's surface and we observe a solar eclipse. A lunar eclipse occurs when the Moon passes behind the Earth so that the Earth blocks the Sun's rays from striking the Moon.

ecosystem – The interactions between animals, plants, micro-organisms and their environment. Ecosystems can be as large as a tropical rainforest or as small as a pond.

electrical circuit – A closed loop through which current electricity flows.

electrical current – Flow of electrical charge carried by mobile electrons in wires.

electrical resistance – A measure of the opposition to flow of electrons in a wire, depending on which metal the wire is made from. Resistance increases with increasing length and decreasing width.

electrical voltage – Measure of the energy carried by the electrical charge. It is supplied by the battery and used by the components (e.g. the bulb) in a circuit.

electromagnetic radiation – Energy-carrying wave that does not need a medium to travel through. It includes radio waves, light waves, X-rays and infrared radiation.

electron – A subatomic particle. Electrons have negligible mass, orbit the atomic nucleus and carry a negative electrical charge.

element – A chemical substance made up of one type of atom (e.g. iron, oxygen and carbon).

embryo – An organism in the early stages of development, from implantation to birth. In humans, the embryo is known as a foetus after eight weeks.

emulsion – A mixture of two or more liquids that are immiscible (will not blend; e.g. oil and water).

energy – An attribute of objects or systems that enables work to be done. Energy can be transformed from one form to another (e.g. chemical energy in food to heat energy in the body) but cannot be destroyed.

enzyme – Enzymes are proteins that increase the rate of reactions that take place in organisms, remaining unchanged themselves.

erosion – A wearing down of rocks by wind, water or other natural means.

evolution – Changes that take place in a species over a long period of time in response to the environment. Genetic changes in a community can result in the development of a new species.

excretion – The process of eliminating waste products from an organism. For example, carbon dioxide (the by-product of respiration) is excreted by the human lungs.

exoskeleton – An external skeleton supporting and protecting an animal's body. Crabs and insects have exoskeletons.

exuvia – Remains of an exoskeleton after the organism (generally an insect, spider or crustacean) has moulted.

fertilisation – Fusion of cells, the sperm and the ovum, in sexual reproduction of animals and flowering plants.

food chain – Feeding relationships between species in an ecosystem. Food chains are drawn to show the direction of energy flow, from the sun to producers and then consumers, then decomposers.

food web – Different food chains in an ecosystem link up with each other to form food webs. Food webs describe the complexity of the feeding relationships in an ecosystem.

force – A force is a push, pull or twist that can cause an object to change its speed, its direction of movement or its shape.

fossil – Any preserved evidence of life from an earlier geological age. It might be an impression of an organism embedded in rock or the mineralised remains of a plant or animal.

fossil fuel – Non-renewable fuels, such as coal, oil and natural gas, formed from organisms alive around 300 million years ago; found in deposits beneath the earth.

fungi – A kingdom of living things or organisms that are more closely related to animals than plants. They are largely invisible apart from their fruiting bodies (e.g. toadstools). Fungi feed on organic matter and reproduce via spores (e.g. yeasts, moulds and mushrooms).

galaxy – A massive system of stars. They are remains of dead stars and interstellar gas held together by a strong gravitational field often with a distinct shape. Our Sun and Solar System are part of the spiral-shaped Milky Way galaxy.

gastric juice – A strongly acidic liquid secreted by the stomach lining to break down food in the stomach.

genetic code – Patterns along the DNA molecule which define a distinct individual.

geothermal energy – Heat from within the Earth, generated in the Earth's core and released via hot springs or geysers. Geothermal heat pumps can be used to extract geothermal energy to heat buildings.

germination – The process by which a dormant seed starts to sprout and grow into a seedling. For this to happen, the seed needs water, oxygen and warmth.

global warming – The increase in the average temperature of the Earth attributed to the release of carbon dioxide through human activity (e.g. burning of fossil fuels).

glucose – A simple sugar (produced in photosynthesis) used by living cells as a source of energy.

gravity – A force of attraction between one mass and another. A property of all matter. Gravity gives weight to objects and keeps the Earth and planets in orbit round the Sun.

greenhouse gas – Gas in the atmosphere (e.g. water vapour, carbon dioxide and methane) that absorbs and holds thermal (heat) energy.

habitat – The place where an organism lives is called its habitat. Habitats have specific conditions of temperature, water, geography, etc., which suit the organisms that inhabit them.

haemoglobin – Protein in red blood cells which holds oxygen for transport round the body.

herbivore – Animal that feeds only on autotrophs (primary producers) such as plants and algae.

hormone – Chemical messengers that act as a signal in multicellular organisms. For example, serotonin regulates mood, appetite and sleep.

igneous rock – Rock solidified from lava or magma (e.g. granite, pumice and basalt).

inheritance – Process by which certain features are transmitted from parent to offspring via the genetic code.

invertebrate – An animal without a vertebral column (backbone). This includes 98% of all animal species, that is, all except fish, reptiles, amphibians, birds and mammals.

kinetic (movement) energy – Energy an object possesses by virtue of its motion (e.g. a moving car, football or planet).

lever – A rigid bar resting on a pivot. When pressure is applied to one end a heavy load resting on the other can be lifted.

light year – A measure of distance – the distance light travels in a vacuum in one year – about ten trillion kilometres. The nearest known star to the Sun is Proxima Centauri, about 4.22 light years away.

longitudinal wave – Waves that oscillate (vibrate) in the same direction in which they travel (e.g. sound waves and seismic waves produced by earthquakes).

luminous – A luminous object emits its own light. To do this it needs a source of energy. Candles, torches and the Sun are luminous objects.

lux – Measure of the intensity of light (e.g. 1 lux =full Moon overhead and 10,000–25,000 lux = full daylight).

magnet – An object or material that can create a magnetic field and repel another magnet.

magnetic – An object or material can be described as magnetic if it is attracted to a magnet.

metamorphic rock – Rock that has undergone a physical change due to extreme heat or pressure (e.g. marble from limestone, slate from shale and gneiss, usually from granite).

metamorphosis – Change. Complete metamorphosis is the process some animals go through when they change from the immature to the adult form (e.g. tadpole to frog or caterpillar to butterfly).

meteor – Small particle of debris (from sand grain to pebble) that falls into the Earth's atmosphere. Often called a 'shooting star' because it glows as it burns up in the atmosphere. If it falls to the ground, it is called a meteorite.

micro-organism – Often single-celled organisms, too small to be seen by the human eye. They include bacteria, fungi, algae, plankton and amoeba.

mixture – Two or more substances mixed together but not combined chemically (e.g. solutions, suspensions and colloids). Mixtures can usually be separated by simple mechanical means such as filtering (e.g. flour in water).

molecule – Group of at least two atoms held together by strong chemical bonds. Some elements only exist as combinations of two or more atoms (e.g. oxygen).

mollusc – Invertebrates with body divided into three parts: a head, a central area containing the major organs and a foot for movement. They include gastropods (snails and slugs), cephalopods (squid and cuttlefish) and bivalves (mussels and oysters).

natural selection – The process by which favourable, inheritable characteristics become common in successive generations.

nebula – An interstellar cloud of dust and gas where materials clump together to form larger masses and eventually new stars.

neutron – Subatomic particle contained in the nucleus of the atom that has no electrical charge and a mass slightly larger than the proton.

non-renewable energy – Energy generated from finite resources such as fossil fuels (e.g. coal, oil and gas). See also *renewable energy*.

nuclear energy – Energy released by splitting (fission) or merging together (fusion) of the nuclei of atoms. On Earth, nuclear energy is produced by splitting the atoms of uranium or plutonium. The Sun produces vast amounts of energy by nuclear fusion using hydrogen as a fuel.

omnivore – Creature that eats both plants and animals. Generally, omnivores are opportunistic feeders not especially adapted to eat meat or plants exclusively (e.g. bears, pigs and humans).

ossification – Process by which bones are formed from connective tissue such as cartilage. Blood brings minerals such as calcium and deposits it to form hard bones.

oxidation – Chemical reaction between oxygen molecules and other substances (e.g. rusting); also, the loss of at least one electron when two or more substances interact.

peristalsis – A rhythmic contraction of muscles that move substances through the digestive system.

phloem – Living tissue in plants that transports the products of photosynthesis (sugars) to all parts of the plant. In trees, phloem is a green layer between the bark and the woody xylem.

photoelectric (voltaic) effect – When electrons are emitted from a material exposed to light. Utilised in solar (photovoltaic) cells to convert sunlight directly into electricity.

photosphere – The Sun is a ball of gas and does not have a well-defined surface. The photosphere is defined as the diameter at which the Sun appears to be opaque. Beyond this is the corona which becomes visible during a solar eclipse.

photosynthesis – Process by which plants convert water and carbon dioxide into organic compounds (especially sugars), using energy from sunlight.

phytoplankton – Autotrophic plankton (drifting organisms in the oceans) containing chlorophyll and so capable of photosynthesising.

pitch – Frequency of vibration of a sound. Measured in Hertz (Hz) as vibrations per second. The adult ear can hear from 20 to 16,000 Hz.

pollination – The transfer of pollen from the male anther to the female stigma of a flower so that fertilisation can take place.

pollinator – Animal which transfers pollen from the male anther to the female stigma of a flower so that fertilisation can take place (e.g. bees and bats).

potential (stored) energy – Energy stored within a system which has the potential to be converted into other forms of energy (e.g. energy stored in the bonds between atoms or in a compressed spring).

predator – An animal that lives by eating or preying on another animal.

prey – An animal that is hunted and killed by another animal.

primary consumer – Organisms that obtain energy from plants (primary producers). See also *secondary consumer* and *tertiary consumer*.

primary producer – An organism that produces organic compounds from simple molecules using energy from light or chemical reactions (e.g. green plants and some bacteria, also known as autotrophs).

protein – Chains of amino acids (found in meat, fish, eggs, dairy products, legumes, pulses and seeds) make up proteins essential for the growth of cells and tissue repair.

proton – Positive subatomic particle in the atomic nucleus with an electrical charge and mass.

pulley – A mechanical device consisting of a wheel with a rim over which a rope is passed to aid in lifting heavy objects.

radiant energy – The energy of electromagnetic waves from radio waves to gamma rays and including solar heat and light.

reflection – A wave travelling in a straight line 'bounces' back as it strikes a new medium. For smooth surfaces, the angle at which the wave strikes will be the same as the angle at which it is reflected (e.g. reflection in mirrors or echoes in sound).

relativity – Theory of Albert Einstein published from 1905 to 1907 on the nature of gravitation, space and time. Presented amongst others the idea that energy and mass are equivalent and interchangeable.

renewable energy – Energy generated from natural, sustainable sources (e.g. sunlight, wind, rain, tides or geothermal heat). See also *non-renewable energy*.

reproduction – Biological process by which new individual organisms are produced. Fundamental to all life; may be sexual (requires two individuals one of each sex) or asexual (by cell division).

respiration – Cellular respiration, a process that takes place in all living cells where sugars are chemically combined with oxygen (oxidised) to release energy for growth, movement, reproduction and repair. Carbon dioxide and water are waste products.

ruminant – Mammal that is able to digest plant-based foods (in particular cellulose). Food is initially softened in a first stomach (the rumen) and then re-chewed as cud (e.g. by sheep or cattle).

secondary consumer – Organism that obtains energy from other consumers, usually a carnivore.

sedimentary rock – Is formed by the deposition of sediment in water in rivers, lakes and oceans. It is usually deposited in layers and often contains fossils (e.g. limestone, sandstone and shale).

solar energy – See *radiant energy*.

solvent – A liquid or a gas that dissolves a solid, liquid or gas solute, most commonly water.

species – Basic unit of biological classification – a group of organisms capable of interbreeding.

spectrum – Of light; visible frequencies of electromagnetic radiation ranging from red through to violet. A spectrum is produced when a beam of light is split into its constituent frequencies (colours). A rainbow displays the visible spectrum.

starch – A carbohydrate made of long chains of glucose molecules. It is a major source of food (energy) for humans. Plants store glucose – the product of photosynthesis – as insoluble starch.

static electricity – Electric charge resulting from electrons building up on the surface of an object as a result of friction (when materials are pulled apart or rubbed together).

supernova – Stellar explosion of great intensity. Occurs either when an ageing star collapses in on itself and then heats and explodes or when a small, very hot star overheats and undergoes runaway nuclear fusion. Supernovas seed galaxies with material and can trigger the formation of new stars.

tertiary consumer – Organism that obtains energy from secondary consumers. Tertiary consumers are known as 'top predators' to indicate their position in the food chain.

thermodynamics – The study of the conversion of energy from one form to another. The total amount of energy in the universe remains constant: energy can be exchanged between systems and transformed from one form to another but cannot be created or destroyed.

tilt of the Earth – The Earth is tilted on its axis and is at an angle of about 23.5 degrees to the vertical. This results in the seasons.

transverse wave – Wave that oscillates at 90 degrees to the direction of travel (e.g. electromagnetic waves – light).

ultrasound – Frequencies above the range of human hearing (about 20,000 Hz). Used in medical imaging. Many animals are capable of hearing well above this limit (such as bats, dogs and dolphins).

upthrust – Force exerted on a floating object by the water it displaces.

vertebrate – Animal with a backbone or spinal column. They include bony fish, sharks, amphibians, reptiles, mammals and birds.

virus – Sub-microscopic particle that contains DNA but no nucleus. It needs to infect a host cell to replicate itself (unlike bacteria). They are the cause of infections such as sore throats, Ebola and HIV/AIDS.

water cycle – The process by which water continuously circulates between the Earth's oceans, atmosphere and land. This involves atmospheric water falling as rain and snow (precipitation), draining in streams and rivers to the sea and then returning to the atmosphere by evaporation and transpiration.

wave motion – Distortion in a material or medium when the individual parts vibrate but the waveform itself moves through the material (e.g. a wave passing across a pond). Wave length is the distance between successive wave peaks, amplitude is the height of the wave and frequency is the speed of vibration.

weathering – The disintegration of rocks at their surface. Physical weathering is caused by changes in temperature or the action of wind, rain or waves. Chemical weathering is caused by rainwater (naturally slightly acidic from dissolved carbon dioxide) or acid rain itself. Biological weathering is the result of the action of plant roots and stems.

weight – The force of gravity acting on a mass.

INDEX

Page numbers in **bold** denote glossary entries.